LAW IN A COM

Approximately half of the total UK pop
welfare benefits, giving rise to the largest
ture. The law and structures of social secu   ...highly complex, made more
so by constant adjustments as government pursues its often conflicting economic, political and social policy objectives. This complexity is highly problematic. It contributes to errors in decision-making and to increased administrative
costs and is seen as disempowering for citizens, thereby weakening enjoyment
of a key social right. Current and previous administrations have committed to
simplifying the benefits system. It is a specific objective of the Welfare Reform
Act 2012, which provides for the introduction of Universal Credit in place of
diverse benefits. However, it is unclear whether the reformed system will be
either less complex legally or more accessible for citizens.

This book seeks to explain how and why complexity in the modern welfare
system has grown; to identify the different ways in which legal and associated
administrative arrangements are classifiable as 'complex'; to discuss the effects
of complexity on the system's administration and its wider implications for
rights and the citizen–state relationship; and to consider the role that law can
play in the simplification of schemes of welfare. While primarily focused on
the UK welfare system it also provides analysis of relevant policies and experience in various other states.

Law in a Complex State
Complexity in the Law and Structure of Welfare

Neville Harris

·HART·
PUBLISHING
OXFORD AND PORTLAND, OREGON
2013

Published in the United Kingdom by Hart Publishing Ltd
16C Worcester Place, Oxford, OX1 2JW
Telephone: +44 (0)1865 517530
Fax: +44 (0)1865 510710
E-mail: mail@hartpub.co.uk
Website: http://www.hartpub.co.uk

Published in North America (US and Canada) by
Hart Publishing
c/o International Specialized Book Services
920 NE 58th Avenue, Suite 300
Portland, OR 97213-3786
USA
Tel: (+1) 503-287-3093 or toll-free: (1) 800-944-6190
Fax: (+1) 503-280-8832
E-mail: orders@isbs.com
Website: http://www.isbs.com

British Library Cataloguing in Publication Data

Data Available

ISBN: 978-1-84946-445-1

Typeset by Hope Services, Abingdon
Printed and bound in Great Britain by
Page Bros Ltd, Norwich UK

Preface

In the continuing evolution of the welfare state in the 70 years since the Beveridge Report, the complexity of the UK welfare system has become one of its most marked features. This complexity is manifested, in the area of social security, in a complicated legal framework of growing intricacy and a diverse pattern of multiple benefits/credits and elaborate administrative processes. The problems arising from complexity in this context centre on its association with, amongst other things, increased administrative burdens and costs, an enhanced risk of error and fraud, and a reduced capacity among citizens to take up benefits to which they are entitled, exercise choices, fulfil their obligations as claimants, and plan financially for the future. A previous attempt to simplify the welfare system, or at least part of it, was made by the Conservative Government via its benefit reforms of the 1980s, but any gains were very short-lived. The 1997–2010 Labour Administration also favoured simplification of the system and in its final five years established a Benefit Simplification Unit within the Department for Work and Pensions to examine the scope for reducing complexity and to advise policy-makers accordingly. However, only piecemeal improvements occurred, and little was achieved. Now, under the Coalition Government comes the first serious attempt at simplification, although, as with other reforms to welfare in recent decades, a wide range of economic and social policy objectives are also being pursued.

Starting in 2013, huge changes are being introduced which will transform the welfare system, a system which at any point in time is providing at least some support to around half the population of the United Kingdom, so any change to it has potentially wide-ranging social implications. As this book goes to press, the phased introduction of a new form of support known as universal credit is underway, although the National Audit Office has recently reported significant problems with the programme's management and information technology framework which are adversely affecting the process (*Universal Credit: early progress* (HC 621) (London, The Stationery Office, 2013)). The credit is replacing a raft of means-tested benefits, including income support, income-based jobseeker's allowance, housing benefit, working tax credit and child tax credits. While it represents the Coalition's central reform to welfare, many other changes are also being implemented, including a new council tax support system, a new disability benefit known as personal independence payment, and an overall cap on the amount of benefit that a household may receive. Since this is a rule-based area of governance dominated by an extensive and detailed legislative framework, inevitably the implementation of wholesale changes to the system of the kind that we are seeing has necessitated a vast array of legislative provisions, including typically complex transitional arrangements.

This book is not merely an attempt to analyse various aspects of these reforms; it also aims to throw some light on the nature of complexity in state governance more broadly and on its significant implications for the relationship between citizens and the state. Social security is not the only area of governance bedevilled by complexity: taxation and immigration, for example, are also afflicted. Yet the reach of social security is particularly wide, and the implications of complexity are perhaps most significant in this sphere. The first chapter explores the problem of complexity in relation to welfare. It also considers the meaning of 'complexity' in a conceptual sense, particularly in the context of law. Chapters two and three look at the causes and sources of complexity in the welfare system, the changing structure of which is mapped out. One area of particular focus in chapter three is the use of complex rules in the system. Chapter three also looks at the measurement of complexity.

Across the next three chapters (four to six), the book assesses the impact of complexity on welfare claimants' engagement with the system as they seek to secure the entitlements derived from their fundamental social rights in this area – rights which are attached to their status as citizens. Thus, these chapters look at how complexity affects the so-called 'customer journey' through the system and in negotiating the processes involved in claiming entitlement and, by satisfying the onerous conditions attached to awards, retaining it. This is a field where erroneous decisions are made but can be corrected through processes such as revision, review or appeal to the First-tier Tribunal. The appeal path, for example, was followed in 370,800 cases in 2011–12 and is projected to be trodden by as many as 800,000 claimants per annum by 2015–16. Therefore, the analysis includes a review of the arrangements for bringing a challenge against an administrative decision on a benefit claim and the assistance available to appellants in accessing and utilising the appeal system, including the implications of recent legal aid cutbacks.

Since various other states have also to varying degrees sought to grapple with the complexities of their social security system, the book also discusses, in chapter seven, examples of simplification measures and strategies that have been adopted in a number of them. The chapter covers, among other things, the codifications of social security law, or significant parts of it, in Australia, Germany and Sweden and reforms to benefits in Ireland, Italy and New Zealand. Chapter eight, the final chapter, attempts to bring the various strands of analysis together and to consider the trade-offs involved between complexity and simplicity in this field of provision.

This book was completed against a background of wide-ranging legislative change and intense political and media debate in the United Kingdom about the direction and impact of welfare reform. This made the subject matter both highly topical but also very challenging to cover. (The judgment in *R (MA) v Secretary of State for Work and Pensions* [2013] EWHC 2213 (Admin) on the 'bedroom tax' became available too late for inclusion in the main text.) I am very grateful to have had a twelve-month Leverhulme Research Fellowship (February 2012 to January 2013) in which to concentrate on the research and undertake much of the writing. I therefore acknowledge with particular thanks the Leverhulme Foundation's support. I also wish to state my indebtedness and gratitude to a number of people who in various ways provided me with advice or assistance in connection with this project – especially Mel Cousins, Eberhard Eichenhofer, Thomas Erhag, Fabrizio Fracchia, Judge Rune Lavin, Frans Pennings, Felix Welti, Nick Wikeley and Penny Wood – although they are not of course to blame for any errors or omissions. I am also very grateful for the support of colleagues at the University of Manchester and for that of Richard Hart and his colleagues in agreeing to commission the book and guiding it through to publication. Finally, but certainly not least, to Marie Harris I simply say thank you for so much.

Neville Harris
September 2013

Table of Contents

List of Tables and Figures

Figures

Tables

List of Abbreviations

AAC	Administrative Appeals Chamber
AJTC	Administrative Justice and Tribunals Council
ASPI	*Assicurazione sociale per l'impiego* (Italy)
ATLAS	Automated Transfers to Local Authority Systems
BSU	Benefit Simplification Unit
CBJSA	Contribution-based jobseeker's allowance
Claims and Payments Regulations 2013	Universal Credit, Personal Independence Payment, Jobseeker's Allowance and Employment and Support Allowance (Claims and Payments) Regulations 2013 (SI 2013/380)
CJEU	Court of Justice of the European Communities
DLA	Disability living allowance
DMA Regulations 1999	Social Security and Child Support (Decisions and Appeals) Regulations 1999 (SI 1999/991)
DMA Regulations 2013	Universal Credit, Personal Independence Payment, Jobseeker's Allowance and Employment and Support Allowance (Decisions and Appeals) Regulations 2013 (SI 2013/381)
DWP	Department for Work and Pensions
ECHR	European Convention for the Protection of Human Rights and Fundamental Freedoms (European Convention on Human Rights)
ESA	Employment and support allowance
ESA Regulations 2008	Employment and Support Allowance Regulations 2008 (SI 2008/794)
ESA Regulations 2013	Employment and Support Allowance Regulations 2013 (SI 2013/379)
FaCSIA	Department of Families, Community Services and Indigenous Affairs
FTT	First-tier Tribunal
HMRC	Her Majesty's Revenue and Customs
ICESCR	International Covenant on Economic, Social and Cultural Rights
JSA	Jobseeker's allowance
JSA Regulations 1996	Jobseeker's Allowance Regulations 1996 (SI 1996/207)
JSA Regulations 2013	Jobseeker's Allowance Regulations 2013 (SI 2013/378)
LEL	Lower earnings limit

LRC	Lowest rate care component
LTAHAW	'Living together as husband and wife'
NAO	National Audit Office
N/SVQ	National/Scottish Vocational Qualification
PIP	Personal independence payment
PO	Presenting officer
RTI	Real Time Information
SBG	*Sozialgesetzbuch* (Social Code) (Germany)
SSAC	Social Security Advisory Committee
UNCRC	United Nations Convention on the Rights of the Child
Universal Credit Regulations	Universal Credit Regulations 2013 (SI 2013/376)
UT(AAC)	Upper Tribunal (Administrative Appeals Chamber)
WFI	Work-focused interview
WRAG	Work related activity group

Table of Cases

Decisions of the Social Security and Child Support Commissioners

Table of Legislation

European Union

Treaties, Charters

Secondary Legislation

1

Complexity and Welfare

I. Introduction

The title of this book carries a dual meaning. It refers, first, to complexity in how a state is organised to conduct its functions – in this instance, the provision of welfare support (specifically social security). Secondly, it alludes to the complexity inherent in the laws through which policy is administered, particularly those that define the bases and extent of entitlement to the various welfare benefits. For reasons which this book explores, complexity is a dominant characteristic of the modern welfare system in the United Kingdom and elsewhere.[1] Indeed, the 'inherent complexity of social security' has been recognised by the European Union,[2] which has included social security legislation in the areas covered by a programme of simplification under its Better Regulation policy initiative.[3]

[1] On the concept of the 'welfare state' from a legal perspective, see R Cranston, *Legal Foundations of the Welfare State* (London, Weidenfeld and Nicolson, 1985) 4; N Harris et al, *Social Security Law in Context* (Oxford, Oxford University Press, 2000) ch 1; and N Wikeley, 'The Welfare State' in P Cane and M Tushnet (eds), *The Oxford Handbook of Legal Studies* (Oxford, Oxford University Press, 2003) 397–412.

[2] Regulation (EC) No 987/2009 of the European Parliament and of the Council of 16 September 2009 laying down the procedure for implementing Regulation (EC) No 883/2004 on the coordination of social security systems, recital 9.

[3] The emphasis has first been on codification and latterly 'moving towards a more integrated approach to simplification where the aim is to examine the entire body of legislation that affects a policy area to identify overlaps, gaps, inconsistencies, obsolete measures, and potential for reducing regulatory burdens': European Commission, COM (2009) 15 Final, Communication from the Commission to the European Parliament, the Council, the European Economic and Social Committee and the Committee of the Regions, *Third Strategic Review of Better Regulation in the European Union*, Brussels, 28.1.2009. See further below ch 2.

Complexity has long been pervasive in the UK social security system, being found in the various benefit schemes and in the administrative processes governing claims and decision-making.[4] Seventy years ago, the Beveridge Report recognised that despite the unification and simplifications proposed in its comprehensive plan for social security, the system would 'still be a machine with many parts and complications to deal with all the complexities of need and variety of persons'.[5] In the late 1970s, the team established by the Secretary of State to review the scheme of supplementary benefit, which at that time was the principal (means-tested) 'safety net' benefit, set as one of its objectives 'to produce a simpler scheme which would be more readily comprehensible to claimants and staff'.[6] Yet complexity grew and by the mid-1980s was regarded by government as one of the key reasons that the social security system as a whole had 'lost its way'.[7] Although the reforms that followed under the Social Security Act 1986 were intended to simplify the system, such gains as were achieved were short-lived.[8]

In 2002 the Social Security Advisory Committee[9] concluded that 'the complexity of the social security system must remain a significant cause of concern'.[10] The issue of complexity attracted the attention of the National Audit Office, which undertook a comprehensive review,[11] and in 2006 the House of Commons Public Accounts Committee called for new solutions to 'reverse the drift towards greater complexity' in the benefits system.[12] Government commitments were forthcoming to address the issue, although as shall be discussed, little was actually achieved.[13] Currently, the most far-reaching reform to the system for over half a century is taking place through the phased introduction of 'universal credit'. This reform will bring the key

---

[4] In this book, the term 'welfare system' is used to denote the structures and arrangements for the delivery of welfare provision, with specific reference to social security. The alternative albeit narrower term 'benefits system' (or 'benefit system') is also used, particularly when referring to the policy of simplification of welfare benefits.

[5] WH (Lord) Beveridge (Inter-departmental Committee on Social Insurance and Allied Services), *Social Insurance and Allied Services* (Cmnd 6404, 1942) para 397.

[6] Department for Health and Social Security Review Team, *Social Assistance: A Review of the Supplementary Benefits Scheme in Britain* (London, DHSS, 1978) para 1.1.

[7] Secretary of State for Social Services, *Reform of Social Security, Vol 1* (Cmnd 9517, 1985) paras 1.1–1.2.

[8] M Hill, 'The 1986 Social Security Act 1986: Ten Years On' (1996) 15 *Benefits* 2.

[9] The Committee is an independent statutory body charged with advising and assisting the Secretary of State 'in connection with his functions under the relevant enactments' and with scrutinising and commenting on draft social security regulations that are referred to it: Social Security Administration Act 1992, s 170. On its role in scrutinising and commenting on regulations, see further below ch 2, n 6.

[10] Social Security Advisory Committee, *Fifteenth Report, 2002* (Leeds, Corporate Document Services, 2002) para 1.6.

[11] National Audit Office (NAO), *Department for Work and Pensions: Dealing with the Complexity of the Benefits System*, HC 592 (London, Stationary Office, 2005).

[12] House of Commons Committee of Public Accounts, *Tackling the Complexity of the Benefits System*, (2005–06, HC 765) 5.

[13] See below s V.

means-tested benefits and tax credits into one scheme and seeks not only to ease the transition from welfare dependency to work but also to effect a considerable reduction in complexity by creating a much simpler framework. However, a significant degree of complexity is likely to remain in the system, as discussed in later chapters. Universal credit is not the only reform which is currently underway, however, and other changes also impact on the legal and structural complexity of the modern welfare system.

For a whole range of reasons outlined below and discussed in more detail throughout this book, complexity matters a great deal in this context. Although it can be viewed as both inevitable and merely reflecting the system's attempt to respond to complex social phenomena[14] in a manageable way,[15] it is also generally seen as highly problematic for both government and citizen. Complexity pervades this area of state provision in which key social rights are embedded and on which so many citizens depend for their material welfare, and it is therefore a particularly important subject for investigation. Such an exploration affords an opportunity but also generates a need to consider the nature and meaning of 'complexity' with reference to law, particularly public legislation. It has significance beyond the area of social security, since simplification strategies have, for example, been pursued in recent years in the fields of both taxation law and immigration law,[16] while the complexity of legislation in general has prompted a 'good law' initiative by the Office of the Parliamentary Counsel which aims to combat the difficulty experienced by the full range of those who engage with legislation.[17] One of the key concerns relating to an area of the law concerned with state provision such as social security and tax credits is that its inherent complexity has a negative overall impact on the rights of the citizen by threatening their realisation in practice.

---

[14] See, eg, L Kaplow, 'A Model of the Optimal Complexity of Legal Rules' (1995) 11(1) *Journal of Law, Economics and Organization* 150, 161: 'Complexity often is discussed as an evil to be minimized, as in commentary on the income tax. Of course, less complexity is to be preferred if the same substantive rules can be applied. But much complexity . . . arises because of the benefits from rules that are more precisely tailored to particular behavior. To talk of minimizing complexity in this context is misguided.'

[15] See, for example, the discussion below in ch 2 regarding the use of information technology in the welfare system.

[16] On taxation law, see below s IV. On immigration law, see Home Office UK Border Agency, *Simplifying Immigration Law: The Draft Bill* (Cm 7730, 2009).

[17] Office of the Parliamentary Counsel, 'Good Law', www.gov.uk/good-law?utm_source=Sign-Up.to&utm_medium=email&utm_campaign=1317-221121-Judicial+Intranet+update+19+April+2013, which states that the idea is that all those involved in law-making, 'in government, in Parliament and beyond', will work more closely to ensure that legislation is necessary, clear, coherent, effective and accessible. See also Office of the Parliamentary Counsel, *When Laws Become Too Complex: A Review into the Causes of Complex Legislation* (London, Cabinet Office, 2013).

II. Law and the Goals of Welfare

The relationship between law and the modern welfare state is important. The law guarantees individual entitlement when prescribed conditions apply and legitimises the bureaucratic decision-making involved in the governance of provision. It therefore serves the realisation of the welfare system's underlying aims in relation to a key responsibility and function of the modern state. Welfare systems operated by or under the aegis of the state in modern industrialised nations exist to fulfil normative expectations about how the basic requirements of human social organisation and personal welfare and development can be met; and this is the case whatever the political or social forces that gave rise to their establishment and the plurality of views about how such a system should be organised and operated. The key areas of state welfare provision all rest on very simple ideas, or at least are intended on the face of it to meet straightforward objectives, as for example conceptualised in Beveridge's notional slaying of 'five giant evils' of Want, Disease, Ignorance, Squalor and Idleness.[18] The required provision is seen as concerning 'things we all need, and which not all of us can guarantee to provide for ourselves either all the time or at the time they are needed'.[19] Welfare systems have the core aims of 'reducing destitution; providing for social contingencies; and promoting greater income and consumption equality'.[20]

However, it is also important to recognise that regardless of the different models of the welfare state that have emerged to deliver such goals,[21] there are other, broader social and economic aims that are simultaneously advanced by the modern state. Prominent among them are increases in personal social

---

[18] Beveridge (above n 5) para 8.

[19] N Timmins, *The Five Giants: A Biography of the Welfare State* (London, HarperCollins, 1995) 2.

[20] D Ghai, *Social Security Priorities and Patterns: A Global Perspective*, DP 141/2002 (Geneva, ILO, 2002) 4.

[21] See in particular G Esping-Andersen, *The Three Worlds of Welfare Capitalism* (Cambridge, Polity Press, 1990), identifying the three systems as conservative (state provision, but preserves class and social institutional frameworks) (eg, France, Germany and Italy), liberal (universalism limited, private provision encouraged and means-testing a dominant feature) (eg, USA and Canada), and social-democratic (universalistic and egalitarian) (eg, Scandinavian states). This typology is, however, seen as not easily accommodating the UK welfare state. See A Cochrane, 'Comparative Approaches and Social Policy' in A Cochrane and J Clarke (eds), *Comparing Welfare States: Britain in International Context* (London, Sage, 1993) 9. Nevertheless, the UK welfare state has arguably moved most squarely into the liberal category. Many of the welfare states (eg, the Netherlands and Switzerland) are seen by Arts and Gelissen as predominantly hybrids of these models: W Arts and J Gelissen, 'Three Worlds of Welfare Capitalism or More? A State-of-the-Art Report' (2002) 12(2) *Journal of European Social Policy* 137, which contains a comprehensive review of critiques of Esping-Andersen's classification.

responsibility and collective economic advancement. It has been said that where 'policymakers have multiple objectives for the tax system, then a substantial degree of complexity is unavoidable'.[22] This is equally true of the welfare system. The diverse policy aims attached to many areas of social security in the United Kingdom have contributed to the development of the welfare state into a hugely complex structure with an intricate legal framework. The evolution of a mixed economy of welfare[23] has had added further complexity. The contracting-out of areas of service provision and the increasing involvement of private actors in welfare provision,[24] which are part of a growing trend in governance (and will be discussed further in chapter two below), have added complexity both to the relationships between state, providers and citizens and in terms of regulatory co-ordination.[25]

Definitional problems with regard to fundamental matters such as poverty and human need will in any event have a bearing on the complexity of the relevant arrangements. Concepts such as poverty and well-being have been described as 'intrinsically complex and vague' in themselves, because 'they involve a plurality of interrelated variables, dimensions and spaces with no clear-cut boundaries between and within them'.[26] Thus legal conceptions of need are in turn likely to be complex, particularly under rules seeking to establish such 'clear-cut boundaries' in order to target support with some precision, as predominate within the UK welfare system. Rules may appear to be well suited to perform the kind of delineating and boundary-defining task assigned to them within such a sphere. Denis Galligan, however, in analysing the role of discretion in governance, discusses the idea that the modern state in seeking to achieve its economic and social goals 'has to deal with matters that are too complex to allow for the generalizations characteristic of rules'.[27]

The comparative benefits and de-merits of rules and discretion in relation to social welfare provision have been the subject of a 'rules versus discretion' debate, which was at its peak in the 1970s. Although it is not within the remit of this work to review that debate,[28] it may be noted that the essential conflict is between rules on the one hand, which may operate too rigidly and thus

---

[22] J Mirrlees et al, *Tax by Design: The Mirrlees Review* (Oxford, Oxford University Press, 2011) 43. Also available at www.ifs.org.uk/mirrleesReview/design.

[23] That is, where welfare is delivered through a combination of state and private provision, including employer schemes and regulated private insurance arrangements.

[24] See N Harris, 'Welfare's Mixed Economy in the UK: Public Rights and Private Actors' in F Pennings, T Erhag and S Stendahl (eds), *Non-Public Actors in Social Security Administration* (Alphen aan den Rijn, Wolters Klewer, forthcoming).

[25] See, eg, P Vincent-Jones, 'The New Public Contracting: Public Versus Private Ordering?' (2007) 14(2) *Indiana Journal of Global Legal Studies* 259.

[26] EC Chiappero-Martinetti, 'Complexity and Vagueness in the Capability Approach: Strengths or Weaknesses?' in F Comim et al (eds), *The Capability Approach: Concepts, Measures and Applications* (Cambridge, Cambridge University Press, 2008) 268. See also M Tomlinson and R Walker, *Coping with Complexity: Child and Adult Poverty* (London, CPAG, 2009).

[27] DJ Galligan, *Discretionary Powers: A Legal Study of Official Discretion* (Oxford, Clarendon Press, 1986) 81–82.

[28] See Harris et al (above n 1) 35–37.

undermine the welfare objectives of social security and the doing of individualised justice, and discretion on the other hand, which through its uncertainty
and weak guarantees of entitlement undermines key social rights and threat-
ens social justice through an increased risk of inconsistency.[29] Discretion is
also associated with a lower amenability to legal challenge as a compared
with rule-based decision-making, on the basis that a failure to adhere to a
rule may be more easily questioned than the exercise of discretion.[30] At the
same time, there is an argument that the exercise of discretion may be associated with an increased risk of challenges on the basis that decisions are more
difficult to defend. The Ministry of Justice, for example, has argued in connection with its Justice Impact Test, 'The more discretion a decision-maker
has, the more potential scope there is to challenge decisions.'[31]

The contribution of discretion to complexity in the welfare system may
arise from the fact that while it may be conducive to greater responsiveness, it
'is often associated with increased costs and complexity.'[32] Officials may be
able to take account of a wide range of factors when deciding on the entitlement of an individual claimant, but that may be a more onerous task than
merely following rules. Moreover, as Peter Schuck argues, discretion may be
associated with increased complexity because of the potential involvement of
courts and judges as challenges are brought,[33] giving rise to an overlay of
judicial guidance on issues of uncertainty. Yet all these factors and outcomes
are equally associated with the application of detailed legal rules,[34] especially
in relation to a system such as that of social security in the United Kingdom,
which generates a high volume of appeals. This issue will be considered further in chapters three and eight, but the basic point to be made here is that
there is some uncertainty as to whether a legal framework for discretion-
based decision-making involves, either intrinsically or in practice, more or
less complexity than one based around more tightly worded rules. This is also

---

[29]   Ibid; CE Schneider, 'Discretion and Rules: A Lawyer's View' in K Hawkins (ed), *The Uses of Discretion* (Oxford, Oxford University Press, 1992) 47–88; and N Lewis, 'Discretionary Justice and Supplementary Benefits' in M Adler and A Bradley (eds), *Justice, Discretion and Poverty* (Abingdon, Professional Books, 1976) 77–89.

[30]   See Harris et al (above n 1); Schneider (ibid); and Lewis (ibid).

[31]   Ministry of Justice, *Justice Impact Test Guidance* (London, Ministry of Justice, 2010) 10. The Justice Impact Test, which is still in use at the time of writing, is a 'tool to help policymakers find the best way of achieving their policy aim, while minimising the impact on the justice sys-tem': ibid, 2. The guidance (above) states that if a policy is likely to increase the volume of cases before the courts, there will be a 'justice impact' (3).

[32]   CJ Jewell, 'Assessing Need in the United States, Germany, and Sweden: The Organization of Welfare Casework and the Potential for Responsiveness in the "Three Worlds"' (2007) 29(3) *Law & Policy* 380, 381.

[33]   P Schuck, 'Legal Complexity: Some Causes, Consequences and Cures' (1992) 42(1) *Duke Law Journal* 1, 16–17.

[34]   The Justice Impact Test also acknowledges this, identifying 'legislative complexity' as likely to have a justice impact: 'Legislation may itself generate litigation. This is more likely to occur if legislation further complicates the wider relevant area of law or an already obtuse area of the law. Also the volume and rate of change of legislation in the area may cause significant disrup-tion and confusion': Ministry of Justice, *Justice Impact Test Guidance* (above n 31) 11.

true of an alternative dichotomy, noted by Isaac Ehrlich and Richard Posner, between precise rules and general 'standards'.[35]

The evolution of the welfare state in the United Kingdom took a distinctly legalistic turn in the early 1980s in relation to social security and has been following that path relentlessly. Indeed, welfare benefits have been governed by ever more numerous and complex rules. According to the National Audit Office, in the years 2000–04 alone, the law of social security was affected by six new Acts of Parliament and 364 new statutory instruments,[36] although Trevor Buck et al counted eight such Acts and 359 statutory instruments during the period 2001–04 (excluding Northern Ireland).[37] The disparity between these two surveys could perhaps be due to definitional differences but might also reflect the obscurity of some parts of the law. In any event, the rules themselves have become more elaborate and prescriptive, particularly those concerned with means-tested benefits and tax credits. As will be discussed in chapter two, the reasons have their roots in the drive for increased central control of expenditure, linked to standardised decision-making and the curtailment of administrative discretion.[38] Although partly rationalised during the reforms of the 1980s with reference to the citizen's right to a clear understanding of the bases of entitlement, the shift from discretion to complex and frequently amended rules, particularly in relation to means-tested benefits, in practice soon resulted in considerable public uncertainty and confusion.[39] This is perhaps not surprising since, as Julia Black has observed, rules may not always be particularly clear or easily intelligible to administrators or citizens, and so their complexity may increase the uncertainty that detailed prescription and greater precision were intended to minimise.[40] As Paul Wilding has noted with reference to the perspective of Richard Titmuss, 'The ultimate effects of measures depend on the small print of regulations or conditions rather than on the broad principles enunciated with euphoria and self-satisfaction by the politicians.'[41]

Concern about the legal complexity surrounding social security predates the shift towards rules in the 1980s – for example, it was referred to in Harry

---

[35] I Ehrlich and RA Posner, 'An Economic Analysis of Legal Rulemaking' (1974) 3 *Journal of Legal Studies* 257, 258: 'A standard indicates the kinds of circumstances that are relevant to a decision on legality and is thus open-ended. That is, it is not a list of all the circumstances that might be relevant but is rather the criterion by which particular circumstances presented in a case are judged to be relevant or not.'

[36] NAO, *Department for Work and Pensions* (above n 11) para 2.7.

[37] T Buck, D Bonner and R Sainsbury, *Making Social Security Law* (Aldershot, Ashgate, 2005) 224.

[38] These kinds of hierarchical controls are also evident in immigration law: see R Thomas, 'Agency Rule-Making, Rule-Type, and Immigration Administration' (2013) *Public Law* 135.

[39] R Berthoud, *Reform of Social Security: Working Papers* (London, Policy Studies Institute, 1984).

[40] J Black, *Rules and Regulators* (Oxford, Clarendon Press, 1997) 25.

[41] P Wilding, 'Richard Titmuss and Social Welfare' (1976) 10(3) *Social and Economic Administration* 147, 150.

Street's seminal work, *Justice in the Welfare State* in 1975[42] and the following year by Sir Robert Micklethwait, who highlighted a number of areas of social security where the law was complex and expressed a concern that as a result of people's uncertainty and lack of clarity about the law its complexity could lead to 'injustice'.[43] As rules replaced much of the discretion within the law governing supplementary benefit, this area was said to 'rival . . . revenue law in its complexity and incomprehensibility to the ordinary person'.[44] Even the agency responsible for benefits administration acknowledged that claimants might need advice and support in consequence.[45] Since that time, the general perception has been that legal complexity in this field has grown markedly, as noted, for example, in a survey in the mid-2000s of the Social Security and Child Support Commissioners.[46]

The judiciary itself has contributed to the overall complexity of social security law, but the precise impact in this regard is difficult to measure. This issue will be returned to in chapter three, but it may be noted here that there is a plethora of case law arising from the decisions of the courts and especially (on appeal from appeal tribunals – now the First-tier Tribunal (Social Entitlement Chamber) (FTT)) the Commissioners and now the Upper Tribunal (Administrative Appeals Chamber).[47] According to Buck et al, part of the rationale for having a specialist second-tier appellate body is the technical complexity of social security law.[48] The second-tier tribunal judges, whose rulings are binding on the FTT, are able to bring some clarity by applying their expertise to the interpretation of legislation, the resolution of difficult questions relating to the handling of evidential or procedural matters[49] and the effects of the European Convention on Human Rights (ECHR) on domestic law.[50] This is particularly the case when new areas of uncertainty

---

[42]   H Street, *Justice in the Welfare State* (London, Stevens, 1975).

[43]   Sir RM Micklethwait, *The National Insurance Commissioners* (London, Stephens, 1976) 79 and, more generally, chs 8 and 9.

[44]   L Lustgarten, 'The New Legislation II: Reorganising Supplementary Benefit' (1981) *New Law Journal* 96. A similar hierarchy of complexity was referred to by one of the Social Security Commissioners quoted in Buck et al's research: Buck, Bonner and Sainsbury (above n 37) 220.

[45]   Supplementary Benefits Commission, *SBC Annual Report 1979* (London, HMSO, 1980) para 2.8.

[46]   T Buck, 'Evaluating the Commissioners' (2005) 12(4) *Journal of Social Security Law* 156–75, 171. The Commissioners were replaced by the Upper Tribunal (Administrative Appeals Chamber) (UT(AAC)) in November 2008 under the Tribunals, Courts and Enforcement Act 2007. The Commissioners in service at the time became judges assigned to the UT(AAC). See below ch 5.

[47]   The jurisdiction of the UT(AAC) is wider than that of the Commissioners but is still predominantly concerned with social security cases. N Wikeley, 'The Role of the Upper Tribunal (AAC)' (2011) *Family Law* 1255–58 notes that 80–90% of the UT(AAC)'s caseload is accounted for by social security appeals and applications for permission to appeal from the First-tier Tribunal (Social Entitlement Chamber).

[48]   Buck, Bonner and Sainsbury (above n 37) 221.

[49]   For example, how to deal with fluctuating effects from health conditions in the assessment of work capability: see, eg, Commissioner's Decision *R(IB) 2/99*.

[50]   Particularly Art 1 of the First Protocol, which includes a right not to deprived of one's possessions – effectively a right to property – which is considered to apply to both contributory and

arise as a result of changes in the legislation. In this regard it be noted that the Ministry of Justice referred in March 2010 to the 'litigation impact' of legislation, in terms of potential increases in number of legal challenges to public bodies' decisions, and has identified 'legislative complexity' as one of the factors.[51] Social security is clearly an area where there is a high risk of litigation in the broad sense, which includes tribunal appeals as well as court action. The frequent new regulations fit the Ministry of Justice's description of legislation that 'further complicates the wider relevant area of law or an already obtuse area of the law' and also contributes to 'the volume and rate of change of legislation in the area may cause significant disruption and confusion.'[52] It was envisaged by the Ministry that departments of state would need to factor-in potential costs arising from this litigation impact when making policy. Despite the clarity at the micro level that such judicial involvement can bring, it is also the case that at the macro level, the accumulation of decisions – which nowadays are widely accessible online – and the lack of consistency across them on certain specific questions of social security law[53] add further complexity.

III. Social Security, Fundamental Rights and the Citizen

Social security law[54] remains, with some exceptions, a somewhat neglected area so far as professional legal practice and, although to a lesser extent, the

non-contributory state benefits. See *Stec v United Kingdom* (Application Nos 65731/01 and 65900/01); *R(RJM) v Secretary of State for Work and Pensions* [2008] UKHL 63. See also Art 14, which provides that Convention rights and freedoms 'shall be secured without discrimination on any ground such as sex, race, colour, language, religion, political or other opinion, national or social origin, association with a national minority, property, birth or other status'. See further *RJM* (above); *R (Carson) v Secretary of State for Work and Pensions* [2005] UKHL 37; and M Cousins, 'The European Convention on Human Rights, Non-Discrimination and Social Security: Great Scope, Little Depth? (2009) 16(3) *Journal of Social Security Law* 120.

[51] Others are the engagement of human rights, discretion exercised by the decision-maker, judicial discretion (in the sense that the courts are invited to apply legislation on a case-by-case basis), the effect of policy on the allocation of resources and the existence of 'organised opposition': Ministry of Justice, *Justice Impact Test Guidance* (above n 31).

[52] Ibid, 11.

[53] Buck, Bonner and Sainsbury (above n 37) 223, although an improvement in consistency in more recent years is observed by those authors.

[54] For the purposes of this book and as generally understood by lawyers and advisers working in the field, 'social security law' includes the law governing tax credits for those in work but on inadequate incomes.

academic study of law are concerned.[55] This has always been an area of the law in which legal advice and assistance for citizens has for the most part been provided not by legal firms but by a range of voluntary bodies or local authority services. Nevertheless, these providers have always had to cope with low budgets and often declining state support, while the involvement of the legal profession, already very limited, has been significantly undermined by the cutbacks to civil legal aid made by the Coalition Government.[56] Yet social security is of fundamental social importance, as recognised in a range of international instruments. A right to social security was, for example, adopted in the United Nations Declaration on Human Rights in 1948[57] and was subsequently enshrined in the International Covenant on Economic, Social and Cultural Rights (ICESCR) as a right of 'everyone'.[58] As noted in the previous section, social security rights and the right to enjoy them on an equal basis are also protected under the European Convention on Human Rights.[59] Moreover, the UN Convention on the Rights of the Child (UNCRC) recognises the right of children to 'benefit from social security, including social insurance',[60] as well as to 'a standard of living adequate for their physical, mental, spiritual moral and social development'.[61] In the European context, the EU Charter of Fundamental Rights 'recognises and respects the entitlement to social security benefits' and to 'social and housing assistance so as to ensure a decent existence for all those who lack sufficient resources',[62] while the social security rights of migrants and certain others are protected by other EU law.[63]

---

[55] Despite the continued publication of the *Journal of Social Security Law* (Sweet and Maxwell, 1994–) and of articles on aspects of social security law in journals such as the *Modern Law Review* and the *Journal of Law and Society*, the most recent comprehensive academic work on the subject in the UK was published a decade ago: N Wikeley, *The Law of Social Security*, 5th edn (London, Butterworths Lexis Nexis, 2002).

[56] See Ministry of Justice, *Proposals for the Reform of Legal Aid in England* (Cm 7967, 2010); and the Legal Aid, Sentencing and Punishment of Offenders Act 2012, Sched 1, Part 2, para 15, which excludes 'civil legal services provided in relation to a benefit, allowance, payment, credit or pension under – (a) a social security enactment'. See further below ch 5.

[57] UN Declaration on Human Rights (1948), Art 22. See also Art 25, which provides for 'a right to a standard of living adequate for health' and to 'security in the event of unemployment, sickness, disability, widowhood, old age or other lack of livelihood in circumstances beyond [the individual's] control'.

[58] International Covenant on Economic, Social and Cultural Rights (1966), Art 9.

[59] See above n 50.

[60] UN Convention on the Rights of the Child (1990), Art 26.1. See further N Harris, 'Social Security and the UN Convention on the Rights of the Child' (2000) 7(1) *Journal of Social Security Law* 9–34; and J Fortin, *Children's Rights and the Developing Law*, 3rd edn (Cambridge, Cambridge University Press, 2009) 122–26.

[61] UN Convention on the Rights of the Child (ibid) Art 27.1.

[62] Charter of Fundamental Rights of the European Union (2000/C 364/01), Art 34. But see the limiting effect of Protocol 30 on the UK's Charter obligations: S Peers, 'The "Opt-Out" that Fell to Earth: The British and Polish Protocol Concerning the EU Charter of Fundamental Rights' (2012) 12(2) *Human Rights Law Reports* 375.

[63] See in particular Regulation 883/2004 on the co-ordination of social security systems (corrected version) [2004] OJ L200/1; and Art 42 of the EC Treaty (now Art 48 of the Treaty on the Functioning of the European Union post the Treaty of Lisbon): see RCA White, 'The New European Social Security Regulations in Context' (2010) 17 *Journal of Social Security Law* 144.

The realisation of the right to social security is essentially dependent on the provision made by the nation state in question. But there are no firm international standards against which to measure such provision.[64] An exception perhaps is the revised European Social Charter, which although requiring the maintenance by a state of a social security system 'at a satisfactory level' nevertheless expects that level to be at least equal to that prescribed in the European Code of Social Security.[65] In the case of the United Kingdom, which is not a signatory to the Code,[66] there is in any event a highly advanced welfare system. Regardless of one's view on its success in providing the security inherent to this right's objective[67] and putting to one side the Joint Committee on Human Rights' criticism of the Government's failure to conduct a detailed analysis of the compatibility with the international standards in such instruments as UNCRC and ICECSR of the provisions of what became the Welfare Reform Act 2012,[68] British social security law provides a guarantee of a basic level of entitlement for those unable to support themselves adequately or at all via paid work. This is seen as a critical facet of the social rights attached to UK citizenship, as one of its three categories of rights – civil, political and social – per TH Marshall's much analysed concept.[69] The guarantees of entitlement also continue to reflect the universalist vision of the Beveridge welfare state ('the Plan for Social Security . . . covers all citizens . . . but has regard to their different ways of life'),[70] although the increasing conditionality and individual responsibility attached to the rights in question in recent years represent 'citizenship's increasingly

---

See also Directive 2004/38 of 29 April 2004 on the Right of Citizens of the Union and Their Family Members to Move and Reside Freely within the Territory of the Member States [2004] OJ L 158/77; and P Minderhoud, 'Directive 2004/38 and Access to Social Assistance Benefits' (2011) 18(4) *Journal of Social Security Law* 153. See further below ch 2.

[64] See the discussion in the various chapters of J Van Langendonck (ed), *The Right to Social Security* (Antwerp, Intersentia, 2007).

[65] European Social Charter (Revised) (1996), Art 12; and European Code of Social Security (Revised) (1990).

[66] France, Germany and the Netherlands are among the signatories, but to date only one state, the Netherlands, has ratified it.

[67] See, for example, the criticism by the UK Children's Commissioners when reporting on the UN Convention on the Rights of the Child, Art 27, regarding the level of child poverty across all four countries of the UK: UK Children's Commissioners, *UK Children's Commissioners Report to the UN Committee on the Rights of the Child* (London, UK Children's Commissioners, 2008) paras 117–27 and RR 75–80. Note also the concern about this expressed by the Committee on the Rights of the Child in its report *Concluding Observations: United Kingdom of Great Britain and Northern Ireland*, CRC/C/GBR/CO/4 (Geneva, Centre for Human Rights, 2008) paras 64 and 65.

[68] Joint Committee on Human Rights, *Legislative Scrutiny: Welfare Reform Bill* (2010–12, HL 233, HC 1704) paras 1.35 and 1.36.

[69] TH Marshall, 'Citizenship and Social Class' in TH Marshall and T Bottomore (eds), *Citizenship and Social Class* (London, Pluto, 1992) 3–51. Civil rights provide, for example, for equality under the law and for access to legal remedies, while political rights are, for example, concerned with universal suffrage and fair elections. See further the discussion below in ch 8.

[70] Beveridge (above n 5) paras 17–19.

disciplinary quality'[71] and, on one view, indicate the 'revocation of social citizenship'.[72]

The very many in the United Kingdom who are engaged with rights derived from social security law at the present time include, for example, 28.5 million people paying National Insurance contributions (whose contribution record will help them to establish potential entitlement to a range of contributory welfare benefits),[73] the 12.7 million people in receipt of state retirement pension,[74] and the nearly 8 million families receiving child benefit in respect of almost 14 million children.[75] The Institute for Fiscal Studies calculates that at any one time about '30 million people in the UK – approximately half the total population – receive income from at least one social security benefit'.[76] Furthermore, social security and child support cases represent the largest category of new appeals made to tribunals. As will be discussed further in chapter five, the First-tier Tribunal (Social Entitlement Chamber) received 418,500 such appeals in 2010–11, and the fall to 370,800 in 2011–12 was reportedly partly due to processing problems at the Department for Work and Pensions (DWP) and is expected to be temporary; indeed, projected annual increases suggest that by 2015–16 the annual number of appeals lodged will peak at over 800,000.[77]

Maintaining the welfare of citizens through the provision of financial support in the form of social security benefits is one of the key tasks of government. The administration of the welfare system was supported by 104,000 full-time equivalent DWP staff as at 31 March 2012,[78] as well as by large numbers of local authority and Her Majesty's Revenue and Customs (HMRC) staff. The system consumes a huge amount of public expenditure. Indeed, at a

[71] R Lister, 'The Age of Responsibility: Social Policy and Citizenship in the Early 21st Century' in C Holden, M Kilkey and G Ramia (eds), *Social Policy Review 23* (Bristol, Policy Press, 2012) 79.

[72] G McKeever, 'Social Citizenship and Social Security Fraud in the UK and Australia' (2012) 46(4) *Social Policy and Administration* 465, 479. See also P Larkin, 'The Legislative Arrival and Future of Workfare: The Welfare Reform Act 2009' (2011) 18(1) *Journal of Social Security Law* 11, 14–15 and 31–32; and P Larkin, 'Incapacity, the Labour Market and Social Security: Coercion into "Positive" Citizenship' (2011) 74(4) *Modern Law Review* 385, 409.

[73] Department for Work and Pensions (DWP) Statistics for April 2010 (most recent available as at August 2012), calculated with the DWP tabulation tool: statistics.dwp.gov.uk/asd/index.php?page=tabtool

[74] Department for Work and Pensions Statistics for February 2012, calculated with the DWP tabulation tool (ibid). Of these, 7.7 million were women, and 5.0 million were men.

[75] HM Revenue and Customs, *Child Benefit Statistics: Geographical Analysis, August 2011* (London, HMRC, 2012), available at www.hmrc.gov.uk/stats/child_benefit/chb-geog-aug11.pdf. The figures relate to the UK.

[76] J Wenchao, P Levell and D Phillips, *A Survey of the UK Benefit System* (London, Institute for Fiscal Studies, 2010) 4. These figures are for the UK.

[77] R Carnwath, *The Senior President of Tribunals' Annual Report* (London, Ministry of Justice, 2013) 29–30. These figures are for the UK. Child support appeals only amounted to 3,700 of the 418,500 appeals received in 2010–11: Ministry of Justice, *Quarterly Tribunal Statistics, 4th Quarter, 2010–11* (London, Ministry of Justice, 2011) table 1.1c.

[78] Department for Work and Pensions, *Department for Work and Pensions Annual Report on Accounts, 2011–12* (London, TSO, 2012) table 5.

total of £188 billion in 2009–10, expenditure on social security represented over 28 per cent of the UK government's spending total, making it the largest single area of government expenditure.[79] (Health was next at 18 per cent.[80]) This level of financial commitment makes social security particularly vulnerable to national economic pressures, as well as to ideological forces directed at limiting the role of the state. Government policy on social security throughout the past three decades has been strongly influenced by the wish to contain and where possible reduce the burden on the public purse that this represents.

IV. The Problem of Complexity

The combined policy goal of reducing complexity and simplifying the benefits system has resulted from an increasing realisation that the system and the rules under which it operates have become too complicated for effective and efficient administration and for ordinary citizens properly to understand. As such, complexity has come to be seen as 'reduc[ing] the value of the benefits system as a whole'.[81] Even the present Government has acknowledged in its White Paper on welfare, 'Complexity undermines trust in the system.'[82]

An investigation by the National Audit Office (NAO) found that the complexity of the system gives rise to a 'high administrative burden'.[83] Means-tested benefits and credits, which are a major feature of the UK welfare system, are particularly prone to complex interaction, which exacerbates the high administrative costs associated with them.[84] One aspect of this inter-action concerns the way that entitlement to some means-tested benefits, such as income-based jobseeker's allowance, can provide a 'passport' to other enti-tlements such as free school meals or sight tests. This basically simple idea of passporting benefits has, however, given rise to a system that, according to the Social Security Advisory Committee, is 'complex to understand, establish entitlement, and administer'.[85]

---

[79] Wenchao, Levell and Phillips (above n 76).

[80] Ibid.

[81] Joseph Rowntree Foundation, 'Memorandum Submitted by the Joseph Rowntree Foundation' in House of Commons Work and Pensions Committee, *Benefits Simplification* (2006–07, HC 463II) Oral and Written Evidence (London, TSO, 2007) Ev 153–58.

[82] Department for Work and Pensions, *21st Century Welfare* (Cm 7913, 2011) ch 2, para 28.

[83] NAO, *Department for Work and Pensions* (above n 11) para 3.18.

[84] National Audit Office, *Means Testing: Report by the Comptroller and Auditor General* (2010–12, HC 1464) 6.

[85] Social Security Advisory Committee, *Universal Credit: The Impact on Passported Benefits (Report by the Social Security Advisory Committee and Response by the Secretary of State for Work and Pensions)* (Cm 8332, 2012) ch 2, para 7.

In addition to increasing the cost of administration, complexity is also regarded as having made the system more susceptible to fraud: 'Opportunistic Rule-Breaking can thrive in complex systems.'[86] Moreover, complexity is seen as contributing to errors in decision-making in individual cases.[87] The Administrative Justice and Tribunals Council (AJTC) has observed that as a result of having to administer complex legislation, 'officials . . . often struggle to get decisions right first time'.[88] There is also likely to be a problem with delays in the processing of claims as administrators struggle with 'interpreting and applying complex and changing regulations'.[89] Indeed, officials have had to be supported in their role by copious DWP guidance on social security, reportedly totalling 8,690 pages across 14 separate manuals.[90] The Government has referred to the way that the system's complexity 'generates inefficiency'.[91] Complexity has also been found to hinder attempts to improve the quality of decision-making.[92] All in all, argues Cornelius Kerwin, 'Complex rules hurt the government.'[93] The problem of complexity also extends beyond the rules governing particular benefits and the interaction of benefits to 'the complicated arrangements for review, revision and reconsideration of decisions, which are not fully understood even by decision makers themselves'.[94]

Complexity may not, however, be a problem only for central government and the relevant departments – currently the Department for Work and Pensions and HMRC, in the case of tax credits (but see section V below, as well as chapter two). For example, the complexity of the system of passported benefits, referred to above, is acknowledged to have impacted on claimants and welfare rights advisers in addition to those responsible for provision.[95] The NAO has found that the inherent complexity of benefit rules and the

---

[86] HM Government, *Tackling Fraud and Error in Government: A Report of the Fraud, Error and Debt Taskforce* (London, Cabinet Office, 2012) 36.

[87] See HC Committee of Public Accounts (above n 12); and DWP/Her Majesty's Revenue and Customs, *Tackling Error and Fraud in the Benefit and Tax Credit Systems* (London, DWP/HMRC, 2010).

[88] AJTC, *Securing Fairness and Redress: Administrative Justice at Risk?* (October 2011) para.37.

[89] NAO, *Department for Work and Pensions* (above n 11) para 3.39.

[90] D Martin, *Benefit Simplification: How and Why It Must Be Done* (London, Centre for Policy Studies, 2009) 5.

[91] See Department for Work and Pensions, *Universal Credit: Welfare that Works* (Cm 7957, 2010) ch 1, para 20.

[92] House of Commons Work and Pensions Committee, *Decision-Making and Appeals in the Benefits System* (2009–10, HC 313) para 57.

[93] CM Kerwin, *Rulemaking: How Government Agencies Write Law and Make Policy* (Washington, DC, CQ Press, 2003) 97.

[94] HC Work and Pensions Committee, *Decision-Making and Appeals in the Benefits System* (above n 92) Memorandum submitted by the Administrative Justice and Tribunals Council (DM 32), Ev 147, para 18.

[95] Social Security Advisory Committee, *The Impact on Passported Benefits* (above n 85) ch 1, para 24.

claims process has generated considerable uncertainty and confusion among the public.[96] Moreover, the new rules on universal credit are regarded as imposing more detailed and onerous reporting requirements on small businesses and the self-employed – requirements that are said to 'fly in the face of simplicity'.[97] Complexity is also seen as a barrier to the take-up of employment, on the basis of public misunderstanding of the potential support available to workers through in-work benefits or credits[98] or due to 'the burden of re-applying for, and the risk of losing benefits'.[99]

The courts have frequently complained about the abstruseness of modern social security law and its unintelligibility to claimants and professionals alike, as for example in Maurice Kay LJ's comment, 'In the field of social security, primary and secondary legislation are notoriously labyrinthine. Sometimes the substantive entitlement to a statutory benefit is clothed in complexity and can be determined after an interpretive journey that few are equipped to travel.'[100] Lord Donaldson MR considered the problem to be particularly acute for ordinary citizens:

> Rules and regulations which govern entitlement to welfare benefit in a modern state are necessarily numerous, highly complex and subject to frequent variation and amendment . . . Those whom they are designed to benefit are among the least able to unravel their mysteries.[101]

More recently, Lady Hale similarly commented that '[f]ew people can be expected to understand even their own entitlements and how these have been worked out, let alone the system as a whole.'[102] As Schuck argues, 'if the complex legal landscape contains many pitfalls for the governors, it is *terra incognita* for the governed.'[103]

It is indeed important to consider complexity through a non-governmental lens, not merely because of its general social impact but also since perceptions of complexity may vary in accordance with individuals' different backgrounds and perspectives. Benefit claimants may perceive complexity in different ways to officials, specialist lawyers or welfare rights advisers, although, for example, 'even welfare advisers and professionals working with older people are, at times, unable to understand the system.'[104]

---

[96] NAO, *Department for Work and Pensions* (above n 11) paras 3.32–3.33.

[97] Comment by A Gotch of the Chartered Institute of Taxation quoted in V Houlder and S Neville, 'Complex New Benefit Rules Attacked', *Financial Times* (3 September 2012) 4.

[98] DWP, *Welfare that Works* (above n 91) ch 1, paras 17–21.

[99] N Keohane and R Shorthouse, *Sink or Swim? The Impact of the Universal Credit* (London, Social Market Foundation, 2012) 73. See www.smf.co.uk.

[100] *Secretary of State for Work and Pensions v Morina and Anr* [2007] EWCA Civ 749 [1].

[101] *R v Legal Aid Board ex parte Bruce* [1992] 1 All ER 133, 134.

[102] *Hinchy v Secretary of State for Work and Pensions* [2005] UKHL 16 [48].

[103] Schuck (above n 33) 22.

[104] National Audit Office, *Tackling Pensioner Poverty: Encouraging Take-Up of Entitlements (Report by the Comptroller and Auditor General)* (2002–03, HC 37) para 2.4.

Regardless of whether complexity is something that can be identifiable or measurable on some objective basis,[105] individuals' subjective experience of a rule or system is, as noted by Schuck[106] and Emmanuel Towfigh[107] respectively, an important consideration in judging complexity. The problem of perceived complexity is particularly acute in relation to pensions. In the United Kingdom, such a perception of pension provision appears to be universally held, reflecting the objective evidence that this state has 'the most complex pension system in the world'.[108] The need for simplification of the state pension derives from the difficulty people experience in planning for retirement or choosing to continue working beyond pension age as a result of the present complexity.[109] This problem forms part of the Government's rationale for the proposed introduction of a new single-tier state pension,[110] discussed below. In one large-scale recent survey, 'the majority (63 per cent) of respondents felt that "sometimes pensions seem so complicated that I cannot really understand the best thing to do"'.[111] Claimant ignorance or confusion caused by the complexity in the rules governing social security more generally can also result in a breach of the obligation to report relevant changes in personal circumstances,[112] often resulting in overpayments, which are recoverable, as discussed below in chapter two. Moreover, although not in this respect a contributor to increased costs, complexity also hinders effective engagement with the benefits system in general among eligible citizens. It may prejudice access to the system, thereby weakening enjoyment of a key social right. As the previous Government acknowledged, complexity can 'disempower people' and 'restrict choices'.[113] Indeed, in relation to areas where citizens' choice has been a notable feature of the political rhetoric on public services and underscored by some substantive rights (for example, in areas such as education, health and social care), its exercise has been found to be significantly hampered by

---

[105] See the discussion below s VI and ch 3, s III.

[106] Schuck (above n 33) 3.

[107] EV Towfigh, 'Complexity and Normative Clarity, Or: Legal Statutes are Made for Lawyers', MPI Working Paper (Bonn, Max Planck Institute, 2008).

[108] Pensions Commission, *Pensions: Challenges and Choices (The First Report of the Pensions Commission)* (London, Stationery Office, 2004) 210.

[109] Department for Work and Pensions, *The Single-tier Pension: A Simple Foundation for Saving* (Cm 8528, 2013), para 4; Department for Work and Pensions, *A State Pension for the 21st Century* (Cm 8053, 2011) 8; A Weyman et al, *Extending Working Life: Behaviour Change Interventions*, DWP Research Report No 809 (London, DWP, 2012) 37; and A Thomas, J Hunt and A Coulter, *A Simpler State Pension: A Qualitative Study to Explore One Option for State Pension Reform*, DWP Research Report No 787 (London, DWP, 2012) 18.

[110] DWP, *The Single-Tier Pension* (ibid).

[111] P Macleod et al, *Attitudes to Pensions: The 2012 Survey*, DWP Research Report No 813 (London, DWP, 2012) 4.7.1.

[112] See M Boath and H Wilkinson, *Achieving Good Reporting of Changes in Circumstances*, DWP Research Report No 457 (London, Corporate Document Services, 2007) 10.

[113] Department for Work and Pensions (DWP), *Raising Expectations and Increasing Support: Reforming Welfare for the Future* (Cm 7506, 2008) para 2.3.

complexity.[114] Complexity can thus affect an aspect of social participation that is a key element of citizenship. Moreover, by undermining public trust in the acceptability of laws and in the state, complexity can impact negatively on the moral dimension of the citizen–state relationship,[115] and where it obscures legislative changes, it can undercut their 'democratic legitimacy'.[116]

How the United Kingdom has ended up with such a complex welfare system is the subject for later discussion (see chapters two and three below). What is clear is that there is a seemingly universal view that reducing the level of complexity would be beneficial. One should, however, note the evidence from the field of taxation, which, like social security, is bedevilled by a fiendishly complex and frequently changing legal framework.[117] In that context, it has been argued that complexity cannot be tackled merely by simplifying the rules without also looking at the entire system and the underlying policy.[118] Simon James and Allison Edwards, for example, criticise a tendency to assume that 'the solution to the problem of complexity in the tax system is largely a matter of simplifying tax law'.[119] A Tax Law Rewrite Project was initiated in the 1990s in response to concerns about the scale and increasing complexity of tax legislation.[120] By its conclusion in 2010, seven Acts had been rewritten.[121] Yet there were doubts at the outset that rewriting tax legislation would 'cure' complexity, since rewriting does not address all its causes;[122] and now that the project has concluded, there is disagreement as to how much has been achieved.[123] It is clear, in any event, that the process of simplifying the tax system is far from complete, as illustrated by the Coalition Government's decision to establish in July 2010 an Office for Tax Simplification (OTS) as an independent part of the Treasury. Its role, according to its

---

[114] D Boyle, *The Barriers to Choice Review: How Are People Using Choice in Public Services?* (London, Cabinet Office, 2013) 24, 26, 47 and 52.

[115] U Karpen, 'Improving Democratic Development by Better Regulation' in C Stefanou and H Xanthaki (eds), *Drafting Legislation* (Aldershot, Ashgate, 2008) 151.

[116] C Harlow and R Rawlings, *Law and Administration*, 2nd edn (London, Butterworths, 1997) 164.

[117] See, eg, F Chittenden and H Foster, *Is There a Way Out of the Tax Labyrinth?* (London, ACCA, 2009) 9.

[118] BJ Arnold, 'Australia Tax Rewrite' (2009) 19(1) *Revenue Law Journal* 1, 1: 'Often tax legislation is complex and confusing because the underlying policy is complex and confused.' See also N Lee, 'The New Tax Credits' (2003) 10(1) *Journal of Social Security Law* 7, 41, referring to the rewriting of tax legislation: 'no amount of re-writing will simplify a system that is inherently complex'.

[119] S James and A Edwards, 'Developing Tax Policy in a Complex and Changing World' (2008) 38(1) *Economic Analysis and Policy* 35, 43.

[120] D Salter, 'The Tax Law Rewrite in the United Kingdom: Plus ça change plus c'est la même chose?' (2010) *British Tax Review* 671, 671.

[121] See N Lee, *Revenue Law Principles and Practice*, 28th edn (Hayward's Heath, Bloomsbury Professional, 2010) 1.22.

[122] J Avery Jones, 'Tax Law: Rules or Principles?' (1996) 17(3) *Fiscal Studies* 63, 66.

[123] See Salter, 'The Tax Law Rewrite' (above n 120); and D Salter, 'The Ipsos Mori Review of Rewritten Income Tax Legislation: Contrasting and Converging Viewpoints' (2011) *British Tax Review* 622.

Framework Document, is to 'advise the Chancellor on delivering a simpler tax system, providing independent advice on options for addressing existing complexity in the tax system'.[124]

V. The Policy Context: Simplifying Welfare

The present Government has followed the 1997–2010 Labour administrations in the pursuit of simplifying the welfare system. Labour established a Benefit Simplification Unit (BSU) in 2005. It was a small unit; in 2007, it had four full-time staff, while two other civil servants contributed to its work.[125] Annual 'simplification plans' were published,[126] and an intra-departmental simplification practice guide was issued.[127]

The first edition of the practice guide, issued in 2006, stipulated that the design of future welfare policies should 'always include practical responses to the challenges posed by the need for simplification' and should be 'fully tested against adding any unnecessary complexity'.[128] Despite its avowed focus on simplification, in reality the practice guide was concerned more with avoiding further complexity as new policies were brought in – for example, by encouraging consistency with existing provision in relation to process and rules – rather than in reforming existing policies and legislation to make them simpler. The principal mechanism of enforcement was to require any policy submissions concerned with effecting changes to be referred to the BSU before being put to ministers. The guide also prescribed a format for proposals and required elements. Proposals would, for example, have to provide a rationale for any change which increased complexity.[129] The consequences of proposed changes for simplification also had to be explained when they were put before the Social Security Advisory Committee.[130]

[124] HM Treasury, *Office of Tax Simplification Framework Document* (London, HM Treasury, 2010) 1.

[125] House of Commons Work and Pensions Committee, *Benefits Simplification* (2006–07, HC 463-I) para 63.

[126] Department for Work and Pensions, *Simplification Plan 2006–07* (London, DWP, 2006); Department for Work and Pensions, *Department for Work and Pensions Simplification Plan 2007–08* (London, DWP, 2007); Department for Work and Pensions, *Department for Work and Pensions Simplification Plan 2008–09* (London, DWP, 2008); Department for Work and Pensions, *Department for Work and Pensions Simplification Plan 2009–10* (London, DWP, 2009).

[127] Benefit Simplification Unit, *Simplification Guide to Best Practice* (London, DWP, 2006); and Benefit Simplification Unit, *Simplification Guide to Best Practice (Revised)* (London, DWP, 2007).

[128] Benefit Simplification Unit, *Simplification Guide to Best Practice* (ibid) 8.

[129] Ibid, 11.

[130] Ibid, 12.

When the practice guide was revised in May 2007, the Minister and the Permanent Secretary jointly proclaimed that the guide had 'made a real difference', since simplification was 'now receiving greater prominence in DWP policy and delivery decisions than ever before', and ministers were now 'getting a much clearer picture of how proposals will impinge on complexity'.[131] At the same time, it was announced that benefits for people above pension age, who were not previously within the Unit's remit, would now be included. The revised version of the practice guide was more prescriptive as to the explanations that were required from those proposing changes which would increase complexity; for example, they had to specify why less complex alternatives were not favoured. If the BSU disagreed with a proposed change, it would indicate to ministers less complex options, and the proposer of the reform would have to include a statement as to why the BSU's alternative was rejected.

Although the introduction of this guide and procedure may have implied that a fairly rigorous policy of eliminating complexity would be pursued, particularly since 'customer-focused' proposals for simplification reforms had been commissioned,[132] the House of Commons Work and Pensions Committee was unconvinced. In its report *Benefits Simplification*, published in July 2007,[133] it noted that various small-scale reforms involving the alignment of administrative requirements related to different benefits had been announced by the Government and that the DWP regarded them a 'very major set of simplification changes'.[134] But the evidence suggested that progress towards simplification had been disappointing and that there was not an over-arching high-level strategy.[135] The Committee concluded that there was a 'lack of vision and drive within DWP and across Government to simplify the benefit system', and while the BSU was helping to prevent the introduction of further complexity, 'this was a very long way from having a plan to systematically introduce simplification'.[136]

The Government rejected these criticisms, claiming instead that simplification had high prominence and was playing a 'crucial role' in its 'ambitious programme of welfare reform', while the DWP was 'devoting more resource and attention to this issue than for many years'.[137] Yet it was unable to counter the criticism that it had failed to evince a coherent simplification strategy. Simplification measures which were subsequently implied to have been

---

[131] Benefit Simplification Unit, *Simplification Guide to Best Practice (Revised)* (above n 127) 2 (Foreword).
[132] See S Royston, *Benefits Simplification and the Customer* (London, DWP/Benefit Simplification Unit, 2007).
[133] Work and Pensions Committee, *Benefits Simplification* (2006–07, HC 463–I).
[134] Ibid, para 68.
[135] Ibid, paras 70–78.
[136] Ibid, para 79.
[137] Work and Pensions Committee, *Benefits Simplification: Government Response to the Committee's Seventh Report of Session 2006–07* (2006–07, HC 1054) para 7.

associated with the Unit included the introduction of employment and support allowance and the local housing allowance in the housing benefit scheme,[138] both of which can in fact be considered to have increased complexity rather than reducing it (as discussed below and later in chapter six).

Despite the limited impact of the BSU, there was nevertheless a growing and expressed governmental commitment to rationalising benefits for people of working age.[139] Some of the impetus for such reform was derived from the Government-commissioned Freud report,[140] arising out of an independent review of the welfare-to-work strategy and related benefits provision. David Freud examined possible restructuring of benefits for persons of working age. The report called for a 'simpler, more flexible system'.[141] Three possible models were identified for working age benefits: separate benefits with a common rate; one benefit with a single rate; and one benefit with short-term and long-term rates.[142] The report did not come down in favour of one particular model, recommending instead further debate and analysis.[143] But it asserted that regardless of the model selected, 'there would be opportunities to simplify the benefit rules to produce greater clarity and certainty for the individual claimant and improve the efficiency of administration.'[144]

The Government also showed interest in proposals by Roy Sainsbury and Kate Stanley for a single working-age benefit in place of separate mainstream out-of-work benefits, including incapacity benefits – a reform for which simplification provided a powerful motive.[145] Indeed, the DWP may have been able to draw support for a reform of this kind from the research it commissioned from Sainsbury and Katherine Weston into public attitudes towards such a benefit, which was in fact published shortly after the 2010 general election.[146] The research was based on discussions with claimants and advisers about a possible new benefit with a simple structure comprising a basic component, which was the same for all regardless of the reason for not being in work, plus an 'extra needs' component that recognised the extra expenses incurred by reason of, for example, disability, ill health or family/caring responsibilities. This simple benefit found favour with interviewees, who had had '[n]egative experiences . . . deriving from the complexity of individual

---

[138] See HC Deb 2 March 2010, vol 506, col 1026W (J Shaw MP). See also Department for Work and Pensions, *Departmental Report 2009* (Cm 7594, 2009) para 25.

[139] See, for example, HM Government, *Building Britain's Recovery: Achieving Full Employment* (Cm 7751, 2009).

[140] D Freud, *Reducing Dependency Increasing Opportunity: Options for the Future of Welfare to Work* (Leeds, Corporate Document Services, 2007).

[141] Ibid, 99.

[142] Ibid, 100–5.

[143] Ibid, 99.

[144] Ibid, 105.

[145] R Sainsbury and K Stanley, *One for All: Active Welfare and the Single Working-Age Benefit* (London, IPPR, 2007).

[146] R Sainsbury and K Weston, *Exploratory Qualitative Research on the 'Single Working Age Benefit'*, Department for Work and Pensions Research Report No 659 (London, DWP, 2010).

benefits, complexity in the benefit structure, and from aspects of organisation and delivery'.[147]

The DWP also adopted an 'error reduction strategy', which identified the tackling of complexity as a 'key element' in seeking to reduce error within the benefits system.[148] Furthermore, simplification was linked into wider managerial reforms, such as the DWP's Change programme,[149] and the introduction via pathfinders of 'lean' techniques.[150] But while some areas of simplification were achieved by the Labour Government, including rationalisation of the claims process for certain benefits, the reforms were relatively limited in scale.[151] As the BSU's final strategy document admitted, 'there is . . . much more to do.'[152] Nevertheless, this was the first time that an attempt had been made to respond actively to the problem of complexity in the benefits system.

Analysis by the Economic Dependency Working Group, established by the right-leaning Centre for Social Justice,[153] fed into the comprehensive proposals by the new Coalition Government post-May 2010 to simplify the system and remove its 'structural propensity towards error'.[154] The Government recognised that the kind of piecemeal simplification that had been attempted previously was insufficient to resolve the problem of complexity in the welfare system.[155] The principal structural changes, which are now underway (see chapter two below), involve replacing a raft of means-tested benefits and working tax credit with a new 'universal credit' and rationalising the administrative arrangements for benefits by concentrating them in the DWP alone rather than being spread across local authorities and two central agencies (the DWP and Her Majesty's Revenue and Customs).[156] The Economic Dependency Working Group estimated that such reforms could result in the state's administrative bill falling by 15 per cent, saving £900 million per annum.[157] The Government's subsequent estimate was more conservative but still envisaged significantly reduced costs: 'The greater simplicity of the Universal Credit system will lead to a streamlined

---

[147] Ibid, 31.

[148] DWP, *Raising Expectations and Increasing Support* (above n 113) para.2.4.

[149] Introduced in 2007, it was set up to 'drive up levels of customer service' and to improve the Department's efficiency: DWP, *Simplification Plan 2009–10* (above n 126) para 47. Elements included developing improved online services for customers, more effective telephone services and better handling of information requested from customers.

[150] 'Lean is shorthand for a commitment to eliminating waste, simplifying procedures and speeding up processes. Lean's approach to continuous improvement uses staff expertise and experience to improve how the Department works by encouraging staff to review their own work processes and environment': DWP, *Simplification Plan 2009–10* (above n 126) para 48.

[151] See, for example, the piecemeal changes listed in DWP, *Simplification Plan 2007–08* (above n 126) Annex A; and DWP, *Simplification Plan 2008–09* (above n 126) Annex A.

[152] DWP, *Simplification Plan 2009–10* (above n 126) 5 (Foreword).

[153] Economic Dependency Working Group (EDWG), *Dynamic Benefits* (London, Centre for Social Justice, 2009) esp ch15.

[154] DWP, *Welfare that Works* (above n 91) ch 1, para 23.

[155] DWP, *21st Century Welfare* (above n 82) 16, para 33.

[156] Ibid; and DWP, *Welfare that Works* (above n 91).

[157] EDWG, *Dynamic Benefits* (above n 153) 301.

administration, which we anticipate will lead to savings of more than £0.5 billion a year.'[158] The involvement of 'multiple agencies' in individual cases has, according to the Government, generated expenditure of 'valuable resources to gather and manage essentially the same information'.[159] Claimants are reported to have reacted positively to this aspect of the reforms, on the basis that 'simplification could mean being passed around the system less.'[160]

The Government stated in its White Paper on universal credit towards the end of 2010, 'There are more than 30 benefits and many more potential combinations of benefits and additional premiums. Some simplifications have been made but much more can and must be done.'[161] Bringing different means-tested (or income-related) welfare benefits, each governed by separate sets of detailed legal provisions, together into one scheme will also simplify the overall legal structure of social security, as will the combining of rules on factors that need to generate variations in support, particularly in relation to disability. For example, under the universal credit system, there are just two rates of additional support for people with disabilities, based on degree of work capability, with the higher rate available to those with the most severe disabilities – in place of the various separate and overlapping disability-related additions in each of diverse income-related benefits at present. Also, unlike under the separate benefit regimes being replaced, universal credit will be paid or be credited monthly.

One key question, however, is how far the system's inherent legal complexity will be ameliorated by these changes, particularly given the need for similarly detailed rules on entitlement and the lack of an explicit commitment to alter the form in which the legislation is drafted. In particular, reducing the number of separate rules due to the combining of separate benefits into a single benefit may on the face of it simplify the legislation, but if the single benefit still covers as wide a set of circumstances and needs as that targeted by the separate benefits previously, the intrinsic complexity of individual rules, which stems from that diversity of circumstances and needs, is likely to remain. Moreover, the experience of tax law rewriting has shown that reducing the length of legislation and modernising the language do not on their own make it simpler. The rules governing universal credit will be considered in more detail in later chapters.

Structural changes have also been pursued in the field of state pensions. As noted above, this field is widely regarded as especially complex, including by ordinary citizens. The main proposed reform, announced in January 2013 and to be effected by the Pensions Bill, which was published in May 2013, involves the introduction of a new single-tier state retirement pension for all those retiring in or after April 2016. It is intended to 'simplify the system,

[158] DWP, *Welfare that Works* (above n 91) ch 7, para 7.
[159] Ibid, ch 1, para 24.
[160] Keohane and Shorthouse (above n 99).
[161] DWP, *Welfare that Works* (above n 91) ch 1, para 6.

enabling people to know what they will get from the state and be more certain they will benefit from saving' and to 'remove outdated or complex aspects of the current system'.[162] State second pension and various other contracted-out and additional pensions will cease, and the level of the single-tier pension will be set above the rate of the pension credit, which will result in far fewer pensioners having eligibility for this credit. Qualification for the pension will be personal in each case, meaning that inheriting or deriving entitlement through the National Insurance contributions of a spouse or civil partner will cease.

The experience of the past 30 years of benefit reform in the United Kingdom has shown that when such structural simplification has occurred, it has tended to be used to rationalise provision and to shift resources away from particular groups of claimants,[163] whether directly or as a consequence of a reduction in a benefit's sensitivity to individual circumstances. A current example of such an approach is the reduction in the number of separate rates of disability benefit. In 2012, disability living allowance (DLA) was being paid to approximately 3 million people, but according to the DWP, its '11 possible different rates of benefit . . . make the benefit complex to administer'.[164] The Welfare Reform Act 2012 provides for DLA to be replaced by a new benefit known as 'personal independence payment' (PIP), with fewer separate rates. PIP will not, for example, offer the equivalent provision to that made by the lowest rate of the care component of DLA, which nearly 700,000 people receive, and on that ground, it has been criticised for raising of the threshold of entitlement to benefit.[165] It is simpler than DLA in structure but will remove a whole category of claimants from entitlement. It is estimated by the Government that of the 560,000 recipients of DLA reassessed under PIP by October 2015, 170,000 (30 per cent) will not receive the new benefit,[166] which is being phased in, from April 2013.

Another earlier example of structural simplification within a scheme is the creation of an age dividing-line (at 25 years) in the income support personal allowance rates (which was introduced in 1987) and, subsequently, in jobseeker's allowance, so that single claimants under that age would receive a significantly lower rate than the standard rate paid to their older counterparts. The rule is therefore simpler than the previous one, which sought to base rates of benefit on whether or not someone was a 'householder', which

---

[162] DWP, *The Single-Tier Pension* (above n 109) paras 32 and 34. The implementation date was originally set at April 2017, but it was announced in the Budget Statement in March 2013 that it was being brought forward to April 2016: HM Treasury, *Budget 2013*, HC 1033 (London, Stationery Office, 2013) para 2.80. For an outline of the reform, see below ch 2.

[163] See, eg, Harris et al (above n 1) ch 4.

[164] Department for Work and Pensions, *Disability Living Allowance Reform* (Cm 7984, 2010) 9.

[165] Acknowledged in Department for Work and Pensions, *Government's Response to the Consultation on Disability Living Allowance Reform* (Cm 8051, 2011) 17–18.

[166] HL Deb 13 December 2012, vol 741, col 1193 (Parliamentary Under-Secretary of State, Department for Work and Pensions, Lord Freud) Statement.

required a range of factors to be considered, such as sharing of accommodation and contractual arrangements.[167]

Another example of a change designed to remove detailed consideration by officials of individual circumstances was the introduction in the housing benefit scheme of a 'local housing allowance' (on a pilot basis in 2003 and nationally in 2008). It limited the amount of rent available within housing benefit to private rented-sector tenants to the median level for rents in the broad rental market area for the size of property, regardless of the rate that they were actually paying.[168] It represented 'a significant simplification'[169] by replacing earlier schemes designed to limit the amount paid out by setting an appropriate rent for each individual property, which involved provisions that were complex and costly to administer.[170] However, more recently, national caps were prescribed on the level of rent covered by housing benefit, at a set amount for properties of different sizes, such as £340 for any three-bedroom property.[171] The policy aim is for levels of benefit which are 'fairer and more sustainable', with the rationale for the former being that in the absence of such limits people had been 'able to enter into rental commitments that people earning a reasonable wage would not consider'.[172] The caps are estimated to save £65 million per annum.[173] Blanket rules of this kind tend to be simple, although ironically, by qualifying an existing rule, they actually add an element of complexity. This in fact illustrates how complexity can result from competing policy objectives, in this case simplification on the one hand and cost and demand control on the other.

---

[167] See NS Harris, *Social Security for Young People* (Aldershot, Ashgate, 1989) 74–76.

[168] There was, however, an allowed excess of up to £15 where the contractual rent exceeded the LHA, but this has been abolished and other restrictions have been imposed. The rates applicable from April 2013 in the different areas are listed at www.voa.gov.uk/corporate/RentOfficers/LHARates/april2013lha.html.

[169] S Rahilly, 'From Rent Stop to a Rent Allowance: The Government's Plans to Introduce Choice and Responsibility in Housing Benefit' (2003) 10 *Journal of Social Security Law* 124, 133.

[170] S Rahilly, 'New Limits on Benefit for Rents: The Cap that Doesn't Fit?' (2011) 18 *Journal of Social Security Law* 118, 119.

[171] Claimants have enjoyed nine months of transitional protection against the effects of the caps.

[172] Work and Pensions Committee, *Local Housing Allowance: Government Response to the Committee's Fifth Report of Session 2009–10* (2009–10, HC 509) 8.

[173] Department for Work and Pensions, *Impact Assessment, Housing Benefit: Changes to the Local Housing Allowances* (London, DWP, 2010), available at www.dwp.gov.uk/docs/lha-impact-nov10.pdf, cited in ibid.

VI. Analysing Complexity

Across areas of governance, the laws and arrangements for their administration are commonly described as 'complex' or perhaps even 'highly complex' without any real sense of what these terms mean. As noted above, the status of complexity of the kind with which we are concerned here as an empirical phenomenon appears to be based primarily on perception rather than scientific measurement.[174] There is a realisation among policy-makers that various negative consequences are attributable to the perceived 'complex' state of a system. At the same time, there is a belief that these negative consequences can be ameliorated through a process of simplification. But if, as has become the case, simplification is adopted as a specific policy goal, it is reasonable to assume that the impact of actions taken in its pursuit can be judged with a reasonable level of accuracy. Identifying the causes of complexity in the system – which in the case of the welfare system would include its diverse range of benefits, the inter-relationships between them and the complicated rules which govern entitlement – is merely the start. The next stage would be to gauge accurately the observable effects of complexity, such as delays or errors in decision-making or significant levels of public confusion about entitlement. The impact of simplification policy could then be assessed with reference to how far the effects or symptoms of complexity are perceived to have been reduced as a result of it. This process would include making a judgement based on comparison of the system before and after changes are made to it.

The House of Commons Committee on Public Accounts considered that if the DWP was to have an effective strategy for tackling complexity, it needed 'to have a clearer idea of the scale of the problem it faces', and the Committee called for an 'easy to understand' basis of measurement of complexity.[175] However, as will be noted below in chapter three, while the DWP gave consideration to the construction of a 'complexity index', it reportedly lacked feasibility, and the idea was abandoned.

---

[174] However, there have recently been claims that organisational complexity in the public sector can be judged with reference to 18 'drivers' of complexity: Simplicity Partnership, *The Public Sector Complexity Review: The True Cost of Complexity to the Taxpayer* (2012), available at www.simplicity-consulting.com/wp-content/files_mf/1340881652PublicSectorComplexityRevie wIA8Feb2012.pdf. The independence of this report is unclear, but it claims to be based on a survey covering 150 civil servants across 15 central departments. It states that across the largest departments, the worst affected in terms of complexity are, surprisingly, not the DWP and HMRC but rather the Ministry of Defence, the Department for Transport and the Department for Business, Innovation and Skills.

[175] HC Committee of Public Accounts (above n 12) para 6 and Conclusions and Recommendations no 7.

Legal complexity warrants special consideration, for as we have seen, the law lies at the heart of the complexity of the welfare system. The law prescribes the various forms of support that the system is to provide in the form of benefits or credits and governs the procedural processes and institutional framework for their administration. It serves both to structure the system at the macro level and determine its detailed procedures and entitlements at the micro level. We have seen that complexity has become viewed in governmental eyes as problematic, warranting a policy response based around structural rationalisation/simplification, including reductions in the number or length of rules. Yet structural complexity, even if resulting from legislation, is distinct from legal complexity per se. This distinction may be illustrated by the rewriting of tax legislation, which aimed to make it easier for professionals and taxpayers to understand and officials to apply. This reform has looked primarily to the legal form in which policy is expressed rather than at the structure of the tax system itself. This singular focus is seen by some as an underlying reason for the rewrite's failure to precipitate a significant reduction in complexity, which was noted above. A major reform of social security legislation in Australia, effected in 1991, was similarly focused, aiming to rewrite and reformulate the legislation in order to make it easier to understand, while leaving unchanged the broad structure of eligibility for the relevant pensions and benefits.[176] It is regarded as having failed to deal sufficiently with the problem of complexity, leading to further simplification initiatives (discussed further below in chapter seven).

Where social security in the United Kingdom is concerned, attention has been paid to the law in addition to the structure – but for the most part only in relation to its role in implementing and operationalising policy. Whilst the rules on social security inter-relate with each other in a complex way, reflecting the structural intricacy of the benefit system and the inter-dependency of different elements within it, it is also the case that many of the rules are themselves very complex. This fact will not change under the proposed universal credit reforms, and consequently, as discussed in later chapters, government claims of radical simplification should be viewed with caution.[177]

Across the academic literature there has been less analysis of legal complexity than might be anticipated, although it has been considered in a variety of different theoretical contexts. In relation to regulation, for example, one finds reference to the complexity of rules and some attempt to define it. Black has observed that a rule's complexity or simplicity is dependent upon 'the number of factual situations or assessments involved in the determination of the rule's applicability',[178] while in the analysis of Louis Kaplow, 'the complexity of legal rules refers to the number and difficulty of distinctions

---

[176] See below ch 7.
[177] DWP, *Welfare that Works* (above n 91) Executive summary, para 2.
[178] Black (above n 40) 23.

the rules make'.[179] More broadly, William Twining and David Miers' study of legal rules refers to their 'structural and linguistic' complexity: 'very complicated, often involving exceptions, qualifications, provisions and double negatives'.[180] Complexity and simplicity have also been referred to in analysis of legislative drafting, for example in discussing the case for the use of plain language in statutes[181] and the issue of the primacy of the goal of certainty over simplicity.[182] The latter issue leads on to the question of rule precision, which has also been analysed. One of the difficulties in relation to the social security system arises from the need to have rules which are sufficiently precise to enable officials to make the kinds of clear distinctions called for in the determination of questions of entitlement. Looking at disability insurance benefit in the United States, Colin Diver found an increased use of bright-line rules to determine disability, but that such rules 'achieve their objective only at the cost of enormous complexity'.[183] That of course increases the transaction costs of employing such rules (as measured by, in particular, the burdens involved in drawing up the rules and in working out how to apply them), even if a major factor in shaping them was a desire to minimise those costs. As Diver points out, much of the administrative burden may come from gathering and assessing relevant medical and other evidence to determine a claim, which would also be required under simpler legal definitions.[184]

The link between the lack of clarity in legislation, which is associated with complexity, and the rule of law, has also been highlighted.[185] The connection is underpinned by the notion that a system committed to the rule of law in a formal sense must have laws with various formal qualities, including that they are 'general, equal and certain' (Hayek)[186] and are clear and capable of being understood (Fuller).[187] (Notably, however, such qualities are also 'not incompatible with dictatorship', as Martin Loughlin has pointed out.[188])

---

[179]   Kaplow (above n 14) 150.
[180]   W Twining and D Miers, *How to Do Things with Rules*, 4th edn (London, Butterworths, 1999) 413.
[181]   Eg, B Hunt, 'Plain Language in Legislative Drafting: An Achievable Objective or a Laudable Ideal?' (2003) 24(1) *Statute Law Review* 112; and Office of the Parliamentary Counsel, 'Good Law' (above n 17).
[182]   The Renton Committee report stated that those who draft legislation 'must never be forced to sacrifice certainty for simplicity': Renton Committee, *The Preparation of Legislation: Report of a Committee Appointed by the Lord President of the Council* (Cmnd 6053, 1975) para 11.5. See also H Xanthaki, 'On the Transferability of Legislative Solutions: The Functionality Test' in Stefanou and Xanthaki (eds) (above n 115) 12–14.
[183]   CS Diver, 'The Optimal Precision of Administrative Rules' (1983) 93(1) *Yale Law Journal* 65, 92.
[184]   Ibid.
[185]   Lord Neuberger of Abbotsbury MR, 'General, Equal and Certain: Law Reform Today and Tomorrow', Annual Lord Renton Lecture (2011); and Office of the Parliamentary Counsel, 'Good Law' (above n 17) 1.
[186]   F Hayek, *The Political Idea of the Rule of Law* (Cairo, National Bank of Egypt, 1955) 34.
[187]   LL Fuller, *The Morality of Law*, 2nd edn (New Haven, Yale University Press, 1969) ch 2, cited in M Loughlin, *Foundations of Public Law* (Oxford, Oxford University Press, 2010) 335.
[188]   Loughlin (ibid) 335.

Lord Neuberger sees practical as well as constitutional advantages to greater legislative clarity, such as a reduced amount of litigation and lower regulatory compliance costs, together with 'a more readily understandable and accessible framework within which people can lead their lives'.[189] These views were expressed in the Annual Lord Renton Lecture, which marks the contribution of the eponymous reformer as chair of the Committee on the Preparation of Legislation in 1975.[190] In commenting on the failure to implement his committee's report, Lord Renton himself commented:

> If our Acts of Parliament cannot be understood, even by experts, it brings not only the law into contempt, it brings Parliament into contempt – and it is, moreover, a disservice to our democracy. It weakens the rights of the individual, it eases the way for wrongdoers and it places honest people at the mercy of the bureaucratic state.[191]

Indeed, it has been suggested that the opacity of laws and their unintelligibility due to complexity serve to alienate lay citizens and to undermine the legitimacy of laws themselves.[192] Paul Craig, also linking legal certainty to formal conceptions of the rule of law, argues that sacrificing clear, general norms because the best way to achieve a particular objective is to have a more open-textured, more discretionary framework would involve undermining aspects of the rule of law, but this may be considered justifiable in those circumstances.[193] A further link is between congruence and complexity, in the sense that rules should regulate to the intended end without over-prescription, which tends to increase complexity, through unnecessary extension ('over-inclusiveness').[194]

Much of the more theoretical academic analysis of legal complexity has been undertaken by US scholars. Twenty years ago, Shuck commented that 'consideration of legal complexity in the academy is still in an embryonic stage'.[195] In his attempt to analyse it, he found legal complexity a relative concept that was 'hard to define, much less to measure'.[196] Despite the apparent elusiveness of a definition, Schuck has nevertheless identified four features of legal complexity: denseness of the law, technicality, institutional differentiation (where it is derived from a number of different sources) and indeterminacy (involving rules that are open-textured and fluid, making possible outcomes of their application less certain).[197] As noted earlier, Schuck has also identified but does not expressly advocate an alternative approach to

---

[189] Lord Neuberger (above n 185).

[190] Renton Committee (above n 182).

[191] Sir D Renton, 'Failure to Implement the Renton Report', address to the Statute Law Society (6 April 1978) 8, www.francisbennion.com/pdfs/fb/1979/1979-004-002-renton-part1.pdf.

[192] Schuck (above n 33) 22–23.

[193] P Craig, 'Formal and Substantive Conceptions of the Rule of Law: An Analytical Framework' (1997) *Public Law* 467, 469.

[194] Kerwin (above n 93) 95. See also Thomas (above n 38).

[195] Schuck (above n 33) 3.

[196] Ibid, 2.

[197] Ibid, 4.

defining complexity based on the subjective experience of those subjected to a rule.[198]

Another of the relatively few authors to analyse the nature of legal complexity in depth is Richard Epstein. In *Simple Rules for a Complex World*,[199] he states that neither simplicity nor complexity are capable of precise definition, adding, perhaps somewhat unhelpfully, that 'the opposite of simplicity is complexity'.[200] The same may of course be said of other opposing concepts, such as 'good' and 'bad', the meaning of which will also depend on context. In any event, Epstein is able to 'identify some of the critical elements that mark a set of legal rules as complex',[201] such as their density and technicality (in reference specifically to US social security law), although he also points to rules which may be short but the application of which to particular circumstances can be a complex process. But he also suggests that legal complexity is related not exclusively to the formal properties of rules but also to the rules' effects, namely 'how deeply they cut into the fabric of ordinary life'.[202] This must be correct, since as previously discussed, judgements of complexity arise from its social impact as the rules in question are applied in practice.

Legal complexity has also been analysed from a law and economics perspective. Particular attention has been given to determining an optimal level of complexity at which programmes of regulation can function effectively[203] and to the inter-relationship between the level of complexity and the international harmonisation of rules of individual nation states.[204] This work reinforces the possibility at least that complexity within legislative schemes may be capable of effective empirical and objective measurement. One author to have pursued this further is Eric Kades, who suggests that a mathematical theory of complexity known as 'computational complexity theory' may offer solutions to the problem of determining the levels of complexity arising from the application of laws to particular cases, especially what he refers to as 'large' cases, such as those involving the establishment of priorities between creditors, which could prove 'intractable' if presented for adjudication.[205] However, it is unclear how readily this theory could be applied to the kind of citizen-versus-state cases that arise in the field of social security; such cases may revolve around a single legal question, and though there may be a range

---

[198] Ibid, 3.

[199] RA Epstein, *Simple Rules for a Complex World* (Cambridge, MA, Harvard University Press, 1995).

[200] Ibid, 24.

[201] Ibid.

[202] Ibid, 29.

[203] RA Epstein, 'The Optimal Complexity of Legal Rules', John M Olin Law and Economics Working Paper No 210, University of Chicago (2004).

[204] B Crettez, B Deffains and R Deloche, 'On the Optimal Complexity of Law and Legal Rules Harmonization' (2009) 27 *European Journal of Law and Economics* 129.

[205] E Kades, 'The Laws of Complexity and the Complexity of Laws: The Implications of Computational Theory for the Law' (1997) 49 *Rutgers Law Review* 403.

of factual issues to consider, hardly any (indeed most probably none) of such cases will be incapable of being resolved.

Another area of theory which may appear at least to have relevance to an analysis of legal and structural complexity is 'complexity theory'. While it has been suggested that 'there is no one identifiable complexity theory',[206] the basic idea that has gained currency is that of 'a scientifically and technologically established conceptual model that draws attention to particular features derived from study of naturally occurring complex systems, features that might be employed in descriptions of complex social situations and events'.[207] It examines the ways in which the internal dynamics of a system create outcomes which are unpredictable.[208] Such as system would be classed as 'complex', as distinct from one that is 'complicated'. In a 'complicated' system,

> ... interactions between elements or variables is (sic) generally linear and in manipulating particular variables we can observe the effects in the system and calculate on arriving at an expected result. We can 'manage' the situation by attending to particular variables, ie, those that are within our control.[209]

On the assumption that the welfare state is a 'system' for the purposes of complexity theory,[210] it could be argued that it is a system that is 'complicated' in the sense that, even though it may be difficult to do so, it is possible to predict the outcomes resulting from the variables and interactions within the system, such as those arising from the inter-relationship between different benefits or rules. If that description is correct, it would suggest that a simplification strategy can perhaps be planned and implemented reasonably effectively, since the effects of planned changes can be predicted with a degree of certainty. Equally, complexity theory might offer a possible explanation for any failure of simplification strategies adopted for the welfare system. If the system is complex in the sense that there may be unpredictable and therefore difficult to manage interactions, it may be difficult for simplification changes, which are essentially linear, to achieve their objectives. Robert Geyer argues that issues to do with resource allocations or debates over the scope of welfare bring the welfare state into that category.[211] Complexity theory also alerts us to the importance of recognising the possibility that simplification measures themselves may have unpredictable effects.

---

[206] SM Manson, 'Simplifying Complexity: A Review of Complexity Theory' (2001) 32 *Geoform* 405, 405.

[207] M Radford, 'Action Research and the Challenge of Complexity' (2007) 37(2) *Cambridge Journal of Education* 263, 264.

[208] See, eg, R Geyer and S Rihani, *Complexity and Public Policy: A New Approach to 21st-Century Politics, Policy and Society* (London, Routledge, 2010).

[209] Radford (above n 207).

[210] It is considered to be one by R Geyer, 'Europeanisation, Complexity, and the British Welfare State', paper presented to the UACES/ESRC Study Group on the Europeanisation of British Politics and Policy-Making, Department of Politics, University of Sheffield (19 September 2003) 40, available at aei.pitt.edu/1719/1/Geyer.pdf.

[211] Ibid.

Complexity theory would, however, be most concerned with the response that the welfare system represents to the social phenomena that it is designed to deal with, such as poverty and unemployment. Its critique is concerned with the linear cause-and-effect assumptions made by political and social scientists, which are seen as reductionist in nature.[212] The Newtonian concepts of cause and effect are based on the idea that predicable and repeatable outcomes arise from the behaviour of a system. Thus complexity theory questions the assumption that 'social phenomena are primarily orderly and therefore controllable and predictable to a high level of detail'.[213] Geyer and Samir Rihani contend that the failure to modify the linear approach – which is evident in, for example, 'health targets that force doctors to treat patients like machines, to teaching philosophies which assume that all children develop uniformly, orderly solutions to complex problems [which] infect our politics and daily lives' – lies behind 'policy actors' continual frustration over their inability to fully control and direct society'.[214] Thus the capacity of public policy to order the wider social world is considered to be limited by the complexity arising from wide-scale unpredictable and nonlinear interactions,[215] while public policy actors are 'caught between the demands of orderly, rational central criteria and the messy reality of day-to-day local conditions and contradictions'.[216]

The law is clearly part of this attempt to bring control or order, not least by prescribing the 'rational central criteria' which are applied to the phenomena or system in question. Complexity theorists have questioned how the law should be constructed for the purpose of policy responses to complex social phenomena.[217] In particular, the question is whether laws of similar complexity (in the sense used in the theory) to the phenomena in question are required.[218] JB Ruhl adopts an affirmative position, favouring an adaptive system involving 'less hierarchical, flatter, and more decentralized power structures'.[219] Byron Holz, however, takes a different view, arguing that it would be impracticable and

---

[212] Geyer and Rihani (above n 208) 6. Geyer, 'Europeanisation, Complexity, and the British Welfare State' (above n 210) explains reductionism as meaning that 'the behaviour of a system could be understood, clockwork fashion, by observing the behaviour of its parts. There are no hidden surprises; the whole is the sum of the parts, no more and no less'.

[213] Geyer and Rihani (above n 208). See also the analysis of the EU's constitutional dynamics from a complexity perspective in G Martinico, *The Tangled Complexity of the EU Constitutional Process* (London, Routledge, 2013) esp 36–54.

[214] Geyer and Rihani (above n 208) 4 and 6.

[215] R Geyer, 'Beyond the Third Way: The Science of Complexity and the Politics of Choice' (2003) 5(2) *British Journal of Politics and International Relations* 237.

[216] Geyer and Rihani (above n 208) 4.

[217] See, eg, JB Ruhl, 'Law's Complexity: A Primer' (2008) 24 *Georgia State University Law Review* 885; and B Holz, 'Chaos Worth Having: Irreducible Complexity and Pragmatic Jurisprudence' (2006) 8(1) *Minnesota Journal of Law, Science and Technology* 303.

[218] Holz (ibid).

[219] JB Ruhl, 'The Fitness of Law: Using Complexity Theory to Describe the Evolution of Law and Society and Its Practical Meaning for Democracy' (1996) 49 *Vanderbilt Law Review* 1407, 1418.

unworkable for the law to seek to be adaptive to the unpredictable behaviour of the social or natural system that it is intended to regulate.[220] Instead, he concludes, agencies would wish to ensure a sufficient degree of control and certainty.[221]

In terms of the British welfare system, it is clear that the law is used to establish such a regime of control and certainty, but at the same time, it is expected to be adaptive as new or unpredicted situations arise. There are plenty of examples in the field of social security when established rules have had to be reformulated or reinterpreted in their application to new situations. Frequent small-scale amendments are made to the law in response not only to minor policy shifts but also to loopholes or 'unpredicted' outcomes which arise from its application. This aspect of the evolutionary process of social security law is one of reasons that we now see a legal framework that is perceived as complex in the more general sense used in this book.

VII. Conclusion

This chapter has sought to explain how and why complexity in the law and structure of the welfare system – specifically the legal (rule-based) and administrative frameworks governing the provision of welfare benefits – is an important issue worthy of detailed analysis. In doing so, it has pointed to the critical role of the modern welfare system in providing support for millions of citizens – around half the total population of Great Britain at any point in time. It has also showed how citizens' entitlement is underpinned by a framework of fundamental rights under a range of international instruments. It has focused on the wide-ranging concerns about complexity and provided some introductory discussion of the policy responses to it. The chapter has also discussed some key definitional issues around complexity and alluded to problems concerning its measurability. It has highlighted a range of relevant conceptual perspectives to show the difficulties inherent in defining and measuring complexity in contexts such as this one.

The next two chapters focus more directly on the specific factors that give rise to complexity in the highly legalistic social security system of the United Kingdom. Chapter two maps out the current UK benefits system and its legislative framework and shows the complexity both in its design and continual

---

[220] Holz (above n 217) 331.
[221] Ibid, 332.

development and in the management of welfare. Chapter three discusses further the notion of complexity in the context of rules and rule-making, giving examples from the current law of the different ways in which legal complexity manifests itself. It also explores ways of measuring such complexity.

Chapter four is the first of three chapters that discuss the impact of complexity on the 'customer journey' into and across the benefit system. It looks at the impact of complexity on claims for benefits and credits, including its deterrent effect on benefit take-up. Welfare complexity has a democratic impact arising from the ways that it creates barriers to citizens' understanding of the welfare system and thus in knowing their rights and accessing their entitlement. The complexity of the claims process reflects both the nature of the benefit schemes themselves and also the extensive controls that are applied. The chapter also focuses on the impact of complexity on the administration of claims and especially on decision-making, including its contribution to increased cost and error and to consequential under- or overpayment of benefit. Chapter five discusses the following stage in this journey, when a claimant is confronted with a decision with which he or she disagrees and seeks to have it changed. Complexity has justice implications for claimants, and this increases the importance of an independent appeal process. Chapter six discusses the impact of complexity on the obligations of benefit recipients. Even though a claimant may have secured entitlement, the journey continues, since the conditions which are attached to receipt of benefits require on-going engagement with the system, whether, for example, as a result of the activation measures which create work-search or work-preparation obligations, or requirements to attend for medical or disability assessment, or the requirement to report changes in personal circumstances. The chapter focuses in particular on the obligations imposed on those claimants classed as incapable of work due to sickness or disability. The relationship between claimant and state which arises from an award of benefit is also analysed. In chapter seven, the response to welfare complexity that has occurred in a range of other states is outlined and assessed with a view to drawing lessons from the various attempts at simplification of welfare made by the governments concerned.

Chapter eight, the concluding chapter, aims to show both how complexity remains difficult to remove from modern welfare systems and how it has positive as well as negative implications. The chapter seeks to suggest that changes in the law and the way it is constructed could enhance understanding and accessibility and thereby ameliorate some of the key problems arising from complexity. It proposes a new approach to social security legislation that attempts to meet both the demands of efficient and accurate governance of welfare and the need for clear and intelligible bases of entitlement enshrined in law which are more accessible to ordinary citizens.

2

The Design, Structure and Management of the Welfare System

I. Introduction

In her judgment in *Hinchy v Secretary of State for Work and Pensions*, Baroness Hale of Richmond commented on the social importance of the benefits system and on the role that its design and administration play in meeting its central objective:

> The benefits system is there for anyone who has or may have a claim upon it. In practice that is almost everyone. This is not just law for the poor. Many claimants are wholly dependent on benefits and have no other resources available to them. Many are old, ill, disabled or struggling to bring up children on their own. Benefits are there to guard against the eventualities which make it difficult for people to be self-sufficient. But they do this in a number of different ways, by a mixture of universal, contributory and non-contributory, non-means-tested and means-tested benefits or tax credits. This means that almost everyone at some time in their lives will have a valid claim to some form of benefit. We are all potential claimants as well as contributors. This means that it is in all our interests that the system be well designed and well administered so that everyone receives what they are properly entitled to, neither more nor less. It also means that the system is enormously complicated . . .[1]

The previous chapter referred at various points to the causes and indicators of complexity, one of the defining features of the welfare system in the United

---

[1] *Hinchy v Secretary of State for Work and Pensions* [2005] UKHL 16, para 48.

Kingdom, which, as Lady Hale stated, is there for all. This chapter considers these factors in more detail.

It has been argued that regardless of whether complexity in the system is defensible, some aspects of it 'are there anyway, like the weather and the tides, and there is not much hope of changing them'.[2] Means testing, for example, is one of the major sources of complexity in the system, as was noted in chapter one, and even though there is scope for some simplification of it,[3] a modern framework of welfare benefits without it is inconceivable. Some of the complexity in the system is therefore inherent, as will be explored further in this chapter.

Rules embody the kind of distinctions that are required in the process of rationing or targeting support that, for example, occurs via means-testing. The contribution of rules to complexity therefore warrants analysis, and this forms much of the content of chapter three. Included in both chapters is a further explanation of how social security and tax credits law is constructed. The nature and sources of the rules governing entitlement and administration make the overall scale of delegated legislative activity in this field probably unequalled in any other area of governance. The apparent omnipotence of government in bringing such legal changes into effect has in the general sphere long prompted concerns regarding 'government by moonlight'[4] and the associated lack of supervision and accountability,[5] although many social security regulations are subject to the scrutiny of the Social Security Advisory Committee (SSAC).[6]

Government has frequently identified the constituents and causes of complexity when setting out proposals for reform of the welfare system or specific

[2] P Spicker, 'Five Types of Complexity' (2005) 13(1) *Benefits* 5, 6.

[3] See J Millar, 'Simplification, Modernisation and Social Security' (2005) 13(1) *Benefits* 10, 13.

[4] See, eg, E Laurie, 'Judicial Responses to Bright Line Rules in Social Security: In Search of Principle' (2009) 72(3) *Modern Law Review* 384, 404–5.

[5] But see the examples of successful challenges to the vires of regulations, below s II.

[6] The SSAC has no power of veto or amendment of legislation. Normally, proposed social security regulations must be referred in draft to the Committee, who will issue comments on them in a report. The Secretary of State may proceed to make the regulations prior to receiving the Committee's report if after referring them to the Committee he or she considers it expedient to make them on the grounds of urgency: Social Security Administration Act 1992, s 173(3). Furthermore, draft regulations do not need to be referred to the Committee before being made either if the Committee agrees to this or 'if it appears to the Secretary of State that by reason of the urgency of the matter it is inexpedient so to refer them': Social Security Administration Act 1992, s 173(1). Once such regulations are made, however, they must be referred to the SSAC as soon as practicable thereafter, unless the Committee is content with non-referral: s 173(2). The Secretary of State is under a duty to lay before Parliament any draft regulations together with the SSAC's report on them and his or her response to it: s 174. The SSAC has no formal remit over HMRC-administered tax credits but does offer informal advice to HMRC on regulations relevant to tax credits under a Memorandum of Understanding (signed 7 January 2009): ssac.independent.gov.uk/pdf/keydocs/MOU.pdf. The SSAC chair has argued that scrutiny of tax credits should be placed on 'exactly the same terms' as that of social security regulations: Social Security Advisory Committee (SSAC), *Twentieth Report: 2007* (Leeds, Corporate Document Services, 2003) vi. For an assessment of the SSAC role, see A Ogus, 'SSAC as an Independent Advisory Body: Its Role and Influence on Policymaking' (1998) 5(4) *Journal of Social Security Law* 156.

parts of it, but more comprehensive and independent analyses have been undertaken by two Parliamentary committees[7] and the National Audit Office (NAO).[8] Paul Spicker[9] has also provided a short but nevertheless valuable typology of the various kinds of complexity within the social security system, although like the other analyses, his does not address legal complexity in any detail. The discussion in this and the next chapter attempts to fill that gap.

The various elements of complexity in the welfare system can be grouped into four areas. The first of them concerns the design of the system, in particular its attempts to cover a wide range of often inter-connected social needs and circumstances through both contributory and non-contributory schemes. Secondly, there is so-called 'extrinsic complexity' arising from the inter-connection between individual benefits and credit schemes and the interfaces between different administrative agencies. Thirdly, complexity arises from the management of the system. A notable issue in this regard is the use of information technology to 'manage complexity'. These three elements are discussed in sections II, III and IV below. Chapter three tackles the fourth area, namely the extensive use of highly complex rules, mostly in very detailed secondary legislation, governing all elements of entitlement, as well as claims and their adjudication.

II. Design

The design of the welfare system is commonly agreed to be a major factor in its complexity.[10] Its design reflects the system's primary purpose of meeting, through the administration of benefit payments or tax credits, the relief of poverty and financial insecurity related to a wide range of factors and circumstances. As the House of Commons Work and Pensions Committee has put it, the intrinsic complexity of the welfare system

> reflects, to some degree, the complexity of the circumstances it is dealing with. It deals with contingencies that can be difficult to identify or classify, such as work

[7] House of Commons Committee of Public Accounts, *Tackling the Complexity of the Benefits System* (2005–06, HC 765); and House of Commons Work and Pensions Committee, *Benefits Simplification, Vol I* (2006–07, HC 463–I).

[8] National Audit Office (NAO), *Department for Work and Pensions: Dealing with the Complexity of the Benefits System*, HC 592 (London, Stationery Office, 2005).

[9] P Spicker, *How Social Security Works: An Introduction to Benefits in Britain* (Bristol, Policy Press, 2011); and Spicker, 'Five Types of Complexity' (above n 2).

[10] Spicker, *How Social Security Works* (ibid); and Spicker, 'Five Types of Complexity' (above n 2). See also F Bennett and J Millar, 'Social Security: Reforms and Challenges' in J Millar (ed), *Understanding Social Security: Issues for Policy and Practice* (Bristol, Policy Press, 2009) 20.

status, personal relationships and disability. It often deals with changing circumstances. Relationships change, for example through divorce and repartnering. Personal needs change: disability can be different from one week to the next. Income fluctuates. Some people are in marginal employment, shifting between casual and irregular work . . .[11]

On this basis, there is an argument that complexity may be rationally defended as an unavoidable consequence of responding to myriad, varying social circumstances.[12] Moreover, the benefits system is not alone in having to deal with the financial consequences and needs related to the complexities of people's lives. Other systems that are also highly complex in structure and operate against a broad and diverse social background include the tax system and the periodically reformed child support scheme.[13] The former has been subject to a law rewrite process, as noted in chapter one, while the latter is about to undergo yet further reform under proposals which aim to institute a 'much simpler, more efficient statutory child maintenance scheme . . . with one set of rules'.[14]

The broad range of factors that the benefit system is designed to deal with, and the way that the system responds to them in the course of a claim, can be illustrated by the example of a person who becomes unemployed and needs the state's financial help to maintain an income. At this point we need to distinguish between the two basic forms of social security in the United Kingdom. They are divided into *contributory* benefits, so called because those who seek support must have a record of (sufficient) National Insurance contributions (see below), and *non-contributory* benefits. While contributory benefits are almost entirely non-means-tested, non-contributory benefits comprise both means-tested benefits (among which universal credit and the benefits it is replacing are the most significant) and non-means-tested benefits (key examples being child benefit and disability living allowance or its replacement, personal independence payment). How all the various benefits and credits map onto this classification is shown later in the chapter (see in particular Figure 2).

In the case of a newly unemployed person, the entitlement that will probably be sought initially is contribution-based jobseeker's allowance (JSA), which has been the main unemployment benefit since 1996. Entitlement to this benefit and to certain others, including state retirement pension and contribution-based employment and support allowance, is based in part on satisfaction of conditions related to the payment of National Insurance contributions – or for some purposes, being credited with such contributions. The system will attempt to identify whether those conditions, which in themselves are complex, have

---

[11] Work and Pensions Committee, *Benefits Simplification* (above n 7) para 8.
[12] See Spicker, 'Five Types of Complexity' (above n 2) 6.
[13] See N Wikeley, *Child Support: Law and Policy* (Oxford, Hart, 2006); and N Wikeley, 'Child Support: The Brave New World' (2008) *Family Law* 1024.
[14] Department for Work and Pensions, *Supporting Separated Families: Securing Children's Futures* (Cm 8399, 2012) ch 8, para 3.

been met.[15] Individual contribution records can span a number of years, and in some cases, links are made between contributions by individuals and by their spouses: this 'adds complexity' to the contributions system.[16] Spouses' contributions are a particularly relevant issue where survivors' benefits are concerned, since a person's entitlement to a bereavement allowance is in large part based on their late spouse's or civil partner's contribution record.[17]

Returning to our example of a recently unemployed claimant, if he or she does not have the necessary contributions record, or if he/she did but entitlement has expired due to receipt of the benefit for the maximum duration of six months, the claimant would need to rely on means-tested benefit. Prior to the full introduction of universal credit, the relevant benefit would be income-based JSA. For this benefit, and also for universal credit, the nature and extent of the claimant's needs will require assessment. The determination of need under the benefits system may bring into play a whole range of issues related to the claimant's family status, health, liability as a tenant, other financial commitments, the extent of any other sources of income or savings or other capital, and so on. The design of means-tested benefits thus presents policy-makers with difficult trade-offs. For example, they may have to choose 'between tighter targeting of benefits (often linked to greater design complexity) and other impacts such as take-up levels, administrative costs and incentives to work'.[18]

The NAO contends that '[s]erious risks to value for money can result if departments fail to take account of how different design choices affect outcomes and costs across government.'[19] The NAO has shown how the different bases for assessing means against standard criteria span a continuum of complexity (see Figure 1). Not all the elements of means-testing are reflected in

---

[15] Only class 1 contributions will provide entitlement to contribution-based JSA (CBJSA). Contributions may be credited in various situations, for example during periods of entitlement to JSA itself or to employment and support allowance. The contribution conditions are based on an 'earnings factor', which is the total amount of earnings below a prescribed upper limit on which class 1 contributions have been paid. For CBJSA, the claimant must (1) have paid, during at least one of the preceding two tax years, contributions on earnings equal to 26 times the prescribed 'lower earnings limit' (LEL) for the year in question (the LEL was £107 per week in 2012–13), effectively meaning that a total of at least 26 weeks paid work must have occurred during one of those two tax years; and (2) have paid or been credited with contributions which together produce an earning factor which represents at least 50 times the LEL in each of the preceding two tax years before the current benefit year. The benefit year generally runs from the first Sunday in January for the next 52 weeks, whilst the tax year runs from 6 April until the next 5 April. See the Jobseekers Act 1995, s 2; the Jobseeker's Allowance Regulations 1996 (SI 1996/207) (hereafter 'JSA Regulations 1996') reg 45A, or Jobseeker's Allowance Regulations 2013 (SI 2013/378) reg 34; and the Social Security (Contribution Conditions for Jobseeker's Allowance and Employment and Support Allowance) Regulations 2010 (SI 2010/2446), all as amended.

[16] NAO, *DWP: Dealing with the Complexity of the Benefits System* (above n 8) para 2.10.

[17] Social Security Contributions and Benefits Act 1992, s 38B.

[18] National Audit Office, *Means Testing Report by the Comptroller and Auditor General* (2010–12, HC 1464) 24, para 3.3.

[19] Ibid, 7.

Figure 1. For example, only one source of income is referred to. Note that part-time work, which has become increasingly prevalent in the United Kingdom,[20] may involve a fixed or fluctuating number of hours per week, and the system must consider how and to what extent it should affect entitlement to benefit. It will also be noted that one of the identified areas of complexity arises from self-reporting of changes of circumstances, an issue which is discussed later.

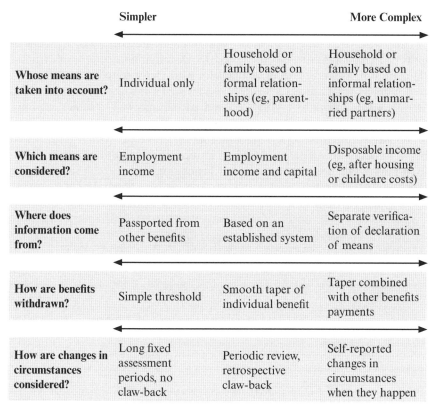

	Simpler ⟵————————————————————⟶ More Complex		
Whose means are taken into account?	Individual only	Household or family based on formal relation-ships (eg, parent-hood)	Household or family based on informal relation-ships (eg, unmar-ried partners)
Which means are considered?	Employment income	Employment income and capital	Disposable income (eg, after housing or childcare costs)
Where does information come from?	Passported from other benefits	Based on an established system	Separate verifica-tion of declaration of means
How are benefits withdrawn?	Simple threshold	Smooth taper of individual benefit	Taper combined with other benefits payments
How are changes in circumstances considered?	Long fixed assessment periods, no claw-back	Periodic review, retrospective claw-back	Self-reported changes in circumstances when they happen

Source: Adapted from National Audit Office, *Means Testing: Report by the Comptroller and Auditor General*(HC 1464, 2011) 9.

Figure 1: Designing A Means Test (National Audit Office)

---

[20] In the period from June/August 2007 to June/August 2012 the number of people in full-time employment fell by 355,000 while the number in part-time work increased by 724,000: Office for National Statistics (ONS), *Labour Market Statistics* (October 2012), www.ons.gov.uk/ons/dcp171778_279723.pdf. Of those in part-time work in 2012, 18.5% wanted a full-time job: ONS, 'Summary of Labour Market Statistics', www.ons.gov.uk/ons/publications/re-reference-tables.html?edition=tcm%3A77-222515 (last updated October 2012).

The welfare system also embodies various policy principles, and as the SSAC has noted, the continuing complexity of the legislation in this field in part reflects 'the underlying complexity of the policies it expresses'.[21] One broad policy is to support only those whose unemployment is genuinely involuntary and to maintain pressure on claimants to seek and secure work. Therefore, whether what is being sought is contribution-based JSA or universal credit (or before the latter's introduction, income-based JSA), it will be necessary to consider whether there was in effect an element of 'fault' in the claimant's unemployed status, such as when employment was lost due to misconduct. In such cases, separate rules involving disqualification from benefit may be invoked.

There is also a strong element of conditionality attached to entitlement to universal credit (as with income-based JSA), requiring, for example, that a claimant is registered as being available for work, has entered into a 'claimant commitment' (or a jobseeker's agreement under JSA) with the agency[22] and is actively seeking work by taking the required steps, as well as subjecting himself or herself to the onerous attendance/interview requirements.[23] (The conditionality within the employment and support allowance regime is discussed below in detail in chapter six.) Failure to meet such conditions can lead to a fixed-period sanction, involving loss of benefit for four weeks or longer.[24] The sanctioning regime itself is said to be responsible for a 'great deal of complexity in benefits system' and to be misunderstood by claimants.[25]

---

[21] SSAC, *Twentieth Report: 2007* (above n 6) para 1.19.

[22] On the claimant commitment, see the Welfare Reform Act 2012, s 14; and the Universal Credit Regulations 2013 (SI 2013/376), regs 15 and 16. In order to qualify for universal credits, 'all claimants will be required to agree to a Claimant Commitment, which will record all activities they are required to undertake, including, where appropriate, doing all that can reasonably be expected of them to find work or prepare for work. In exceptional circumstances, where a claimant is unable to accept a Claimant Commitment, for example where they lack capacity to do so, the requirement to accept the Commitment may be removed': Explanatory Memorandum to the Universal Credit Regulations 2013 (etc), para 7.10. The commitment will be personalised as has been the case with the jobseeker's agreement under JSA.

[23] Regarding universal credit, see the Welfare Reform Act 2012, s 15 ('work-focused interview requirement'), s 16 ('work preparation requirement'), s 17 ('work search requirement') and s 18 ('work availability requirement'); and the Universal Credit Regulations 2013, Pt 8, ch 1 ('work-related requirements'). Regarding JSA, see the Jobseekers Act 1995, ss 6–10; and the JSA Regulations 1996 (above n 15), as amended, or the Jobseeker's Allowance Regulations 2013 (SI 2013/378) (hereafter 'JSA Regulations 2013'). Under the Mandatory Work Activity scheme, for example, a JSA claimant may be placed by a Jobcentre Plus adviser in a workplace for four weeks; non-participation without good cause will result in automatic loss of benefit: Jobseeker's Allowance (Mandatory Work Activity Scheme) Regulations 2011 (SI 2011/688).

[24] Jobseekers Act 1995, ss 19A and 19B (inserted by the Welfare Reform Act 2012, s 46(1)) and either (i) the JSA Regulations 1996, regs 69A, 69B and 70 as inserted or substituted by the Jobseeker's Allowance (Sanctions) (Amendment) Regulations 2012 (SI 2012/2568) or (ii) the JSA Regulations 2013, Pt 3. In the case of universal credit, see the Welfare Reform Act 2012, ss 26 and 27; and the Universal Credit Regs 2013, Pt 8, ch 2. Both JSA and universal credit make provision for hardship payments in certain situations when sanctions have been imposed under these conditions: see in particular the Welfare Reform Act 2012, s 28; the Universal Credit Regs 2013, Pt 8, ch 3 (universal credit); and the Jobseekers Act 1995, s 19C, inserted by s 46 of the 2012 Act (JSA).

[25] Child Poverty Action Group (CPAG), "No One Written Off: Response to the July 2008 Welfare Reform Green Paper' (CPAG, 2008) 29. See also SSAC, 'Universal Credit and

In relation to all these factors, therefore, the benefits system is designed to be responsive to need but also to ensure that need is met by the state only when there is no alternative and on the basis that claimants are doing everything possible to limit their welfare dependency. It therefore reflects a range of different aims which, stepping back further, also include minimising the cost to the state. When it comes to determining entitlement in individual cases, the various relevant issues or factors affecting entitlement will need to be assessed in a consistent way, since the system also aims to ensure distributive justice through parity between people in like circumstances. Ensuring this will happen is a function of the bureaucratic and legal frameworks, as discussed below. Thus in the design and management of the welfare state, 'policymakers have had to contend with balancing the institutional values of accountability and individualization', namely to ensure that decisions can be justified in terms of being consistent and not arbitrary, while ensuring that individual circumstances are properly responded to.[26]

The present-day distinction between benefits that are based on National Insurance contributions and those that are non-contributory (whether means-tested or non-means-tested) reflects both the original Beveridge design and the specific purpose of the benefits in question. Under Sir William Beveridge's scheme of social insurance, contribution-based benefits were to 'guarantee the income needed for subsistence in all normal cases'.[27] There was a separate scheme of means-tested 'national assistance' as a residual benefit originally expected to cover needs not met by the comprehensive scheme of social insurance. The importance and scope of means-tested benefit grew significantly from the 1960s onwards as long-term unemployment grew and the insurance system failed to adjust to the changed social and economic climate. Means-tested assistance, which was increasingly sought as a top-up to inadequate payments of insurance benefits, burgeoned through new schemes such as housing benefit (introduced in 1983[28]), family income supplement (1971) and in-work tax credits for the low paid (1999).[29]

Conditionality', Occasional Paper No 9 (August 2012), ssac.independent.gov.uk/pdf/universal-credit-and-conditionality.pdf.

[26] CJ Jewell, 'Assessing Need in the United States, Germany, and Sweden: The Organization of Welfare Casework and the Potential for Responsiveness in the "Three Worlds"' (2007) 29(3) *Law & Policy* 380, 381.

[27] WH (Lord) Beveridge (Inter-departmental Committee on Social Insurance and Allied Services), *Social Insurance and Allied Services* (Cmnd 6404, 1942) para 23.

[28] Through the Social Security and Housing Benefits Act 1982.

[29] Two of the tax credits introduced in 1999 under the Tax Credits Act 1999, namely working families tax credit and disabled person's tax credit, replaced social security in-work benefits (that is, benefits paid to people undertaking at least a prescribed minimum number of hours of work per week) – family credit (which had itself replaced family income supplement in 1988) and disability working allowance (introduced in 1992) respectively: see N Harris et al, *Social Security Law in Context* (Oxford, Oxford University Press, 2000) ch 4; and N Wikeley, *The Law of Social Security*, 5th edn (London, Butterworths Lexis Nexis, 2002) ch 10. There was also a childcare tax credit that aimed to encourage take-up and retention of employment by contributing to the cost of childcare. The pre-universal credit 2013 tax credits – working tax credit (incorporating a

While the insurance principle has been retained in a number of areas, including benefits designed to meet short-term interruptions of work due to unemployment or sickness, it has been progressively eroded within the modern benefits system, and its role continues to diminish. For example, entitlement under a claim for contribution-based JSA runs for only for the first six months of unemployment; unemployment benefit, which it replaced in 1996, was available for a year. Furthermore, recently a maximum duration of entitlement to contribution-based employment and support allowance (ESA) of 365 days has been introduced, whereas previously it was unlimited, provided the conditions continued to be met.[30] Although contributory benefits have nevertheless deliberately been very largely omitted from the reforms surrounding the introduction of universal credit,[31] many recipients of contributory benefits also require mean-tested assistance which has been available via benefits such as housing benefit and in due course (but not in relation to council tax) will have to be sought via universal credit. If they received universal credit whilst in work, because their wages were low, the transition to out-of-work entitlement would only involve an adjustment being made by the system. In other cases they would need to make a fresh claim for the credit. The retention of separate insurance benefits therefore limits the structural simplification sought via the design of universal credit.

Aside from the computation of contribution records, the assessment of entitlement to contributory and other non-means benefits is on the face of it much more straightforward than it is in the case of their means-tested counterparts; the latter have complex structures designed to recognise levels and kinds of need, albeit to prescribed extents only. Nevertheless, there are exceptions to this generalisation. For example, there is the complicated assessment of needs and capacity related to disability that occurs in the case of personal independent payment (see below). Moreover, some of these benefits now incorporate an element of means-testing. In particular, as described more fully in chapter three, provision is made within the contributory ESA scheme for benefit to be reduced on account of any occupational pension above a certain weekly limit (£85) received by the claimant; moreover, what effectively amounts to an income threshold for entitlement to child benefit (but is in fact an income tax charge –

childcare element and extra support for disabled workers) and child tax credit – emanated from the Tax Credits Act 2002: see N Lee, 'The New Tax Credits' (2003) 10(1) *Journal of Social Security Law* 7.

[30] Welfare Reform Act 2007, s 1A, as inserted by the Welfare Reform Act 2012, s 51(1). Note that (i) the maximum prescribed period specified in the Act can be varied by the Secretary of State by order; (ii) a period or periods when the claimant is a member of the ESA 'support group' (meaning that he or she is not capable of undertaking a work-related activity, in other words those with the greatest incapacity for work) do not count towards the 365 days; and (iii) a person can re-qualify for contribution based ESA after a further complete tax year during which the relevant number of contributions or credits have accrued.

[31] See Department for Work and Pensions (DWP), *Universal Credit: Welfare that Works* (Cm 7957, 2010) ch 6, paras 4–8.

the 'high-income child benefit charge' – related to the amount of child benefit received) was introduced by the Coalition Government in January 2013.[32]

A Map of Benefits and Credits

It is appropriate at this point in the discussion to map out the structure of the British social security system in more detail. The diverse welfare benefits and credits provided by the system are shown in Figure 2. Due to the introduction of universal credit, the structure will undergo its most far-reaching changes since the Beveridge reforms of the 1940s. As was explained in chapter one, a range of means-tested (or income-related) benefits and tax credits is being abolished and replaced by universal credit.[33] The aim of this redesign is to have a simpler system that is easier to administer and facilitates and encourages entry into employment for claimants.[34] Important elements of reform include the alignment of rules and a single taper whereby increases in earnings reduce a claimant's combined benefit (by 65 per cent per £1 in net earnings above a prescribed level). Eligibility to universal credit is not dependent on work status per se. Thus the idea is that making the transition from unemployment to work is facilitated, since entitlement may continue on entry into work: the level of support will simply be adjusted.

Figure 2 shows the planned transition of individual benefits and credits to universal credit, as well as the classification of benefits with reference to their basic entitlement conditions. Many in the first group, the income-related benefits and credits (which are primarily intended to provide relief from poverty, including help with particular kinds of expenses), are in the process of being subsumed within universal credit. As the author has discussed elsewhere, there are alternative classifications of benefits based on their principal purpose (earnings replacement, meeting extra costs and poverty relief) or the customer or claimant groups at which the benefit is aimed (elderly, long-term sick and disabled, short-term sick, families, unemployed and survivors and

---

[32] The charge is one per cent of each £100 of income in excess of £50,000 per annum; but if income exceeds £60,000 the charge is equal to the amount child benefit entitlement – effectively meaning a complete loss of child benefit: Income Tax (Earnings and Pensions) Act 2003, ss 681B–H, inserted by the Finance Act 2012, Sch 1. The charge is incurred if the recipient of child benefit or his/her partner has an income above £50,000 per week. Child benefit will thus be declarable via a tax return, but a claimant will have the option of electing not to receive child benefit (Social Security Administration Act 1992, s 13A, inserted by the Finance Act 2012, Sch 1), and thus if the charge was the only reason for needing to complete a form, they would thereby avoid having to do so. HMRC estimated that 1.2 million households would lose out and that 70% of them would in effect lose an amount equal to all their child benefit entitlement: HMRC, 'Child Benefit: Income Tax Charge for Those on Higher Incomes' (HMRC, 2012), www.hmrc.gov.uk/budget 2012/tiin-0620.pdf.

[33] Welfare Reform Act 2012, s 33, which will be phased in and subject to transitional arrangements.

[34] DWP, *Welfare that Works* (above n 31).

I. Income-Related Benefits and Credits

Before Coalition Reforms	After Coalition reforms*
Income support Income-based jobseeker's allowance (JSA) Housing benefit	Universal Credit
Council tax benefit	Local authority-based council tax support schemes
State pension credit →	Continues but now also includes 'housing credit' following the abolition of housing benefit
Income-based employment and support allowance (ESA) Working tax credit Child tax credit	Universal Credit
Passported benefits (not all are social security benefits) →	Will continue, with adjusted eligibility tailored to Universal Credit
Social fund (SF) for those on income-related benefit	Partly replaced by local authority schemes

II. Non-Contributory (Non-Means-Tested or Substantially Non-Means-Tested) Benefits

Before Coalition Reforms	After Coalition reforms
Child benefit →	Continues but is subject to income tax charge if income is above £50,000
Disability living allowance	Personal independence payment**
Attendance allowance Carer's allowance Guardian's allowance SF winter fuel payments	

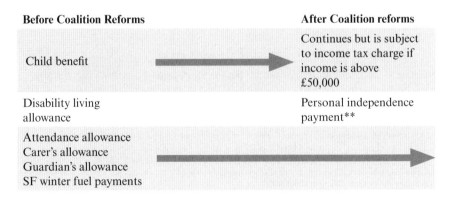

III. Contributory Benefits

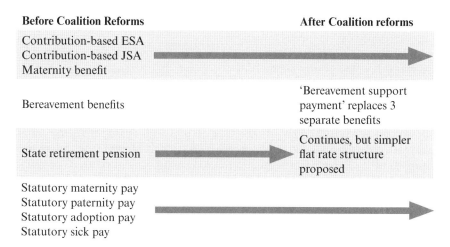

* Many changes will be phased in, so for a time, both pre- and post-reform benefits will be in payment to different claimants.
** DLA is to continue for under 16s, however (DWP (March 2012) n 58 below, 12).

Figure 2 Principal Social Security Benefits in Great Britain Before and After the Coalition Government's Planned Reforms

others).[35] However, these classifications work less well as a result of the introduction of universal credit, particularly in light of the structure of the transition, as illustrated by Figure 2. Figure 2 assumes that the planned separate reforms to state retirement pension[36] and bereavement benefits,[37] among others, will be carried through. (A brief explanation of the individual benefits and an indication of the main legislation applicable to them will be shown below in Table 1.[38])

The breakdown of different benefit schemes in Figure 2 into three separate categories perhaps gives a false sense of the coherence of the benefits system. As we saw from the example of the unemployed claimant above, the structural divisions do not necessarily correspond with the circumstances of individual lives. Contributory benefits, for example, reflect the links between life events and the loss of income derived from one's own or one's spouse's or civil

[35] Harris et al (above n 29) 155–65.

[36] See Department for Work and Pensions (DWP), *The Single-Tier Pension: A Simple Foundation for Saving* (Cm 8528, 2013).

[37] See Department for Work and Pensions, *Public Consultation: Bereavement Benefit for the 21st Century* (Cm 8221, 2011); and Department for Work and Pensions, *Government Response to Bereavement Benefit for the 21st Century* (Cm 8371, 2012).

[38] Figure 2 and Table 1 exclude industrial injuries benefits in order to keep within manageable limits. On these, see S Clarke et al, *Welfare Benefits and Tax Credits Handbook, 2012–13* (London, Child Poverty Action Group, 2012) ch 18; and S Jones, 'Social Security and Industrial Injury' in Harris et al (above n 29).

partner's employment – as in the case of bereavement benefits or retirement pension. Yet in many cases, they fail to obviate the need for support from income-related benefits. For example, income from state retirement pension may be topped up via means-tested pension credit, although fewer would need it under the proposed new flat-rate pension.[39] Entitlement to mainstream contributory benefits is time-limited, in any event. If circumstances permit the take-up or resumption of employment, an individual may become eligible for other means-tested support in the form of (currently) tax credits; and an entitlement to support with rent may continue but at a reduced rate by virtue of the adjustment of income. The introduction of universal credit, replacing (inter alia) tax credits, is intended to remove the need to make fresh claims on a transition to work. Some benefits are not linked to employment status or capacity for work but are designed to meet additional costs and therefore may be retained during employment; these include disability living allowance/personal independence payment (which is intended to help with the extra expenses related to care and mobility of living with a disability) and child benefit (which aims to assist with the cost of child-rearing).

The Social Fund, which paid out over £3 billion in 2011–12,[40] is a distinct element of the welfare system with different features to other benefits. In particular, the *discretionary* part of it has been subject to an overall expenditure limit, and much of the provision made by it has taken the form of loans: crisis loans to meet expenses arising in an emergency or disaster; and budgeting loans to meet intermittent or one-off costs for items such as furniture/household equipment or clothing. Grants have, however, also been available under the discretionary part: community care grants, intended to meet specific costs related to acute needs. The *regulated* part of the fund – which provides grants for funeral expenses[41] and maternity expenses, cold weather payments and winter fuel payments – is set to continue. However, the discretionary part is being abolished.[42] Budgeting loans, for which people in receipt of income-related benefits for six months or longer have been eligible to apply, will no longer be available after introduction of universal credit.[43] Instead, a universal credit claimant, if he or she has been in receipt of 'benefit' (as defined) for such a period, may be eligible for a 'budgeting advance'.[44] Social fund crisis loan alignment payments (payments to cover immediate needs prior to the commencement of a new entitlement to a social security benefit) are also

[39] See DWP, *The Single-Tier Pension* (above n 36).

[40] Department for Work and Pensions, *Annual Report by the Secretary of State for Work and Pensions on the Social Fund (2011–2012)* (London, Stationery Office, 2012) para 6.1.

[41] See below ch 3, s II.

[42] Welfare Reform Act 2012, ss 70–72.

[43] The transitional arrangements post-April 2013 are in the Welfare Reform Act 2012 (Commencement No 6 and Savings Provisions) Order 2102 (SI 2012/3090) (C123).

[44] Social Security (Payments on Account of Benefit) Regulations 2013 (SI 2013/383), pt 3. Limiting factors include a maximum earnings threshold. 'Benefit' here is defined in reg 3 as universal credit, ESA, income support, JSA or state pension credit.

being replaced,[45] by advances of benefit known as 'payments on account of benefit'.[46] Other crisis loans, along with community care grants, are being replaced by provision made by local authorities and the devolved administrations in Scotland and Wales,[47] funded centrally at the same level as previously.[48] Local authorities do not have to make these payments in the form of loans,[49] and the Government has warned them against doing so because of the high costs of administering them.[50] The Government expects this devolved system to include – via partnerships – local voluntary provision involving foodbanks, furniture re-use organisations and credit unions.

Notably, the House of Commons Work and Pensions Committee has found that the plan for localised provision to replace elements of the social fund 'would potentially add further complexity to the benefits system'.[51] The Committee is critical of the 'uncertainty and inconsistency in the way that support is administered' that will result from giving local authorities such a free rein over this new form of support.[52] It certainly seems redolent of the local forms of relief operating over 50 years ago, such as local rate rebate schemes.

Each of the welfare system's various benefits and credits therefore has a specific role. They will generally not cover all areas or causes of need, although as discussed later, universal credit offers a greater breadth of coverage than has been available hitherto[53] and may help to counter to some extent

---

[45] Subject to transitional arrangements under which applications made before 1 April 2013 can continue to be determined: Welfare Reform Act 2012 (Commencement No 6 and Savings Provisions) Order 2102 (SI 2012/3090).

[46] Social Security (Payments on Account of Benefit) Regulations 2013 (SI 2013/383), pt 2; and the Welfare Reform Act 2012, s 101(1), amending the Social Security Administration Act 1992, s 5(1). (S 101(2) of the 2012 Act repeals the Welfare Reform Act 2009, s 22, which provided for payments on account but was never implemented.)

[47] See Department for Work and Pensions, *Local Support to Replace Community Care Grants and Crisis Loans for Living Expenses: A Call for Evidence* (February 2011), webarchive.national-archives.gov.uk/+/http://www.dwp.gov.uk/docs/social-fund-localisation-call-for-evidence.pdf. Local knowledge (thereby enabling the making of 'better links with other services and funds where appropriate') and an ability to target the most vulnerable people who need support are the reasons put forward for this devolved administration: Department for Work and Pensions, *Localising Crisis Loans and Community Care Grants: Impact Assessment* (February 2011) 1, www.parliament.uk/documents/impact-assessments/IA11-022AO.pdf.

[48] Department for Work and Pensions, *Local Support to Replace Community Care Grants and Crisis Loans for Living Expenses in England: Government Response to the Call for Evidence* (June 2011), webarchive.nationalarchives.gov.uk/+/http:// www.dwp.gov.uk/docs/social-fund-localisation-response.pdf. See further C Grover, 'Abolishing the Discretionary Social Fund: Continuity and Change in Relieving "Special Expenses"' (2012) 19(1) *Journal of Social Security Law* 12.

[49] DWP, *Local Support to Replace Community Care Grants and Crisis Loans: Government Response* (ibid) para71. The Government has said that it does not propose to place a duty on local authorities to provide local payments: para 136

[50] Ibid, paras 72 and 73.

[51] House of Commons Work and Pensions Committee, *Universal Credit Implementation: Meeting the Needs of Vulnerable Claimants* (2012–13, HC 576-I) para 209.

[52] Ibid, para 212.

[53] But note that at one time, in the days before the introduction of housing benefit (in 1983 under the Social Security and Housing Benefits Act 1982), supplementary benefit, the forerunner of the income support scheme, included a rent element (rent allowance), which universal credit now also does. See Harris et al (above n 29) 111–13.

the 'pervading sense of a loss of cohesion', which the chairman of the Social Security Advisory Committee attributed in large part to the 'size, complexity and dispersion of the benefits system'.[54] Table 1 below describes the principal benefits in force prior to and after the reforms being introduced by the Coalition Government,[55] which will be phased in during the period from 2013 to approx 2017 (some more rapidly than others).[56] Table 1 also identifies the main legislation governing the benefits in question; separate legislation (not listed) governs the administration of benefits, particularly in relation to the claims, decision-making and payment processes, as discussed later.

Universal credit was due to be introduced for new claims in four pathfinder areas in April 2013, although the start was delayed until July 2013 in three of them.[57] Its national introduction, planned for October 2013, has also been delayed; only six more areas will be covered from then. Benefits due to be replaced by universal credit are expected to continue to be paid to those who are receiving them when the credit is introduced, but recipients will be transferred to universal credit (assuming they qualify) between April 2014 and October 2017. Personal independence payment is due to be phased in between April 2013 and the end of 2017.[58]

---

[54] Social Security Advisory Committee, *Seventeenth Report: 2004* (Leeds, Corporate Document Services, 2004) Foreword, para 12.

[55] As was also the case with Figure 2, industrial injuries benefits and war pensions are deliberately omitted from Table 1.

[56] See for example the timetables for the introduction of universal credit and personal independence payment (below) and note that new council tax reduction schemes in place of council tax benefit came into operation in April 2013. See below n 123.

[57] See the Universal Credit (Transitional Provisions) Regulation 2013 (SI 2013/386) Pt 2 chs 2 and 3. Tameside (Ashton under Lyme) is the first pathfinder area to operate universal credit, to be followed in July 2013 by Oldham, Wigan and Warrington: DWP, 'Universal Credit: Pathfinder Update', press release (28 March 2013). An estimated 1,500 new universal credit claims per month were expected to be dealt with across the four pathfinder areas: DWP, 'Iain Duncan Smith: Early Roll-Out of Universal Credit to Go Live in Manchester and Cheshire', press release (24 May 2012) www.dwp.gov.uk/newsroom/press-releases/2012/may-2012/dwp057-12.shtml.

[58] From April 2013, but only in prescribed administrative areas, only new claims for PIP, not disability living allowance (DLA), will be possible for 16–24 year olds. The prescribed areas are Cheshire, Cumbria, Merseyside, North East England and North West England. In June 2013 this will be extended the remainder of the UK. It is expected that from October 2013 if a claimant seeks to renew a fixed period of award or reports a change in his or her condition that requires a reassessment, any new or changed award will be of PIP only. From October 2015 anyone still in receipt of a DLA award will be contacted by the Department to be invited to apply for PIP. Reassessments in such case will be completed by the end of 2017. See DWP, *Personal Independence Payment: Reassessment and Impacts* (13 December 2012), webarchive.nationalarchives.gov.uk/+/http://www.dwp.gov.uk/docs/pip-reassessments-and-impacts.pdf. Previously it was announced that the reassessment of DLA would initially start in October 2013 as a pathfinder exercise for 30,000 claimants followed by a phased reassessment for others, starting in January 2014: see DWP, *DLA Reform and Personal Independence Payment: Completing the Detailed Design* (March 2012), www.dwp.gov.uk/docs/pip-detailed-design-consultation.pdf.

Table 1: The Principal Benefit and Tax Credit Schemes and Relevant Entitlement Legislation in Great Britain Before and After the Coalition Government's Planned Reforms

(Bold type denotes benefits continuing or introduced under the Coalition reforms, including planned changes but excluding transitional arrangements.)

I. Income-Related Benefits and Tax Credits

Name	Description	Legislation
Universal credit	**Paid/credited monthly to jobseekers, people too sick or disabled to work and those in work earning below a prescribed threshold. May include elements regarding housing costs, work incapacity and caring responsibilities.**	**Welfare Reform Act 2012** **Universal Credit Regulations 2013**
Income support	Basic weekly assistance for those not working and not required to be available for work.	Social Security Contributions and Benefits Act 1992 as amended (SSCBA 1992) Income Support (General) Regulations 1987
Income-based JSA	Weekly assistance for those available for work who have no right to contribution-based JSA.	Jobseekers Act 1995 Jobseeker's Allowance Regulations 1996
Housing benefit	Assistance regarding rent liability.	SSCBA 1992 Housing Benefit Regulations 2006
Council tax benefit (CTB)	Assistance towards council tax liability.	SSCBA 1992 Council Tax Benefit Regulations 2006
Local authority council tax support schemes	**Replaces CTB and has same role.**	**Local Government Finance Act 1992 as amended** **The regulations covering England and Wales listed at note 123 below** Council Tax Reduction (Scotland) Regulations 2012 Council Tax Reduction (State Pension Credit) (Scotland) Regulations 2012

Table 1: (*cont.*)

State Pension Credit (SPC)	**Weekly assistance for persons of (female) retirement age.**	**SPC Act 2002** **State Pension Credit Regulations 2002**
Income-based employment and support allow-ance	Weekly benefit for people of working age who have a limited capability for work on health/disability grounds.	Welfare Reform Act 2007 Employment and Support Allowance Regulations 2008
Passported benefits [including benefits outside social security system]	**Entitlement to specific welfare benefits and diverse local benefits including free school meals, transport costs and health costs (eg, eye tests)**	**Education Act 1996** **Education (Free School Lunches) (Working Tax Credit) (England) Order 2009 (SI 2009/830)** **Various other legislation**
Working tax credit (WTC)	Paid weekly to persons working above a prescribed number of hours per week on low earnings.	Tax Credits Act 2002 WTC (Entitlement and Maximum Rate) Regulations 2002
Child tax credit	Basic credit for those with a dependent child/young person under age 20.	Tax Credits Act 2002 Child Tax Credit Regulations 2002
Social fund (SF)	**Regulated scheme of funeral and maternity grants and cold weather payments. (SF winter fuel payments are in section II below.) Discretionary loans (crisis loans and budgeting loans) and grants (community care grants) now covered by local authority schemes.**	**SSCBA 1992** **SF Cold Weather Payments (General) Regulations 1998** **SF Maternity and Funeral Expenses (General) Regulations 2005**

II. Non-Contributory (Non-Means-Tested or Substantially Non-Means-Tested) Benefits

Name	Description	Legislation
Child benefit	**For those with a dependent child or 'qualifying young person'**	**SSCBA 1992** **Child Benefit (General) Regulations 2006**
Disability living allowance (DLA)	Weekly allowance for disabled people needing extra support. Includes care (three rates) and mobility (two rates) components.	SSCBA 1992 Social Security (DLA) Regulations 1991
Personal independence payment	**Function as per DLA. Two components (daily living and mobility), each with two rates.**	**Welfare Reform Act 2012** **Personal Independence Payment Regulations 2013.**
Attendance allowance	**Weekly allowance for disabled people needing extra support who are aged 65 or older**	**SSCBA 1992** **Social Security (AA) Regulations 1991**
Winter fuel payment	**Single annual payment for older people, but rates vary depending on age and whether sharing home.**	**SSCBA 1992** **Social Fund Winter Fuel Payment Regulations 2000**

III. Contributory Benefits

Name	Description	Legislation
Contribution-based ESA	**Weekly benefit paid to people of working age who have a limited capability for work on health/disability grounds**	**Welfare Reform Act 2007** **Employment and Support Allowance Regulations 2013**
Contribution-based JSA	**Weekly assistance for up to 6 months for those not required to be available for work who have a sufficient record of contributions.**	**Jobseekers Act 1995** **Jobseeker's Allowance Regulations 2013**

Table 1: (*cont.*)

Name	Description	Legislation
Bereavement benefits	A lump sum and weekly payments to survivors; also includes widowed parent allowance if survivor has child/is pregnant.	SSCBA 1992 Social Security (Widow's Benefit and Retirement Pensions) Regulations 1979
Bereavement support payment	**Replaces bereavement benefits; under current plan, will include a lump sum and monthly payments for 12 months.**	**Pensions Bill 2013/14, part 3 (Regulations to be made)**
State retirement pension	**Weekly pension based on claimant's National Insurance Contributions; new flat-rate pension due from 2016.**	**SSCBA 1992** **Pensions Bill 2013/14, parts 1 and 2** **Various statutory instruments**
Statutory maternity/ paternity/ adoption pay (SMP/SPP/SAP); Maternity allowance	**Earnings-replacement benefits (maximum of 39 weeks but usually only 2 weeks for SPP) paid via employer before and after a birth or adoption. Maternity allowance is available in the case of no SMP entitlement.**	**SSCBA 1992** **SMP (General) Regulations 1986** **SPP and SAP (General) Regulations 2002** **Social Security (Maternity Allowance) Regulations 1987**
Statutory sick pay	**Earnings-replacement benefit for up to approximately 28 weeks via employer.**	**SSCBA 1992** **Statutory sick pay (General) Regulations 1982**

The structure of universal credit as it relates to a single claimant is shown in Figure 3 (below page 54). Entitlement is subject to the overall benefits cap introduced via the Welfare Reform Act 2012.[59] As will be examined in chapter four below, claims for universal credit by members of a couple must normally be made as a joint claim, and the relevant conditions need to be applied to each member. Each of the elements and conditions is subject to detailed prescription and definition in the regulations (including exceptions, such as a minimum age of 16 in some cases). The incorporation of income-based ESA and housing benefit into universal credit is occurring via the inclusion of capability for work and housing costs elements respectively, while the child element replaces child tax credits. The standard allowance is higher for people aged 25 or over and there are different couple rates, as under JSA and income support.

Alteration and Reform of Social Security Benefits

The range of different benefits and tax credits shown in Table 1 does not suggest a simple system. Nonetheless, there are additional elements that further aggravate the complexity of this structure. The first factor involves its near-constant state of flux due to the continual process of adjustment and reform. The system of benefits shown in Table 1 is the product not of a single design but of the piecemeal evolution of its constituent parts. For example, in terms of implementation, income support dates from 1987, disability living allowance (DLA) from 1992, JSA from 1996 and ESA from 2008. There has been significant amendment to the law governing each of these over the ensuing years. Recent major reforms have related to personal independence payment and universal credit (noted above). A further reform, currently in prospect,

[59] See the Welfare Reform Act 2012, ss 96 and 97. Section 96 empowers regulations to be made to provide for a cap on the amount of benefits to which a couple or single person may be entitled. See the Universal Credit Regs 2013, Pt 7. Under s 96(2), 'applying a benefit cap to welfare benefits means securing that, where a single person's or couple's total entitlement to welfare benefits in respect of the reference period exceeds the relevant amount, their entitlement to welfare benefits in respect of any period of the same duration as the reference period is reduced by an amount up to or equalling the excess'. See also the Benefit Cap (Housing Benefit) Regulations 2012 (SI 2012/2994) (as amended by SI 2013/546), inserting Pt 8A into the Housing Benefit Regulations 2006 (SI 2006/213). The cap will be applied via the housing benefit system (but not in respect of prescribed categories of persons including those in receipt of disability living allowance/personal independence payment or ESA support component) until a claimant is receiving universal credit. (Some claimants affected by the cap may nevertheless be able to secure 'further financial assistance . . . in order to meet housing costs' via a discretionary housing payment from the local authority (see the Discretionary Financial Assistance Regulations 2001 (SI 2001/1167), reg 2 et seq), for which the Government allocated an additional £65 million in 2013–14.) The cap is related to average take-home pay across the working population and has been set at £350 per week for single people and £500 per week for couples and lone-parent households. Under universal credit these will be converted to monthly amounts: £2,167 for couples and lone parents; £1,517 for single adults. See Universal Credit Regs 2013, reg 79. See also DWP, *Explanatory Memorandum for the Social Security Advisory Committee* (London, 2012) para 205. The cap was introduced in four London boroughs in April 2013 before a national roll-out in July 2013.

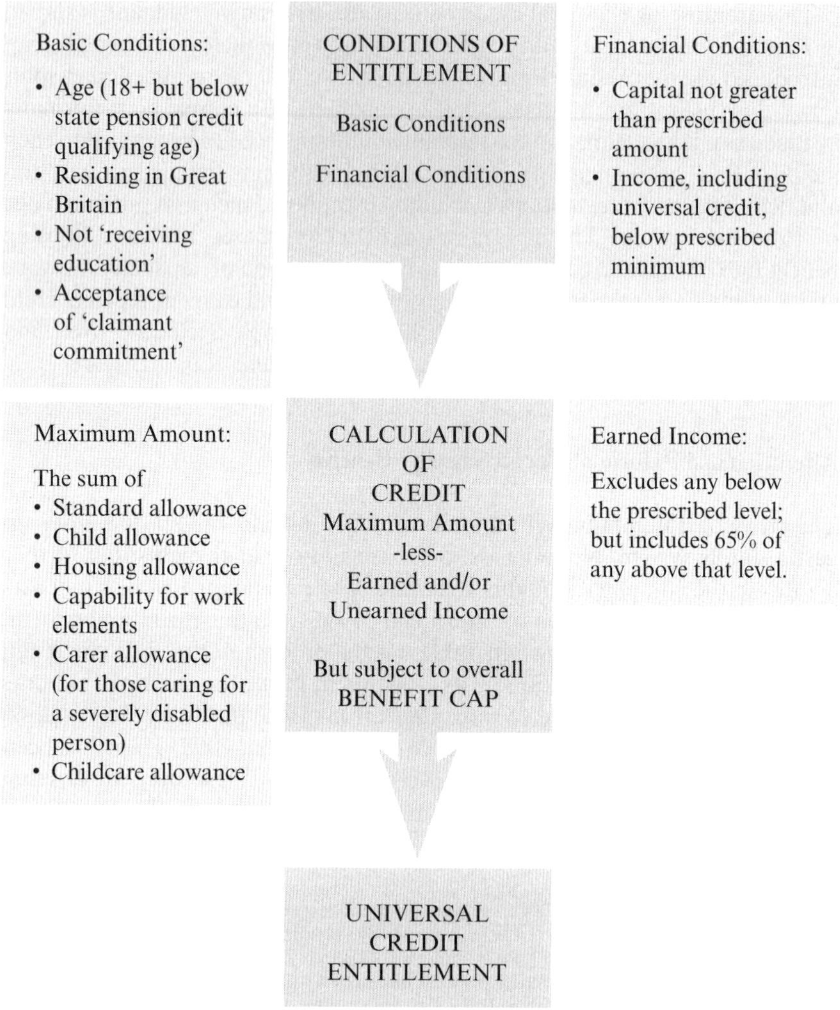

Basic Conditions:

- Age (18+ but below state pension credit qualifying age)
- Residing in Great Britain
- Not 'receiving education'
- Acceptance of 'claimant commitment'

CONDITIONS OF ENTITLEMENT

Basic Conditions

Financial Conditions

Financial Conditions:

- Capital not greater than prescribed amount
- Income, including universal credit, below prescribed minimum

Maximum Amount:

The sum of
- Standard allowance
- Child allowance
- Housing allowance
- Capability for work elements
- Carer allowance (for those caring for a severely disabled person)
- Childcare allowance

CALCULATION OF CREDIT
Maximum Amount
-less-
Earned and/or Unearned Income

But subject to overall BENEFIT CAP

Earned Income:

Excludes any below the prescribed level; but includes 65% of any above that level.

UNIVERSAL CREDIT ENTITLEMENT

Figure 3: Universal Credit under the Welfare Reform Act 2012 and the Universal Credit Regulations 2013

involves retirement pensions, with the proposed introduction of a single-tier, flat-rate state retirement pension in place of the current pension, for those retiring from 2016 onwards.[60]

Since reforms to parts of the system have knock-on effects due to the interaction of benefits (discussed below), the process of implementing change is particularly complex and generates uncertainty and potential confusion for

---

[60] See above ch 1.

both administrators and claimants alike. Thus, for example, the estimated savings of £2.5 billion from reforms to housing benefit being introduced in advance of the introduction of universal credit would be partly offset by the administrative costs involved in adjusting to the reforms.[61]

Transitional arrangements, mostly set out in separate legislation each time, are needed to manage the process of changing over to a new benefit or the radical reform of an existing benefit and to ensure that changes to the benefits structure do not have a disproportionate impact on claimants in relation to vital areas of support. So-called 'transitional protection' is therefore important, designed to protect households from any loss of income consequent on benefit changes as reform is implemented.[62] However, it is acknowledged to give rise to considerable legal complexity.[63] Indeed, transitional arrangements have been described as 'one of the most technical and complex features of social security law'.[64] The Universal Credit (Transitional Provisions) Regulations 2013,[65] for example, deal with a number of difficult issues during the period from 29 April 2013 (when the new benefit was introduced in one area and, from July 2013, in three others) when the pathfinder areas are in operation. The purpose of the Regulations includes modification of the tax credits legislation to deal with the problem caused by the end-of-year finalisation of tax credit awards, in relation to someone in work who has transferred onto universal credit. Transitional provisions of this kind compound the problem of complex rules, discussed below.

It is also important to take account of the use of amendment regulations, which give effect to a majority of the changes that are made to the system and which have a 'layering' effect.[66] The 2012–13 edition of Sweet and Maxwell's annotated Social Security Legislation, for example, shows that in the Jobseeker's Allowance (JSA) Regulations 1996[67] as then in force, the general definition provision (regulation 1) contains 73 amendments spanning 16 years to April 2012;[68] there was not one year in which new amending regulations did not alter regulation 1.

[61] National Audit Office (NAO), *Department for Work and Pensions: Managing the Impact of Housing Benefit Reform*, HC 681 (London, Stationery Office, 2012) paras 1.15–1.16.

[62] In the case of universal credit, as claimants are moved onto it, the level of entitlement will be compared with that under the previous benefits, and if it is now lower the difference will be paid, although without annual up-rating until universal credit entitlement becomes higher. Claimants who come off universal credit and later reapply for it cannot claim transitional protection. See further DWP, 'Universal Credit Briefing Note' (10 December 2012) webarchive.nationalarchives. gov.uk/+/http://www.dwp.gov.uk/docs/ucpbn-transitional-protection.pdf.

[63] House of Commons Committee of Public Accounts, *Getting It Right, Putting It Right: Improving the Quality of Benefit Decisions and Reporting on Performance* (2003–04, HC 406) 4.

[64] A Ogus, 'Transitional Protection is Not Just a Technical Problem' (1999) 6(3) *Journal of Social Security Law* 111, 111.

[65] SI 2013/386.

[66] SSAC, *Twentieth Report: 2007* (above n 6) para 1.19.

[67] Above n 15.

[68] P Wood et al, *Social Security Legislation 2012/13, Volume II: Income Support, Jobseeker's Allowance, State Pension Credit and the Social Fund* (London, Sweet and Maxwell, 2012) 873–89.

Moreover, the legislation underpinning this benefits structure is not only highly technical but expansive and, as noted above, dominated by secondary legislation, which facilitates the constant process of change. The aforementioned JSA Regulations 1996,[69] for example, comprised 172 separate regulations and 8 schedules but were only one of 18 sets of social security regulations issued in 1996 covering JSA and its interaction with other benefits. The Housing Benefit Regulations 2006[70] comprised 122 separate regulations and 10 Schedules, and there is a separate set of housing benefit regulations of similar length for people old enough to receive state pension credit.[71]

When housing benefit is abolished and the equivalent support included within universal credit, the regulations governing state pension credit will contain amendments to include such support in the form of 'housing credit'.[72] The Universal Credit Regulations 2013 themselves are shorter than the JSA or housing benefit regulations above, although they do not include the contributory versions of JSA and ESA, each of which are covered by separate statutory instruments. By combining the rules on matters such as the calculation of income and capital previously contained in separate sets of regulations governing different benefits, the Universal Credit Regulations effect a significant overall reduction in the number of individual provisions. Yet they still comprise a total of 119 separate provisions and 11 schedules. They are also highly technical. While the length of legislation does not in itself make it complex, as noted in chapter one, length and technicality in combination almost invariably will do so.

The European Dimension

A further element of complexity arises from the impact of the United Kingdom's membership in the European Union and thus of European law on UK social security law, particularly as regards the entitlement of migrants.[73] This interaction between the UK benefits system and the European Union, in the context of the policies of co-ordination and free movement,[74] has included

---

[69] Above n 15.

[70] Above n 59.

[71] Housing Benefit (Persons who have attained the qualifying age for state pension credit) Regulations 2006 (SI 2006/214).

[72] See State Pension Credit Act 2002, s 3A, inserted by the Welfare Reform Act 2012, Sch 4, para 4. The 2012 Act has also made an amendment which bars a person from claiming state pension credit if he or she is a member of a couple whose other member has not attained the qualifying age for the credit: s 4(1A) of the 2002 Act, as inserted by Sch 1, para 64 of the 2012 Act.

[73] As noted above in ch 1: see in particular n 63. See also below n 76. Based on the size of the EU legislation (but seemingly not taking into account its significance), the DWP is, however, reported to have been one of the government departments least affected by new EU regulations between 2010–12: Office of the Parliamentary Counsel, 'When Laws Become Too Complex: A Review into the Causes of Complex Legislation' (London, Cabinet Office, 2013) 8–10.

[74] See in particular Art 48 of the Treaty on the Functioning of the European Union.

adaptation of UK social security law in the light of EU requirements.[75] It has manifested in some highly difficult and complex issues of law. Some have concerned the classification and status of different kinds of benefits under EU law,[76] which is itself highly complex[77] and whose social security provisions are, as noted in chapter one, among those which are the subject of a rolling programme of simplification as part of the EU Better Regulation initiative.[78]

A key issue concerning the impact of EU law has been its application to specific benefits in the United Kingdom. The position of universal credit in this regard has been queried by the Social Security Advisory Committee, and the Government has responded defensively that 'it is not a straightforward task to assess all the implications of EU legislation'.[79] At the same time, the Government has reported that the Department for Work and Pensions (DWP) has classed the credit as lying outside the scope of the EU co-ordination regulation[80] and thus not exportable. Whether this conclusion is correct will surely be subjected to juridical assessment.

Another critical issue to date has been the social security rights of EU citizens from outside the United Kingdom who are living in its territory.[81] The legal position in respect of foreign nationals who seek social security support in the United Kingdom has proved particularly problematic and continues to throw up new questions, as illustrated by the Supreme Court's recent decision

[75] See, for example, the 'right to reside' test discussed below.

[76] Specifically, Regulation 1408/71 on the application of social security schemes to employed persons, to self-employed persons and to members of their families moving within the Community [1971] OJ L149/2 (and implementing regulation, Regulation 574/72) and now (since 1 May 2010) Regulation 883/2004 on the co-ordination of social security systems (corrected version) [2004] OJ L200/1 (implementing regulation, Regulation 987/2009). See further T Hervey, 'Social Security: The European Union Dimension' in Harris et al (above n 29) 231–56; and RCA White, 'The New European Social Security Regulations in Context' (2010) 17(3) *Journal of Social Security Law* 144.

[77] See White (ibid).

[78] Simplification measures have included (i) amendments to Regulation 883/2004 (above n 76) intended to simplify rules and processes for the co-ordination of national social security systems within the EU; and (ii) the implementing regulation (Regulation 987/2009), whose recitals refer to facilitating the adoption of simplified procedures and administrative arrangements in Member States and increased electronic communication and which also aims to increase the co-operation between social security institutions in order to enable insured persons to access their rights as quickly as possible. White (above n 76) argues that these two instruments have failed to pass the test of modernisation and simplification which rests on 'whether someone coming new to Regulations 883/2004 and its Implementing Regulation will find its provisions clear and helpful without any prior knowledge of the predecessor regulations' (162).

[79] Social Security Advisory Committee (SSAC), *The Draft Universal Credit Regulations 2013; the Benefit Cap (Housing Benefit) Regulations 2012 (SI 2012/2994); the Draft Universal Credit, Personal Independence Payment, Jobseeker's Allowance and Employment and Support Allowance (Claims and Payments) Regulations 2013: Report by the Social Security Advisory Committee* (London, Stationery Office, 2012) Government response, para 21.

[80] Regulation 883/04 (above n 76).

[81] As in 'right to reside' cases – cases in which benefit is denied to claimants on the basis that they do not satisfy a residence requirement, which is a condition of entitlement, because they do not have a right to reside in Great Britain: see below.

in *Saint Prix v Secretary of State for Work and Pensions*.[82] Here the Court referred to the Court of Justice of the European Union (CJEU) questions of law concerning the entitlement of a French woman to income support, which she claimed after giving up employment in nursery schools due to considering the work too strenuous in view of her pregnancy. The basic issue was whether she fell within some category of 'worker' for the purposes of Article 7 of the EU Citizenship Directive.[83] As such, she would not be classifiable as a 'person from abroad' (such persons being excluded from the benefit) under the income support legislation,[84] itself described as 'complex' by Lady Hale.[85] A substantial body of case law indicated that in general, once employment is lost, a person ceases to be a 'worker' for the purpose of Article 7, [86] yet the House recognised the vulnerability of someone in this claimant's position: 'she will be left destitute if income support is not available.'[87]

Another case that illustrates some of the complexities arising from the EU–domestic law interface is *The Commissioners for Her Majesty's Revenue and Customs v Ruas*.[88] It concerned the entitlement to child benefit of a Portuguese national living in Great Britain whose children lived in Portugal. The claimant, Mr Ruas, came to Britain in 2000 with his wife and youngest daughter. His two elder daughters, born in 1988 and 1992 respectively, remained in Portugal. Mr Ruas held employment in the United Kingdom, paying National Insurance contributions, until 2004, when he became unable to work due to ill health. In 2006 he claimed child benefit for all three daughters. His application in respect of the two elder daughters was refused on the grounds that the Social Security Contributions and Benefits Act 1992, the relevant legislation, required that the children for whom a claimant is responsible be 'in Great Britain'.[89] The principal question was whether Mr Ruas should nevertheless be entitled by virtue of EC Council Regulation 1408/71 of 14 June 1971 (the Regulation).[90] Article 73 of the Regulation provides:

> An employed or self-employed person subject to the legislation of a Member State shall be entitled, in respect of the members of his family who are residing in another Member State, to the family benefits provided for by the legislation of the former State, as if they were residing in that State, subject to the provisions of Annex VI.

[82] *Saint Prix v Secretary of State for Work and Pensions* [2012] UKSC 49.
[83] Directive 2004/38/EC of the European Parliament and of the Council on the right of citizens of the Union and their family members to move and reside freely within the territory of the Member States (OJ 2004 L158/77).
[84] Various provisions of the Income Support (General) Regulations 1987 (SI 1987/1967), read with the Social Security Contributions and Benefits Act 1992, s 124.
[85] *Saint Prix* (above n 82) [4].
[86] In particular, *Secretary of State for Work and Pensions v Dias* [2009] EWCA Civ 807; *Johnson v Chief Adjudication Officer* (Case C-31/90) [1991] ECR I-3723; and *Martinez Sala v Freistaat Bayern* (Case C-85/96) [1998] ECR I-2691.
[87] *Saint Prix* (above n 82) [4].
[88] *The Commissioners for Her Majesty's Revenue and Customs v Ruas* [2010] EWCA Civ 291.
[89] Social Security Contributions and Benefits Act 1992, s 146, read with s 141. There were prescribed exceptions to this condition, but none of them applied to this claim.
[90] As noted above in n 76, new cases would be covered by Regulation 883/2004.

Child benefit was a 'family benefit' for this purpose, but there was a question as to whether Mr Ruas fell within the definition of being an 'employed or self-employed person'. Article 1(a) of the Regulation contained three alternative definitions. When this case was before the Upper Tribunal, Judge Mesher held that Mr Ruas was covered by the second one:

> (ii) any person who is compulsorily insured for one or more of the contingencies covered by the branches of social security dealt with in this Regulation, under a social security scheme for all residents or for the whole working population, if such person:
>
> - can be identified as an employed or self-employed person by virtue of the manner in which such scheme is administered or financed, or
> - failing such criteria, is insured for some other contingency specified in Annex I under a scheme for employed or self-employed persons, or under a scheme referred to in (iii), either compulsorily or on an optional continued basis, or, where no such scheme exists in the Member State concerned, complies with the definition given in Annex I.

Judge Mesher considered that as Mr Ruas had paid National Insurance contributions while working and was being credited with contributions while receiving benefit subsequently, he could 'be identified as an employed person by virtue of the way that the British scheme is financed and administered, through his actual earnings-related contributions as an employed person and his credited earnings'.[91] Therefore he was covered by the first subparagraph and it was not necessary to consider the second subparagraph.

On appeal to the Court of Appeal, the Commissioners of Her Majesty's Revenue and Customs (HMRC) contended that Mr Ruas did not fall within the definitions in Article 1. In relation to definition (ii) quoted above, they contended that while he was covered by the general part – since child benefit was a benefit available under a social security scheme for all residents – he did not fall within the first subparagraph. This was because the child benefit scheme, as a scheme within which inclusion was not dependent on having a contributions record as an employed person, did not distinguish between employed/self-employed persons and others. Etherton LJ, giving the only substantive judgment in the Court of Appeal (in 65 paragraphs), reviewed large tracts of EC legislation and the complex EC case law on employed and self-employed status in the context of social security. Distinguishing a number of the judgments, his Lordship concluded that Judge Mesher's interpretation[92] was correct and was consistent with the underlying policy of the Regulation:

> [A]lthough the Regulation is an instrument for co-ordination rather than harmonisation, the policy underlying the Regulation is that, in support of the freedom of

---

[91] Cited in Regulation 883/2004 (above n 76) para 19.
[92] Which relied in particular on the European Court of Justice's approach in *Martinez Sala v Freistaat Bayern* (above n 86).

movement of workers who are nationals of Member States, employed persons and self-employed persons moving within the Community should be subject to the social security scheme of only one single member state in order to avoid the over-lapping of national provisions and ensuing complications, and that the exceptions to the general rule should be as limited as possible . . . The Judge's interpretation, far from depriving limb (ii)(a) of any force . . . provides it with a meaning and effect which reflect a coherent policy.[93]

Thus Mr Ruas' two children fell to be treated 'as if they were residing in' the United Kingdom (per Article 73 of Regulation 1408/71) for the purposes of entitlement to child benefit. The outcome was therefore relatively simple, but the thought processes that led to it, taking in the difficult interaction of EC and domestic law, was most definitely not. (At the time of writing, the Government is reported to be trying to find 'a way that is legal' to prevent or limit further the exporting of child benefit by foreign nationals living in the United Kingdom.[94])

III. 'Extrinsic Complexity'

The complexity arising from the interactions between two or more individual benefits/credits and the interfaces between different administrative agencies has been described as 'extrinsic complexity'.[95] This is perhaps a misnomer insofar as most of these interactions take place within the social security sys-tem itself and are an intrinsic feature of it. On the other hand, there is cur-rently a jurisdictional division within the system between the DWP (which administers most welfare benefits), HMRC (which administers tax credits and some benefits, most notably child benefit) and local authorities (which have responsibility for housing benefit administration). A decision by one agency can affect that of another; information may need to pass between them; and claimants may have to deal with more than one of them in connec-tion with a single claim.

Complexity also arises from amendments to the legislation governing one particular benefit/credit, which may generate a need for consequential changes

---

[93] *Ruas* (above n 88) para 61.

[94] G Osborne, Chancellor's speech in Sittingbourne, Kent, reported in M Savage, 'Tories Come Out Fighting on "Dependency Culture"', *The Times* (3 April 2012) 8. Note that the official version of the speech published on the Treasury website does not include anything on this particular issue: www.gov.uk/government/speeches/chancellor-speech-on-changes-to-the-tax-and-benefit-system.

[95] Spicker, 'Five Types of Complexity' (above n 2); and Spicker, *How Social Security Works* (above n 9).

to the inter-related provisions applicable to another benefit or credit. For example, the introduction of tax credits contributed significantly to the growing complexity of the benefits system: not only may tax credits be treated as income for the purposes of various income-related benefits, but some elements of means-tested benefits have been transferred into the tax credits system (eg, the replacement of child allowances under the income support scheme with child tax credits).[96]

The interaction between different parts of the system is particularly important for claimants. For example, it can be especially problematic for a claimant who needs 'to report a change of circumstance at different times for tax credit and Housing Benefit/Council Tax Benefit'[97] or where there is a risk that such a change may not be reported to the correct agency or department. In Figure 1 above, provision for self-reporting of such changes is identified as an element of complexity in the specific context of means-tested benefits, but it is the case across all benefit and credit areas.[98] Where a material change of circumstances that may affect entitlement is not notified by a claimant, it is likely that the appropriate consequential adjustment to their benefit will not occur. If the change of circumstances, assuming it is known to the claimant,[99] has, for example, involved an improved level of income – such as from an increase in part-time earnings – a failure to notify the relevant office could result in overpayment of benefit, dating from the date of the change.[100] Such overpaid benefit may later be recoverable from the claimant.[101] Recovery usually occurs via deductions from benefit; despite the impoverishment this could cause, it

[96] NAO, *DWP: Dealing with the Complexity of the Benefits System* (above n 8) para 2.22.

[97] Ibid, para 2.23.

[98] See, eg, HM Revenue and Customs and DWP, *Tackling Fraud and Error in the Benefit and Tax Credit Systems* (London, HMRC/DWP, 2010) ch 2, para 8.

[99] That the claimant must be aware of them was confirmed in Commissioners' Decision CIS/4348/2003.

[100] See in particular the Social Security Administration Act 1971, s 71 (overpayments resulting from failure to disclose or misrepresentation of material fact) and s 71ZA (overpayment out of social fund), both read with the duty to provide information on changes in circumstances in the Universal Credit, Personal Independence Payment, Jobseeker's Allowance and Employment and Support Allowance (Claims and Payments) Regulations 2013 (SI 2013/380), regs 37–39 or the Social Security (Claims and Payments) Regulations 1987 (SI 1987/1968), regs 32 and 32ZZA (whichever set of regulations is applicable at the time). For housing benefit, see the Housing Benefit Regulations 2006 (SI 2006/213), pt 13.

[101] See in particular the Social Security Administration Act 1971 (as amended by the Welfare Reform Act 2012, s 105) ss 71, 71ZA and 71ZB. Regarding the mode of recovery, see s 71ZC (deduction from benefit), s 71ZD (deduction from earnings) and s 71ZE (court action). And see, for example, *B v Secretary of State for Work and Pensions* [2005] EWCA Civ 929, where it was held that the Secretary of State was entitled to recover overpayments totalling £4,626.74 from a claimant who had reduced mental capacity and had failed to appreciate the need to report that her children had been placed in the care of the local authority. Note that the Secretary of State has discretion as to whether to recover an overpayment. In *B* Sedley LJ appeared critical of the failure to apply it. See further the Social Security (Overpayments and Recovery) Regulations 2013 (SI 2013/384), pt 2; and the Social Security (Payments on Account, Overpayments and Recovery) Regulations 1988 (SI 1988/664), as amended. Regarding housing benefit, see the Housing Benefit Regulations 2006 (SI 2006/213).

appears not to be in breach of the European Convention on Human Rights (ECHR).[102] For a claimant whose culpable failure or negligence is the cause of an overpayment (an estimated 500,000 cases per annum),[103] if he or she has 'not taken reasonable steps to correct the error', there is also now the risk of a civil penalty of £50 (whilst a criminal sanction continues to be a possibility in a fraud case).[104] On the other hand, if a change in circumstances has made a claimant's financial situation worse, a shortfall in benefit through non-adjustment that results from a failure to notify the relevant authority cannot generally be rectified beyond a limited period of backdating, normally one month.[105] This inconsistency with the backdating of recoverable overpayments has been described as a 'case of double standards'.[106]

Some claimants may, through ignorance or confusion, fail to appreciate when they need to report changes[107] or which changes need to be reported.[108] But the problem with reporting changes of circumstance extends beyond this:

[102] *McGrath v Secretary of State for Work and Pensions* [2012] EWHC 1042 (Admin). Cranston J held that in the light of *B v Secretary of State* (ibid), recovered overpayment was not a 'possession' for the purposes of Art 1 of the First Protocol (which protects against deprivation of one's possessions – benefit being classed as a possession for this purpose: see *Stec v United Kingdom*, App Nos 65731/01 and 65900/01, noted above ch 1, n 50). But he considered that even if the contrary was the case, the deductions were in accordance with the law and in the public interest; moreover, the deprivation that occurred did not impose a 'disproportionate burden' on the claimant such as would have stuck an unfair balance between the public interest and individual rights (paras 26 and 32).

[103] Welfare Reform Bill Deb 19 May 2011, col 1041.

[104] See the Social Security (Civil Penalties) Regulations 2012 (SI 2012/1990) and ss 115C and 115D of the Social Security Administration Act 1992, inserted by the Welfare Reform Act 2012, s 116. According to the Minister, 'We aim to stop claimants thinking it is acceptable for them not to respond to a request for information, or to delay telling the Department or local authority about a change in circumstances, and so needlessly incur overpayments. This simple penalty is all about helping us to achieve those aims': Draft Social Security (Civil Penalties) Regulations 2012 Deb, 19 June 2012, col 3 (C Grayling MP). The regulations also enable a civil penalty of £50 to be imposed for failing, 'without reasonable excuse', to disclose information or provide evidence which results in an overpayment.

[105] The basic rule in such cases where mainstream benefits are concerned is that the necessary supersession of the award (under s 10 of the Social Security Act 1998) cannot be backdated more than one month: Social Security and Child Support (Decisions and Appeals) Regulations 1999 (SI 1999/991) reg 7(2)(a). However, in limited circumstances, that period could be extended to 13 months: reg 8(4)–(6). Different rules apply in the case of housing benefit, council tax benefit, child benefit and guardian's allowance.

[106] R Sainsbury, 'Social Security Decision Making and Appeals' in Harris et al (above n 29) 222.

[107] G Fimister, *Reporting Changes in Circumstances: Factors Affecting the Behaviours of Benefit Claimants*, DWP Research Report No 544 (2009). In this research, 40% of those surveyed had little knowledge of the reporting requirements. In a large minority of cases, claimants did not know that particular changes of circumstances would affect entitlement. See also A Irvine, J Davidson and R Sainsbury, *Reporting Changes in Circumstances: Tackling Error in the Benefits System*, DWP Research Report No 497 (2008) ch 2.

[108] In Fimister (ibid), 70% did not believe that it was necessary to report short-term changes. See also M Boath and H Wilkinson, *Achieving Good Reporting of Changes in Circumstances*, DWP Research Report No 457 (2007) 10: 'Two types of confusion were noted firstly, that claimants sometimes did not understand which changes they ought to report and secondly . . . confusion because of differences in rules for different benefits and tax credits.'

a claimant may not understand that the changes may need to be reported to more than one office, since a communications link over such matters between different branches of the administration cannot be assumed. Despite these serious problems, the reporting of changes of circumstances occurs on a considerable scale: the NAO found that it happens in thousands of cases every week, including 6,000–7,000 cases in Jobcentre Plus claims handled in the Derby region alone.[109] To Spicker, the problems over the reporting of changes of circumstance epitomise 'the claimant experience', which he identifies as another of his 'five types of complexity'.[110] This issue is linked to the interactions between parts of the benefits system as a whole.

The lack of administrative cohesion across the benefits system has resulted in real problems in the past, highlighted in particular by the case of *Hinchy*.[111] Miss Hinchy's income support award had included a severe disability premium.[112] She qualified for the premium because she had been awarded the care component of DLA at the middle rate on account of her disability, which was related to a bowel condition. Her DLA was awarded for five years, but when that period expired, the award was not renewed. An appeal by Miss Hinchy against the non-renewal failed. Miss Hinchy's weekly income support should have gone down by £48.50 per week from the date of the non-renewal of DLA, but the officials in her local social security office in Hackney were not aware that DLA had been terminated until it was revealed by a spot check in 2000. By this time, Miss Hinchy had been overpaid a total of £3,555.40. The Secretary of State sought to recover this amount on the grounds of Miss Hinchy's failure to disclose to the relevant office the material fact that her DLA award had expired.[113] When Miss Hinchy appealed on the grounds that she had told the office by telephone about the change and that in any event disclosure of the DLA termination could not reasonably have been expected from her due to her ill health and lack of understanding of the benefits system, her appeal was rejected. The tribunal concluded that the absence of a record of her call at the office made it unlikely that the information had been communicated in this way. Moreover, the standard order book for income support issued to Miss Hinchy had referred in the instructions to the importance of informing the office of any changes, including if benefit 'goes up or down'. The tribunal had considered that she was not incapable of understanding this and of taking the required action. Furthermore, if, as she claimed, she had not read the instructions, it was reasonable for her to have done so. Finally, the case law, in a range of decisions by the Social Security

[109] NAO, *Dealing with the Complexity of the Benefits System* (above n 8) para 2.33.

[110] Spicker, 'Five Types of Complexity' (above n 2) 8; and Spicker, *How Social Security Works* (above n 9) 142–43.

[111] Above n 1.

[112] Under the Income Support (General) Regulations 1987 (SI 1987/1967) reg 17 and Sch 2, still in force at the date of writing.

[113] Social Security Administration Act 1971, s 71(1).

and Child Support Commissioners, held that disclosure of information must be made to the appropriate office.

When the case reached the Court of Appeal it was held that disclosure of the information relating to DLA did not need to be made to the Secretary of State via the office dealing with income support, since that information was already in his officials' possession, in the DLA office, and it was reasonable for a claimant to believe therefore that the termination of the award of DLA would be known. In the House of Lords, Lord Scott of Foscote did not consider that the instructions made it sufficiently clear that the claimant should inform a specific office about the cessation of payment of a benefit to her; moreover, by instituting recovery in such circumstances, the Secretary of State was in effect 'seeking . . . to remedy the consequences of the inefficiencies of his own Departmental officials'.[114] However, Lord Scott was in a minority of one. The other four judges disagreed with the Court of Appeal. Lord Hoffmann said that the principles applicable to these kinds of case, which had been developed by the Social Security Commissioners, who had specialist experience of the benefit system, were 'entitled to great respect'.[115] There was an onus on the claimant to report changes, and the official was 'not deemed to know anything which he did not actually know'.[116] Lords Hope and Walker concurred with Lord Hoffmann. Baroness Hale was the other majority judge. She was not convinced that the instructions in the order book referring to the reporting of circumstances when benefit went up or down would be sufficiently clearly understood to require notification of a non-renewal of a separate benefit award. Alluding to the different approaches of Lords Scott and Hoffmann, she said that 'two highly literate and intelligent Law Lords have interpreted it differently. How can a poor claimant expect to know what it means?'[117] But as to whether Miss Hinchy ought reasonably to have known that she should report the termination of her DLA award, Baroness Hale was content to leave that matter to the judgment of a tribunal rather than the House.[118]

Hinchy therefore highlights the lack of cohesiveness in the system, which contributes to the complexity within it. 'Joined-up' governance, part of the broad political vocabulary in the United Kingdom, has been slow to enter the welfare system and indeed its electronic data systems. The NAO has found the computer systems of the different agencies to be 'at best, only partially linked',[119] and Mark Rowland and Robin White have commented in relation to overpayments of benefit:

---

[114] Above n 1, para 46.
[115] Ibid, para 30.
[116] Ibid, para 32.
[117] Ibid, para 57.
[118] Ibid, para 58.
[119] NAO, *Dealing with the Complexity of the Benefits System* (above n 8) para 2.24.

The advent of computerised data systems with easy national access has not yet reached the point where the possibility of data matching within the Department will provide much protection for claimants where overpayments arise because of the inter-relationship of conditions of entitlement to different benefits.[120]

Hinchy also illustrates the disadvantage of this aspect of complexity for claimants. As the House of Commons Work and Pensions Committee has explained, 'Viewing the system from the claimant's perspective . . . the complexity arises not just from [the] structure, but also from the individual's experience of the process, and whether or not the letters they receive are clear and comprehensible.'[121] Having to deal with different agencies, or even different offices within the same agency, is another source of complexity for claimants.[122]

Whether such problems may be alleviated with the coming of universal credit is not yet clear. As noted in chapter one, the role of the three agencies in administering benefits and tax credits will be combined within the DWP, but some parts of the system will lie outside this framework – although they are expected to interact with it. For example, council tax benefit has been replaced from 1 April 2013 by locally designed rebate schemes, termed 'council tax support' by the Government.[123] Local authorities have faced the risk of court action challenging the introduction of their schemes, which in the

---

[120] M Rowland and R White, *Social Security Legislation, 2012–13, Volume III: Administration, Adjudication and the European Dimension* (London, Sweet and Maxwell, 2012) 90.

[121] Work and Pensions Committee, *Benefits Simplification* (above n 7) para 10.

[122] Ibid, para 15.

[123] Local authorities in England are under a duty to make schemes reducing council tax liability for people in financial need: Local Government Finance Act 1992 (the 1992 Act), s 13A(2) and Sch 1A (as inserted by the Local Government Finance Act 2012), which prescribes particular matters which a scheme must include. The Government has a power to apply a default scheme to all local authorities which failed to devise their own individual scheme by 31 January 2013: see the 1992 Act, Sch 1A para 4(6). The default scheme is contained in the Council Tax Reduction Schemes (Default Scheme) (England) Regulations 2012 (SI 2012/2886), as amended by the Council Tax Reduction Schemes (Prescribed Requirements and Default Scheme) (England) (Amendment) Regulations 2012 (SI 2012/3085). Basic requirements for all council tax rebate schemes, including provision for pensioners in need and a small number of administrative arrangements, are prescribed by the Council Tax Reduction Schemes (Prescribed Requirements) (England) Regulations 2012 (SI 2012/2885), as amended by SI 2012/3085 (above), made under the 1992 Act, Sch 1A para 2(8). Transitional arrangements applicable from 1 April 2013 were made by the Council Tax Reduction Schemes (Transitional Provision) (England) Regulations 2013 (SI 2013/215). In Wales, see the 1992 Act, as amended, s 13A(4) and Sch 1B; the Council Tax Reduction Schemes and Prescribed Requirements (Wales) Regulations 2012 (SI 2012/3144) (W.316); and the Council Tax Reduction Schemes (Default Scheme) (Wales) Regulations 2012 (SI 2012/3145) (W.317). In Scotland, a national council tax reduction scheme has been prescribed. The Scottish Government decided, however, to prescribe arrangements designed to ensure that persons who would have been entitled to council tax benefit (some 565,630 people in May 2012) would be liable for the same net rate of council tax on the abolition of that benefit: Scottish Government, Local Government and Communities, 'The Council Tax Reduction (State Pension Credit) (Scotland) Regulations 2012 (SSI 2012/319)', policy note (November 2012), www.legislation.gov.uk/ssi/2012/319/pdfs/ssipn_20120319_en.pdf. See the Council Tax Reduction (Scotland) Regulations 2012 (SSI 2012/303) and the Council Tax Reduction (State Pension Credit) (Scotland) Regulations 2012 (SSI 2012/319), both as amended.

majority of cases will offer less generous support than council tax benefit;[124] an unsuccessful legal challenge was brought in February 2013 to the London Borough of Haringey's scheme.[125]

For claimants, changes in circumstances that could affect entitlement to council tax support and universal credit will have to be reported to both the local authority and the DWP, unless information reported to one can be shared with the other. By introducing separate locally devised schemes in place of a national (albeit locally administered) scheme, the council tax support reform has been criticised for precipitating 'the sort of complexity and lack of transparency that the Government says it wants to reduce'.[126] The variation across local schemes will 'add complexity to earnings incentives', thus working against an objective of universal credit of enabling claimants to identify the financial advantages of entering employment.[127] Furthermore, it is still unclear what the arrangements will be, governing eligibility for benefits currently passported through entitlement to some of the mainstream means-tested benefits which universal credit will replace. We cannot yet tell whether the arrangements will ameliorate or exacerbate the 'complexity and lack of coordination in the current system' found by the SSAC in its review of passported benefits.[128] Unless, for example, local authorities receive data from the DWP about a person's universal credit, to enable passporting of council tax support to them in the way that income support or income-based JSA entitlement has passported claimants into full council tax benefit, they will have an additional means-testing burden, thereby increasing complexity at a time when welfare reform aims to do the opposite.[129]

[124] In 2013–14 under the new framework, the Government is providing local authorities with funding covering only 90% of the amount provided to them for council tax benefit in 2012–13. According to research for the Joseph Rowntree Foundation, only around one in five local authorities will provide those liable for council tax with the level of support previously provided under council tax benefit; and 2.4 million of the 2.9 million council tax benefit recipients in England will face an extra liability of an average of £138 per annum as a result of the new system: S Bushe, P Kenway and H Aldridge, *The Impact of Localising Council Tax Benefit* (York, Joseph Rowntree Foundation, 2013), www.jrf.org.uk/publications/impact-localising-council-tax-benefit. See also M Pennycook and A Hurrell, *No Clear Benefit: The Financial Impact of Council Tax Benefit on Low-Income Households* (London, Resolution Foundation, 2013), www.resolutionfoundation.org/publications, which contains similar findings.

[125] See S Neville, 'Councils Face Court over Changes to Tax Benefit: Haringey Test Case', *Financial Times* (1 February 2013); and *R (M and S) v London Borough of Haringey* [2013] EWHC 252 (Admin). Underhill J's decision that there was no lack of fairness in the consultation process followed by Haringey was upheld by the Court of Appeal: *R (Stirling) v London Borough of Haringey* [2013] EWCA Civ 116.

[126] M Brewer, J Browne, and J Wenchao, 'Benefit Integration in the UK: An Ex Ante Analysis of Universal Credit' in T Callan (ed), *Budget Perspectives 2013* (Dublin, Economic and Social Research Institute, 2012) 45.

[127] HC Work and Pensions Committee, *Universal Credit Implementation* (above n 51) para 206.

[128] Social Security Advisory Committee, *Universal Credit: The Impact on Passported Benefits* (Cm 8332, 2012) 35, para 6.1.

[129] Pennycook and Hurrell (above n 124). See further the discussion of information technology below.

The House of Commons Work and Pensions Committee has commented that working out how to administer passported benefits under universal credit is 'a complex issue' with 'no easy answers', but the Government should ensure that 'fair and workable criteria' are put in place 'to avoid adding complexity' to the benefit and the risk of reduced work incentives.[130] The House of Commons Communities and Local Government Committee has subsequently recommended that the DWP should prioritise passporting between universal credit and council tax support systems, not merely to avoid administrative duplication but also 'to help claimants and limit confusion resulting from the separation of housing and council tax benefits'.[131]

IV. Management of Welfare

Spicker's list of the types of complexity within the welfare system[132] includes what he terms 'management issues'. Two such issues are the restructuring of agencies responsible for administration and decision-making and the streamlining of services delivery.[133] Renaming agencies is also likely to add to complexity from a claimant's perspective. Another aspect of management complexity concerns the contracting out of work such as health assessments for ESA and of work preparation for JSA claimants. This arguably also falls within the area of extrinsic complexity discussed in the previous section, since claimants may have to deal with organisations that are distinct from the welfare system but acting under its aegis. Nevertheless, contracting-out is now a fundamental part of how many welfare agencies manage their functions. The use of information technology also has a bearing on issues relating to complexity in the system and its management.

---

[130] HC Work and Pensions Committee, *Universal Credit Implementation* (above n 51) para 194.

[131] House of Commons Communities and Local Government Committee, *Implementation of Welfare Reform by Local Authorities* (2012–13, HC 833) para 102.

[132] Spicker, 'Five Types of Complexity' (above n 2) 7–8; and Spicker, *How Social Security Works* (above n 9) 141.

[133] Currently, within the DWP, Jobcentre Plus is responsible for most benefits for persons of working age; the Pension Service covers state retirement pensions and state pension credit; and the Disability and Carers Service covers disability living allowance and personal independence payment and attendance allowance. Before October 2011, Jobcentre Plus and a combined Pensions, Disability and Carer Service had formal executive agency status, but now their various services fall under a single DWP Departmental Board and Executive Team.

Contracting-Out and Commissioning

Quite complex arrangements have been entered into for the commissioning and management of contracts concerning health/disability-related assessment and welfare-to-work.[134] Concerns have arisen over the effectiveness of the arrangements, in particular the Government's failure to hold contractors to account for, among other things, the operation of the Pathways to Work programme for people on incapacity benefits.[135]

The Coalition Government introduced the Work Programme for people who have been receiving JSA or ESA for a minimum period, in order to prepare them for and ease them into taking up employment. Claimants are assigned to one of eight groups related to the barriers to employment they face. The programme operates under contracts with external bodies, whose remuneration rates are related to the group to which a claimant belongs.[136] Despite better controls than under previous contracted arrangements, there is still a risk of fraud.[137]

The purchasing of health assessments for incapacity benefits and now for ESA is another major feature of the contracting-out approach, which has been part of a broad trend under 'the changing state'.[138] The DWP negotiated with Atos Healthcare, a private company, in 2005 for the provision of medical services in a contract worth £100 million. In 2009–10, the payment to Atos for assessment reports and related work totalled £24.4 million,[139] and in 2011–12, 738,000 assessments were conducted by Atos at a cost to the DWP of £112.4m.[140] Atos has conducted all the health assessments for ESA since its introduction in 2008, and its contract has been extended to 2015. The total number of assessments conducted by May 2011 was over 1.25 million.[141]

---

[134] See, eg, Department for Work and Pensions, *DWP Commissioning Strategy* (Cm 7330, 2008).

[135] See National Audit Office, *Support to Incapacity Benefit Claimants through Pathways to Work: Report by Comptroller and Auditor General* (2010–11, HC 21); and House of Commons Public Accounts Committee, *Support to Incapacity Benefits Claimants through Pathways to Work* (2010–11, HC 404).

[136] See House of Commons Work and Pensions Committee, *Work Programme: Providers and Contracting Arrangements* (2010–12, HC 718).

[137] National Audit Office, *Department for Work and Pensions: Preventing Fraud in Contracted Employment Programmes* (HC 90, 2012).

[138] See C Harlow and R Rawlings, *Law and Administration*, 3rd edn (Cambridge, Cambridge University Press, 2009) ch 2.

[139] House of Commons Work and Pensions Committee, *The Role of Incapacity Benefit Reassessment in Helping Claimants into Employment* (2010–12, HC 1015-I) para 83.

[140] House of Commons Committee of Public Accounts, *Department for Work and Pensions: Contract Management of Medical Services* (2012–13, HC 744) para 1.

[141] Some 929,500 initial assessments and 336,500 repeat assessments: Department for Work and Pensions, *Employment and Support Allowance: Work Capability Assessment by Health Condition and Functional Impairment (Official Statistics)* (2011) tables 1a and 2.

The DWP monitors the work of Atos and can impose financial penalties for underperformance.[142] Despite such checks and a generally positive assessment from an independent review,[143] there have been some concerns about both the relatively high success rate for appeals in ESA cases (approximately 40 per cent[144]), which is suggestive of inaccurate assessment by Atos in a good number of cases, and claimants' experiences with Atos. Indeed, the Public Accounts Committee has concluded that the DWP has not been managing the contract with Atos with sufficient rigour.[145] The Work and Pensions Committee has found that 'many claimants have not received the standard of service from Atos which they can reasonably expect'.[146] Complaints have centred on the short time allocated to assessments, failure to provide claimants with adequate opportunities to discuss their problems and a mechanistic, 'tick box' approach.[147] There is also evidence that claimants often misunderstand the assessment process and what their assessment means; for example, being found not to have a limited capability for work is often understood by claimants to imply, wrongly, that they are healthy.[148] The way in which a sanction for failure to attend an Atos medical examination is imposed by Jobcentre Plus has added complexity.[149] The non-attendance is reported by Atos, but the reason for it is established by Jobcentre Plus. As a result, in some cases, claimants whose medical assessment appointment was cancelled by Atos have wrongly received a benefit sanction from Jobcentre Plus for non-attendance.[150]

When personal independence payment is introduced, Atos and another company, Capita, will have contracts for carrying out disability-related assessments.[151] The involvement of contractors in this sort of 'customer-facing' role adds to the range of organisations with which welfare claimants

[142] HC Work and Pensions Committee, *The Role of Incapacity Benefit Reassessment* (above n 139) para 87.

[143] M Harrington, *An Independent Review of the Work Capability Assessment* (London, Stationery Office, 2010).

[144] DWP, *Employment and Support Allowance: Work Capability Assessment by Health Condition and Functional Impairment* (above n 141) para.3.3.1.

[145] HC Committee of Public Accounts, *DWP: Contract Management of Medical Services* (above n 140) para 5.

[146] HC Work and Pensions Committee, *The role of Incapacity Benefit Reassessment* (above n 139) para 92.

[147] Ibid; and Harrington (above n 143) ch 5.

[148] HC Work and Pensions Committee, *The Role of Incapacity Benefit Reassessment* (above n 139) para 25.

[149] The claimant would fall to be treated as not having a limited capability for work, meaning that he or she will be barred from entitlement to ESA, unless there was a 'good cause' for the claimant's non-attendance: Employment and Support Allowance Regulations 2008 (SI 2008/794) reg 23(2) and 24.

[150] HC Work and Pensions Committee, *The Role of Incapacity Benefit Reassessment* (above n 139) para 65.

[151] S Cassidy, 'Half a Million Disabled People May Lose Benefits under Reforms', *The Independent* (3 August 2012), www.independent.co.uk/life-style/health-and-families/health-news/half-a-million-disabled-people-may-lose-benefits-under-reforms-8002288.html.

must engage, thereby increasing the complexity of the process from their per-spective, as well as increasing the complexity of the management of the sys-tem itself.[152]

Information Technology

Information technology (IT) plays a critically important role in the manage-ment of a modern welfare system that caters for very large numbers of peo-ple. The UK welfare system requires a large administrative apparatus to manage the processing, assessment and resolution of the millions of claims for benefit. The central agencies responsible for the management of large parts of the welfare system, namely the DWP and HMRC, represent 'machine bureaucracies' – that is, hierarchical organisations coping with a 'large, repet-itive, and routine workload'.[153] The use of standardised, automated proce-dures is favoured by such bodies. Indeed, the welfare system is said to have become 'absolutely impossible to deliver . . . without considerable reliance on [IT]'.[154] The role of IT is set to become even more pronounced when universal credit is fully rolled out by 2017, not least because most claims for the credit will be expected to be made online, as discussed below.

In principle, as the NAO has explained, the use of IT 'offers a prospect of managing complexity, shielding both staff and customers from it'.[155] IT facil-itates the handling of claims by giving administrators quick access to the pro-gress of cases. Moreover, a major potential benefit can be that of facilitating information-sharing within the relevant agency and between agencies. The use of IT within the welfare system has, however, been problematic to date due to technical problems and the disruptive effects of modernisation programmes. As has been the case with the role of IT in the child support scheme,[156] the design and implementation of effective IT systems for social security is difficult, due to the complexity of the processes which they need to cover. Moreover, the continuing lack of a workable link-up between different systems or a common access point limits the scope for information-sharing[157] and for the detection of incorrect information provided by claimants (which might be indicative of fraud in some cases).[158]

Nevertheless, the design of benefits structured around bright-line rules that seek, where possible, to ensure sharp distinctions across the wide range of

---

[152] See further the discussion below ch 6.

[153] R Thomas, 'Agency Rule-Making, Rule-Type, and Immigration Administration' (2013) *Public Law* 135, 141.

[154] J Hudson, 'Social Security and Information Technology' in Millar (ed) (above n 10) 296.

[155] NAO, *DWP: Dealing with the Complexity of the Benefits System* (above n 8) para 3.24.

[156] See, eg, House of Commons Work and Pensions Committee, *The Performance of the Child Support Agency* (HC 44, 2005).

[157] NAO, *DWP: Dealing with the Complexity of the Benefits System* (above n 8) para 3.26.

[158] House of Commons Committee of Public Accounts, *Achieving Value for Money in the Delivery of Public Services* (2005–06, HC 742) para 38.

issues that may arise in a claim may in part be directed towards the use of computers; state pension credit is cited as an example.[159] Carol Harlow and Richard Rawlings have commented, 'Computers . . . speak the language of rules'.[160] Eric Kades also argues that formal mechanical rules such as one finds in much of social security law are particular suited to the use of this technology, 'to manage more and more complexity with fewer and fewer (human) headaches'.[161] The NAO has explained that IT systems can reduce the need for detailed knowledge of benefit rules among benefit staff, 'allowing eligibility and award recommendations to be made for more complex cases'.[162]

However, the continual process of benefit reform generates significant problems for IT. The complexity of the benefit system means that reform is complicated, and this can hamper the installation of new IT systems. Indeed, sorting out the IT in anticipation of changes has on occasion led to delays in introducing the new rules and benefits.[163] Once an intricate IT system is set in place, it is in any event inherently more likely to experience problems and failure and ultimately generate increased costs.[164] Part of the problem in the past has been the relatively poor quality of the IT used in the social security system – being 'far from cutting- edge' and using, for the main processes, equipment that is often 'well over a decade old'.[165] In May 2012, the Government admitted that the IT system used for DLA claims was 'outdated'.[166] The limitations of the IT systems used to date include their inability to, for example, upload copies of paper documents; this means that a claim may have two files, one paper and one computerised.[167]

Far from ameliorating complexity, therefore, IT management has been shown in practice to increase it. Part of the problem is that policy development has taken insufficient account of the IT implications, and in some instances, late adjustments of policy have hampered the technical design.[168] Yet the demands placed on IT for the management of social security are only going to increase. For example, reforms to housing benefit in 2012–13, including the introduction in the social rented sector of the so-called 'bedroom tax',[169] were set to increase the number and kinds of notifications local

[159] NAO, *DWP: Dealing with the Complexity of the Benefits System* (above n 8) para 3.28.
[160] Harlow and Rawlings (above n 138) 198.
[161] E Kades, 'The Laws of Complexity and the Complexity of Laws: the Implications of Computational Theory for the Law' (1007) 49 *Rutgers Law Review* 403, 409.
[162] NAO, *DWP: Dealing with the Complexity of the Benefits System* (above n 8) para 3.31.
[163] Hudson (above n 154) 298; NAO, *Universal Credit: early progress* (HC 621) (London, TSO, 2013).
[164] NAO, *DWP: Dealing with the Complexity of the Benefits System* (above n 8) para 3.29.
[165] Ibid.
[166] House of Commons Work and Pensions Committee, *Government support towards the additional living costs of working-age disabled people: Government Response to the Committee's Seventh Report of Session* 2010–12 (2012–13, HC 105) 3.
[167] Spicker, *How Social Security Works* (above n 9) 141.
[168] NAO, *DWP: Dealing with the Complexity of the Benefits System* (above n 8) para 3.27.
[169] This reform, described by the Government as involving the removal of what it has termed a 'spare room subsidy', relates to the size of accommodation which the Government considers

authorities need to receive via the DWP's automated data-sharing system, known as ATLAS (Automated Transfers to Local Authority Systems). Local authorities are reported to receive 20 million such notifications each year, and some authorities are already experiencing difficulties in managing them; but levels of automation vary across authorities.[170] The effective sharing of information between the IT systems operated by local authorities and the DWP is said to be 'critical to the implementation of welfare reform'.[171] Implementing universal credit successfully is regarded by the House of Commons Work and Pensions Committee as being partly dependent on the efficient transfer of data between DWP IT systems and ATLAS and between the former and HMRC's 'Real Time Information' (RTI) system, although the Committee harbours doubts as to whether the interface between the systems is 'robust'.[172]

There is also scope for the use of IT in an 'outward-facing' role, such as through the provision of information to the public via the internet. At a time of major reforms to the benefit system, online services could have a particularly important role in providing information about changes that are expected to have a significant impact on many households, although a survey by the NAO found local authority websites 'varied significantly' in their coverage of the reforms to housing benefit in advance of the introduction of universal credit.[173] Interactive benefit calculation facilities are now available for existing or potential claimants, although the complexity of some schemes and their reform may result in gaps. For example, as the aforementioned reforms to

should be funded for particular categories of household in the social rented sector. Working-age tenants considered to have accommodation which is regarded as too large will have their housing benefit entitlement reduced by 14% or 25% depending on the number of surplus bedrooms – a controversial reform widely referred to as the 'bedroom tax'. The reform was expected by the Government to achieve total savings to the Exchequer of £1bn per annum by 2014/15: DWP, *Explanatory Memorandum to the Housing Benefit Amendment Regulations 2012, 2012 No 3040* (London, DWP, 2012) para 4.1. This change was effected by the Housing Benefit (Amendment) Regulations 2012 (SI 2012/3040) from 1 April 2013. Some exceptions to the 'bedroom tax' restrictions applicable in both the social and private sector have since been made by the Housing Benefit (Amendment) Regulations 2013 (SI 2013/665), in relation to the need for an extra bedroom due to a requirement for overnight care of a partner, the placement of a child by a local authority or fostering, or the intended return of a non-dependant son/daughter or stepson/stepdaughter in the armed forces who is away on operations. (Equivalent exceptions have been made to the corresponding 'bedroom tax' provisions within the universal credit scheme by the Universal Credit (Miscellaneous Amendments) Regulations 2013 (SI 2013/803).) Other housing benefit reforms in 2012–13 included extending the shared accommodation rate for rent (based on assumed sharing of accommodation regardless of whether the claimant shares or lives alone) to single people aged 25–34; and the administration of the general benefits cap related to the composition of the household (see above n 59).

[170] NAO, *DWP: Managing the Impact of Housing Benefit Reform* (above n 61) paras 1.17–1.19.
[171] HC Communities and Local Government Committee, *Implementation of Welfare Reform by Local Authorities* (above n 131) para 132.
[172] HC Work and Pensions Committee, *Universal Credit Implementation* (above n 51) para 232.
[173] NAO, *DWP: Managing the Impact of Housing Benefit Reform* (above n 61) para 2.7 and fig 8.

housing benefit were being introduced, the public could use online tools to calculate the impact of some of them.[174] However, due to the complex nature of the calculations involved, the DWP could not include two of the key elements – the social sector size criteria[175] and the non-dependant deduction.[176]

IT can also be used to enable claims to be made online. As mentioned above, this is planned to become the normal method for making universal credit claims. 'Digital by default' is the Government's policy.[177] By the Government's estimate, at the national launch of universal credit in October 2013 (but now delayed), around 50 per cent of claims will be online, rising to 80 per cent by full implementation.[178] As will be discussed in chapter four, the process involved in claiming benefits, particularly the length and complexity of the forms to be completed, has long been regarded as problematic for claimants. It is not clear that online claiming will make the process less complex overall for claimants, especially since one in five universal credit claimants are not expected to have the capacity or resources to use it. Some claimants may need to rely on support for online claiming, which is apparently going to be made available in offices and via the telephone.[179] Various groups have been identified as particularly vulnerable and most in need of such assistance (in addition to needing help in learning how to budget under

---

[174] Ibid, para 2.9. The local housing allowance (see above ch 1, nn 168–70 and associated text) and the benefit cap are, however, included. But in relation to the local housing allowance, it does not enable the effects of the changes to the shared accommodation rules to be factored in: ibid.

[175] See above n 169.

[176] This is an amount deducted from the claimant's eligible rent to determine his or her 'maximum housing benefit'. The deduction is intended to reflect the capacity of a non-dependant aged 18 or over, typically a son or daughter, to contribute to the housing costs. A much higher deduction is made where the non-dependant is in employment: in 2012–13 it was, eg, £26.25 where the non-dependant's gross weekly income was £124–£182.99, rising incrementally to £73.85 where income was £394 or higher. If the non-dependant is not in remunerative employment, a standard deduction of £11.45 is made. See the Housing Benefit Regulations 2006 (SI 2006/213), as amended, regs 3, 70 and 74.

[177] Cabinet Office, 'Digital by Default Proposed for Government Services', press release (23 November 2010). This policy is based on the recommendations of the report for the Government by Martha Lane Fox, *Directgov2010 and Beyond: Revolution not Evolution: An Independent Report* (Cabinet Office and Efficiency Reform Group, 2010), www.gov.uk/government/publications/directgov-2010-and-beyond-revolution-not-evolution-a-report-by-martha-lane-fox. The Government's digital strategy was published in November 2012: Cabinet Office, *Government Digital Strategy* (2012), publications.cabinetoffice.gov.uk/digital/strategy/government-digital-strategy.pdf. It states that 'digital by default' means 'digital services that are so straightforward and convenient that all those who can use them will choose to do so whilst those who can't are not excluded' (2).

[178] HC Work and Pensions Committee, *Universal Credit Implementation* (above n 51) oral evidence (17 September 2012), Q202–Q205 (Iain Duncan Smith).

[179] On the need for help with IT under universal credit, see M Rotik and L Perry, *Insight to Support Universal Credit User-Centred Design*, DWP Research Report No 799 (DWP, 2012); and T Tu and S Ginnis, *Work and the Welfare System: A Survey of Benefits and Tax Credits Recipients*, DWP Research Report 800 (DWP, 2012). See further below ch 3. People aged 65 or over, for example, are much less likely than younger people to have internet experience, since far fewer of them have internet access at home: National Audit Office, *Digital Britain 2: Putting Users at the Heart of Government's Digital Services* (2012–13, HC 1048) para 3.3.

the new paid-monthly system).[180] Such support is intended to be delivered through local authority-led partnerships with DWP funding.[181] It is also planned that recipients of universal credit will have an 'online account through which they will be able to access information about their claim and their . . . payments, much like the options that online banking services currently offer'.[182] Recipients of the credit will also be expected to report online any significant changes of circumstances: as explained earlier, this reporting is an important obligation for claimants.[183]

The IT system is expected to have the sophistication to provide automatic, reliable assessment of entitlement when such information is inputted, as well as making initial award calculations so that staff can concentrate on 'complex cases or those where there is a risk of fraud or error'.[184] Its capacity to function in this way will, however, be dependent on a combination of factors, not all of which are within the Government's control: robust well-designed IT programs, which will require a significant improvement on the system's record to date; sufficient simplicity in the structure of the credit's different elements and how they inter-relate; and wide-scale claimant access to the internet (although 'Internet Access Devices' are being installed in Jobcentres to help those who cannot access the internet at home[185]) and competence among claimants in using it.

Given that the universal credit reforms will roll a number of separate benefits into one, the failure of the IT system could 'potentially expose large numbers of service users to the risk of financial hardship', and back-up arrangements will be important.[186] Such arrangements will of course partly offset any cost savings to be made from an increased use of IT. Indeed, it has been argued that while IT holds the promise of lower cost in administering a claim, the true cost should reflect the number of transactions that are likely to occur as individual claimants experience problems as a result of using the

---

[180] Including those with mental health problems, addiction, learning or language difficulties, domestic violence victims, over-18 care leavers, homeless people, the 'severely indebted' and those in 'rural isolation': DWP, *Universal Credit Local Support Services Framework* (11 February 2013) Annex C, www.dwp.gov.uk/docs/uc-local-service-support-framework.pdf. See also Social Security Advisory Committee, *The Implementation of Universal Credit and the Support Needs of Claimants: A Study by the Social Security Advisory Committee*, Occasional Paper No 10 (May 2013) ch 2.

[181] Ibid (DWP). See also below ch 3.

[182] DWP, *Welfare that Works* (above n 31) ch 4, para 8.

[183] Ibid, para 9.

[184] Ibid, para 7.

[185] In February 2013, the Government reported that 2,167 devices had been installed across 706 sites: Department for Work and Pensions, *Government Response to the House of Commons Work and Pensions Select Committee's Third Report of Session 2012–13, Universal Credit Implementation: Meeting the Needs of Vulnerable Claimants* (Cm 8537, 2013) para 15.

[186] A Tarr and D Finn, *Implementing Universal Credit: Will the Reforms Improve the Service for Users?* (York, Joseph Rowntree Foundation/Centre for Social Inclusion, 2012) 57–58. See also the SSAC recommendation (no 28) that 'the Government . . . ensure that it has sufficient resources in place to support those claimants who are initially unable to make claims online because of capability or accessibility difficulties, to make claims by telephone or, where appropriate, through a home visit': SSAC, *Report by the Social Security Advisory Committee* (above n 79).

digital system: 'The failure of the web-based service to resolve individuals' problems will multiply those transactions, generating massive amounts of failure demand as vulnerable citizens keep returning . . .'.[187]

V. Conclusion

This chapter began with a quotation from Lady Hale in which she noted the important role played by the welfare system in meeting a diversity of need across the population. She commented that almost every person may at some point in his or her life have a valid claim upon the system. Some parts of the media and some politicians may portray the UK welfare benefits system as enabling large numbers of citizens to enjoy a parasitic existence on the state at the expense of economically active citizens. This is a cruel misrepresentation of what is for the majority of claimants an unwanted dependence on the lifeline of welfare support, even if the system does need to have checks in place to ensure that support is genuinely needed and to prevent abuse. Such checks include elaborate conditions surrounding entitlement and the claims process. As the discussion in later chapters will show, these elements contribute significantly to the complexity of the system.

In this chapter we have seen how complexity manifests in the design of the system and in continual and often piecemeal adjustment and reform. In seeking to target needs and provide the necessary lifeline in what is considered to be the most appropriate way, the system has developed a complex structure of benefits and credits. Complexity is inherent in the individual schemes and in the way they and the systems for their administration inter-relate. It is also evident in the management of the system. The use of information technology is heralded as an antidote to bureaucratic complexity, but it is not problem-free and may bring new burdens for claimants.

The introduction of universal credit (and accompanying rationalisation of the administrative framework) represents the first significant attempt to introduce greater coherence into the UK welfare system. However, the changes to council tax benefit and the social fund are to some extent undermining this objective, and the structural simplification that the reform represents masks an underlying, continuing, legal complexity. The pervasive rules variously governing all aspects of the system are perhaps the most significant principal manifestation of its complexity. They are the main focus of the next chapter.

[187] J Seldon and B O'Donovan, 'The Achilles' Heel of Scale Service Design in Social Security Administration: The Case of the United Kingdom's Universal Credit' (2013) 66(1) *International Social Security Review* 1, 11.

3

Rules and the Measurement of Complexity

I. Introduction

The previous chapter explored three of the four elements that contribute to the complexity of the welfare system: its design, including the impact of continual reform; the 'extrinsic complexity' arising from the interactions and inter-relationships between different parts of the system and its constituent institutions; and the arrangements for the management of welfare, especially the use of contracting-out and information technology. The fourth contributory element, the use of complex rules, will be discussed in the present chapter. This chapter also focuses on the measurement of complexity and the various attempts that have been made to find an effective basis for it. As stated in chapter one, such measurement could aid the effective gauging of progress in simplification, which remains a key policy objective. Indicators of various complexity levels within the welfare system, which could be used in this process of assessment, are among the factors which are discussed.

II. Complex Rules

As previously stated, the law is at the heart of the complexity of the welfare system. It determines the system's structure and gives effect to the frequent changes to it that government sees fit to make. It also determines key aspects of administration and decision-making – including many of the processes by which claims may be made and determined. More importantly, it aims to set out in generally very precise terms, through rules which for the most part are tightly drafted, when and to whom there is a duty to pay an individual benefit and of what amount. The rules therefore prescribe the entry conditions of entitlement to the various benefits and credits, including eligibility factors related to such matters as age, country of residence, health, disability and status (eg, as tenant, student and parent). They also cover the matters that are to determine the level of support the system must confer on an individual, providing in relevant cases for the assessment of means and seeking to define in that context what counts as income and capital and its possession. The rate of benefit or credit to be paid and the duration of entitlement are also prescribed. Often prescription includes exceptions to general rules, which increases complexity.[1]

As discussed above, many of these elements are a reflection of the need to build a system attuned to the hugely diverse circumstances and needs across the claimant population, as well as to various underlying social and economic policy goals and values. There are nevertheless practical limits to prescription, particularly since policy delivery may be best served by flexibility in some circumstances, while the full range of possible situations that might give rise to need cannot always be identified in advance. For example, the housing benefit scheme has not covered liability for rent under a tenancy which is 'not on a commercial basis';[2] effectively, the assessment of this issue has had to be made on a case-by-case basis since 'it is probably not possible to definitively state when an agreement is commercial and when it is not'.[3] There is, however, guidance in the case law and a requirement in the regulations that in deciding this issue, regard must be had, inter alia, to whether the terms of occupancy 'include terms which are not enforceable by law'.[4] The law on overpayments offers another example of an area where the rules themselves are, in social security terms at least, reasonably succinct but which careful and extensive judicial consideration has revealed to hide considerable complexity.[5] On the other hand, policy and operational ends may be well served by relatively simple, 'fact-insensitive', rules,[6] such as providing that an adult of state pension

---

[1] P Spicker, *How Social Security Works: An introduction to Benefits in Britain* (Bristol, Policy Press, 2011) 140.

[2] Housing Benefit Regulations 2006 (SI 2006/213) reg 9(1)(a).

[3] L Findlay, *CPAG's Housing Benefit and Council Tax Benefit Legislation, 24th edn (2011–12)* (London, CPAG, 2011) 253.

[4] Housing Benefit Regulations 2006 (SI 2006/213) reg 9(2).

[5] See the necessarily very extensive commentary given in M Rowland and R White, *Social Security Legislation (2012–13), Volume III: Administration, Adjudication and the European Dimension* (London, Sweet and Maxwell, 2012) 56–104.

[6] P Sales and B Hooper, 'Proportionality and the Form of Law' (2003) 119 *Law Quarterly Review* 426, 428. Sales and Hooper state, 'A law's fact sensitivity is the degree to which the outcome of applying it depends on the detailed factual context in which it is applied. A general law that is expressed in simple and rigid terms by reference to precise concepts is fact insensitive.'

credit age who is ordinarily resident in Great Britain has an entitlement to a winter fuel payment.[7]

By specifying the bases of entitlement, the legal framework provides assurances of consistency and equal treatment between claimants in like circumstances. Denis Galligan has argued that 'the primary virtue of rules is guidance', and officials are best guided by precise rules which serve and embody aims such as stability and consistency of application and are 'not changed too often, known publicly, and not unduly complex'.[8] Rules may be prescribed that apply strict central controls to this massive area of governance in which many thousands of decisions are made each day by front-line administrators. Minimising the scope for the exercise of discretion through the use of detailed, bright-line rules to control decision-making reduces the risk of an 'implementation deficit', which occurs when front-line decision-makers 'adapt in particular ways the goals and rules included in the body of legislation or programmes they are required to implement' and in so doing reduce the 'extent to which the application of the law in question corresponds with the legislator's objectives'.[9] In *Alvi*, Lord Walker of Gestingthorpe noted the tension between flexibility and predictability in relation to decision-making in the public law context and observed that in recent decades, there has been a 'marked tendency of government' to favour the latter over the former.[10] This was true of immigration control, where predictability of outcome was desirable. But it came 'at a considerable price in terms of rigidity and complexity'.[11] Such a perspective has equal validity in the context of social security.

A rule-based system that aims to ensure consistent and accurate decision-making reflects the 'bureaucratic rationality' model of administrative justice identified by Jerry Mashaw.[12] The UK social security system is frequently associated with this model, although it also fits with Robert Kagan's 'bureaucratic legalism' model, under which centrally devised rules aim to ensure hierarchical

---

[7] Social Security Contributions and Benefits Act 1992, s 138(2); and the Social Fund Winter Fuel Payment Regulations 2000 (SI 2000/729), as amended, reg 2 (a provision the drafting of which has nonetheless been described as 'quite unnecessarily opaque': P Wood et al, *Social Security Legislation (2012–13), Volume II: Income Support, Jobseeker's Allowance, State Pension Credit and the Social Fund* (London, Sweet and Maxwell, 2012) 1374).

[8] DJ Galligan, *Discretionary Powers: A Legal Study of Official Discretion* (Oxford, Clarendon Press, 1986) 161.

[9] P Van Aerschot, *Activation Policies and the Protection of Individual Rights: A Critical Assessment of the Situation in Denmark, Finland and Sweden* (Farnham, Ashgate, 2011) 22–23.

[10] *R (Alvi) v Secretary of State for the Home Department (Joint Council for the Welfare of Immigrants intervening)* [2012] 1 WLR 2208 [111].

[11] Ibid [112].

[12] JL Mashaw, *Bureaucratic Justice: Managing Social Security Disability Claims* (New Haven, Yale University Press, 1983). The bureaucratic rationality model of administrative justice recognises a decisional process with the legitimating goals of accuracy and efficiency. Rule-based decision-making fits with this model: Mashaw (above) 26. It contrasts with Mashaw's 'professional treatment' model and 'moral judgment' model, noted below.

control of decision-making in order to ensure a uniform approach.[13] Indeed, the latter is consistent with the achievement of 'goal congruence': that is, when the operative goals of front-line officials are congruent with the formal goals of policy-makers.[14] Nevertheless, there has been a partial shift in discrete parts of the system in recent years towards another of Mashaw's models, that of 'professional judgment'. This model is based on contextual interpretation, whereby a professional applies his or her expertise related to the needs of a client to form a professional judgment – a process underpinned by the legitimating value of 'service'.[15] Two areas in particular have been associated with this trend. The first is health assessment for incapacity benefits,[16] although as Jackie Gulland has argued, under employment and support allowance (ESA), the assessment is 'heavily constrained by low-level bureaucratic rules which leave little room for the kind of judgements (sic) we would expect in a professional model'.[17] The second is the enforcement of work search and related 'activation' conditions.[18] The latter is also an area governed by managerialism – officials working to targets as part of performance management – which Michael Adler has identified as a separate model of administrative justice.[19]

Judicial Interpretation and Intervention

As noted in chapter one, the complexity of rules may give rise to uncertainty about precisely how they should be applied in particular situations. It may

---

[13] RA Kagan, 'The Organisation of Administrative Justice Systems: The Role of Political Mistrust' in M Adler (ed), *Administrative Justice in Context* (Oxford, Hart, 2010) 164–65.

[14] See MK Meyers, N M Riccucci and I Lurie, 'Achieving Goal Congruence in Complex Environments: The Case of Welfare Reform' (2001) 11(2) *Journal of Public Administration Research and Theory* 165.

[15] Mashaw (above n 12) 26–29. Mashaw's other model of administrative justice is the 'moral judgment' model (29–31). This model's primary goal is conflict resolution, and it has a legitimating value of fairness. As will be noted below, ch 5, this model is associated with courts and tribunals as neutral decision-makers.

[16] T Buck, D Bonner and R Sainsbury, *Making Social Security Law: The Role and Work of the Social Security and Child Support Commissioners* (Aldershot, Ashgate, 2005) 216.

[17] J Gulland, 'Ticking Boxes: Decision-Making in Employment and Support Allowance' (2011) 18(2) *Journal of Social Security Law* 69, 86. Although one might argue that in the context of social security cases (such as those concerned with capacity for work), the decision-maker is a different person to the professional and is only using the judgement of the health professional in the context of rule-based decision-making, in practice the evidence shows that the former tends to follow the latter's view in a majority of cases. See Gulland (above) 76 and 86.

[18] See M Adler, 'The Justice Implications of "Activation Policies" in the UK' in S Stendahl, T Erhag and S Devetzi (eds), *A European Work-First Welfare State?* (Gothenburg, Centre for European Research, 2008) 95–127.

[19] Ibid. See also M Adler, 'A Socio-Legal Approach to Administrative Justice' (2003) 25(4) *Law and Policy* 323–52; and M Adler, 'Understanding and Analysing Administrative Justice' in Adler (ed) (above n 13) 129–59. The managerial model has the legitimating goal of improved performance and a mode of accountability based on performance indicators and audit. Managerial autonomy characterises the mode of decision-making in this model, according to Adler.

also provide enhanced scope for error, which could give rise to appeals by claimants to the First-tier Tribunal (Social Entitlement Chamber), the latest in a line of appellate bodies charged with adjudication of social security cases.[20] The tribunal is a neutral and independent appellate body of the kind associated with the third of Mashaw's models, that of 'moral judgment', whose primary goal is conflict resolution and a 'full and equal opportunity to obtain one's entitlements', with a legitimating value of fairness.[21]

It may be the case that with the intensification of bureaucratic rationality in a social security system increasingly based on bright-line rules and with reduced scope for the application of a broad principle of 'fairness', moral judgment has suffered in its shadow, as Trevor Buck, David Bonner and Roy Sainsbury have contended[22] – notwithstanding its role in some decisions, as noted above. Faced with such rules, the response of the judiciary has in general been deference, even in cases in which the rules make broad-brush distinctions, which can give rise to unfairness among some of those caught by them and notwithstanding the subjection of the legislation to a test of proportionality under the European Convention on Human Rights (ECHR).[23] Such deference is perhaps understandable when rules are straightforward and easily applied, since Parliament's intention that they operate in the way adopted by the administration can more legitimately be assumed, and judges are in any event traditionally wary on constitutional grounds of straying into resource allocation issues in the fields of social or economic policy.[24] But

---

[20] As discussed below ch 5.

[21] Mashaw (above n 12) 31.

[22] Buck, Bonner and Sainsbury (above n 16) 220.

[23] See E Laurie, 'Judicial Responses to Bright-Line Rules in Social Security: In Search of Principle' (2009) 72(3) *Modern Law Review* 384; and R Thomas, 'Agency Rule-Making, Rule-Type, and Immigration Administration' (2013) *Public Law* 135, citing in particular *Huang v Secretary of State for the Home Department* [2007] UKHL 11; [2007] 2 AC 176. Furthermore, Sales and Hooper (above n 6) note that the European Court of Human Rights 'takes a relatively tolerant attitude towards rigid laws in benefit systems' (443).

[24] See, eg, *Stewart v Secretary of State for Social Security* [2011] EWCA Civ 907, in which the Court of Appeal did not wish to 'expose the court to the charge that it is trespassing in territory in an area of social policy that is properly the preserve of the legislature' (per Sir Henry Brooke, giving the only substantive judgment, at para 35). See also *Stec v United Kingdom* (Application Nos 65731/01 and 65900/01) para 52: 'A wide margin is usually allowed to the State under the Convention when it comes to general measures of economic or social strategy . . . Because of their direct knowledge of their society and its needs, the national authorities are in principle better placed than the international judge to appreciate what is in the public interest on social or economic grounds, and the Court will generally respect the legislature's policy choice unless it is "manifestly without reasonable foundation".' In *R (RJM) v Secretary of State for Work and Pensions* [2008] UKHL 63 [54] and [56], Lord Neuberger expressed the view that social policy was 'an area where a wide measure of appreciation is accorded . . . to the state' by the Strasbourg court and that a court 'should be very slow to substitute its view for that of the executive'. For exceptions, see *Willis v United Kingdom* (Application No 36042/97) (2002) EHRR 21 (gender discrimination in entitlement to the widow's payment and widow's mother's allowance); and in the UK courts, *Burnip v Birmingham City Council and Others* [2012] EWCA Civ 629 (local housing allowance limit based on number of bedrooms allowed for various private-sector tenants and their household members discriminated on disability grounds and could not be justified as fair or proportionate). See also the discussion below ch 8.

there is also evidence that, at the judicial level, complexity can push decision-making in the opposite direction, through judges seeking creatively to decide the kinds of cases that are inherently difficult to resolve correctly.

An example is *Moyna v Social Security Commissioner*,[25] in which at issue was the claimant's entitlement to the care component (lowest rate) of the disability living allowance (DLA). One route to qualification involves a claimant being 'so severely disabled physically or mentally that . . . (ii) [she] cannot prepare a cooked meal for [herself] if [she] has the ingredients'.[26] This 'bizarre statutory formulation'[27] represents what has generally been known as the 'cooking test'. An assessment of the capacity to prepare a meal will continue to form part of the assessment of disability under the personal independence payment scheme, which is replacing DLA, as discussed below. The Department for Work and Pensions (DWP) has not published independent figures on the numbers receiving the care component of DLA on the basis of satisfying this test, but in 2012 they were likely to have been in the region of 750,000.[28]

The apparent straightforwardness of the test that the wording of the statute suggests belies a provision of considerable complexity in its application to individual cases. For example, it is not immediately apparent what the position would be if a claimant has no prior experience of cooking. But case law indicates that such experience or lack of it should be discounted for the purposes of the test.[29] Indeed, case law also refers to the test as a hypothetical one, so that a claimant's cooking *skill* is irrelevant.[30] Other issues include the kind of a meal that the claimant needs to be able to cook and by what means. Again, there has been some judicial clarification concerning such matters.[31] The meaning of 'prepare' has also required elucidation; thus in one case, it was held to include 'the peeling and chopping of fresh vegetables'.[32] What if the claimant cannot stand for a sufficient period? Once again, case law has

---

[25] *Moyna v Social Security Commissioner* [2003] UKHL 44; [2003] 1 WLR 1929.

[26] Social Security Contributions and Benefits Act 1992, s 72(1)(a)(ii).

[27] N Wikeley, 'Social Security and Disability' in N Harris et al, *Social Security Law in Context* (Oxford, Oxford University Press, 2000) 384.

[28] Based on 911,000 people being in receipt of the lowest rate care component (LRCC) in February 2012, according to statistics on the Department for Work and Pensions (DWP) website (83.244.183.180/100pc/dla/ccdate/carepay/a_carate_r_ccdate_c_carepay.html) and the fact that 80–85% of those in receipt of this component satisfied the cooking test according to a detailed study: K Swales, *A Study of Disability Living Allowance and Attendance Allowance Awards* (London, HMSO, 1998) 22. The alternative basis of entitlement to the LRCC is that a person 'requires in connection with his bodily functions attention from another person for a significant portion of the day': Social Security Contributions and Benefits Act 1992, s 72(1)(a)(i).

[29] *R v Secretary of State for Social Security, ex p Armstrong* (1996) Admin LR 626 (CA).

[30] Commissioner's Decision R(DLA)2/95.

[31] Ibid, where the Commissioner refers to it being a 'labour intensive reasonable main daily meal freshly cooked on a traditional cooker' for one person and says that the 'test includes activities auxiliary to the cooking such as reaching for a saucepan, putting water in it and lifting it on and off the cooker' [8]. But see also Commissioner's Decision CDLA/2367/2004, which suggests that use of a microwave oven could be sufficient for the purposes of the test; and *KS v Secretary of State for Work and Pensions* [2011] UKUT 29 (AAC) on the use of a slow-cooker.

[32] R(DLA)2/95 (above n 30) [9].

assisted, by indicating that the test would take account of the possibility of sitting on a high stool or chair for periods while preparing food and cooking it.[33] A further issue is when a risk to health or welfare arising from preparing a meal might prevent a claimant from being able to cook; a risk of an asthma attack from cooker heat was held sufficient in one case,[34] but in another it was held not to be unreasonable for a person with haemophilia to incur the additional risk to his safety in preparing a meal.[35] One Commissioner's decision also indicates that a lack of motivation due to laziness would not amount to an inability to cook, but where it stems from a physical or mental disability, the position might be different.[36]

Moyna looked at the position of a claimant who has an ability to cook only on some days of a typical week. The claimant's disability was derived from a heart condition (angina) and arthritis, among other problems, and between one to three days per week, she was unable to prepare a main meal. Kay LJ, giving the judgment of the Court of Appeal, said that if someone's inability to prepare such a meal was intermittent or occasional, that would not satisfy the cooking test, but where there was a 'clear pattern', as in the present case, that the claimant could not provide for himself or herself in the relevant way 'on a regular basis', the matter would be different, since it could have 'very real consequences for [their] long-term wellbeing'.[37]

When *Moyna* reached the House of Lords, Lord Hoffmann, giving the court's judgment, disagreed with the Court of Appeal's approach. He indicated that the test was 'a notional test, a thought experiment, to calibrate the severity of the disability'.[38] He said that although the test related to one's ability *throughout* the relevant period, it could not be said that not being able to prepare or cook on one occasion would satisfy the test. Rather, the test would involve the question whether 'in a general sense' there was the relevant inability, which required 'an exercise in judgment rather than an arithmetical calculation of frequency'.[39] In effect, therefore, a decision should be made in the round. The reasons that help would be needed were as relevant as the number of occasions when it would be required.[40] Lord Hoffmann concluded:

> In any case in which a tribunal has to apply a standard with a greater or lesser degree of imprecision and to take a number of factors into account, there are bound to be cases in which it will be impossible for a reviewing court to say that the tribunal must have erred in law in deciding the case either way.[41]

[33] Commissioner's Decision CDLA/2267/95.
[34] Commissioner's Decision CDLA/20/94.
[35] Commissioner's Decision R(DLA)1/97.
[36] Commissioner's Decision CSDLA/725/2004.
[37] *Moyna v Secretary of State for Work and Pensions* [2002] EWCA Civ 408 [32] and [34].
[38] *Moyna v Social Security Commissioner* (above n 25) [17].
[39] Ibid [18].
[40] Ibid [19].
[41] Ibid [20].

Citing Lord Reid's well known dictum in *Brutus v Cozens* on statutory interpretation ('The meaning of an ordinary word of the English language is not a question of law . . .'[42]), Lord Hoffmann said that it was 'the meaning to be ascribed to the intention of the notional legislator in using [a particular] word which is a statement of law', and that 'because of the nature of language . . ., in trying to ascertain the legislator's meaning, it is seldom helpful to make additions or substitutions in the actual language he has used'. Accordingly, it was 'unhelpful for the Court of Appeal to construe the statutory language as if it included words like "daily" or "regularly"'.[43]

The logic of the House of Lords' approach in *Moyna* is that the law provides considerable flexibility to decision-makers, such that, for example:

> Wherever judgment has to be exercised in deciding whether a given set of facts meets a statutory threshold, it is inevitable that two tribunals, each applying the law correctly, might reach different conclusions. It cannot be said that either is wrong unless its judgment is outside the bounds of reasonableness.[44]

A first-instance decision-maker is likely to be relying heavily on a health professional's opinion, and moreover, any tribunal dealing with a DLA appeal has both a medical and a disability member, as will be the case with personal independence payment (PIP) appeals. Thus what we see is that contrary to the predominant character of social security law as dominated by rules and administered on the basis of 'bureaucratic rationality', there are areas such as this where the exercise of 'professional judgment' and discretion come into play. But more importantly, we see that the relatively flexible rules of the kind at issue here have an inherent complexity in their application; and no one can easily ascertain in advance whether the law is on their side.

So far as the future of the cooking test itself is concerned, while it was not expected to appear in its DLA form under the PIP when this new benefit was introduced, especially since there is no equivalent to the lowest rate care component under PIP, it is not disappearing altogether. The assessment of PIP is based on criteria or descriptors linked to specific activities, to which points are attached in a similar way to the work capability assessments under ESA and in respect of the capability for work elements of universal credit.[45] For both the daily living and mobility components of PIP,[46] there are total points score thresholds for the 'standard' and 'enhanced' rates at which each of these elements of the benefit is paid.[47] One of the daily living activities to

---

[42] *Brutus v Cozens* [1973] AC 854, 861.

[43] *Moyna v Social Security Commissioner* (above n 25) [24] and [28].

[44] D Thomas, 'Case Analysis: *Ramsden v Secretary of State for Work and Pensions* and *Moyna v Secretary of State for Work and Pensions*' (2004) 11 *Journal of Social Security Law* 37, 44.

[45] See above ch 2, Figure 3.

[46] Welfare Reform Act 2012, ss 78 and 79.

[47] The entitlement thresholds for both the daily living component and the mobility component are 8 points for the standard rate and 12 points for the enhanced rate: Personal Independence Payment Regulations 2013 (SI 2013/377), regs 5(3) and 6(3). See also the Department for Work and

be considered under the initial draft regulations[48] was 'preparing and cooking,' to which there was a list of descriptors relating to a 'simple meal' or, in one descriptor, a 'simple snack'. In the second version of the draft regulations,[49] the activity was changed to 'preparing food and drink', and the descriptors were also based around the notion of a 'simple meal', defined as 'a cooked, one-course meal for one using fresh ingredients';[50] this definition is now in the regulations as made.[51] 'Prepare' in relation to food was defined as 'the activities required to make food ready for cooking or eating', but the regulations now in force contain the slightly neater formulation: '"prepare", in the context of food, means make food ready for cooking or eating'.[52] Either way, some of the judicial clarifications concerning the DLA cooking test are adopted in the PIP regulations.

What, however, of a claimant whose ability varies from day to day, as in *Moyna*? This was not addressed in the first draft regulations, but the regulations now in force provide, in rather complex rules, that in order for a descriptor or combination of descriptors to be satisfied, they must in effect apply to a claimant on 'over 50% of the days of the required period'.[53] That would appear to suggest that a mathematical test is to be extended to the *Moyna* situation – a mechanistic approach that could involve a rather difficult factual calculation. It may not, however, remove the need for the broader *Moyna* approach to determining the question whether a descriptor is satisfied on any particular day, since the logic of that approach is that over a period, a claimant may need to be deemed not to be able to prepare food or cook a meal even on some days when such activity may be possible.

There are also examples of cases in which the courts, when confronted with a social security provision whose meaning is obscure, have adopted a somewhat interventionist position when basic entitlement is threatened.[54] One such case is the combined case *Chief Adjudication Officer v Clarke; Chief*

Pensions (DWP), *Personal Independence Payment: Assessment Thresholds and Consultation* (DPW, 2012) para 1.4.

[48] Department for Work and Pensions, *Personal Independence Payment: Initial Draft of Assessment Regulations* (DPW, 2011).

[49] Department for Work and Pensions, *Personal Independence Payment: Second Draft of Assessment Regulations* (DPW, 2011).

[50] The first version referred to 'fresh or frozen ingredients'.

[51] Personal Independence Payment Regulations 2013 (SI 2013/377), Sched 1, para 1.

[52] Ibid.

[53] Ibid, reg 7(1)–(2). The rules also determine the number of points to be credited from the descriptors. For example, where more than one descriptor is satisfied for at least 50% of the 'required period', the points that count are those attached to the descriptor carrying the most/ greater points. The required period basically runs from 3 months before the claim to 9 months after it: ibid, reg 7(3). The rules need to be read with the Welfare Reform Act 2012, s 80 and with regs 12–14, which set out the basic 3+9 months 'required period condition' which normally applies for entitlement to PIP under ss 78, 79 and 81 of the Act. The exception, in s 82, covers persons who are terminally ill, as defined.

[54] See further Laurie (above n 23) 392–93.

Adjudication Officer v Faul,[55] where the questions were whether for the purposes of the Income Support (General) Regulations 1987[56] the appellants, students at the University of East Anglia, had ceased to attend their course or had 'abandoned' it and thus ceased to be ineligible for entitlement to benefit due to being a 'student'.[57] The students had had a significant period of intercalation from their studies; a key question was whether this constituted abandonment. In a majority decision, the Court of Appeal held that they should not be classed as attending the course while intercalating, and thus they were not students at that time, although their Lordships unanimously rejected the argument that they had abandoned the course. Hoffmann LJ (as he then was), one of the majority judges, referred to the appellants' probable ineligibility for student support during the period of intercalation; if they were also to be denied entitlement to income support, 'there would be an anomalous class of people who for no obvious reason were left to destitution without state support of any kind'.[58]

Similarly, in *ex p Joint Council for the Welfare of Immigrants (JCWI)*,[59] there was a challenge to regulations that were designed to prevent most asylum seekers from securing entitlement to an urgent-cases payment of income support.[60] One of the key arguments was that the regulations were in conflict with the Asylum and Immigration Appeals Act 1993, which gave a right to asylum seekers not to be removed from or required to leave the United Kingdom until their claims for asylum had been determined. By a majority, the Court of Appeal declared the regulations to be ultra vires. In the lead majority judgment, Simon Brown LJ considered the regulations to be 'uncompromisingly draconian' and that 'rights necessarily implicit in the 1993 Act are now inevitably being overborne'.[61] He stated:

> Parliament cannot have intended a significant number of genuine asylum seekers to be impaled on the horns of so intolerable a dilemma: the need either to abandon their claims to refugee status or alternatively to maintain them as best they can but in a state of utter destitution.[62]

Similarly, Waite LJ concluded:

> The effect of the regulations upon the vast majority [of asylum seekers] will be to leave them without even the most basic means of subsistence . . . rendering their ostensible statutory right to a proper consideration of their claims in this country

---

[55] *Chief Adjudication Officer v Clarke; Chief Adjudication Officer v Faul* [1995] ELR 259.

[56] SI 1987/1967.

[57] Ibid, reg 61.

[58] *Clarke* (above n 55) 264E.

[59] *R v Secretary of State for Social Security, ex p Joint Council for the Welfare of Immigrants (JCWI)* [1997] 1 WLR 275.

[60] The Social Security (Persons from Abroad) Miscellaneous Amendment Regulations 1996 (SI 1996/30).

[61] *ex p JCWI* (above n 59) 293.

[62] Ibid.

valueless in practice by making it not merely difficult but totally impossible for them to remain here to pursue those claims.[63]

Another example of judicial intervention is found in *Hourigan v Secretary of State for Work and Pensions*,[64] in which the Court of Appeal had to determine the effect of another part of the Income Support (General) Regulations 1987 in the case of a claimant who had bought her house with the assistance of a 5/6ths contribution towards the cost from her son. Regulation 52 provided that 'where a claimant and one or more persons are beneficially entitled in possession to any capital asset', they were to be 'treated as if each one of them were entitled in possession to the whole beneficial interest therein in an equal share', with a consequential effect on the calculation of capital. The Secretary of State deemed the claimant to own 50 per cent of the value of the house, which meant that she had a level of capital excluding her from entitlement to income support. But the court disagreed with this approach, and Brooke LJ said that in his judgment, 'it would need very much clearer words in the regulation if a court were to be constrained to interpret it in the unfair way for which the Secretary of State contends'.[65] Similarly, Sedley LJ criticised the Secretary of State's 'crude calculation', which could be 'a source of real unfairness'.[66]

Nick Wikeley has referred to the 'complexity of regulation 52',[67] but he sees it primarily as an example of a wider attempt in the reform of the system in the 1980s, whence it originated, to facilitate decision-making by establishing an inflexible rule that could be applied repeatedly to many cases.[68] Nevertheless, the lack of clarity combined with the need for judicial interpretation has added complexity to the rule's administration.

Indeed, while judges have a freer hand over questions of interpretation in such cases, it can over time increase overall legal complexity,[69] due to their diverse conclusions on the law. There is also the overall diffusion of the law that arises from the growing body of case law. This has been the case in relation to the decisions of the Upper Tribunal and especially the Social Security Commissioners in the past.[70] Social security has also been a field

---

[63] Ibid, 293–94.

[64] *Hourigan v Secretary of State for Work and Pensions* [2002] EWCA Civ 1890, [2003] 1 WLR 608.

[65] Ibid [21].

[66] Ibid [28].

[67] N Wikeley, 'Co-ownership of Property and Entitlement to Means-Tested Benefits' (2001) 8 *Journal of Social Security Law* 95, 122.

[68] Ibid, 122–24.

[69] P Schuck, 'Legal Complexity: Some Causes, Consequences and Cures' (1992) 42(1) *Duke Law Journal* 1, 16–17.

[70] See, eg, National Audit Office, *Tackling Pensioner Poverty: Encouraging Take-Up of Entitlements (Report by the Comptroller and Auditor General)* (2002–03, HC 37) para 3.2: 'Attendance Allowance and Disability Living Allowance are also complex because of their detailed entitlement rules and also because the interpretation of those rules can be changed by court judgements (sic) and decisions of the Social Security Commissioners, some of which are contradictory.'

where challenges to the vires of regulations are relatively common. This has indirectly contributed to complexity, since where the provision in question has been struck down, the governmental response has very often been to rewrite it,[71] as happened following the *Clarke and Faul* and *JCWI* rulings above[72] and in February 2013, when the Court of Appeal held in *Reilly and Wilson* that the regulations[73] governing work-for-your-benefit arrangements for those in receipt of jobseeker's allowance (JSA) – non-participation in which can lead to a benefit sanction – were ultra vires.[74]

The judgment in *Reilly and Wilson* was handed down on the morning of 12 February 2013, and the same day, the Government promulgated amendment regulations to correct the legal flaws and ensure that the arrangements could continue whilst also evincing an intention to appeal to the Supreme Court. The regulations themselves stated that they were made that day at 4:19 pm, were laid before Parliament at 6:15 pm and came into force at 6:45 pm also on that day.[75] The Government also rapidly steered an amendment Act through

---

[71] See, for example: (i) the response to the ruling in *R v Secretary of State for Social Services, ex p Cotton and Waite, The Times* (5 August 1985), in which restrictions to entitlement to payments covering board and lodging charges under the supplementary benefit scheme were struck down: discussed in N Harris, *Social Security for Young People* (Aldershot, Avebury, 1989) 76–84; (ii) the amendments made to an earlier version of reg 52 above in the wake of the combined decision in *Tucker* (CIS/15936/1996), *Wilkinson* (CIS/263/1997) and *Moharrer* (CIS/3283/1997): see Wikeley, 'Co-ownership of Property' (above n 67); (iii) and the recasting of reg 27 of the Social Security (Incapacity for Work) (General) Regulations 1995 (SI 1995/311), which set out the exceptional circumstances under which a person assessed as not incapable of work was to be treated as incapable, following the ruling in *R v Secretary of State for Social Security, ex p Moule* (unreported but noted in D Bonner, I Hooker and R White, *Social Security Legislation (2007), Volume 1* (London, Sweet and Maxwell, 2007) 729). The coda to the reg 27 story is that the amendment regulations that altered this regulation were themselves declared ultra vires in *Howker v Secretary of State for Work and Pensions* [2002] EWCA Civ 1623, because they had wrongly not been laid before the Social Security Advisory Committee (SSAC), as the Committee had been misled by the DWP that the amendments were not 'adverse' to claimants and therefore did not need to be formally referred to the Committee.

[72] Via, respectively, the Social Security Benefits (Miscellaneous Amendments) Regulations 1995 (SI 1995/1742) reg 2; and the Asylum and Immigration Act 1996, s 11 and Sch 1.

[73] Jobseeker's Allowance (Employment, Skills and Enterprise Scheme) Regulations 2011 (SI 2011/917).

[74] *R (Reilly and Wilson) v Secretary of State for Work and Pensions* [2013] EWCA Civ 66. In the main substantive judgment, Pill LJ said that s 17A of the Jobseekers Act 1995 'contemplates regulations which make provision for schemes of a prescribed description and which impose on claimants for Jobseeker's Allowance a requirement to participate in such schemes' [36]; that the Secretary of State had specified only one scheme – the Employment, Skills and Enterprise Scheme – and had announced a series of sub-schemes 'in order to achieve the complete flexibility sought by the Secretary of State in the administration of the Act' [37]. But there was an issue as to 'whether the Scheme named in the Regulations satisfies the requirements for specificity in section 17A by way of being "prescribed"' [48]. Pill LJ concluded: 'Simply to give a scheme a name cannot, in context, be treated as a prescribed description of a scheme in which claimants may be required to participate, within section 17A(1)' [51]. He stated, 'The statutory requirement is that the prescribed description is in the regulation' [52]. Sir Stanley Burton added inter alia that a proper description of a scheme was necessary to ensure proper Parliamentary scrutiny of the work of the administration [76].

[75] The Jobseeker's Allowance (Schemes for Assisting Persons to Obtain Employment) Regulations 2013 (SI 2013/276). Reg 3 lists and provides details of the schemes.

Parliament to prevent having to incur liability of £130 million in respect of benefit sanctions imposed, or which would have been imposed, for non-compliance with the arrangements which the court had found ultra vires.[76]

This longstanding process of exerting legislative power in response to unfavourable court decisions was referred to a number of years ago as 'legislative overkill'.[77] The effect of such rulings on complexity has been referred to by the National Audit Office (NAO): 'By creating the need to add new pieces to existing regulation and implementation, case law, by definition, adds to the complexity of a benefit.'[78] Such changes would be expected to have prospective effect. Moreover, the impact of test cases unfavourable to the Government has been minimised as a result of the 'anti-test case' rules that were introduced over a decade ago and were designed to prevent a claimant from benefiting, in terms of his or her own entitlement, from the effect of a test case for any period prior to the date of the test case ruling.[79]

Where Complexity Lies

In general the complexity of a rule is self-evident and revolves such matters as: (i) the difficulty in following its sense because of the way it is expressed, particularly where there are a number of conjunctive or disjunctive elements to it, and its length and density; (ii) the way that the rule's effect is dependent on the requirements of another rule such that two or more rules would need to be considered simultaneously, a problem not merely related to the need to consult definition provisions; and (iii) whether there are amendments to the rule which have effect from a prescribed date, meaning that the correct version to be applied to a set of facts may not be easy to discern.

The Social Security Advisory Committee (SSAC), which, as noted above, scrutinises a great deal of secondary legislation on social security, has commented, 'Once detailed consideration of the regulations is underway, the complexity of the benefits system is immediately apparent.'[80] There are so

---

[76] Jobseekers (Back to Work Schemes) Act 2013. The figure of £130 million is taken from the Jobseekers (Back to Work Schemes) Bill Explanatory Notes (2013) para 3, www.publications. parliament.uk/pa/bills/lbill/2012-2013/0091/en/13091en.pdf.

[77] C Smith, 'Discretion or Legislation?' (1974) *New Law Journal* 219. See also T Prosser, 'Politics and Judicial Review: The Atkinson Case and its Aftermath' (1979) *Public Law* 59.

[78] National Audit Office (NAO), *Department for Work and Pensions: Dealing with the Complexity of the Benefits System*, HC 592 (London, Stationary Office, 2005) para 2.16.

[79] See the Social Security Act 1998, s 27; and the Child Support, Pensions and Social Security Act 2000, Sch 7, para 18. The rule works by limiting the precedent effect of the ruling in the test case ('A') on a subsequent case, 'B' or any others. The decision-maker in case B must assume that even though the ruling in case A might suggest that the initial decision in case B was wrong, that was not the case for any period prior to the case A ruling. Thus entitlement that the claimant in case B might have expected to have as a result of the impact of case A cannot accrue for any period prior to the case A ruling.

[80] Social Security Advisory Committee (SSAC), *Twentieth Report (2007)* (Leeds, Corporate Document Services, 2007) para 1.19.

many highly complex rules within social security and tax credits law in the United Kingdom that it is difficult to identify the most egregious. The following two examples have been selected as reasonably representative illustrations of the genre. The first example focuses on two regulations governing funeral expenses payments under the social fund. The second is a shorter set of rules dealing with the treatment of notional capital under income-related benefit schemes.

Example 1: Funeral Expenses

The rules on entitlement to funeral expenses payments 'clearly give rise to considerable complexity', despite the relatively modest level of support they provide.[81] As Baroness Hale has remarked, funeral payments provide 'a good illustration' of the trend towards increased complexity in the benefits system, as provision is increasingly targeted.[82] The system currently makes a claimant who is responsible for the costs of a funeral and who is in receipt of any one of a number of welfare benefits (a qualifying benefit), potentially eligible for a funeral expenses payment.[83] Funeral expenses payments are non-repayable grants made under rules within the regulated social fund. But, in addition, since May 2012, loans to cover funeral expenses have been possible under the discretionary social fund as 'budgeting loans',[84] although such loans are being replaced under forthcoming reforms to the discretionary social fund under the Welfare Reform Act 2012, as noted in chapter two. The discussion which follows is concerned with the payments under the regulated social fund.

In 2012–13, there were 35,000 funeral expenses awards totalling £43.1 million,[85] compared with 61,618 awards in 1995–96 costing £49 million.[86] The average individual award in 2012–13 was £1,225. This is well below the average cost of a funeral. The only slightly lower figure of £1,217 in 2010–11 represented but 39 per cent of the average cost of a funeral that year.[87] Over the years and especially following amendments to the regulations in 1997, the

[81] A Ogus, 'Funeral Expenses' in SSAC, *Fourteenth Report (2001)* (Leeds, Corporate Document Services, 2001) Annex D, para 15.

[82] *Kerr v Department for Social Development (Northern Ireland)* [2004] UKHL 23, 56.

[83] For discussion of the background to these payments, see T Buck, *The Social Fund: Law and Practice* (London, Sweet and Maxwell, 2009) ch 8; and for a brief historical account, see Ogus (above n 81) Annex D.

[84] Due to the amendment of the Social Security Contributions and Benefits Act 1992, s 138(1) by the Welfare Reform Act 2012, s 71. Maternity expenses payments, which also fall under the regulated social fund, are similarly now also eligible for payment as budgeting loans under the amendment.

[85] DWP, *Annual Report by the Secretary of State for Work and Pensions on the Social Fund (2012/2013)* (London, Stationery Office, 2013) Annex 1.

[86] Department for Social Security, *Annual Report by the Secretary of State for Social Security on the Social Fund* (Cm 3320, 1996) Annexes 1 and 2.

[87] Calculated from the figures in University of Bath, *Cost of Dying Special Report: 'Affording a Funeral' – Social Fund Funeral Payments* (London, Sun Life Direct, 2012) 11.

rules have been tightened up, and while the fall in awards over this period is partly down to a reduced number of applications, it is also attributable to a reduced success rate for claimants, which stood at 66 per cent in 1995–96 but at only 54.3 per cent in 2012–13.[88]

The rules governing funeral expenses payments are in Part III (regulations 7–10) of the Social Fund Maternity and Funeral Expenses (General) Regulations 2005.[89] The regulations define what specific expenses may be claimed for and the amounts that are to be allowed.[90] To illustrate the complexity of the regulations, however, it is necessary only to look at regulations 7 and 8, which govern eligibility. They set out who may qualify for a funeral expenses payment in respect of the prescribed costs. They reflect a policy intention not to provide support from the welfare system where there is another family member or friend of the deceased whom it is reasonable to expect to meet the funeral expenses. These provisions are therefore, like many other detailed rules in this area, aimed at controlling the demands on and abuse of the benefits system.

The rules begin in regulation 7 by defining key terms, including 'funeral' ('a burial or cremation') and 'funeral payment' ('a social fund payment to meet funeral expenses of a deceased person').[91] They then provide that, subject to regulation 8 (below), a funeral payment 'shall be made where each of the conditions referred to in paragraphs (3) to (9) is satisfied'.[92] There are six conditions, and they are logically referred to in regulation 7 as 'first condition', 'second condition' and so on. Since they are intended to limit entitlement by identifying the persons who are or are not to be regarded as responsible for a funeral and eligible to receive support from the state to fund it, the description by Lord Hope of Craighead of the identical equivalent provisions in Northern Ireland as 'a series of filters' is not inapt.[93]

The first condition relates primarily to a claimant being in receipt of a qualifying benefit. The claimant or his/her partner must be a person to whom regulation 7(4) applies – namely, a person with an award of one or more qualifying benefits.[94] The condition of having to be in receipt of a qualifying benefit in order to secure a funeral expenses payment has been the subject

---

[88] Department for Social Security (above n 85) Annex 1; and DWP, *Annual Report on the Social Fund (2012/2013)* (above n 86) Annex 1.

[89] SI 2005/3061, as amended.

[90] SI 2005/3061, as amended, regs 9 and 10.

[91] Ibid, reg 7(1).

[92] Ibid, reg 7(2).

[93] *Kerr* (above n 82) [4].

[94] SI 2005/3061, as amended, regs 7(3) and (4)(a): income support; state pension credit; income-based jobseeker's allowance; working tax credit, which includes the disability element or the severe disability element of the credit; child tax credit payable at a rate higher than the family element; housing benefit; and universal credit (added from 1 April 2013 by the Social Fund (Maternity and Funeral Expenses) (Amendment) Regulations 2013 (SI 2013/247), which also removed council tax benefit from the list and revoked reg 7(4)(b), which had provided an alternative means of meeting the first condition by being a person to whom various provisions relating to council tax benefit applied).

of challenges under the Human Rights Act 1998, although none have succeeded.[95]

The second condition is that the claimant must be 'ordinarily resident in the United Kingdom at the date of . . . [the] death'.[96] 'Ordinarily resident' is not defined, although there is case law governing it.[97] The third condition is that 'the claim is made within the prescribed time for claiming a funeral payment'.[98] The regulations do not explain what the 'prescribed time' is, nor where the time is prescribed. The time is in fact prescribed separately in the Social Security (Claims and Payment) Regulations,[99] which stipulate that a claim for funeral expenses must be made during 'the period beginning with the date of death and ending 3 months after the date of the funeral'.[100]

The fourth condition is that 'the claimant is the responsible person or the partner of the responsible person'.[101] 'Responsible person' is defined as 'the person who accepts responsibility for the funeral expenses'.[102] With regard to the definition of 'partner', this term is now established in social security law and is defined here as meaning 'the other member of a couple' or any other member of a polygamous relationship.[103] The word 'couple' is also defined, in terms of opposite sex and same-sex relationships. A couple comprises (a) a man and a woman who are either (i) both married to each other and 'members of the same household', or (ii) not married to each other but 'living together as husband and wife'; or (b) two people of the same sex who are (i) civil partners and 'members of the same household', or (ii) not civil partners but 'living together as if they were civil partners', provided 'they would be regarded as living together as husband and wife if they were instead two people of the opposite sex'.[104]

---

[95] See, eg, Commissioner's Decision CIS/3280/2001 in which the claimant had not been entitled to income support because she lived in a local authority residential home, not an independent home; consequently, she was denied a funeral payment. Mr Commissioner Bano rejected her claim to have been discriminated against for the purposes of Art 14 of the ECHR, read with Art 1 of the First Protocol, since she could not claim a 'status' merely by living in such a residence. In *Stewart* (above n 24), the appellant's son died while she was serving a prison sentence, and her claim for a funeral expenses payment was denied because, as a prisoner, she was not in receipt of a qualifying benefit. The Court of Appeal accepted that there had been indirect discrimination against her as a prisoner. However, it considered that there was a rational justification for it: the administrative complication and cost of establishing a mechanism for prisoners; the wider implications of departing from the basic condition concerning qualifying benefits; and the alternative provision for the state to help with funerals where there is no entitlement to a funeral payment.

[96] SI 2005/3061, reg 7(5).

[97] See Wood et al (above n 7) 1397.

[98] SI 2005/3061, reg 7(6).

[99] SI 1987/1968, as amended.

[100] Ibid, reg 19(1) and Sch 4, para 9.

[101] SI 2005/3061, reg 7(7).

[102] Ibid, reg 7(1).

[103] SI 2005/3061, reg 3(1). Note that the second definition (member of polygamous relationship) does not apply where the claimant is entitled to universal credit (amendment made by SI 2013/247).

[104] SI 2005/3061, reg 3(1).

The pivotal phrase 'living together as husband and wife', which is used in the definition of 'couple' across social security and tax credits law,[105] is not in itself defined. It has been the subject of copious case law indicating the range of factors in a relationship that are to be taken into account and which thus require investigation by first-tier decision-makers, thereby contributing to complexity (as shown in Figure 1 in chapter two above in relation to means-testing). The factors include membership of the same household, any financial arrangements, child caring responsibilities, the permanency of the relationship and how the relationship is perceived by others known to the parties.[106] However, as Penny Wood et al explain, its meaning 'is among the most contentious issues in the whole of social security law'.[107] A review of fraud and error in the benefits system in 2010 found that the lack of a definition of 'living together as husband and wife' contributed to claimants' failure to report its occurrence to the relevant department as a change in their circumstances, and '[t]he complexity here is compounded by the fact that DWP and HMRC apply the concept in slightly different ways'.[108]

The fifth condition is enshrined in the most complex provisions.[109] It looks to the relationship between the person who has now deceased and the responsible person. It covers the following scenarios:

(a) The responsible person was the partner of the deceased at the date of death.

This brings into play the term 'partner', considered above, but is otherwise straightforward. The next relates to cases in which the deceased was a child:

(b) In a case where the deceased was a child and –

  (i)   there is no absent parent, or
  (ii) there is an absent parent who, or whose partner, is a person to whom paragraph (4) applied as at the date of death,

  the responsible person was the person, or the partner of the person, responsible for that child for the purposes of Part IX of the Act as at the date of death.

These provisions are not quite as straightforward as they seem. First, one needs to know who counts as a 'child'. The regulations define 'child' as a person under the age of 16 or a 'young person' within the meaning of two prescribed provisions,[110] which unfortunately define 'young person' in a highly

---

[105] For example, see also the Social Security Contributions and Benefits Act 1992, s 137(1).

[106] See N Harris, 'Unmarried Couples and Social Security in Great Britain' (1996) 18(2) *Journal of Social Welfare and Family Law* 123; Wood et al (above n 7) 220–26; and most recently, *VG v Secretary of State for Work and Pensions* [2012] UKUT 470 (AAC).

[107] Wood et al (above n 7) 220.

[108] Her Majesty's Revenue and Customs (HMRC) and Department for Work and Pensions (DWP), *Tackling Fraud and Error in the Benefit and Tax Credit Systems* (London, HMRC/DWP, 2010) ch 2, para 4.

[109] SI 2005/3061, reg 7(8).

[110] For example, at the time of writing: 'regulation 14 of the Income Support Regulations' (defined separately in the regulations as the Income Support (General) Regulations 1987) and

technical way.[111] Secondly, the general words at the end bring into play another pivotal issue under social security and tax credits law, that of responsibility for a child. This is, for example, a key issue concerning entitlement to child benefit, the benefit that is the subject of 'Part IX of the Act', namely the 1992 Act.[112] Part IX contains a definition, for the purposes of that Part, of 'person responsible for a child'.[113]

The next head under which the fifth condition may be satisfied is simple:

(c) In a case where the deceased was a still-born child, the responsible person was a parent, or the partner of a parent, of that still-born child as at the date when the child was still-born.

Then we come to another way of satisfying this condition, which again looks quite straightforward but is not altogether unproblematic:

(d) In a case where the deceased had no partner and neither sub-paragraph (b) nor (c) applies, the responsible person was an immediate family member of the deceased, and it is reasonable for the responsible person to accept responsibility for those expenses.

The definition of 'immediate family member' in the regulations is 'a parent, son or daughter'.[114] The question of the reasonableness of accepting responsibility for the relevant expenses is covered by regulation 8(5): 'Whether it is reasonable for the responsible person to accept responsibility for meeting the expenses of a funeral shall be determined by the nature and extent of his contact with the deceased.' This brings into these bright-line rules another imprecise test, based on an objective view of a relationship in terms of the nature and extent of the contact between the family members in question. However, it would be difficult to prescribe all the factors over the lifetime of a relationship that should count towards the determination of this issue. Case law indicates that one should look at the whole history of the relationship, not just at its nature during the final years of the deceased person's life.[115]

'regulation 76 of the Jobseeker's Allowance Regulations' (defined as meaning the self-same regulations of 1996): SI 2005/3061, reg 3(1). Note that the definition of young person under the revised JSA scheme (non-contributory) is now in the Jobseeker's Allowance Regulations 2013 (SI 2013/378) reg 2(2).

[111] See, eg, the Income Support (General) Regulations 1987 (SI 1987/1967), as amended, reg 14(1): 'Subject to paragraph (2), a person of a prescribed description for the purposes of section 20(11) of the Act [SSCBA, s 137(1)] as it applies to income support (definition of the family) and section 23(1) and (3) of the Act [SSCBA, s 126(1) and (3)] is a person who falls within the definition of qualifying young person in section 142 of the Contributions and Benefits Act (child and qualifying young person), and in these Regulations such a person is referred to as a "young person" . . .'

[112] Ie, the Social Security Contributions and Benefits Act 1992.

[113] Ibid, s 143.

[114] SI 2005/3061, reg 3(1).

[115] Commissioner's Decision R(IS)3/98.

The final situation in which the fifth condition may be satisfied is:

(e) In a case where the deceased had no partner and none of sub-paragraphs (b), (c) and (d) applies, the responsible person was either –

(i) a close relative of the deceased, or
(ii) a close friend of the deceased,

and it is reasonable for the responsible person to accept responsibility for the funeral expenses.

So this provision also requires consideration of regulation 8(5) as to the issue of reasonableness in accepting responsibility for the funeral expenses. Here, the responsible person would be seeking funeral expenses in respect of a close relative or close friend. Neither 'friend' nor 'close friend' is defined in the regulations, but the meaning of 'close relative' is prescribed.[116] Although it includes the relatives who would be classed as 'immediate family members', it extends more broadly to include, for example, the deceased's brother or sister.

The circumstances covered in the last two of these sets of situations, namely (d) and (e), nevertheless have to be read subject to other provisions, namely regulation 8(4)–(9). Taking regulation 8(9) first, it provides that when the responsible person is the partner of the close relative, close friend or immediate family member of the deceased, 'references to the responsible person are to be construed as references to the responsible person's partner'. The effect is that the partner of a close relative, etc is to be treated as the close relative, provided that his or her partner is the responsible person – that is (per the definition above), the person who accepts responsibility for the funeral expenses. Moving on to regulation 8(4),[117] it prescribes circumstances in which the deceased must be treated as having had no partner:

The deceased had a partner at the date of death and –

(a) no claim for funeral expenses is made by the partner in respect of the death of the deceased; and
(b) that partner dies before the date upon which the deceased's funeral takes place.

Without this rule, the fact that the partner had been living at the date of the deceased's death might prevent another family member from having entitlement to a payment even when that partner died prior to the deceased's funeral. Regulation 8(5), setting out a test as to the reasonableness of a person accepting responsibility for meeting the cost of the funeral, has already been considered.

---

[116] It means 'a parent, parent-in-law, son, son-in-law, daughter, daughter-in-law, step-parent, step-son, step-son-in-law, step-daughter, step-daughter-in-law, brother, brother-in-law, sister, or sister-in-law': Social Fund Maternity and Funeral Expenses (General) Regulations 2005 (SI 2005/3061), reg 3(1).

[117] As so provided by Social Fund Maternity and Funeral Expenses (General) Regulations 2005 (SI 2005/3061), reg 8(3).

Regulation 8(6) provides that if the deceased had one or more close relatives, the position is covered by regulation 8(7) and (8):

(7) If, on comparing the nature and extent of any close relative's contact with the deceased and the nature and extent of the responsible person's contact with the deceased, any such close relative was –

    (a) in closer contact with the deceased than the responsible person,
    (b) in equally close contact with the deceased and neither that close relative nor his partner, if he has one, is a person to whom regulation 7(4) applies,

the claimant shall not be entitled to a funeral payment.

(8) However, paragraph (7) shall not apply where the close relative who was in –

    (a) closer contact with the deceased than the responsible person, or (as the case may be)
    (b) equally close contact with the deceased,

is at the date of death of a description specified in any of sub-paragraphs (a) to (h) of paragraph (2).

The above two sub-paragraphs interact in a rather complex way. Sub-paragraph (7) requires a comparison to be made between the contact that the claimant had with the deceased and that which a close relative had. If the close relative's contact was closer, the claim must fail.[118] If the contact was equally close, and neither the close relative nor his/her partner (if there is one) is receiving a qualifying benefit, etc (per the first condition above), the claim again would fail.[119] But in both these cases, the rule is subject to an exception if the close relative in question falls within the list in regulation 8(2)(a)–(h)[120] (the policy clearly being, as noted below, that such a person should not be expected to meet funeral expenses):

    (a) a person who has not attained the age of 18;
    (b) a qualifying young person within the meaning of section 142 of the Act (child and qualifying young person);

---

[118] In R(IS)3/98 (above n 115), Commissioner Heggs did not consider that the claimant's estrangement from his father for 24 years of itself erased the contact between him and his father, who had now died: 'Although the time element is important in considering the extent of the closeness, each case falls to be determined by reference to its own individual facts. Families drift apart for different reasons. In the present case I do not consider it fatal to the claimant's claim that he had not seen his father for 24 years. It does not automatically erase the contact they had in the preceding 30 years. It would be a harsh doctrine which would not allow an only surviving child to assume responsibility for his father's funeral as a final act of reconciliation. I cannot imagine that this was the intention of Parliament' [11].

[119] In *Kerr* (above n 82), the House of Lords held that in such a circumstance the onus was on the department rather than the claimant to establish whether the close relative was on a qualifying benefit.

[120] Social Fund Maternity and Funeral Expenses (General) Regulations 2005 (SI 2005/3061), reg 8(8).

(bb) a qualifying young person under section 10(5) (prescription of qualifying young person) of the Welfare Reform Act 2012;[121]

(c) a person who has attained the age of 18 but not the age of 19 and who is attending a full-time course of advanced education, as defined in regulation 61 of the Income Support Regulations, or, as the case may be, a person aged 19 or over but under pensionable age who is attending a full-time course of study, as defined in that regulation, at an educational establishment;

(d) a person in receipt of asylum support under section 95 of the Immigration and Asylum Act 1999 . . .;

(e) a member of, and fully maintained by, a religious order;

(f) being detained in a prison, remand centre or youth custody institution and either that immediate family member or his partner is a person to whom regulation 7(4) applied immediately before that immediate family member was so detained;

(g) a person who is regarded as receiving free in-patient treatment within the meaning of the Social Security (Hospital In-Patients) Regulations 1975 . . ., or the Social Security (Hospital In-Patients) Regulations (Northern Ireland) 1975 . . ., and either that immediate family member or his partner is a person to whom regulation 7(4) applied immediately before that immediate family member was first regarded as receiving such treatment; or

(h) a person ordinarily resident outside the United Kingdom.

Moving through these categories, one can see references to statuses determined in many cases by provisions in entirely separate regulations, such as young persons (above) and persons attending a course of advanced education for the purposes of regulation 61 of the Income Support Regulations (which contains a range of complex definitions relating to participation in education, itself related to student status). The policy underlying these exceptions to the closer contact rule above is that if the close relative falls within one or more of these categories, he or she should not be considered able to meet the costs of the funeral such as to deprive the claimant of entitlement to a funeral expenses payment for which he or she would otherwise be eligible. Similarly, if any person in one of the above categories (a)–(h) is an immediate family member and is not someone receiving a qualifying benefit (as defined in regulation 7(4)), the claimant will not be prevented from being entitled to a funeral payment by the general exclusionary rule in regulation 8(1). The rule in regulation 8(1) will exclude a claimant, as the responsible person, from entitlement to a funeral expenses payment when he or she is a close relative, close friend or immediate family member of the deceased and –

(a) there are one or more immediate family members of the deceased;

(b) one or more of those immediate family members or their partners are not persons to whom regulation 7(4) applied as at the date of death; and

[121] Inserted by Social Fund (Maternity and Funeral Expenses) (Amendment) Regulations 2013 (SI 2013/247), reg 2.

(c) any of the immediate family members referred to in sub-paragraph (b) was not estranged from the deceased at the date of his death.

Thus, the state in effect expects the immediate family member who is not on benefit and not in one of the exceptional categories (a)–(h) in regulation 8(2) to meet the costs of funeral expenses, but only provided he or she was not 'estranged' from the deceased at the date of the death. This concept of estrangement gives rise to further complexity. The term, which is imprecise, is not defined in the regulations or the relevant primary legislation, but again there is relevant case law, indicating, for example, the need for a proper disengagement rather than a mere disagreement and for it to be for a 'sufficient period of time'.[122]

Finally, the sixth condition concerns the location of the funeral.[123] The funeral must take place in either the United Kingdom or in a case where the responsible person is a migrant worker or within another prescribed category under EU law,[124] in a Member State of the European Union, Iceland, Liechtenstein, Norway or Switzerland. The condition is thus discriminatory against cases in which, for example, burial occurs in any other part of the world. Although Article 8 of the ECHR (in particular, the right to family life) is engaged by the denial of a funeral expenses payment, the discrimination has been held to be justified for Article 14 purposes.[125]

Looking at the above rules as a whole, it is clear that the provisions governing eligibility to a funeral expenses payment are highly complex. The wording is at times tortuous, and there is considerable cross-referencing, both within the rules and externally with a range of other social security provisions. The regulations comprise a mixture of bright-line rules and more flexible and imprecise rules – as in the case of those referring to estrangement or having 'closer contact' – and involve the application of various qualifying provisions. The SSAC warned against the growing complexity of the rules, particularly after the 'immediate family member' test element was introduced in 1997: the scheme became 'increasingly complex and difficult for potential claimants to understand and for Adjudication Officers[126] to apply in practice'.[127] This was 'a

---

[122] Commissioner's Decision (Northern Ireland) C1/01-02(SF), cited in Wood et al (above n 7) 1403. See further the discussion in Wood et al, 1403–4.

[123] Social Fund Maternity and Funeral Expenses (General) Regulations 2005 (SI 2005/3061), reg 7(9) and (10).

[124] (a) A worker for the purposes of Council Regulations (EEC) No 1612/68(2) or (EEC) No 1251/70(3); (b) a member of the family of a worker for the purposes of Council Regulation (EEC) No 1612/68; (c) in the case of a worker who has died, a member of the family of that worker for the purposes of Council Regulation (EEC) No 1251/70; or (d) a person with a right to reside in the United Kingdom pursuant to Council Directive No 68/360/EEC(4) or No 73/148/EEC(5).

[125] *Esfandiari and Others v Secretary of State for Work and Pensions* [2006] EWC Civ 282. See also Commissioner's Decision R(IS)3/02.

[126] The front-line or first-tier decision-makers.

[127] Social Security Advisory Committee (SSAC), *Eleventh Report (1997)* (London, Stationery Office, 1997) para 9.2. See also SSAC, *The Social Security (Social Fund and Claims and Payments) (Miscellaneous Amendments) Regulations 1997 (SI 1997, No 792)* (Cm 3585, 1997).

particular problem since funerals need to be arranged quickly and a potential claimant . . . is unlikely to know in sufficient time whether it is reasonable for them to take responsibility for the funeral expenses'.[128] Claimants are likely to misunderstand their position under the rules, and as the Local Government Association put it in a submission to the Social Security Select Committee when it reviewed the social fund, claimants may 'find themselves unexpectedly and bafflingly refused a payment', giving rise to 'an unpalatable shock at the most grievous of times'.[129] The complexities of the benefit, a recent University of Bath study found, 'could, the participants told us, impact on their grief'.[130] The study also found that in some cases, individuals and families may, due to uncertainty over eligibility, have committed to costs which they may not have done had they understood the rules on the support that the state would provide.[131] Social fund funeral expenses payments therefore provide a good illustration of the social impact of complexity in the benefits system.

The DWP attempts in its guidance for decision-makers to represent these rules in a flow chart, which can barely be squeezed onto two full pages.[132] This merely highlights the complexity of the provisions and the difficulty that arises from the uncertainty often attached to yes/no distinctions which the rules ultimately aim to make. Such factors are arguably further evidenced by the appeal statistics for funeral expenses payments. Recent statistics are not available, but those for 2003 show that for oral hearings, when the tribunal is able to probe for information and assess the circumstances that are relevant under the rules, 28.8 per cent of appeals that were heard and 72.7 per cent when the claimant attended were decided in the claimant's favour, as against 2.4 per cent of cases decided on the papers alone.[133] The success rate for attended oral hearings was the highest for any social security benefit and suggests that until claimants appear before the tribunal, many of them fail to provide all the information that may be relevant to their claims – which is surely suggestive of a misunderstanding on the part of many claimants of the complex conditions governing this benefit.

Example 2: The Diminishing Notional Capital Rule

The assessment of need for the purposes of income-related benefits, such as income support and housing benefit, and in due course universal credit,

---

[128] SSAC, *Eleventh Report (1997)* (ibid) para 9.2.

[129] House of Commons Social Security Committee, *The Social Fund, Minutes of Evidence* (2000–01, HC 232) SF 42, Memorandum submitted by the Local Government Association, para 20.

[130] University of Bath (above n 87) 17.

[131] Ibid, 13.

[132] See DWP, 'Chapter 39: Social Fund Payments' in *Decision-Makers Guide*, www.dwp.gov.uk/docs/dmgch39.pdf.

[133] DWP, *Work and Pensions Statistics 2003* (London, DWP, 2003) 207 and 209.

includes the calculation of a claimant's capital. The treatment of capital is based around a policy that claimants who have a sufficient amount of available, realisable capital should use it or some of it before being permitted to receive state support. The general rule under the Income Support (General) Regulations 1987,[134] for example, is that when a claimant's and/or his or her partner's capital exceeds £16,000, there can be no entitlement to the benefit.[135] If it exceeds £6,000, then entitlement is reduced on the basis of a tariff – that is, the claimant is assumed to have income of £1 for every £250 of capital above that amount.[136]

These rules were replicated in the housing benefit scheme[137] and are found now in the Universal Credit Regulations 2013, which will eventually replace the income support and housing benefit provisions. The tariff under universal credit will be higher, reflecting the fact that the credit will comprise a monthly rather than weekly benefit.[138] All the sets of regulations on the individual means-tested benefits have contained elaborate and intricate rules designed to identify capital and calculate it.[139] They illustrate that the taking account of capital for benefit purposes is problematic:

> The treatment of savings and other forms of capital is particularly difficult . . . [It] differs depending on the definition of capital, how much capital is disregarded for the means test and the thresholds at which support is withdrawn as capital increases. More detailed definitions of capital and lower disregards can help to prevent benefits being paid to wealthy households. But there is a trade-off involved, since the complexity of capital conditions can cause problems for households who do not understand the criteria.[140]

One of the complexities in this area arises from the law's policy of in effect requiring claimants in some circumstances to avail themselves of capital that has been disposed of – so-called 'notional capital'. This form of capital is referred to in regulation 51 of the Income Support (General) Regulations 1987, which provides, 'A claimant shall be treated as possessing capital of which he has deprived himself for the purposes of securing entitlement to income support or increasing the amount of that benefit' except in various prescribed circumstances. The Universal Credit Regulations 2013 retain this concept but also simplify the exceptions to the rule.[141] An example of a classic

---

[134] SI 1987/1967.

[135] Ibid, reg 45.

[136] Ibid, reg 53.

[137] Housing Benefit Regulations 2006 (SI 2006/213), regs 43 and 52. There is a modification of it, however, in the case of certain people in residential homes.

[138] Universal Credit Regulations 2013 (SI 2013/376) regs 18 (capital limit of £16,000 for a single person of couple) and 72 (tariff income of £4.35 for each £250 of capital above £6,000, plus a further £4.35 for any remaining sum if under £250): see below in this section.

[139] In the case of income support, for example, see the Income Support (General) Regulations 1987 (SI 1987/1967) reg 46 and Sched 10.

[140] National Audit Office, *Means-Testing Report by the Comptroller and Auditor General* (2010–12, HC 1464) 25, para 3.9.

[141] Universal Credit Regulations 2013 (SI 2013/376), reg 50. See below.

notional capital situation involves a claimant who, in order to bring the level of his or her capital below the cut-off point for benefit, temporarily transfers a sum from a savings account to that of a child or other relative. But it may not always be easy to determine whether the claimant's purpose in depriving himself or herself of the capital, for example by disposing of it through expenditure, was 'for the purposes of securing entitlement'. There is case law guidance on this issue, however.[142]

In the case of income support, regulation 51A currently sets out the basis for reducing the level of this notional capital to take account of the amounts that are assumed to be used by a claimant towards daily living under the tariff income rule above. This is referred to as the 'diminishing notional capital rule', which has also been present in the schemes for housing benefit,[143] council tax benefit,[144] income-based JSA[145] and state pension credit.[146] Regulation 51A(1)–(3), as amended, deals with this calculation under an existing claim; the other main provisions of regulation 51A concern redetermination of amounts where a subsequent claim is made, and they do not need to be considered here. Regulation 51A is chosen to illustrate the complexity in the technicality and form of the rules. It is also possible to compare it with its replacement under the universal credit scheme.

The basis of the calculation under regulation 51A is the hypothetical amount of income support for which a claimant would have qualified but for the notional capital which falls to be taken into account:

(1) Where a claimant is treated as possessing capital under regulation 51(1) (notional capital), the amount which he is treated as possessing –

(a) in the case of a week that is subsequent to –

(i) the relevant week in respect of which the conditions set out in paragraph (2) are satisfied, or

(ii) a week which follows that relevant week and which satisfies those conditions,

shall be reduced by an amount determined under paragraph (2);

(b) in the case of a week in respect of which paragraph (1)(a) does not apply but where–

---

[142] See, eg, Commissioner's Decision R(SB)9/91, where the claimant had disposed of her property by transferring the beneficial interest by deed of gift to her two daughters. She entered a nursing home and claimed supplementary benefit (SB), which was covered by a similar rule about notional capital as is now in the income support scheme that replaced SB. The house was subsequently sold for £26,000. The Commissioner held that securing entitlement to benefit did not need to be the 'predominant motive' (original emphasis), and although such motive was to advance the claimant's children, 'a significant operative purpose was also to obtain [SB] in the same exercise' [14]; and this was sufficient. See also Commissioner's Decisions R(SB)38/85 and R(SB)40/85.

[143] Housing Benefit Regulations 2006 (SI 2006/213) reg 50.
[144] Council Tax Benefit Regulations 2006 (SI 2006/215) reg 40.
[145] Jobseeker's Allowance Regulations 1996 (SI 1996/207) reg 114.
[146] State Pension Credit Regulations 2002 (SI 2002/1792) reg 22.

(i) that week is a week subsequent to the relevant week, and

(ii) that relevant week is a week in which the condition in paragraph (3) is satisfied,

shall be reduced by the amount determined under paragraph (3).

(2) This paragraph applies to a benefit week or part week where the claimant satisfies the conditions that –

(a) he is in receipt of income support; and

(b) but for regulation 51(1), he would have received an additional amount of income support in that benefit week or, as the case may be, that part week;

and in such a case, the amount of the reduction for the purposes of paragraph (1)(a) shall be equal to that additional amount.

(3) Subject to paragraph (4), for the purposes of paragraph (1)(b) the condition is that the claimant would have been entitled to income support in the relevant week, but for regulation 51(1), and in such a case the amount of the reduction shall be equal to the aggregate of–

(a) the amount of income support to which the claimant would have been entitled in the relevant week but for regulation 51(1); and for the purposes of this sub-paragraph if the relevant week is a part-week that amount shall be determined by dividing the amount of income support to which he would have been so entitled by the number equal to the number of days in the part-week and multiplying the quotient by 7;

(b) the amount of housing benefit (if any) equal to the difference between his maximum housing benefit and the amount (if any) of housing benefit which he is awarded in respect of the benefit week, within the meaning of regulation 2(1) of the Housing Benefit Regulations 2006 (interpretation), which includes the last day of the relevant week;

. . .

(d) the amount of council tax benefit (if any) equal to the difference between his maximum council tax benefit and the amount (if any) of council tax benefit which he is awarded in respect of the benefit week which includes the last day of the relevant week, and for this purpose 'benefit week' means a period of 7 consecutive days beginning on a Monday and ending on a Sunday.[147]

The term 'relevant week', which is used throughout this provision, is defined separately.[148] As regards the meaning of these provisions, the basic position

---

[147] This paragraph incorporates an amendment made on 1 April 2013 in consequence of the abolition of council tax benefit: see the Council Tax Benefit Abolition (Consequential Provision) Regulations 2013 (SI 2013/458) Sched 2, para 1.

[148] Income Support (General) Regulations 1987 (SI 1987/1967) reg 51A(7)(b): 'the benefit week or part-week in which the capital in question of which the claimant has deprived himself within the meaning of regulation 51(1)' was (i) 'first taken into account for the purposes of determining entitlement to income support' or (ii) taken into account on a subsequent occasion in order to determine or re-determine entitlement to income support – and 'where more than one benefit week or part-week is identified by reference to heads (i) and (ii) . . . the later or latest such

immediately following the 'relevant week' is dependent on whether or not the conditions set out in regulation 51A(2) are satisfied. What we might refer to as 'position 1' is when the conditions are satisfied:[149] when a claimant was entitled to income support and would have received an additional amount of income support but for his/her notional capital. In such a case, regulation 51A(2) provides that the capital he or she is treated as possessing (ie, the notional capital) is to be reduced in the week in question by this additional amount (which will equate to the 'tariff' income[150]). What we might call 'position 2' is less clear from the wording, but it involves situations in which the conditions in paragraph (2) are not satisfied, that is where a claimant is not entitled to income support, etc.[151] In such a case, paragraph (3) is brought into play: if the claimant would have received income support but for having notional capital, the notional capital is to be reduced for the week in question by the aggregate of three amounts (set out in regulation 51A(3)(a), (b) and (d)). The first is the amount of income support to which the claimant would have received for that week[152] but for the capital he or she was treated as possessing under regulation 51(1) (ie, the notional capital), followed by amounts of housing benefit and council tax benefit (if any) calculated as prescribed. Thus over time, week by week, notional capital will reduce until, along with any reduction in actual capital (due, for example, to using it to meet living costs), it may bring the claimant's overall capital below the overall limit of £16,000 and thus enable him or her to secure entitlement to some income support.[153] While the position under these provisions can, with care, be discerned, they are far from straightforward.

The Universal Credit Regulations 2013 contain a much simpler form of the diminishing notional capital rule. Regulation 50 reads:

> (3) Where a person is treated as possessing capital in accordance with this regulation, then for each subsequent assessment period (or, in a case where the award has terminated, each subsequent month) the amount of capital the person is treated as possessing ('the notional capital') reduces –
>
> (a) in a case where the notional capital exceeds £16,000, by the amount which the Secretary of State considers would be the amount of an award of uni-

---

benefit week or, as the case may be, the later or latest such part-week'. 'Benefit week' is also defined by cross-referral to other regulations as essentially the week for which the benefit in question is paid to the person entitled to it: reg 2(1), referring to the Social Security (Claims and Payments) Regulations 1987 (SI 1987/1968), Sched 7, para 4.

[149] Income Support (General) Regulations 1987 (SI 1987/1967) reg 51A(1)(a) read with (2).

[150] The income that the regulations assume to be available to the claimant due to the possibility of expending some of his or her capital. This rule reflects the fact that it represents the additional amount that would have been included in income support but for the claimant having been treated as having notional capital under the Income Support (General) Regulations 1987 (SI 1987/1967) reg 51.

[151] Ibid, reg 51A(1)(b).

[152] Or part-week, in which the formula set out in para (3)(a) must be applied.

[153] See Commissioner's Decision CIS/2287/2008; and S Clarke et al, *Welfare Benefits and Tax Credits Handbook (2012–13)* (London, Child Poverty Action Group, 2012) 989.

versal credit that would be made to the person (assuming they met the conditions in section 4 and 5 of the Act) if it were not for the notional capital; or

(b) in a case where the notional capital exceeds £6,000 but not £16,000 (including where the notional capital has reduced to an amount equal to or less than £16,000 in accordance with sub-paragraph (a)) by the amount of unearned income that the notional capital is treated as yielding under regulation 72.

As under income support, £16,000 is the capital cut-off limit for entitlement to the benefit. Paragraph (a) effectively mirrors position 2 in the income support version of the rules above but is reconfigured to take account of universal credit as a single benefit covering costs previously met by different schemes. Thus one would ignore any notional capital and work out what the claimant's universal credit entitlement for the relevant assessment period (a month) would be without it. That amount is then deducted from the notional capital for each subsequent assessment period. Under paragraph (b), if the claimant's notional capital is above £6,000 and less than £16,000 (whether from the start or as a result of the diminution of notional capital under the application of paragraph (a)), then it reduces by the amount of (what the income support scheme refers to as) tariff income calculated under regulation 72. The general rule under regulation 72 is that each £250 of capital above £6,000 and any remaining sum of less than £250 provides a tariff income of £4.35. Therefore if the claimant has notional capital of £7,200, there would be tariff income calculated on £1,200 of it: five multiplied by £4.35, which equals £21.75 per month. That would be the amount by which notional capital reduces each month.

The Implications and Future of Complex Rules

It can be seen from the above examination of the funeral expenses and diminishing notional capital rules that the variously located definitions and the use of cross-referencing both within and across provisions contribute to the complexity of the rules; but at the same time, they minimise the length of the rules by avoiding duplication of content, which would often render the relevant provisions too unwieldy. Either way, the full meaning and purport of such rules is often difficult to discern. There has long been a question as to whether the rules could, while retaining their underlying policy purpose, be satisfactorily redrafted to make them easier to understand and thus apply. The reformulation of the diminishing notional capital rule within the universal credit scheme shows that some simplification is undoubtedly feasible, even though a degree of complexity remains.

While administrators' familiarity with particular rules and their access to guidance and specialist advice may help them to cope with the complexities of some of the rules, many claimants will suffer a level of uncertainty and bewilderment that, as we saw in the case of funeral payments, may be particularly undesirable. In this way, complex rules are liable to have an oppressive effect, which is ironic given that part of the rationale for enshrining policy in closely drafted rules is to ensure simplified and more clearly defined legal entitlement.[154] When the revised scheme of supplementary benefit (later to be replaced by the income support scheme) was introduced in 1980, Lister asked, 'Do [the regulations] herald a new era of a simplified, open scheme based on clear rules of entitlement . . .? I fear not . . . The regulations are complex, the legal entitlement they provide is blurred . . .'[155] This remains the position across many areas of social security, even though, after a period in which complexity has grown, particularly with the increased number of rules as the benefits and tax credits system has diversified and the continuing accumulation of case law,[156] some simplification of rules is now taking place.

Nevertheless, any suggestion that the introduction of universal credit has greatly simplified the rules should be viewed cautiously. When considering whether there would be 'any significant reduction in the rules governing the conditions of entitlement and the assessment of claimants' income and capital', Wood et al concluded that it was 'doubtful', 'since many of the rules are likely to replicate those governing the current benefits'.[157] The new regulations on universal credit largely bear this out, although as exemplified by the diminishing notional capital rule discussed above, complexity has been reduced in some areas. It should at least be easier to amend regulations under universal credit. Take, for example, the Social Security (Habitual Residence) (Amendment) Regulations 2012.[158] Under different sets of regulations governing a range of separate benefits, a person who is 'habitually resident' in the United Kingdom, the Channel Islands, the Isle of Man or the Irish Republic has not been a 'person from abroad' such as would make them ineligible for benefit. A person who has a 'right to reside' must be treated as habitually resident in these jurisdictions unless it is a right to reside falling within pre-

---

[154] See Department of Health and Social Security (DHSS) Review Team, *Social Assistance* (London, DHSS, 1978); Secretary of State for Social Services, *Reform of Social Security, Volume 1* (Cmnd 9517, 1985); and Secretary of State for Social Services, *The Reform of Social Security: A Programme for Action* (Cmnd 9691, 1985).

[155] R Lister, 'The New Supplementary Benefit Regulations I Comment' (1980) *Journal of Social Welfare Law* 341, 341 and 343. In similar vein, Partington referred to the scheme as a 'rule-based scheme of breath-taking complexity': M Partington, 'The Juridification of Social Welfare in Britain' in G Teubner (ed), *Juridification and Social Spheres* (Berlin, Walter de Gruyter, 1987) 429.

[156] As illustrated by the fact that, for example, the 1984 edition of the annotated income-related benefits legislation (which did not cover housing benefits) ran to 428 pages: J Mesher, *Supplementary Benefit and Family Income Supplement: The Legislation* (London, Sweet and Maxwell, 1984). In contrast, the 2012–13 edition (also excluding housing benefit, as well as council tax benefit) spanned 1,461 pages: Wood et al (above n 7). Both of these editions omit provisions that fall outside the remit of the appeal system.

[157] Wood et al (above n 7) x.

[158] SI 2012/2587, in force from 8 November 2012.

scribed categories. The 2012 amendment regulations added a further such category following a ruling by the Court of Justice of the European Union (CJEU),[159] but in order to do so, *eight* separate statutory instruments had to be amended. Under universal credit, there will be fewer benefits and separate rules; thus fewer changes would be needed.

The Government has also explained that the approach to drafting the new Universal Credit Regulations[160] was to 'replace detailed provisions with general principles supported by guidance', and it claims that this means a reduction in the need for frequent amendment of regulations.[161] Nonetheless, reducing the number of rules and/or having broader rules does not necessarily make them more intelligible to citizens, or even to administrators, who already rely on huge volumes of guidance, such as the 'Decision Makers' Guide'.[162] Furthermore, increasing the role of official guidance has constitutional implications by hindering Parliamentary scrutiny, which proposed legislative changes would be expected to receive. Indeed, the courts have declared the application of eligibility criteria governing immigration outside the formal legislative process to be unlawful for this reason.[163] In response to this and subsequent rulings, various matters previously covered by guidance have been brought within the Immigration Rules.[164]

---

[159] C-34/09 *Gerardo Ruiz Zambrano v Office national de l'emploi (ONEm)*. Mr Zambrano was a Colombian national who was refused asylum in Belgium and a work permit. His wife gave birth to two children in Belgium, making these children Belgian and EU citizens. In this case, the Grand Chamber confirmed that Article 20 of the Treaty on the Functioning of the European Union (TFEU) precluded national measures 'which have the effect of depriving citizens of the Union of the genuine enjoyment of the substance of the rights conferred by virtue of their status as citizens of the Union' (para 42). The court held that a 'refusal to grant a right of residence to a third-country national with dependent minor children in the Member State where those children are nationals and reside, and also a refusal to grant such a person a work permit, has such an effect' (para 43). The 2012 Amendment Regulations (ibid) were intended to place someone in the equivalent of Mr Zambrano's position in the category of persons with a right to reside which does not require them to be treated as habitually resident for benefit purposes.

[160] 2013 (SI 2013/376).

[161] Department for Work and Pensions (DWP), *Explanatory Memorandum to the Universal Credit Regulations 2013 (etc)*, www.legislation.gov.uk/uksi/2013/376/pdfs/uksiem_20130376_en.pdf, para 7.77.

[162] Department for Work and Pensions, 'Decision Makers' Guide' (February 2013; new version expected June 2013), www.dwp.gov.uk/publications/specialist-guides/decision-makers-guide/. The DWP/HMRC reported in 2010, 'While efforts have been made to promote simplification in recent years, in 2009 DWP still issued its decision-makers with 8,690 pages worth of instruction manuals to help them apply benefit rules correctly, and the guidance for [HMRC] tax credits staff ran to 1,447 pages.' See HMRC and DWP (above n 108) ch 2, para 7.

[163] See in particular *R (Alvi) v Secretary of State for the Home Department* [2012] UKSC 33, [2012] 1 WLR 2208. The Occupation Codes of Practice were applied to determine the applicant's eligibility for leave to remain. Lord Hope concluded: 'The statements in the Code that all qualifying jobs must be skilled at N/SVQ level 3 or above and that the job of a physiotherapy assistant is below that level both set out rules that ought to have been laid before Parliament under section 3(2) of the 1971 Act. As they were not laid, it was not open to the Secretary of State to rely on them as part of the Immigration Rules' [66].

[164] See R Thomas (above n 23) 151.

Concern about the effect of using guidance to, in effect, steer the application of legislation was articulated by the House of Lords Secondary Legislation Scrutiny Committee in relation to the new rules governing personal independence payment (PIP).[165] According to the Government, there was an intention to retain some 'flexibility around certain terms' by omitting precise definition of them from the rules and instead dealing with them in guidance, as in the pivotal test of being able to perform a particular task 'safely, reliably, repeatedly and in a timely manner'.[166] The Government initially resisted the idea that such a test should be included in the legislation despite the many consultees to the draft regulations who had favoured it.[167] The Government's rather weak argument was that 'the broad definitions we are using are not conducive to a legislative framework and without definitions we could not include them in the Regulations'.[168] However, following the Scrutiny Committee's report, which drew on widespread criticism from the voluntary sector about the omission of the test from the legislation, amendment regulations were published in advance of the commencement date of the new PIP regulations (8 April 2013). They introduced a requirement that a judgment as to whether a person is able to carry out a particular activity should rest on the person's ability to do so '(a) safely; (b) to an acceptable standard; (c) repeatedly; and (d) in a reasonable time period'.[169] While the definitions of two of these criteria – 'safely' and 'repeatedly' – were also included in the regulations, the term 'to an acceptable standard' was not and is instead to be explained by department guidance, which the Scrutiny Committee has warned should be examined carefully to ensure that 'the stated need for legal clarity' that the amendment regulations were intended to reflect is met by the DWP.[170]

In any event, recasting rules to make them more straightforward is not easy given the role that they are expected to play, as discussed earlier. It would take a real commitment of the kind that, for example, was lacking when the

---

[165] House of Lords Secondary Legislation Scrutiny Committee, *Draft Social Security (Personal Independence Payment) Regulations 2013* (2012–13, HL 101) para 25.

[166] Ibid, para 14.

[167] DWP, *The Government's Response to the Consultation on the Personal Independence Payment Assessment Criteria and Regulations* (2012) para 4.11.

[168] Ibid.

[169] Social Security (Personal Independence Payment) (Amendment) Regulations 2013 (SI 2013/455), reg 2, amending the Social Security (Personal Independence Payment) Regulations 2013 (SI 2013/377), reg 4.

[170] House of Lords Secondary Legislation Scrutiny Committee, *National Health Service (Primary Dental Services) (Miscellaneous Amendments and Transitional Provisions) Regulations 2013, Social Security (Personal Independence Payment) (Amendment) Regulations 2013 and National Health Service (Procurement, Patient Choice and Competition) (No 2) Regulations 2013* (2012–13, HL 153) para 13. Under the amendment regulations, '(a) "safely" means in a manner unlikely to cause harm to [the claimant] or to another person, either during or after completion of the activity; and (b) "repeatedly" means as often as the activity being assessed is reasonably required to be completed': Social Security (Personal Independence Payment) (Amendment) Regulations 2013 (SI 2013/455) reg 2, amending Personal Independence Payment Regulations 2013 (SI 2013/377) reg 4.

Labour Government, having to its credit floated the possibility of a pensions law rewrite project, decided to drop the idea when it received a 'mixed response'.[171] The Office of the Parliamentary Counsel, in setting out its vision for 'good law' in general, notes that 'there is no compelling incentive within government or Parliament to avoid generating further complexity'.[172] In the area of social security, an opportunity has nevertheless been taken by government with the regulations on universal credit to tidy up and thereby reduce the complexity within some of the rules, which is to be welcomed.

III. Measuring Complexity?

The discussion above and in chapter two has attempted to explain what is complex about the law and structure of welfare. We know the causes of complexity and how it manifests itself. We saw from the NAO's breakdown of the options in designing means tests, set out in chapter two, that a broad comparison of the levels of complexity involved in different bases of assessing needs can be made. There is also a general consensus that complexity has increased over the past three decades, although this is based on general perception rather than any kind of empirical measurement. Nevertheless, as stated in chapter one, in view of the avowed governmental aim of simplifying the system, it is reasonable to consider whether there is an effective way of measuring complexity in order to facilitate evaluation of policies aimed at reducing it.

The House of Commons Committee of Public Accounts noted in 2006, 'The benefits system appears to be getting more complex, but there is currently no way of measuring the degree of complexity.'[173] As stated in chapter one above, the Committee recommended the formulation and adoption of an 'easy to understand' basis for the measurement of complexity.[174] It identified various criteria related to complexity that could be measured and combined into a

---

[171] DWP, *Simplification Plan (2006–07)* (2006) para 58. It was the pensions industry and CBI that were against it; trade unions were in favour. Those against considered that 'redrafting of current legislation would divert resources from consideration of the underlying policies': DWP, *Security in Retirement: Towards a New Pensions System (Summary of the Responses to the Consultation)* (Cm 6960, 2006) para 26.

[172] Office of the Parliamentary Counsel, 'Good Law' (19 April 2013), www.gov.uk/good-law?utm_source=Sign-Up.to&utm_medium=email&utm_campaign=1317-221121-Judicial+Intranet+update+19+April+2013.

[173] House of Commons Committee of Public Accounts, *Tackling the Complexity of the Benefits System* (2005–06, HC 765) para 6.

[174] Ibid, Conclusions and Recommendations No 7.

'composite indicator', specifically referring to customer satisfaction, error rates, benefit take-up and the accessibility of customer services.[175] The Committee also recommended that other elements could also be taken into account – namely, 'the length of secondary legislation, and the number of linkages with existing regulations'.[176] It was reported by the DWP in 2007 that a priority of its Benefit Simplification Unit[177] over the succeeding year would be to 'conclude the study of the scope for producing a complexity index'.[178] But in oral evidence to the House of Commons Work and Pensions Committee, the Parliamentary Under-Secretary, James Plaskitt MP, dampened expectations:

> **Q298 Chairman:** Is the Department in any way close to defining a measure of complexity?
>
> **Mr Plaskitt:** No.
>
> **Q299 Chairman:** That was a simple answer. That will do.
>
> **Mr Plaskitt:** Perhaps I should explain. I think many people have tried valiantly to define complexity. I think the National Audit Office had a crack at it and concluded they could not do it. It is very difficult. Often what I say is that you know complexity when you run into it, you recognise it when you hit it, but standing back and trying to do almost a sort of abstract definition of what complexity is, in itself is very, very complex and might not contribute anything to the process of achieving simplification.[179]

The apparent inference therefore was that there was no point to attempting to measure something that cannot even be properly defined.

It was later reported that the DWP had found 'no single metric that could act as a suitable measure of complexity', and it regarded the best approach as likely to be 'to focus on the burdens the benefits system imposes on its customers'.[180] Such an approach was recommended in a report commissioned by the Department, which stated, 'Typical customer journeys are more likely to give an indication of complexity for the customer than the complexity of individual benefits.'[181] The report's author separately commented that one way of measuring complexity would be to construct a 'basket of customer journeys' related to different kinds of personal circumstances and potential interactions with the system.[182] The journeys would range from simple ones (at least in benefit terms), such as that experienced when a claimant's partner

---

[175] Ibid, para 6.

[176] Ibid.

[177] The Unit was established at the end of 2005: see further above ch 1.

[178] House of Commons Work and Pensions Committee, *Benefits Simplification* (2006–07, HC 463–II), 'Further Supplementary Note from DWP' (Ev 132).

[179] Ibid, Oral Evidence (18 June 2007).

[180] House of Commons Work and Pensions Committee, *Benefits Simplification: Government Response to the Committee's Seventh Report* (2006–07, HC 1054) paras 11–12. See also Department for Work and Pensions (DWP), *Simplification Plan 2008–09* (2008) para 61.

[181] S Royston, *Benefits Simplification and the Customer* (London, DWP, 2007) para 0.2.1 (sic).

[182] HC Work and Pensions Committee, *Benefits Simplification* (above n 178) Oral Evidence, Q3 (Sue Royston).

leaves him or her, through to more complex ones, such as when a person with disabilities becomes eligible for more than one benefit and there is a potential interaction between them. Complexity would be judged with reference to questions such as:

> How easy was it for the person to find out about benefits? Do benefits get missed? How many contacts does the person have to make in order to claim the benefit? How easy is it to report a change of circumstances? Do they have to go to lots of places? Can they just report it once? . . . Do they have a way of finding out about new entitlement?[183]

A similar distinction between straightforward and more complicated interactions with the system was made by the NAO, although based not so much on the level of complexity actually experienced but rather on the risk of complexity impacting on the claimant. 'Low-risk' factors were: a limited need for interaction with the agency; receipt of a single benefit; responsibility by a single agency; limited requirements to report changes; limited evidence requirements; and straightforward personal circumstances. 'High-risk' factors were: regular interaction with the agency; claims for more than one benefit; jurisdiction by multiple agencies; a requirement to report changes; high evidence requirements; and complex personal circumstances.[184]

It was also suggested by one expert that such matters could be quantified in terms of 'compliance costs' for claimants, such as: the time involved in claiming; the help that may be needed; the need for physical journeys; and the impact on privacy and even dignity.[185] A detailed scoping study aimed at assessing the measurability of compliance costs has identified such costs as spanning three categories: time costs (such as filling in forms and visits to offices), money costs (such as travel, postage, use of the telephone) and psychological costs (such as stress/worry, frustration, fear and depression).[186] Account also needs to be taken of the characteristics of claimants. Their levels of education, access to assistance and information, English language proficiency and personal characteristics such as disability may also affect the level of complexity experienced.[187]

Nonetheless, producing an official basis for measuring complexity seems to have been abandoned in favour of a more general commitment to identify factors that exacerbate the burden on claimants and to tackle them through simplification.[188] The focus therefore seems to be on the aforementioned 'customer

---

[183] Ibid.

[184] NAO, *Dealing with the Complexity of the Benefits System* (above n 78) fig 3.

[185] HC Work and Pensions Committee, *Benefit Simplification* (above n 178) Oral Evidence, Q4 and Q5 (Fran Bennett).

[186] F Bennett, M Brewer and J Shaw, *Understanding the Compliance Costs of Benefits and Tax Credits* (London, Institute for Fiscal Studies, 2009) ch 2.

[187] NAO, *Dealing with the Complexity of the Benefits System* (above n 78) fig 3.

[188] See for example the DWP, *Simplification Plan 2008–09* (above n 180) para 62, which states the DWP's objective of making the system 'more customer-friendly', in line with the DWP's 'objective to become an exemplar of service delivery'.

journey', with a view to making it a smoother, easier one.[189] Yet while the Work and Pensions Committee approved of the idea of putting claimants 'at the heart of the simplification process', it regarded the intended approach as one of 'masking' complexity and considered that it ignored the inconsistencies between different benefits and the need to create a new coherent benefits structure.[190] To the Government, the minimising of differences between rules and the alignment of them formed 'a long-term aim', but there was no specific timetable due to the 'constraints on costs and capacity'.[191]

The notion of 'compliance costs' is associated with regulatory impact, the burden imposed on those affected by new legislation. The regulatory impact assessment process developed under the Regulatory Reform Act 2001. This Act enabled ministers to make regulatory reform orders designed to remove or reduce this burden. The process was directed at public and private sector bodies, charitable/voluntary bodies and small businesses. It was said to be consistent with the Government's aim of regulating only on the basis of necessity and proportionality and effecting simplification whenever possible.[192] Regulations affecting individuals were not covered by the process, however. The House of Commons Committee of Public Accounts described this as 'an unnecessary exclusion given the evidence of the effects of complex benefit regulations on vulnerable individuals and the costs to third parties who assist them'.[193]

The legislation that replaced the 2001 Act, the Legislative and Regulatory Reform Act 2006, gives a power to any minister of the Crown to make an order (a legislative reform order)[194] removing or reducing a burden arising directly or indirectly from any legislation, and it defines 'burden' as, inter alia, 'a financial cost' and 'an administrative inconvenience'.[195] It further provides that, for this purpose, 'a financial cost or administrative convenience may result from any form of legislation (for example, where that legislation is hard to understand)'.[196] The Better Regulation Task Force[197] proposed that all government departments should implement a rolling programme for the identification of regulations that could be simplified or changed in some other way,

---

[189] HC Work and Pensions Committee, *Benefit Simplification* (above n 178) Oral Evidence, Q306 (James Plaskitt, Parliamentary Under-Secretary of State).

[190] House of Commons Work and Pensions Committee, *Benefit Simplification* (2006–07, HC 463–I) para 262.

[191] HC Work and Pensions Committee, *Benefits Simplification: Government Response* (above n 180) para 57.

[192] See the archived webpage at webarchive.nationalarchives.gov.uk/20060715142853/http://www.cabinetoffice.gov.uk/regulation/ria/overview/index.asp [last updated 16 June 2006].

[193] HC Committee of Public Accounts (above n 173) para 21.

[194] Proposed orders are scrutinised by the House of Lords Delegated Powers and Regulatory Reform Committee.

[195] Legislative and Regulatory Reform Act 2006, s1(1)–(3).

[196] Ibid, s 1(4).

[197] Better Regulation Task Force, *Regulation – Less is More: Reducing Burdens, Improving Outcomes* (London, Better Regulation Task Force, 2005).

consolidated or repealed. The Government adopted these recommendations and proposed to use the new measures aimed at reducing administrative burdens etc with a view to effecting simplifications.[198] This commitment was given despite the absence of any reference to simplification in the legislation. Simplification measures might include clarification of legislation, 'ie, resolving doubts and ambiguities about its meaning' and restating the law to improve its 'transparency, coherence and accessibility'.[199] To date, however, no social security legislation or process has been the subject of a legislative reform order. Instead, simplification has become an inherent feature of welfare reform, or at least one of its stated aims.

As noted above, the measurement of the complexity of legislation was referred to by the Committee of Public Accounts both directly, in terms of the length of secondary legislation and the linkages between provisions, and indirectly, in terms of error rates. It was also noted in chapter one how the level of complexity may be related to the burden involved in determining whether and how a rule is applicable and to the denseness, clarity or determinacy of the rule. We also saw how the level of complexity experienced can vary across people with different backgrounds, so that a professional may judge a rule to be less complex than would a typical claimant. This is also related to the aforementioned issue of burden; the claimant may have to expend more time and seek advice in order to understand a rule, whereas a front-line administrator may be sufficiently conversant with it to be able to understand and apply it quickly. It was also suggested above that the difficulty in following the sense of a rule because of the way it is expressed, the rule's interaction with or dependence on another rule or other rules, and the possibility of different versions of rules applicable to different periods of time due to prospective amendments, were all measures of a rule's complexity.

Looking across all these elements of complexity, what stands out is that measuring complexity scientifically is almost impossible, since we are largely forced to base measurements on its impact, on the experience of it, which varies across those affected by it. One might, on that basis, need different measurements of complexity for, say, claimants and administrators. For the former group, one would need to decide whether the measurements should be based on a hypothetical average claimant in terms of intelligence and experience of the system or take greater account of claimant diversity in relation to such matters. Moreover, complexity may not be the sole cause of the particular effects in question; for example, administrative error could be partly due to complexity and partly a weakness in staff training, and the same could be said of the time taken to determine a claim. Thus it may be difficult to separate the effects of complexity from other factors. Where complexity is judged with reference to factors associated with it, such as the length or frequency of amendment of

---

[198] Cabinet Office Better Regulation Executive, *A Bill for Better Regulation: Consultation Document* (London, Better Regulation Executive, 2005) 11.
[199] Ibid.

regulations, the general assumption will not be correct in every case: for example, short rules may be complex if they deal with highly technical matters and if there is a need for cross-referencing to other provisions.

With these caveats, a possible broad framework for gauging complexity levels is offered in Table 2. It shows the likely level of complexity for each of the indicators within the elements of the system that were identified above as inherently complex or particularly affected by complexity. Clearly, adjustments may be needed in light of the particular benefit or relevant legislative provision. Moreover, as mentioned earlier, a claimant's degree of experience, expertise, education and intelligence will obviously have a bearing on the perceived level of complexity; the table assumes that the claimant has neither very high nor very low levels of each.

Table 2 provides a basis for assessing how much complexity there is in parts of the system and its legal framework. A high level of complexity for means-testing, for example, is indicated by the claimant's likely difficulty in understanding the basis for entitlement and need to provide detailed information to the department, while in the case of the department, it is indicated by the range of issues that need to be considered in determining a claim. It would be possible to apply many of the various impact indicators shown in Table 2 to typical claimant 'journeys' through the benefits system and its claims process. (These stages in a journey will be explored further below in chapters four to six.) Using that method, the degree of difficulty likely to be encountered as a consequence of complexity could be assessed. Such a focus is favoured by some and seems to be where government has placed an emphasis in pursuit of a simplification strategy, although under the Coalition Government, the impact on administrators has received additional attention.

IV. Conclusion

As we have seen, social security and tax credits are governed by very detailed and often bright-line rules, although areas of flexibility more amenable to the exercise of professional judgment and discretion are used out of necessity or preference in some areas. This aspect of the system will not change under universal credit, even as alignment and consolidation mean that common issues such as the calculation of capital or income are handled by one set of rules rather than discrete (albeit inter-related) sets of provisions. As we have also seen, there has been a slight shift towards the use of principles supplemented by guidance, which has reduced a little the volume of legislation.

Table 2: Indicators of Moderate and High Complexity Levels within the UK Welfare System

Area of Complexity	Element of Complexity	Impact on Claimant and State	Complexity Level	
			Moderate	High
Design				
Underlying aims	Range of benefits and credits (size of the system)	Claimant: what to claim		√
		State: reform		√
Coverage	Need to identify intended beneficiaries	Claimant: whether entitled		√
		State: cost and error	√	
	Life transitions	Claimant: entitlement effect	√	
		State: benefit transitions	√	
	The EU dimension (migrant workers, etc)	Claimant: knowledge		√
		State: investigation	√	
Basis of entitlement	Contribution conditions	Claimant: understanding		√
		State: computation		√
	Means-testing	Claimant: understanding; provision of information		√
		State: range of issues		√
	Passported entitlement	Claimant: understanding	√	
		State: co-ordination		√
Reform	Changes to structure and to benefits; rapidity of change	Claimant: awareness		√
		State: cost and accuracy		√
	Transitional protection	Claimant: understanding		√
		State: administration		√

Table 2: (*cont.*)

Area of Complexity	Element of Complexity	Impact on Claimant and State	Complexity Level	
			Moderate	High
Extrinsic Complexity				
Agencies	Number of agencies	Claimant: where to go	√	
		State: co-ordination	√	
	The claimant experience (claiming and reporting changes)	Claimant: claims and reporting burden; overpayment		√
		State: discovery and recovery of overpayments	√	
Interaction across the system	Benefits/processes impacting on each other; entitlement to two or more benefits/ credits	Claimant: understanding		√
		State: co-ordination		√
Management				
Organisational structure	Changes to names and structures of agencies	Claimant: knowledge	√	
		State: adjustment	√	
	Contracting out of functions	Claimant: service	√	
		State: control		√
Information management	Development and use of IT	Claimant: not applicable		
		State: cost and effectiveness		√
	IT availability and competence	Claimant: accessibility [if low]	√	[√]
		State: not applicable		

Table 2: (*cont.*)

Area of Complexity	Element of Complexity	Impact on Claimant and State	Complexity Level	
			Moderate	High
Law				
Scope and breadth	Range of issues covered and needing to be considered	Claimant: understanding		√
		State: cost and error		√
	Layering effect	Claimant: understanding		√
		State: adjustment	√	
Form	Flexibility	Claimant: knowledge		√
		State: accuracy; time		√
	Clarity and coherence: length, density, inter-dependence	Claimant: intelligibility		√
		State: accuracy; time		√
	Case law	Claimant: knowledge; accessibility		√
		State: knowledge/ expertise; time		√

Moreover, the Social Security Advisory Committee has reassuringly assessed the regulations governing universal credit as having 'an overall coherence'.[200] Nevertheless, the elaborate UK welfare system has been under continual reform since the 1960s, a process effected via legislative changes of which many are highly technical and detailed and add layers of complexity to an already extremely complex area of the law.

The introduction of universal credit may represent a major landmark, but further change is inevitable. For example, Policy Exchange has recently argued that it would be desirable to reverse the decline in insurance benefits

[200] Social Security Advisory Committee, *The Draft Universal Credit Regulations 2013; the Benefit Cap (Housing Benefit) Regulations 2012 (SI 2012 No 2994); and the Draft Universal Credit, Personal Independence Payment, Jobseeker's Allowance and Employment and Support Allowance (Claims and Payments) Regulations 2013: Report by the Social Security Advisory Committee* (London, Stationery Office, 2012) para 8.1.

by 'building a something for something system that all parts of society believe is fair'; this would involve a strengthening of the contributory principle.[201] Frank Field MP, who has a similar view, launched a private member's Welfare Reform Bill in March 2013; it is aimed at restoring the largely contributory basis of social security. There are some indications that ministers may be considering the possibility that extending contributory welfare might provide a means of restricting the rights of economic migrants to UK benefits without breaching EU law – thereby alleviating the (significantly exaggerated) phenomenon of EU 'benefits tourism'.[202]

In the evolving welfare state after 1945, complexity grew as the range of social security benefits expanded; questions of entitlement became increasingly governed by extensive rules. Indeed, the volume and range of legislation expanded hugely,[203] as illustrated by the fact that around 1,000 pages of secondary legislation have had to be rewritten to accommodate the universal credit reforms.[204] Tax credits were introduced; a comprehensive appeal process has developed and, at the second tier, has spawned copious amounts of case law; increasing levels of conditionality have been attached to welfare entitlement; and administrative controls have intensified via a plethora of new rules on claiming and decision-making. That complexity is an inherent feature of the legislative and administrative frameworks is what one would expect in a system that is so diverse, has such a wide range of functions in catering for particular areas of need across the population, and serves wide-ranging policy objectives concerned with, for example, the alleviation of poverty, increasing pressure to take up employment, the promotion of self-sufficiency and reduced welfare dependency, the enforcement of family responsibility, and the provision of security in old age or when living with disability.

While the measurement of complexity remains problematic, the way that complexity manifests itself is at least far better understood by government than it has been in the past. This will facilitate the planning of simplification and means that the success of such policy may eventually be more accurately gauged.

---

[201] See M Oakley, 'Welfare Reform Must Be Based on the Principle of "Something for Something"', *The Guardian* (7 January 2013). Oakley is the head of economics and social policy at Policy Exchange.

[202] See 'Once More unto the Breach: The Government Wants to Curb Benefits for EU Migrants. But Can It?', *The Economist* (9 March 2013), www.economist.com/news/britain/21573144-government-wants-curb-benefits-eu-migrants-can-it-once-more-unto-breach.

[203] The increasing volume of legislation more generally has been identified by the Office of the Parliamentary Counsel as a feature of growing legal complexity: Office of the Parliamentary Counsel, *When Laws Become Too Complex: A Review into the Causes of Complex Legislation* (London, Cabinet Office, 2013) 6–9.

[204] DWP, *Explanatory Memorandum to the Universal Credit Regulations* (above n 161) para 7.77.

4

Claims and Their Administration

I. Introduction

The idea of assessing the degree of complexity within the welfare system with reference to typical 'journeys' that benefit and credit claimants experience was referred to in the previous chapter. The premise is that the burdens and difficulties that claimants face in their engagement with the welfare system must in part be derived from the complexity within the system's structure and processes and their legislative underpinnings. The burdens have also been conceptualised as 'compliance costs' in the sense that this 'implies the inherent inequality of the position in which claimants of benefits/tax credits usually feel themselves to be, and it also recognises that the costs of complying with benefit and tax credits can continue after the initial claim'.[1]

There has been quite a strong push from within and without the UK Department for Work and Pensions (DWP) to use the claimant experience or journey as a primary indicator of complexity. Examining the issue of complexity from this perspective need not be a purely theoretical exercise, since there is empirical evidence of the impact upon actual or potential claimants. For example, we know that due to the uncertainty or perceived obstacles to which it gives rise, complexity is a factor in the level of benefit take-up. It thus increases the risk that claimants will not gain access to benefit to which they are entitled. We

---

[1] F Bennett and M Brewer, 'Memorandum' in House of Commons Work and Pensions Committee, *Benefits Simplification, Volume II: Oral and Written Evidence* (2006–07, HC 463-II) Ev 90–92, para 8.

also know that the system's complexity 'obscures choices' for claimants.[2] As noted in chapter one, it has been found to deter entry into employment due to the confusion or uncertainty about in-work benefits or credits or the antici-pated risks involved in having to reapply for benefits if, for example, a period of employment proves only temporary. This is now a critical element of the ration-ale for the universal credit reform – to end a system in which 'complexity means that it is difficult for people to know what benefits and Tax Credits they can get', which in turn 'undermines trust in the system and stops people focusing on getting back to work'.[3]

In examining this 'journey', it is important to bear in mind that government would regard itself as having an underlying responsibility, in administering public funds for this purpose, to ensure that support at the appropriate level is paid only to those whom Parliament intended or expected to receive it.[4] Indeed, the legitimacy of targeting those with particular needs or circumstances and thus disfavouring other people is underscored by its potential justification as discriminatory treatment for the purposes of Article 14 of the European Convention on Human Rights (ECHR). For example, in *RJM*, the House of Lords held that a rule depriving disabled homeless people of entitlement to the disability premium payable within income support was not in conflict with Article 14, since, first, it was consistent with the aim of encouraging the home-less to find permanent accommodation, and secondly, the premium was partly intended to meet heating costs, which a homeless person was considered to be much less likely to incur as compared with other income support claimants.[5] Another example is *Reynolds*,[6] which concerned discrimination against claim-ants aged under 25 resulting from their entitlement to a lower rate of income support personal allowance than that applicable to those aged 25 or over. The policy arguments for the rule were explained as follows: on average, the living costs of over-25s are greater; a lower rate of benefit for under-25s reflects age-related wage differentials; and government should discourage sole occupancy of accommodation among under-25s. The House of Lords accepted that tar-geting support in that way was a matter for political judgment and found noth-ing wrong in the use of a bright-line rule that, in this instance, was conducive to legal certainty and much easier to administer than the previous rule, which sought to distinguish between householders and non-householders.

Targeting clearly requires the firm establishment of legally prescribed levels or kinds of need, or accepted contingencies, that are intended to trigger entitle-

---

[2] Department for Work and Pensions (DWP), *No-One Written Off: Reforming Welfare to Reward Responsibility* (Cm 7363, 2008) Executive Summary, para 39.

[3] Department for Work and Pensions (DWP), *Universal Credit: Welfare that Works* (Cm 7957, 2010) ch 1, para 17.

[4] Arrangements that do not reflect Parliament's intention or expectation may be challengeable on that basis or partly on that basis, as in *Chief Adjudication Officer v Foster* [1993] 1 All ER 705.

[5] *R (RJM) v Secretary of State for Work and Pensions* [2008] UKHL 63.

[6] *R (Carson) v Secretary of State for Work and Pensions; R (Reynolds) v Secretary of State for Work and Pensions* [2005] UKHL 37.

ment. Targeting may involve the application of very sophisticated criteria that seek to enable fine distinctions to be made between different sets of circumstances, as we saw in chapter three, for example, in the rules governing social fund funeral payments. Equally, however, legislation can target, albeit less precisely, through wider rules that make broad or blanket distinctions. Such rules may restrict the entitlement of a whole category of potential claimants, as illustrated by *Reynolds*. In recent years, government has regarded such measures as a potential contribution to the effort to curb welfare dependency and spending and as a contribution to the general austerity drive and public debt reduction strategy. Examples include the general benefits 'cap', introduced in April 2013, which is intended to limit overall benefit entitlement of families to a prescribed amount;[7] it is expected to save a total of £531 million between 2013 and 2015.[8] Another example would be the removal of the right of people under the age of 25 to housing benefit or to the housing costs element of universal credit, which replaces it. Such a reform was proposed in 2012 but has not been carried out (although it has remained under active contemplation).[9] Yet such arrangements are not necessarily significantly simpler, as even blanket restrictions may require complex provision for exceptional cases. Lone parents aged 18 or over, for example, have been entitled to the 25 or over rate of income support and income-based jobseeker's allowance (JSA), presumably on the basis that their responsibility for a child or children means that they are more likely to be living in single households, although this provision will change under universal credit.[10] Similarly, in the case of housing support for

---

[7] See the Welfare Reform Act 2012, ss 96 and 97; the Benefit Cap (Housing Benefit) Regulations 2012 (SI 2012/2994), inserting Part 8A into the Housing Benefit Regulations 2006 (SI 2006/213); and the Universal Credit Regulations 2013 (SI 2013/376), Pt 7. For further details of the cap, see above ch 2, n 59.

[8] National Audit Office (NAO), *Department for Work and Pensions: Managing the Impact of Housing Benefit Reform*, HC 681 (London, Stationery Office, 2012) para 1.5, fig 2.

[9] The proposal (along with possible exceptions for limited cases of particular need) was mentioned in a speech by Prime Minister David Cameron on welfare at Bluewater, Kent (25 June 2012), available at www.number10.gov.uk/news/welfare-speech/. See also P Wintour, 'Housing Benefit for Under-25s could be Scrapped, PM to Announce', *The Guardian* (24 June 2012), www.guardian.co.uk/society/2012/jun/24/housing-benefit-under-25s-welfare. In May 2013, it was reported that the Secretary of State for Work and Pensions was 'understood to have offered to restrict housing benefit for the under-25s' in order to help the Government protect spending on the police and the Armed Forces from forthcoming public expenditure cuts: R Winnett, 'Iain Duncan Smith: Cut Welfare to Fund Police and Forces', *The Telegraph* (28 May 2013), www.telegraph.co.uk/news/politics/10083049/Iain-Duncan-Smith-cut-welfare-to-fund-police-and-Forces.html. However, the Chancellor reportedly ruled out further welfare cuts for the time being, due to the Liberal Democrats' unwillingness to accept any unless benefits for the elderly, such as winter fuel payments, are looked at: G O'Donoghue, 'Spending Review Challenges Remain for George Osborne', *BBC News* (28 May 2013), www.bbc.co.uk/news/uk-politics-22686060.

[10] Under universal credit, a person aged 18 to 24 would only benefit from the 25 or over rate as a member of couple, where the other member is 25 or over. A lone parent aged under 25 will not have access to the 25 or over rate, although will receive support for the child(ren) through the 'child element' (plus the disabled child addition, where relevant) as in the case of all parents: Universal Credit Regulations 2013 (SI 2013/376), reg 36.

young people, it was acknowledged that exceptional categories, such as those who were previously in public care or had other vulnerabilities, would need to be established as exceptions to the general restriction.[11]

Much of the targeting in the welfare system is based on means-testing, and this will show no abatement under the universal credit system. Means-tested support has grown in importance, in terms of the numbers of claimants receiving it and the range of provision made by the system, as noted in chapter two. Intensifying the targeting of support through means-testing inevitably makes the claimant journey to entitlement more complex. Arrangements governing means-tested benefits will inevitably place demands on both benefit claimants and the administrative authorities, to varying degrees. The former, for example, will generally have to provide a considerable amount of personal information in connection with their claim; the latter will have to analyse that information with reference to the rules of entitlement. Determinations can give rise to significant 'administrative complexities'.[12] It is largely because of this that means-tested benefits cost more per claim to deliver than other benefits, as discussed in section III below.

In recent years, means-testing has been introduced into benefit areas in which it had no prior history, namely incapacity benefits and, more recently, child benefit. For the former, 50 per cent of the rate of any occupational or personal pension in excess of £85 per week reduces the rate of contributory employment and support allowance (ESA) (as it did incapacity benefit post-1999) by that amount.[13] With regard to child benefit, until January 2013, it was an entirely 'universal' benefit in the sense of being paid to all with responsibility for a child or, depending on various factors, young person. In 2012–13, there was entitlement to £20.30 per week in respect of a claimant's only, elder or eldest child and £13.40 for each other child. However, as had been announced in the 2012 Budget, for couples with one member earning over £60,000, there is now no entitlement, but where the higher or sole income exceeds £50,000 but is not in excess of £60,000, child benefit entitlement is reduced on a sliding scale, thereby 'preventing a cliff-edge effect'.[14] Benefit is to be clawed back from the claimant through the tax system as an income tax

[11] Mr Cameron (above n 9) acknowledged, 'A lot of these young people will genuinely need a roof over their head. Like those leaving foster care, or those with a terrible, destructive home life and we must always be there for them.' But see the Universal Credit Regulations 2013 (SI 2013/376), Sched 4, para 4, which excludes 16- and 17-year-old care leavers from the housing costs element.

[12] P Spicker, *How Social Security Works: An introduction to Benefits in Britain* (Bristol, Policy Press, 2011) 87, who highlights these complexities as including 'the problem of defining the threshold for entitlement', dealing with changes in the claimant's income, 'the treatment of saving', 'the aggregation and distribution of resources in the household' and the treatment of non-dependants in the household.

[13] Welfare Reform Act 2007, ss 2(1) and 3(1); and the Employment Support and Allowance Regulations 2008 (SI 2008/794), reg 74 and 2013 (SI 2013/379), reg 67. The rate has been £85 since this offset was first introduced, in the incapacity benefit scheme, via the Welfare Reform and Pensions Act 1999, s 63.

[14] HM Treasury, *Budget 2012*, HC 1853 (London, Stationery Office, 2012) para 1.177.

charge.[15] The taxpayer would have to include the benefit on a self-assessment tax form; it is estimated that as a result of the reform, some 500,000 people would be completing such a form for the first time.[16] Thus part of the complexity here arises from the interaction of benefit and tax systems – another example of 'extrinsic' complexity, which was discussed above in chapter two. 'Confusion' was expected to be generated among the couples concerned, arising from the fact that the benefit may well not be in payment to the higher earner but to the other member of a couple.[17]

Yet the claimants affected by the introduction of what amounts to a means-tested element in child benefit are in households which are not typical of those likely to be claiming means-tested benefits, or in this case a benefit that is, in effect, partly means-tested. As the National Audit Office (NAO) has explained, 'means-testing concentrates payments on poorer households'.[18] For many of them, complexity may well present particularly acute difficulties, as they are likely to need access to a variety of forms of support; be required to furnish broader information about their financial and domestic circumstances; and face educational, language or cultural barriers. According to the NAO, government departments 'do not systematically consider or measure all of the impacts of means-testing, particularly the burden on claimants'.[19] Most of the impact assessments, which are published at the time of major reforms, 'failed to assess the burden on claimants, such as the costs of completing forms and requesting advice'.[20]

Evidence of the effects of such burdens and costs, in particular the social and economic impact, is analysed in this chapter in discrete contexts that accord broadly with the first stage in the 'journey' that a claimant may need to make, or at least the main elements of it. It starts with the issue of take-up, before moving on to consider the claims process and the assessment of claims, which is obviously an issue for the administrative authorities. It includes consideration of the reforms consequent on the introduction of new claims regulations covering universal credit, personal independence payment, ESA and JSA.[21] This is the first of three chapters examining the claimant journey. A claimant's on-going engagement with the system as a result of the responsibilities placed upon him or her, including those that concern the provision of information, such as information needed beyond the initial phase of an award

[15] Ibid, para 2.89. See the Finance Act 2012, s 8 and Sched 1, inserting new ch 8 into the Income Tax (Earnings and Pensions) Act 2003.

[16] J Hall, 'Child Benefit Changes Lead to "Confusion" among Couples', *Daily Telegraph* (23 October 2012) 14.

[17] Ibid.

[18] National Audit Office (NAO), *Means Testing: Report by the Comptroller and Auditor General* (2010–12, HC 1464, 2011) para 2.2.

[19] Ibid, 'Key Findings', para 10.

[20] Ibid.

[21] The Universal Credit, Personal Independence Payment, Jobseeker's Allowance and Employment and Support Allowance (Claims and Payments) Regulations 2013 (SI 2013/380) (hereafter the 'Claims and Payments Regulations 2013').

of ESA to judge the capability for work of a sick or disabled claimant, is another element, and this will be discussed in chapter six.

Before that, chapter five will examine the appeal process, specifically how complexity bears down on this mechanism for challenging a decision adverse to the claimant. The need to apply complex rules may present problems for adjudicators, but tribunals must engage not only with the rules governing substantive entitlement but also rules of procedure, which can sometimes be almost as troublesome for them. More importantly, there is also the complexity of the appeal process itself from the claimant's perspective. To what extent does complexity deter some claimants from appealing or discourage those who have appealed from opting for an oral appeal hearing? Research into the use of tribunals has shown a general reluctance to utilise judicial processes because of 'anticipated expense and complexity'.[22] The Leggatt Report advocated a more independent and coherent system of tribunals but, consistent with its focus on the user's perspective, also sought an 'accessible and user-friendly' system 'so that most users can understand the process and prepare their case themselves'.[23] Thus, an issue to be addressed in the case of social security and tax credit appeals is the impact on the user of the reforms consequent on the Leggatt Report, effected via the Tribunals, Courts and Enforcement Act 2007.

Other elements and effects of complexity that arise outside the claimant journey (for example, the implementation of reforms to the structure of benefits and rules of entitlement) were discussed in earlier chapters and do not require further elaboration here.

II. Take-Up and Claims

Standardised processes such as those used for benefit claims and their assessment are essential for the efficient operation of an administrative system that caters for large numbers of people. But they should be processes that facilitate rather than hinder access to potential entitlements. Arguably, the state has a positive obligation to citizens to enable them to exercise their rights,[24] whilst it is an essential principle of administrative justice at all levels (including initial decision-making) that procedures operated by the state should be

---

[22] H Genn et al and the National Centre for Social Research, *Tribunals for Diverse Users*, DCA Research series 1/06 (London, DCA, 2006) i.

[23] Sir A Leggatt, *Tribunals for Users: One System, One Service* (London, Stationery Office, 2001) para 4.17.

[24] S Fredman, *Human Rights Transformed* (Oxford, Oxford University Press, 2008) 231.

fair to those who use them.[25] Among other things, a high degree of accessibility is important. Being able to bring a claim is obviously essential to the realisation of one's right to social security, even if there is an argument that social rights of this kind are above all contingent on their enforceability.[26] At the same time, and consistent with the increasing emphasis government policy has placed on the responsibilities of citizens in the public sphere, there is an obligation on claimants to present their claims in the appropriate manner. Thus, for example, if a person wishes to claim universal credit and he or she is a member of a couple, normally only a joint claim by the couple can be made.[27] More generally, all benefit claimants have to provide information needed for the assessment of entitlement. Unfortunately, the complexity of a benefit and the confusion among the public about the criteria determining eligibility and any applicable level of support can result in the omission of key information from claims, which, as a result, may fail (or be wrongly assessed).

The complexity of the benefit claims process itself, in particular the length of forms and the amount and level of detail expected to be included when completing them, has long been problematic.[28] A survey of ESA claimants, for example, found among them 'a general feeling surrounding the wider claim process that the amount of paperwork was excessive'.[29] Most benefit claim forms ask for over 100 pieces of information,[30] although some have been simplified, and telephone claiming has been facilitated for many benefits, including JSA, pension credit and state retirement pension. The Work and Pensions Committee has commented that 'claim forms are long and complex, which would appear to be inevitable in an excessively complex benefit system' and, while welcoming efforts by the department to improve forms, has acknowledged 'the scale of the task given the complexity of the system'.[31] The complexity of the claims process has a cost for claimants in terms of not

---

[25] See, eg, Administrative Justice and Tribunals Council, *Principles for Administrative Justice* (London, AJTC, 2010).

[26] Eg, R Plant, 'Citizenship, Rights and Welfare' in A Coote (ed), *The Welfare of Citizens: Developing New Social Rights* (London, IPPR/Rivers Oram Press, 1992) 15–29.

[27] See the Welfare Reform Act 2012, s 2, read with the Universal Credit Regulations 2013 (SI 2013/376), reg 3(3). One exception to this rule is where the other member of the couple is a prisoner.

[28] See A Corden, *Changing Perspectives on Benefit Take*-up (London, HMSO, 1995); J Ritchie and M Chetwynd, *Claimants' Perceptions of the Claim Process*, DSS Research Report No 68 (London, Stationery Office, 1997); House of Commons Committee of Public Accounts, *Difficult Forms: How Government Departments Interact with Citizens* (2003–04, HC 255); House of Commons Work and Pensions Committee, *Decision-Making and Appeals in the Benefits System* (2009–10, HC 313) paras 62–66; and House of Commons Work and Pensions Committee, *Government Support towards the Additional Living Costs of Working-Age Disabled People* (2010–12, HC 1493-I) para 42.

[29] H Barnes et al, *Unsuccessful Employment and Support Allowance Claims: Qualitative Research*, DWP Research Report No 762 (London, DWP, 2011) 14.

[30] National Audit Office, *Department for Work and Pensions: Dealing with the Complexity of the Benefits System*, HC 592 (London, TSO, 2005) para 2.31.

[31] HC Work and Pensions Committee, *Decision-Making and Appeals* (above n 28) para 66.

only time but also effort and stress. For example, evidence shows that 'for disabled people, claiming benefit can require a degree of physical and mental commitment that would tax perfectly fit people'.[32] A potential psychological cost for claimants arises due to the anxiety that is caused by the uncertainty surrounding the outcome of claims. This problem is compounded by the need in some cases to make renewal claims for benefit or claims for an alternative benefit when a period of entitlement of fixed duration expires.[33]

There is evidence that in general claimants may be deterred from claiming benefits due to the perceived bureaucracy that is involved.[34] This is backed up by evidence relating specifically to state pension credit. The perceived difficulty in claiming this benefit has been identified as one of the reasons behind the relative modest take-up rate.[35] While the primary barriers to claiming it are assumptions by potential claimants that they would be ineligible and concerns that receiving it could affect their existing benefit entitlements and possibly leave them worse off, they are 'reinforced by a number of secondary barriers concerning the perceived complex/intrusive nature of the application process'.[36] Similarly, a recent survey for the Joseph Rowntree Foundation covering access to benefits found that while most respondents managed to complete new and renewal claims, 'a majority felt there were too many forms and that benefit claim forms were unclear, repetitive, time-consuming and unnecessarily long'.[37]

The NAO, however, has commented that while there is evidence that complexity 'plays a role in preventing people from claiming support',[38] one cannot be sure what proportion of cases of non-take-up are directly related to it as opposed to the other factors.[39] There may well be more than one reason why a person who is potentially eligible for a benefit does not claim it. For example, a survey of over 2,000 eligible non-recipients of state pension credit found that the main reason for not claiming this payment given by two-thirds of respondents was a belief that they were ineligible for it. Only two per cent cited the length or complicated nature of the application process. Nonetheless, concerns about the application process did reinforce decisions not to claim, and 58 per cent of respondents (rising to 68 per cent among those aged 85 or

---

[32] NAO, *DWP: Dealing with the Complexity of the Benefits System* (above n 30) para 3.10.
[33] F Bennett, M Brewer and J Shaw, *Understanding the Compliance Costs of Benefits and Tax Credits* (London, Institute for Fiscal Studies, 2009) 26.
[34] NAO, *DWP: Dealing with the Complexity of the Benefits System* (above n 30) 42.
[35] House of Commons Work and Pensions Committee, *Tackling Pensioner Poverty* (2008–09, HC 411-I) para 113.
[36] K Bunt, L Adams and C Leo, *Understanding the Relationship between the Barriers and Triggers to Claiming Pension Credit*, Research Report 336 (Corporate Document Services, 2006) 5, available at research.dwp.gov.uk/asd/asd5/rports2005-2006/rrep336.pdf.
[37] D Finn et al, *Delivering Benefits, Tax Credits and Employment Services: Problems for Disadvantaged Users and Potential Solutions* (York, Joseph Rowntree Foundation, 2008) 37.
[38] NAO, *DWP: Dealing with the Complexity of the Benefits System* (above n 30) para 3.12.
[39] Ibid.

over) thought that the process of applying for pension credit would be 'too long or complicated'.[40] The perceived stigma of claiming a benefit and, especially among older members of minority groups, 'cultural or religious factors' may also be influential.[41]

One of the most complex claims processes that has been identified is that relating to disability living allowance (DLA).[42] It has been estimated that a claim form for DLA takes at least two hours to complete, even with the help of an adviser.[43] The forthcoming introduction of personal independence payment (PIP) in place of this benefit (see above chapter two) is being accompanied by measures to ameliorate the difficulties involved in making a claim. The Government says that the regulations on claims for PIP are aimed at simplifying the initial claims process in a way that supports the benefit's overall objective of targeting support on those who 'face the greatest barriers to leading full, active and independent lives'.[44] The process will be simpler in part because of the way entitlement to PIP is assessed. Since all claimants of PIP will have to undergo disability assessment by specialist professionals, they will not be expected, as under DLA, to provide details of the disabling effects of their condition at the initial stage of their claims. They will, however, be required to indicate any claims being made under the special provision for terminally ill persons and to specify any relevant periods spent in hospital or residential care. In addition, they will have to provide 'personal and contact details' and residence/presence circumstances along with payment details (such as bank details).[45] A claimant's explanation of a condition suffered and how it affects him or her will occur at the second stage, when evidence is gathered as part of the assessment. However, the date of the claim will be linked to the first stage; it will be the date when the initial information was received by the department.[46] If the information is not submitted, the claim may, however, be 'defective' and thus not properly made; but provided the claim is properly made within one month of being notified of the defect, it must be treated as having been so made in the first instance.[47]

---

[40] L Radford, L Taylor and C Wilkie, *Pension Credit Eligible Non-recipients: Barriers to Claiming*, DWP Research Report No 819 (London, DWP, 2012) 8 and 11.

[41] Department for Work and Pensions/HM Treasury/Inland Revenue, *Simplicity, Security and Choice: Working and Saving for Retirement* (Cm 5677, 2002) 21. See also the discussion below.

[42] S Royston, *Benefits Simplification and the Customer* (London, DWP, 2007) 36.

[43] Ibid, 39.

[44] Department for Work and Pensions (DWP), *Explanatory Memorandum for the Social Security Advisory Committee: Claims and Payment Regulations for Universal Credit, Personal Independence Payment, Jobseekers* (sic) *Allowance (Contributory) and Employment and Support Allowance (Contributory)* (London, DWP, 2012) 3.

[45] Ibid, 17.

[46] Claims and Payments Regulations 2013 (above n 21) reg 12. Claims for personal independence payment must be made in writing (using an authorised form) (online claims count as being in writing) or by telephone: reg 11(1).

[47] Ibid, regs 11(3) and (4) and 12(2).

As we saw in chapter two, claims for universal credit will be expected to be made online.[48] Online claiming is consistent with the 'digital by default' principle that has been adopted by the Government for claims and their management.[49] There are potential cost savings for government from online claiming, although perhaps not as substantial as has been predicted.[50] Nonetheless, some claimants appear unwilling to claim online;[51] more importantly, this method is likely to present a considerable barrier for many.[52] The House of Commons Work and Pensions Committee has expressed concern that 'some vulnerable claimants will not have the internet access or skills to be able to use the system and so may be unable to obtain their benefit entitlement'.[53] Online claiming could have potential cost implications for those without home internet access, as they might need to travel to public libraries, internet cafés or advice agencies to make online claims,[54] although as noted in chapter two, the DWP is installing information technology devices in Jobcentres. On the other hand, the universal credit system will obviate the need for separate claims to be made under the different income-related benefit schemes which, with the exception of council tax reduction schemes, the new system is replac-

---

[48] Ibid, reg 9 and Sched 2. Claims may be made by telephone only if they fall within 'a class of case for which the Secretary of State accepts telephone claims or where, in any other case, the Secretary of State is willing to do so': reg 9(2). It is expected that even when made via the telephone, an online claim will be prepared by the telephone agent: see DWP, *Explanatory Memorandum for the Social Security Advisory Committee* (above n 44) 7.

[49] See House of Commons Work and Pensions Committee, *Universal Credit Implementation: Meeting the Needs of Vulnerable Claimants* (2012–13, HC 576-I) para 17.

[50] The cost of an online claim for JSA was reportedly almost three times lower than that arising from a telephone claim, according to the JSA Online project cited in A Tarr and D Finn, *Implementing Universal Credit: Will the Reforms Improve the Service for Users?* (York, Joseph Rowntree Foundation/Centre for Social Inclusion, 2012) 19. However, an evaluation of the JSA online 'Trailblazers' operating in three districts for 12 weeks from May 2012 has found that 'shifts to JSA Online may not necessarily be accompanied by cost savings'. One factor is the way that a 'considerable proportion' of online claims omit some key information needed to assess them, making it necessary for officials to contact the claimants for further details: DWP, *An Evaluation of the Jobseeker's Allowance (JSA) Online Digital Trailblazers (One, Two and Three)*, In-House Research No 15 (May 2013), research.dwp.gov.uk/asd/asd5/ih2013-2014/ihr15.pdf, 9–11.

[51] T Tu and S Ginnis, *Work and the Welfare System: A Survey of Benefits and Tax Credits Recipients*, DWP Research Report 800 (London, DWP, 2012) para 7.3.1, who note that 62% of claimants surveyed were willing to apply online; the most common reason for being unwilling was lack of knowledge or ability to use the internet that way.

[52] Tarr and Finn (above n 50) 30–31, reviewing the evidence of the uneven spread of internet usage competence and confidence across difficult social groupings. For example, among disabled people, internet usage rates are 25% lower than across the general population. See also Tu and Ginnis (ibid); and M Rotik and L Perry, *Insight to Support Universal Credit User-Centred Design*, DWP Research Report No 799 (2012).

[53] HC Work and Pensions Committee, *Universal Credit Implementation: Vulnerable Claimants* (above n 49) para 29.

[54] Bennett, Brewer and Shaw (above n 33) 19; Social Security Advisory Committee (SSAC), *The Draft Universal Credit Regulations 2013; the Benefit Cap (Housing Benefit) Regulations 2012 (SI 2012 No 2994); the Draft Universal Credit, Personal Independence Payment, Jobseeker's Allowance and Employment and Support Allowance (Claims and Payments) Regulations 2013* (London, Stationery Office, 2012) para 7.5.

ing. The Government argues that this can be expected to improve the take-up rate.[55] Nonetheless, the amount of information that will need to be provided when making this single claim will obviously be considerable.

The House of Commons Work and Pensions Committee found evidence that applications for welfare support have 'a degree of complexity' that tends to preclude online claiming by many people.[56] If, as will be the case with universal credit, the various factors that determine the level of entitlement are very wide and penetrate deeply into claimants' circumstances, the burdens attached to claiming are unlikely to be reduced. Moreover, the problems experienced by those most likely to face barriers in bringing claims, such as people with mental health problems or learning or language difficulties,[57] will be just as acute.[58] The DWP does, however, provide support with translation of forms and other information. In addition, the Department will set up a three-way call-back with an interpreter, but as he or she will not have access to the claim documentation, this can hinder the support.[59] Nevertheless, the previous claims regulations made some allowance for people with various kinds of difficulty through exemption from the requirements to comply with the instructions on the claim form and to furnish information or evidence required by it. This applied where a claimant was unable to meet these requirements due to a 'physical, learning, mental or communication difficulty' and 'it is not reasonably practicable for the claimant to obtain assistance from another person to complete the form or obtain the information or evidence'.[60] Under the new regulations, however, no prescribed exceptions are set out; such information or evidence as the Secretary of State 'considers appropriate' may be required from the claimant,[61] which obviously appears to give the Secretary of State some discretion over the matter.

Claimants are also likely to be adversely affected by the firm time limits for claims. The previous rules governing claims restricted, in some cases quite severely, any backdating of benefit and limited it to specific grounds.[62] The rules had originally been more flexible and had enabled claims to be backdated on the basis of 'good cause' for late claiming. But they were later changed due to the '[a]dministrative complexity in dealing with back-dated

---

[55] DWP, *Welfare that Works* (above n 3) ch 2, para 16.

[56] HC Work and Pensions Committee, *Universal Credit Implementation: Vulnerable Claimants* (above n 49) para 21.

[57] Royston (above n 42) Executive Summary.

[58] It has been recommended that claimants with learning difficulties should be offered a face-to-face interview when making a claim for benefit: Royston (above n 42) 70. Whether this happens under universal credit remains to be seen.

[59] Ibid, 70–71.

[60] In the Social Security (Claims and Payments) Regulations 1987 (SI 1987/1968), reg 4(1A) and (1B)(a).

[61] Claims and Payments Regulations 2013 (above n 21) reg 37(2). There are separate general provisions governing persons 'unable to act' (reg 57), as under the 1987 Regulations (ibid), reg 33.

[62] In the Social Security (Claims and Payments) Regulations 1987 (SI 1987/1968), reg 19 and Sched 4.

claims'.[63] The provisions thereafter prescribed various factors that in effect were recognised as constituting a good cause for a late claim. Like these provisions, the new regulations adopt a restrictive basis for time limits, though with some key differences from the arrangements they are replacing, including a slightly more flexible allowance for health or disability factors that hinder the making of claim.[64] One significant difference is that they do not specify many of the factors (such as a domestic emergency, the death of a close relative or the receipt of misleading advice from an officer of the DWP) that previously could give rise to an extension of time.

The Social Security Advisory Committee (SSAC) consulted on the draft regulations and reported that a large number of those providing submissions considered the rules too restrictive and that they could cause hardship, particularly since universal credit payments were to be made one month in arrears.[65] The SSAC recommended the retention of the prescribed good cause grounds in some cases – for example, where a claimant received misleading benefits advice – but this was rejected on the somewhat unconvincing grounds that the 'dynamic online service' for claiming universal credit would enable claims to be made straight away, with the result that backdating would not be needed in such situations.[66]

Providing help and assistance to claimants may be regarded as an important means of enabling them to deal with the complexity of making claims for benefit. Policy in this area has been focused on telephone helplines operated by contact centres, although this form of support is 'not suitable for all customers'[67] and may not be of value where 'complex financial issues and details of personal circumstances' have to be dealt with[68] or for those with specific communication difficulties.[69] Research has found that claimant experience of

---

[63]   M Rowland and R White, *Social Security Legislation (2012/13), Volume III: Administration, Adjudication and the European Dimension* (London, Sweet and Maxwell, 2012) para 2.118.

[64]   Under the first version of the draft regulations, the Secretary of State had to extend time for claiming universal credit if, inter alia, the claimant 'has a physical, learning, mental or language disability and as a result of that disability the claimant was not able to make a claim in the manner prescribed in regulation' and as a result of their disability 'could not be expected to make the claim earlier' (draft Claims and Payments Regulations 2012, reg 24(2) and (3)). However, in the final version, the first part of this ground was simplified to 'the claimant has a disability': Claims and Payments Regulations 2013 (above n 21) reg 26(2) and (3)(b). The maximum period of extension which may be granted by the Secretary of State for a universal credit claim is one month: reg 26(2). In the case of JSA, it is a maximum of three months: reg 29(2). ESA claimants have up to three months from the start of the period of incapacity for which they are claiming in which to submit their claim: reg 28. There is no provision for an extension of time for a personal independence payment claim (reg 27), but the date of the claim will be the date of the notification of an intention to make a claim if the claim is then made by non-electronic or non-telephonic means within one month thereafter or within 'such longer period as the Secretary of State considers reasonable': reg 12(1)(c).

[65]   SSAC (above n 54) paras 7.21–7.22.

[66]   Ibid, 'Statement by the Secretary of State for Work and Pensions', para 110.

[67]   NAO, *DWP: Dealing with the Complexity of the Benefits System* (above n 30) para 4.25.

[68]   J Millar, 'Simplification, Modernisation and Social Security' (2005) 13(1) *Benefits* 10, 12.

[69]   Finn et al (above n 37) 17.

the telephone-based services has been negative at times due to lengthy waiting times for calls to be answered or failure by the department to call back;[70] but there have been some improvements.[71] The cost of making calls to the department by mobile phone (since such calls are free only if made from a landline) is another problem.[72] Also, many contact centre staff follow a set script in dealing with claimants on the telephone, and if a matter falls outside the script, especially if the member of staff lacks the necessary knowledge relevant to the claim, there is an increased risk of error.[73] It can also leave claimants feeling disempowered, unable to explain their problem properly.[74] The House of Commons Work and Pensions Committee has called for staff to be 'better trained than they are now, to provide a more informed and flexible service to claimants and save work further down the line'.[75]

The latest DWP estimates of take-up of income-related benefits, covering 2009–10,[76] show that a considerable amount of benefit was unclaimed and that millions of potential recipients lost out, including 1.2–1.5 million people of pension age who did not claim state pension credit despite being entitled to it. Across the system as a whole, benefits estimated to total between £6.44–11.77 billion were unclaimed in that year, meaning a take-up rate by expenditure of 77–84 per cent. The take-up by caseload (based on a comparison between the numbers receiving a benefit and the numbers who would receive it if they claimed their entitlement) for individual benefits[77] varies quite widely. In the case of pension credit, it ranged in 2009–10 between 62 and 68 per cent, but the take-up of the savings credit element of this benefit was only 43–48 per cent, a significant shortfall. The take-up rate by caseload for other benefits was as follows:

- council tax benefit: 62–69 per cent;
- housing benefit: 78–84 per cent; and
- income-based JSA: 60–67 per cent (although single people without children were significantly more likely to claim than couples with children).

The take-up rate of council tax benefit among pensioners (54–61 per cent) was almost 20 points lower than among non-pensioners.

---

[70] Calling back but being unable to reach the claimant is also a problem for the Department; avoiding it would 'save time and money': Royston (above n 42) 66.

[71] Finn et al (above n 37) 16.

[72] Bennett, Brewer and Shaw (above n 33) 22–23.

[73] NAO, *DWP: Dealing with the Complexity of the Benefits System* (above n 30) para 4.24.

[74] Finn et al (above n 37) 42.

[75] House of Commons Work and Pensions Committee, *Benefits Simplification* (2006–07, HC 463-I) para 226.

[76] Department for Work and Pensions (DWP), *Income Related Benefits: Estimates of Take-Up in 2009–10* (23 February 2012), www.gov.uk/government/publications/income-related-benefits-estimates-of-take-up.

[77] The DWP says that an overall total of take-up across the relevant benefits as a whole is not possible on the model it uses.

Lack of awareness or understanding of a benefit or benefits is another factor in non-take-up – and one which is linked to complexity.[78] The Government argues that one of the reasons that universal credit is likely to lead to improved take-up of benefit is that it is 'much simpler' than the array of separate benefits that it is replacing, making it easier for people to understand whether they may be entitled.[79] There is evidence of misunderstanding in respect of, for example, in-work provision, such as working tax credit or extended payment of housing benefit for those who take up employment.[80] Another area of confusion has been the 'linking rules' for various benefits whereby periods in employment may or may not mean that fresh claims for benefit need to be made when such periods end.[81] It is also evident in relation to benefits claimed by older people,[82] as illustrated by the take-up rate for council tax benefit among this group (above). When the NAO examined the barriers to benefit claims by people of pension age, it found that the influence of complexity was felt through a general reluctance among such people to make a claim unless feeling certain they would qualify, confirmed by 88 per cent of respondents to the survey.[83] Thus the deterrent effect of complexity may often be exacerbated by pensioners' cultural resistance to claiming something that they perceive (wrongly) they may not 'deserve'. One way of overcoming this could be to adopt the practice of giving all claimants a benefit 'check' to identify their entitlement. Sue Royston found that such a check could be 'one of the most important ways in which the complexities of the benefits system could be masked for customers'.[84]

---

[78] NAO, *DWP: Dealing with the Complexity of the Benefits System* (above n 30) para 3.11.

[79] DWP, *Welfare that Works* (above n 3) ch 2, para 16.

[80] G Elam et al, *Getting the Message Across*, DSS Research Report No 85 (Leeds, Corporate Document Services, 1998) 19. The DWP figures above show that the overall take-up rate for housing benefit (HB) among those in employment was only 40–50%, compared with 93–97% among those not in employment: DWP, *Income Related Benefits: Estimates* (above n 76) Table 4.4. However, it is likely that the very high take-up rate among unemployed claimants has increased due to the fact that when DWP-administered income-related benefits have been claimed by telephone, the DWP prepares the claimant's housing benefit claim at the same time and, once a signed copy is returned by the claimant, forwards it to the local authority. This must surely have boosted the take-up rate.

[81] Social Exclusion Unit, *Mental Health and Social Exclusion* (London, Office of the Deputy Prime Minister, 2004) 60–61.

[82] National Audit Office, *Tackling Pensioner Poverty: Encouraging Take-Up of Entitlements (Report by the Comptroller and Auditor General)* (2002–03, HC 37) paras 2.4. See also C Talbot et al, *Encouraging Take-Up: Awareness of and Attitudes to Pension Credit*, Research Report No 234 (Leeds, Corporate Document Services, 2005).

[83] NAO, *Tackling Pensioner Poverty* (ibid) para 2.5.

[84] Royston (above n 42) para 1.1.1.

III. Administration of Claims

Once a claim for benefit or credit has been made, the claimant is at a stage in his or her journey equivalent to being at the 'gateway', awaiting a decision on admission to the system and on what terms. The gateway analogy was adopted by the Labour Government in the late 1990s when it put forward the idea of a 'single gateway into the benefits system for all those of working age',[85] as a means of reinforcing the expected commitment on the part of many benefit recipients to seek and prepare for entry to employment. While a claimant waits at the gateway for a decision, the focus shifts onto the administrative officials charged with the responsibility of assessing the claim.

The administrative framework for decision-making was changed by the Social Security Act 1998 to reduce the complexity and 'confusion' for both staff and claimants arising from the existence of different decision-making roles and officers.[86] In particular, it ended the separate roles of independent adjudication officer and social fund officer and ensured that all benefit decisions were those of the Secretary of State, made by officials working in the relevant DWP agencies (Jobcentre Plus and the Pension, Disability and Carers Service),[87] although decisions about tax credits have been the responsibility of the Commissioners for Her Majesty's Revenue and Customs (HMRC),[88] and those relating to housing benefit and council tax benefit have been under the jurisdiction of local authorities.[89] As noted in chapter two, universal credit will combine within the DWP all these areas of administration, although council tax relief will remain with local authorities under local council tax support schemes, as will some of the provision currently made via the discretionary social fund.

Cost

One of the reasons that complex benefits are comparatively expensive to administer is the greater time that assessment and processing of claims may

[85] Department for Education and Employment/Department of Social Security, *A New Contract for Welfare: The Gateway to Work* (Cm 4102, 1998) ch 1, para 2.
[86] Department of Social Security (DSS), *Improving Decision-Making and Appeals in Social Security* (Cm 3328, 1996) para 3.4.
[87] Jobcentre Plus has responsibility for administering most welfare benefits. Those handled by the Pension, Disability and Carer Service comprise state retirement pension, pension credit, attendance allowance/disability living allowance and carer's allowance.
[88] See, eg, Tax Credits Act 2002, s 2.
[89] Social Security Administration Act 1992, ss 134 and 139.

take.[90] As noted previously, means-tested benefits are particularly problematic in this regard. Through its targeting function, means-testing can restrict entitlement and thus limit public expenditure, but at the same time, the unit cost of administering individual claims tends to be highest for these benefits. This is 'largely due to the greater complexity of assessing eligibility' and the necessity of dealing with changes in claimants' financial circumstances.[91] DWP figures, set out in Table 3, show the contrasting levels of cost between the different categories of benefit and within them. It can be seen that the unit cost of administering means-tested benefits is significantly higher than that

Table 3: Unit Cost of Administering Means-Tested Benefits (2010–11)

Type of Benefit	Type of Claim	Unit Cost (in £)
Means-Tested		
Housing and council tax benefit	All	163
Tax credits	All	78
Income Support	New	181
	Existing	116
Pension Credit	New	351
	Existing	47
JSA	New	92
	Existing	306
Carer's Allowance	New	121
	Existing	33
Non-Means-Tested (Examples)		
Child Benefit	All	11
State Retirement Pension	New	91
	Existing	14

Note: Adapted from NAO, *Means Testing* (above n 18), citing DWP, 'Departmental Resource Accounts: Updating the Costs of Housing and Council Tax Benefit Administration', DWP Research Report 705 (2010). The unit costs for income support, JSA, Pension Credit and Carer's Allowance are described as preliminary departmental estimates and 'include an element of recharged central costs from the [DWP] and the agency responsible': NAO, *Means Testing* (above n 18) 19. The costs for tax credits and child benefit are described as 'based on dividing total administration costs by claimant estimates', possibly making them not directly comparable with estimates for other benefits. In the case of new claims for JSA, the cost 'includes processing and excludes initial interviews and job search reviews'.

[90] NAO, *DWP: Dealing with the Complexity of the Benefits System* (above n 30) para 3.39.
[91] NAO, *Means Testing* (above n 18) para 2.11.

for other benefits, although this is offset to some extent where entitlement is largely passported and consequently the examination of individual circumstances is reduced (as has, for example, been the case with regard to entitlement to housing benefit where a claimant is in receipt of income support or income-based JSA).

The administrative costs of complexity also include those involved in correcting errors.[92] Moreover, some errors will result in appeals, and the average administrative cost per social security appeal was estimated in 2005 – when over 250,000 appeals were received, and nearly 300,000 cases were decided – to be £340.[93] Not all of this cost can be attributed to error at the initial decision stage, however, since over two thirds of appeals are unsuccessful (see below chapter four).

Error and Fraud

Government has in the past declared, 'One of the primary aims of an efficient, modern benefits system should be to provide *the right amount of benefit to the right person, at the right time, every time*.'[94] In analysing the framework for decision-making within the social security system, Roy Sainsbury has invited us to imagine ourselves as a social security claimant who has completed a claim form supplied by the relevant agency (as noted above, the claim is now likely to be made via telephone or the internet) and is awaiting a decision. Sainsbury poses the question to the imagined claimant: 'Can you, sitting at home, be confident that the unknown officials working on your claim will actually reach the correct decision?'[95] As he has pointed out, the claimant may assume that, having provided the information about his or her circumstances required by the form, a 'single, unequivocal decision should surely result'; but in many cases, the decision-making process does not produce a correct decision.[96] Thus, as Sainsbury has argued, processes for overturning incorrect decisions, especially the appeal system (discussed later), are important. Sainsbury has not analysed the factors that underlie incorrect decisions, but as noted at various points in this book, there is much evidence that the complexity of individual benefits and in the rules governing entitlement is an important factor. Accurate decision-making hinges on officials understanding the rules and applying them correctly.

The Government has in the past acknowledged the need for decision-makers to be properly trained and to 'have an appropriate degree of expertise

[92] NAO, *DWP: Dealing with the Complexity of the Benefits System* (above n 30) 'Executive Summary', para 22.

[93] National Audit Office, *Citizen Redress: What Citizens Can Do if Things Go Wrong with Public Services*, HC 21 (London, Stationery Office, 2005) Figs 13 and 14.

[94] DSS, *Improving Decision-Making and Appeals* (above n 86) para 3.1 (original emphasis).

[95] R Sainsbury, 'Social Security Decision-Making and Appeals' in N Harris et al (eds), *Social Security Law in Context* (Oxford, Oxford University Press, 2000) 207.

[96] Ibid.

and knowledge in the application of the law, within the relevant subject area'.[97] Officials in any event have the benefit of guidance in the form of the 'Decision Makers' Guide', noted in chapter three, along with other internal guidance and support. Nonetheless, as we have seen, the rules that officials have to apply are complex, and in many cases, a wide range of factors must be taken into account in reaching decisions. As the then Department of Social Security commented in the mid 1990s, when discussing how social security decision-making could be improved, 'The types of decisions to be taken in future will be no less complex than the individual rules applying to specific benefits.'[98] The administration of complex legislation is difficult, and there can be no certainty that the process will be error-free.

The identification of a link between complexity and error in decision-making is not of recent origin.[99] Such an association is acknowledged as well in other fields, such as immigration.[100] The issue was examined in some depth by the NAO, which found that the errors in the social security system resulting from complexity are caused by both claimants and benefit staff.[101] The types of error made by staff that can be associated with complexity include 'incorrect considerations of fundamental entitlement, problems with the interfaces between benefits systems, incorrect attribution, arithmetic or transcription errors, and the applicable amount (eg, partner or dependants incorrectly omitted/included in the assessment)'.[102] The complexity of various legal concepts and processes and with regard to the interpretation of evidence relevant to a claim leads to inconsistencies of outcome and in some cases to decisions that, if there is an appeal, are particularly likely to be overturned.[103] A process of internal reconsideration of decisions was introduced after 1999, in part to enable errors to be rectified before a case goes to appeal, via a 'second look',[104] which may result in a decision being revised.[105] However, as will be discussed in chapter five, the effectiveness of such 'second looks' is questionable.

According to the NAO, to get a decision right in an individual case would require that the decision-maker has 'seen all the necessary evidence, asked any necessary clarifying questions, correctly determined the facts of the case and considered and applied the appropriate statute and case law – a complex

---

[97] DSS, *Improving Decision-Making and Appeals* (above n 86) para 4.14.

[98] Ibid.

[99] See, for example, R Cranston, *Legal Foundations of the Welfare State* (London, Weidenfeld and Nicolson, 1985) 217; and DSS, *Improving Decision-Making and Appeals* (above n 86) para 3.2.

[100] Home Office (UK Border Agency), *Simplifying Immigration Law: The Draft Bill* (Cm 7730, 2009) para.1.4.

[101] NAO, *DWP: Dealing with the Complexity of the Benefits System* (above n 30) para 3.4.

[102] Ibid, para 3.5.

[103] Ibid, para 3.17.

[104] DSS, *Improving Decision-Making and Appeals* (above n 86) paras 4.16–4.23.

[105] Social Security Act 1998, s 9. See also N Wikeley, 'Decision-Making and Appeals under the Social Security Act 1998' (1998) 5 *Journal of Social Security Law* 104; and the Social Security and Child Support (Decisions and Appeals) Regulations 1999 (SI 1999/991), as amended, regs 3–5.

combination'.[106] As we saw in chapter two, however, not all types of case are conducive to a single 'right' outcome, particularly over issues related to the definition of disabling conditions and the extent of the needs to which they give rise. In any event, it is clear that the law is not always correctly applied. For example, it was reported that in 2011–12, errors in social fund decisions arising from actual or suspected departmental non-compliance with regulations or directions[107] affected £30.33 million of expenditure (just under 1.0 per cent of overall expenditure out of the fund), although this represented a significant improvement on the previous year, when the equivalent amount was £58.87 million (1.41 per cent).[108]

Claimants also contribute to error. Errors arise in particular from their failure to provide relevant information due to ignorance or misunderstanding.[109] If they are unsure about which factors trigger or enhance entitlement, claimants are likely to fail to bring relevant circumstances to officials' attention. As noted in chapter two, such failure can extend to not reporting relevant changes in their circumstances while in receipt of benefit or credit.[110] Resultant errors can be costly for claimants, in terms of receiving inadequate levels of support due to underpayment or being required to reimburse overpaid benefit.

The DWP has estimated that in 2011–12, error by officials led to the overpayment of a total of £800 million (0.5 per cent of total benefit expenditure) and underpayment of £400 million (0.3 per cent),[111] while error attributable to claimants gave rise to a total overpayment of £1.3 billion (0.8 per cent) and to underpayment totalling £900 million (0.5 per cent).[112] These are clearly significant amounts, even if they concern only a small percentage of total expenditure. Error rates varied across different benefits, as shown in Table 4.

---

[106] NAO, *DWP: Dealing with the Complexity of the Benefits System* (above n 30) para 3.16.

[107] Directions made by the Secretary of State under a statutory power (Social Security Contributions and Benefits Act 1992, s 140, as amended) specify various matters relating to payments out of the discretionary social fund, such as when someone will be eligible, which items will be excluded and how much can be paid out.

[108] National Audit Office, *2011–12 Social Fund White Paper Account: Report by the Comptroller and Auditor General* (London, National Audit Office, 2012) 3.

[109] NAO, *DWP: Dealing with the Complexity of the Benefits System* (above n 30) para 3.6. See further below ch 5, s IV concerning the ways that inadequate information elicited from claimants via the DLA claim form can affect the outcome of paper hearings of appeals.

[110] It has been suggested that while over 80 per cent of error and fraud in relation to tax credits relates to changes in claimants' circumstances, HMRC could do more to alleviate the problem. One aspect of the problem is that 'if a parent notifies HMRC that their child has left school at 16 for the purposes of Child Benefit, this change is not registered for tax credit purposes': House of Commons Committee of Public Accounts, *HM Revenue and Customs: Tax Credits Error and Fraud* (2013–14, HC 135) 5.

[111] 'Error by officials' is defined as occurring where benefit 'has been paid incorrectly due to inaction, delay or a mistaken assessment by the DWP, a Local Authority or Her Majesty's Revenue and Customs': DWP, *Fraud and Error in the Benefit System: Preliminary 2011/12 Estimates (Great Britain) Revised Edition* (6 June 2012), statistics.dwp.gov.uk/asd/asd2/fem/fem_preliminary_1112_revised.pdf, para 1.16.

[112] 'Error attributable to claimants' is defined as: 'The customer has provided inaccurate or incomplete information, or failed to report a change in their circumstances, but there is no fraudulent intent on the customer's part': DWP, *Fraud and Error in the Benefit System 2011/12* (ibid).

Table 4: Estimated Underpayment and Overpayment of Key Benefits (2011–12), Shown as Total Amount and Percentage of Total Benefit Expenditure

Benefit	Overpayment				Underpayment			
	Customer Error		*Official Error*		*Customer Error*		*Official Error*	
Income support	1.0%	£70m	0.8%	£50m	0.5%	£40m	0.3%	£30m
JSA	0.6%	£30m	1.7%	£80m	0.1%	£10m	0.4%	£10m
Pension credit	2.0%	£170m	2.1%	£170m	0.9%	£70m	0.8%	£70m
Housing benefit	2.6%	£600m	0.4%	£90m	1.0%	£220m	0.2%	£50m
Incapacity benefits	0.9%	£40m	1.2%	£60m	0.0%	£0m	0.7%	£30m
DLA	0.6%	£80m	0.8%	£100m	2.4%	£300m	0.1%	£10m
State retirement pension	0.1%	£60m	0.0%	£40m	0.0%	£0m	0.2%	£150m
Carer's allowance	1.0%	£20m	0.6%	£10m	0.1%	£0.1m	0.0%	£0m

Note: Drawn from data in DWP, *Fraud and Error in the Benefit System 2011/12* (above n 111). The 0.0% official error rate for underpaid retirement pension is as per the official figures and appears to be rounded down from the actual percentage (0.05%).

The impact of customer error leading to overpayment was greatest in respect of two means-tested benefits – pension credit and housing benefit. But where underpayment was concerned, it was highest in relation to DLA, which perhaps reflects the particularly high level of misunderstanding of this (non-means-tested) benefit among claimants. Where error by the administration was concerned, again it was in the area of means-tested benefit that it was most prominent, in relation to both underpayment and overpayment, although such error also caused an above-average level of overpayment of (largely non-means-tested) incapacity benefits. The extent to which the complexity of state pension credit is a factor in the high official error rate for this benefit is unclear, but it is perhaps significant that in 2011–12, there were 70,000 claimants who were underpaid due to incorrect uprating of elements of the benefit.[113] The DWP reported that in 2008–09, additional staff who 'lacked experience in administering a complex benefit system' were recruited, but interestingly, there was 'no evidence that new staff were more likely to

---

[113] Ibid, para 5.12.

make mistakes than their long-serving colleagues'[114] – an observation that can obviously be read two ways!

It is perhaps reassuring that as a percentage of overall benefit expenditure, overpayment due to official error across the main benefits has in fact steadily declined, from 0.8 per cent to 0.5 per cent since 2006–07.[115] Overpayment due to customer error has remained a constant level over this period (0.8 per cent).[116] Levels of claimant and official error in relation to tax credits administered by HMRC have been similar to those relating to social security benefits and by 2008 had fallen, compared with 2006.[117] More recently, however, HMRC has reportedly 'made little progress in reducing the amount of money it loses due to error and fraud in tax credits'.[118]

The main two aspects of pension credit that produced overpayment due to customer error in 2011–12 were income (in the form of occupational or private pensions) and capital, arguably two of the most complex aspects from a claimant's perspective.[119] Capital, the assessment of which can be notoriously complex, was the leading cause of overpayment of this benefit due to official error[120] and was also the most frequent cause of underpayment of JSA due to customer error.[121] In the case of housing benefit, the largest cause of both overpayment and underpayment due to customer error related to earnings and employment,[122] which again is covered by particularly complex rules. A final figure for that year that is suggestive of the link between complexity and error relates to the total amount in underpaid premiums[123] due to errors by officials: across all the income-related benefits, the total was £42 million – more than twice as high as that relating to any other single area of underpayment.[124] Access to premiums is mostly triggered by entitlement to a particular rate of another benefit, a form of inter-relationship associated with what was identified in chapter two as 'extrinsic complexity'.

The relationship between complexity and fraud was referred to briefly in chapter one. Across the UK benefits system as a whole, an estimated £1.1 billion was paid out as a consequence of fraud in 2011–12.[125] The NAO has stated, 'While it is widely recognised that complexity generates error, the link with benefit fraud appears less clear.'[126] Nevertheless, means-tested benefits,

[114] Ibid, para 5.9.
[115] Ibid, Fig 3.3.
[116] Ibid.
[117] HM Revenue and Customs, *Reducing Error and Fraud in Tax Credits* (London, HMRC, 2008) 14.
[118] HC Committee of Public Accounts, *Tax Credits Error and Fraud* (above n 110) 5.
[119] DWP, *Fraud and Error in the Benefit System 2011/12* (above n 111) Tables 6.3 and 6.4.
[120] Ibid.
[121] Ibid, Table 6.6.
[122] Ibid, Tables 6.3 and 6.6.
[123] These are needs-related additions in respect of factors such as disability or being a carer: see, eg, Income Support (General) Regulations 1987 (SI 1987/1967), Sched 2.
[124] DWP, *Fraud and Error in the Benefit System 2011/12* (above n 111) Table 6.7.
[125] Ibid, 2.
[126] NAO, *DWP: Dealing with the Complexity of the Benefits System* (above n 30) para 3.7.

which are assessed on information provided by claimants and which, as we have seen, are governed by some of the most complex parts of the legislation, are considered particularly susceptible to fraud leading to overpaid benefit.[127] The official figures show that these benefits had the highest levels of fraud in 2011–12: fraud accounted for some 2.8 per cent of the total amount of JSA[128] that was paid out to claimants and 2.7 per cent of the income support total, although in fact, carer's allowance (which is not means-tested) had the highest rate (3.9 per cent).[129] These rates are significantly higher than the overall rate of payments resulting from fraud across the main benefits (0.7 per cent).[130]

The NAO considers that 'the sheer amount of information to be processed in the context of means-testing requires the Department to take certain statements on trust, which may persuade some people that fraud is a risk worth taking'.[131] Furthermore, the burdens involved in reporting changes in circumstances, discussed above in chapter two, are said to 'encourage people to "fall into" fraud'.[132] Research has indicated that claimants decide not to report such changes because they see doing so as involving too much trouble, although there may also be concern about how the changes might affect their entitlement.[133] Gráinne McKeever, however, rejects the idea that 'those committing fraud are doing so as a result of familiarity with the rules of social security and their most vulnerable areas', citing the 'complexity of the system' and 'continuing evidence of claimant ignorance of social security obligations'.[134] Yet she accepts that in addition to a lack of understanding of the system, some claimants tend to be unwilling to 'engage with it beyond what is absolutely necessary to make their claim'.[135]

The association between complexity and both fraud and error is referred to at some length in the universal credit White Paper. There is a direct link in the sense that the 'complex and fragmented nature of the system' generates error, and administrators, when applying the rules governing means-testing, must 'rely on people to let us know about their earnings, savings and non-financial circumstances . . . [which] creates opportunities for fraud and error'.[136] The Government claims that replacing an array of benefit schemes with a single

---

[127] Ibid.
[128] This seems to include contribution-based and income-based JSA, but the vast majority of JSA payments are of the latter (means-tested) form.
[129] DWP, *Fraud and Error in the Benefit System 2011/12* (above n 111) Table 2.1.
[130] Ibid.
[131] NAO, *DWP: Dealing with the Complexity of the Benefits System* (above n 30) para 3.9.
[132] HM Revenue and Customs and the Department for Work and Pensions, *Tackling Fraud and Error in the Benefit and Tax Credit Systems* (London, HMRC/DWP, 2010) ch 2, para 8.
[133] A Irvine, J Davidson and R Sainsbury, *Reporting Changes in Circumstances: Tackling Error in the Benefits System*, DWP Research Report No 497 (2008) ch 4.
[134] G McKeever, 'Balancing Rights and Responsibilities: The Case of Social Security Fraud' (2009) 16(3) *Journal of Social Security Law* 139, 146.
[135] Ibid, 146–47.
[136] DWP, *Welfare that Works* (above n 3) ch 5, para 4.

universal credit and thereby driving down the level of complexity in the system will make it 'much easier for recipients to understand and establish entitlement to payments, meaning much of the error which is currently caused by the complicated interactions between different benefits will be reduced'.[137] Similarly, the use of an 'integrated computer system with integrated process-ing teams' will reduce the fraud and error that is due to the current 'complex interactions' between such systems.[138] Combining benefit/credit administra-tion within one agency (the DWP) will also, it is claimed, avoid duplication of fraud and error policing.[139]

IV. Conclusion

There is considerable evidence that complexity has posed a significant problem for both claimants and administrators, through its impact on the take-up of benefits, the claims process and initial decision-making on claims. Complexity has exacerbated the difficulties people experience in submitting claims – which can inhibit claims from being made, thus affecting overall take-up rates. It is implicated in error in decision-making, often resulting in overpayment or underpayment of benefit. Error arises from factors such as claimants' failure to provide sufficient or correct information and the misapplication of complex rules by officials. There is also evidence of the contribution that complexity makes to administrative costs and to benefit fraud. If, as McKeever has argued when discussing error and fraud in the social security system, the integrity of such a system must in part 'rest on the ability to guide individuals through the maze of relevant provisions',[140] the problems noted above suggest that the UK benefits system has fallen short. However, tackling the problems successfully may be dependent on addressing complexity by changing the system itself.

Current structural changes and the rationalisation of rules as a result of the introduction of universal credit in Britain should at least alleviate some of the problems associated with complexity in the claims process. Rather than having to apply for individual benefits or tax credits, a claimant will be able to make a single claim that will be governed by common rules. However, as noted in chapter two, localisation of council tax relief and some forms of

---

[137] Ibid, para 5.
[138] Ibid, para 6.
[139] Ibid, ch 4, para 32.
[140] G McKeever, 'Social Citizenship and Social Security Fraud in the UK and Australia' (2012) 46(4) *Social Policy and Administration* 465, 471.

assistance previously available via the social fund will undermine the benefits to some extent, and online claiming may also create difficulties. As the House of Commons Communities and Local Government Committee has concluded, having to make a claim for universal credit to the DWP and a separate claim for council tax support to a local authority will 'cause a level of confusion for some claimants'.[141] Moreover, the Government has been criticised for failing to make adequate arrangements to meet the need which some claimants will have for 'face-to-face support when making a claim for Universal Credit'.[142]

The introduction of universal credit is also likely to increase the need and demand for independent advice services. The Government has been urged to provide further support for the advice sector. Increased advice services are seen by the House of Commons Work and Pensions Committee as necessary to 'ensure a successful implementation' of the new benefit.[143] The Government has acknowledged that the introduction of universal credit will necessitate additional advice for claimants, and whilst some funding has been allocated for this purpose to the advice sector,[144] much is being pinned on the development of a local support services framework, based on local partnerships but focused on specific objectives around the idea of a 'single claimant journey':

> The ultimate aim of those providing services under the framework will be the creation of a 'single claimant journey' from dependency to self-sufficiency and work readiness, as far as is possible, behind which all service providers should be aligned. To this end, DWP and delivery partners will identify specific outcomes required by individual claimants to help move them closer to the labour market and financial independence. [For c]laimants with more complex problems . . . the proper alignment of services behind a single claimant journey will be essential in moving them closer to independence, workforce participation and full social inclusion.[145]

This could, of course, be viewed by some as a cynical attempt to control rather than aid claimants. Nevertheless, the specific references to assistance with online claiming, money advice and alternative payment arrangements,[146]

---

[141] House of Commons Communities and Local Government Committee, *Implementation of Welfare Reform by Local Authorities* (2012–13, HC 833) para 97.

[142] HC Work and Pensions Committee, *Universal Credit Implementation: Vulnerable Claimants* (above n 49) para 42.

[143] Ibid, para 51.

[144] The Government's response to the call by the Work and Pensions Select Committee in *Universal Credit Implementation: Vulnerable Claimants* (above n 49) included reference to a £65 million Advice Services Transition Fund created by the Cabinet Office and the Big Lottery Fund 'to support the advice sector across the UK, between April 2013 and April 2015, develop new ways of working such as in partnership with other organisations': Department for Work and Pensions, *Government Response to the House of Commons Work and Pensions Select Committee's Third Report of Session 2012–13, 'Universal Credit Implementation: Meeting the Needs of Vulnerable Claimants'* (Cm 8537, 2013) paras 26 and 27.

[145] Department for Work and Pensions (DWP), *Universal Credit: Local Support Services Framework* (London, DWP, 2013) 11.

[146] Such arrangements might include, for example, more frequent payment of universal credit, since payment on the standard monthly basis may make budgeting difficult for some claimants.

together with triage at the initial contact stage,[147] are at least consonant with the broad notion of helping claimants to take some control over their respective journeys, if not exactly empowering them.

[147] DWP, *Universal Credit: Local Support Services Framework* (above n 145) 11–14.

5

Challenges to Decisions

I. Introduction

The next possible stage in the claimant journey with which we are concerned involves challenges to decisions that are adverse to the claimant. While not all claimants choose to exercise their rights to challenge decisions, increasing numbers are doing so. The principal mechanism for such challenges is an appeal to the First-tier Tribunal. This involves a process that is intended to be straightforward and relatively easily accessible and is expected, in the post-Leggatt era,[1] to put users' interests to the fore. Yet it too has complex elements, particularly from the perspective of appellants, who most frequently will be novices in this sphere. This chapter examines the impact of complexity in the arrangements governing challenges to benefit decisions and includes discussion of the reforms to the system aimed at improving the quality and independence of tribunal adjudication while also facilitating improved accessibility and appellant participation.

An appeal against a decision on a claim, including a decision superseding an initial decision, lies to the First-tier Tribunal (Social Entitlement Chamber), which has appellate jurisdiction over most social security and tax credit decisions on or affecting entitlement.[2] A right of appeal in the British

---

[1] See discussion of the Leggatt Report above ch 4, s I.

[2] Social Security Act 1998, s 12. The decisions against which no right of appeal lies are listed in Sched 2 to this Act, read with the Social Security and Child Support (Decisions and Appeals) Regulations 1999 (SI 1999/991), Sched 2; and the Child Benefit and Guardian's Allowance (Decisions and Appeals) Regulations 2003 (SI 2003/916), Sched 2. They include a decision as to: the day and time a jobseeker should attend at a job centre; the member of a couple who should be the claimant in the event that the couple cannot agree; whether to treat a claim for one benefit as a claim for another. See also below n 32.

social security system can be traced back just over a century.[3] The current framework dates from 2008 and results from the reforms introduced via the Tribunals, Courts and Enforcement Act 2007, which will be outlined below. In practice, not all appeals are determined by the tribunal. Some are resolved through concession by the Department for Work and Pensions (DWP) or are withdrawn by appellants. However, the frequency with which these alternatives occur has recently fallen dramatically, and currently over 80 per cent of appeals proceed to hearing.[4] There is a right of further appeal, with permission,[5] on a point of law to the Upper Tribunal (Administrative Appeals Chamber), whose jurisdiction in this field replaced that of the Social Security and Child Support Commissioners in November 2008.

Council tax benefit appeals have been within the scope of these arrangements, but following the replacement of this benefit with council tax support, that is no longer the case. Council tax support appeals will instead lie to the Valuation Tribunal (despite concerns that it lacks the resources to handle the likely volume of appeals[6]) and then, on a point of law, to the High Court.[7] By establishing an entirely separate route to redress to that applicable to other mainstream welfare benefits, this reform can therefore be regarded as adding complexity to the system for challenging decisions, particularly from a claimant's perspective.

Aside from the new council tax support schemes, one important part of the benefit system not covered by the general social security appellate jurisdiction, nor affected by the reforms under the 2007 Act, has been the discretionary social fund, for which there has been a two-stage review process.[8] As noted in chapter two, this part of the fund is being either localised or abolished. Provision to replace budgeting loans is being made with the

---

[3] See the National Insurance Act 1911, ss 88–90. Claims relating to unemployment benefit were decided by insurance officers. A person whose claim for benefit was refused or whose benefit was stopped could require the insurance officer to refer the matter to a 'court of referees', whose recommendations were to be given effect unless the insurance officer disagreed with them, in which case the insurance office could refer the matter to an 'umpire' appointed under the Act, whose ruling would be 'final and conclusive'.

[4] Senior President of Tribunals, *The Senior President of Tribunals' Annual Report* (London, Ministry of Justice, 2013) 30.

[5] Which can be granted by the First-tier Tribunal or via an application to the Upper Tribunal.

[6] HC Third Delegated Legislation Committee Deb 11 March 2013, cols 6–7 (per A Slaughter MP).

[7] Local Government Finance Act 1992, s 16 and Scheds 1A, para 2(6) and 1B, para 5(1), both inserted by the Local Government Finance Act 2012, Sched 4; the Council Tax Reduction Schemes (Prescribed Requirements) (England) Regulations 2012 (SI 2012/2885), Sched 7, para 8; and the Council Tax Reduction Schemes (Prescribed Requirements) (Wales) Regulations 2012 (SI 2012/3144) (W316), Sched 12, para 10. Note that, astonishingly, as late as March 2013, there was still no formal appeals or review structure in place in Scotland, nor likely to be prior to April 2013, when the support (or reduction) scheme was introduced there. It was expected that arrangements would be in place by the summer of 2013: Scottish Parliament Welfare Reform Committee, *Official Report* (5 March 2013) cols 558–68.

[8] Social Security Administration Act 1992, s 38; Social Fund (Application for Review) Regulations 1988 (SI 1988/34).

introduction of universal credit, in the form of 'budgeting advances', and there is no longer a need for separate internal review. So a detailed assessment of the review process will not be undertaken here. Nevertheless, it is important to note that this has been a significant central jurisdiction (albeit locally administered), and a quite distinct model of redress has been used.[9] Internal review by an officer following an application in writing has comprised the first stage. Applicants have also had the possibility of a second-stage review, conducted independently by a Social Fund Inspector (SFI) within an Independent Review Service. The independence of the SFIs was clearly a strength of this system. Neither review stage involved an oral hearing, which has been seen as undermining the inquisitorial role of the review process,[10] although interviews were held by the SFI in some instances. In 2012–13, there were 192,500 applications for first-tier review, of which 28.4 per cent resulted in a revised decision (although only 22.1 per cent in the case of budgeting loans), and there were 47,720 SFI reviews, 39.7 per cent of which resulted in revision (but only 5.6 per cent in the case of budgeting loans).[11]

Criticism of the system has focused first on the time it has taken for completion of the review process in individual cases,[12] particularly the length of the period before initial decisions are reached – decisions that, after all, have concerned 'payments which by their nature are needed urgently'.[13] Notably, however, second-tier (SFI) review decisions generally have involved considerably shorter waits for claimants than those facing claimants appealing to the First-tier Tribunal (see further section IV below).[14] There has also been some evidence of claimants being dissuaded by officials from taking their cases to the SFIs, leading to a call from what was then the House of Commons Social Security Committee for a right to take applications for review directly to the

---

[9] See T Buck, *The Social Fund: Law and Practice* (London, Sweet and Maxwell, 2009) ch 5; T Buck, 'Undoing the Damage: Review Processes' in T Buck and RS Smith (eds), *Poor Relief or Poor Deal? The Social Fund, Safety Nets and Social Security* (Aldershot, Ashgate, 2003) 131–49.

[10] S Rahilly, 'Social Security, Money Management and Debt' in N Harris et al, *Social Security Law in Context* (Oxford, Oxford University Press, 2000) 457.

[11] Department for Work and Pensions (DWP), *Annual Report by the Secretary of State for Work and Pensions on the Social Fund 2012/2013* (2013) Annex 12. The low percentage of reversals of budgeting loan decisions on review is attributed to changes made in April 1999, including the removal of the requirement to review where there has been a relevant change of circumstances since the decision was made (Social Fund Direction 32) and the statutory change which removed in budgeting loan cases the requirement to take account of the 'nature and extent and urgency of the need' (Social Security Contributions and Benefits Act 1992, s 140(1)): see Buck, 'Undoing the Damage' (above n 9) 137–38.

[12] House of Commons Social Security Committee, *The Social Fund* (2000–01, HC 232) paras 111–12. The Committee said that it was not possible to ascertain where in the system the delays were occurring, nor were there any figures on the average period of delay: para 112.

[13] House of Commons Work and Pensions Committee, *The Social Fund* (2006–07, HC 464) para 68.

[14] It has been calculated that a straightforward case could take about 29 days to go through both review stages: K Legge et al, *The Social Fund: Current Role and Future Direction* (York, Joseph Rowntree Foundation, 2006) 43. This is much less than half the time an average appeal will take: see below. The success rate for oral hearings is also discussed below.

inspectors to be introduced.[15] The Government rejected this recommendation, saying that the review system was 'working well': 'We do not think that there is convincing evidence that people are failing to take up their right to approach the [Independent Review Service].'[16] Trevor Buck, however, offers the sober reflection that social fund applicants

> belong to the most numerous category of persons who will either not have the resources and stamina to pursue a review and/or will be persuaded by the management of the review processes in the district offices that there is no point in pursuing their claims further.[17]

Moreover, while the social fund review process has appeared on the surface to offer a relatively straightforward mechanism for redress, there has been evidence of widespread misunderstanding among claimants about how it operates.[18] Despite criticisms of the review process, it is unlikely to be matched by arrangements set in place under the new local authority-based system of support.[19]

Returning to the subject of social security appeals, there has been an expectation since the 2007 Act reforms that, in their operation, tribunals will place a considerable emphasis on the user's perspective. The Leggatt Report in particular had proposed a 'more user-friendly system' for tribunals in general and stressed the importance of remembering that 'tribunals exist to serve the users, not the other way round'.[20] The Department for Constitutional Affairs, in its 2004 White Paper, noted that tribunal users found that 'a system that should be informal and accessible is legalistic and complicated', and the Department endorsed the idea of changes that would deliver better services.[21] It was proposed that there should be a new unified tribunals service with a tribunals judiciary and judicial leadership (with a Senior President of Tribunals at the helm) together with improved training. To improve appellant access and participation, key performance indicators would include better

---

[15] House of Commons Social Security Committee, *The Social Fund* (2000–01, HC 232) para 113.

[16] Department for Work and Pensions, *Report on the Social Fund: Reply by the Government to the Third Report of the Social Security Committee, Session 2000–01 [HC 232]* (Cm 237, 2001) para 42.

[17] Buck, 'Undoing the Damage' (above n 9) 145.

[18] G Dalley and R Berthoud, *Challenging Discretion: The Social Fund Review Procedure* (London, Policy Studies Institute, 1992).

[19] The social fund review process continues until 1 August 2013 under transitional arrangements. Internal reviews of crisis loan and community care grant decisions on applications made before 1 April 2013 and on budgeting loan decisions were possible after that date. Reviews by a social fund inspector can be applied for only if the application for a payment from the discretionary social fund was made before 1 April 2013; but the role of SFIs will end with effect from 1 August 2013. See the Welfare Reform Act 2012 (Commencement No 6 and Savings Provisions) Order 2012 (SI 2012/3090) (C123).

[20] A Leggatt, *Tribunals for Users: One System, One Service* (London, Stationery Office, 2001) 43.

[21] Department for Constitutional Affairs, *Transforming Public Services: Complaints, Redress and Tribunals* (Cm 6243, 2004) paras 5.10 and 5.30.

information, hearings that were 'not daunting or legalistic' and written decisions that were 'comprehensible'.[22] The White Paper emphasised giving users choices and promoted the idea of 'proportionate dispute resolution', which would involve less formal mechanisms for resolving disputes wherever possible.[23] A key issue of concern to the present discussion is whether, in the context of social security appeals, the claimant's journey – which at this stage is concerned with access to justice – has become less complex and consequently not as burdensome as a result of the changes made.

It should also be noted that with the phased introduction of personal independence payment and universal credit, the Government has laid down new decisions and appeals regulations.[24] They will sit alongside the existing regulations,[25] which will still apply to other benefits. Together they provide key elements of the legal framework governing the right to appeal and various aspects of decision-making, especially in cases when changes to benefit decisions are needed. The Government explained that further amendments to the 1999 regulations in order to accommodate the new benefits and other changes would have been disadvantageous, since those regulations had already been much amended over the years, leading to 'substantial additional complexity in an already complex policy area', and '[t]o have mixed the old and the new would have added to that complexity'.[26] The new regulations adopted the 'tried and tested' substance of the 1999 regulations, but the opportunity is said to have been taken to 'restructure and modernise the drafting'.[27] There has also been alignment of some rules across the different benefits in place of separate specific provision within some of them. Generally the new rules, while still complex, are (for the time being at least) tidier and easier to read than the old provisions.

It is important before focusing more fully on the appeal process to take account of the other ways in which the system in Great Britain enables an administrative decision to be changed or overturned, particularly as the alternatives aim to afford claimants an easier route to rectifying incorrect adverse outcomes. Thus the discussion now turns to revision and supersession of decisions followed by alternative dispute resolution.

---

[22] Ibid, para 6.89.

[23] See further M Adler, 'Tribunal Reform, Proportionate Dispute Resolution and the Pursuit of Administrative Justice' (2006) 69(6) *Modern Law Review* 958; H Genn and G Richardson, 'Tribunals in Transition: Resolution or Adjudication?' (2007) *Public Law* 116.

[24] Universal Credit, Personal Independence Payment, Jobseeker's Allowance and Employment and Support Allowance (Decisions and Appeals) Regulations 2013 (SI 2013/381) (hereafter the 'DMA Regulations 2013').

[25] Social Security and Child Support (Decisions and Appeals) Regulations 1999 (SI 1999/991) (hereafter the 'DMA Regulations 1999').

[26] Department for Work and Pensions, *Explanatory Memorandum to the Universal Credit, Personal Independence Payment, Jobseeker's Allowance and Employment and Support Allowance (Decisions and Appeals) Regulations 2013* (2012) para 7.2.

[27] Ibid, para 7.3.

II. Revision and Supersession

A claimant may benefit from the revision of a decision by the Secretary of State,[28] if the claimant applies for it within one month of the decision[29] or if it is initiated by the relevant official within that time.[30] This means that a decision can be changed notwithstanding the absence of an appeal. Revision of a decision is also permitted where there is an appeal that has not yet been decided.[31] The other grounds permitting a revision of a decision, the provisions on which have been streamlined under the new regulations, include (a) that it arose from an official error, (b) that it was made in ignorance of or based on a mistake as to some material fact and in consequence was more advantageous to the claimant than it would otherwise have been or (c) that it was a prescribed non-appealable decision.[32] Generally, a revision takes effect from the date of the original decision.[33]

A process for the reconsideration of initial decisions outside the context of formal appeals was proposed in the 1996 Green Paper *Improving Decision-Making and Appeals in Social Security* on the basis that a decision-making process needs a 'simple' mechanism for changing decisions quickly if they are thought to be wrong.[34] Such a mechanism would offer a means of avoiding tribunal cases since 'the emphasis should be on encouraging individuals who think decisions are wrong to say so before seeking to appeal'.[35] Informal reviews were introduced into the decision-making and appeal regime following the reforms to it under the Social Security Act 1998, which established the current arrangements for revisions (and supersessions: see below). As Nick Wikeley has explained, the reform was 'designed to provide the Secretary of State with maximum flexibility to correct decisions which are wrong for any reason and to prevent them entering the appeals system unnecessarily'.[36]

---

[28] Under the DMA Regulations 1999, decisions of HMRC, officially 'the Board', defined as the 'Commissioners of Inland Revenue' (reg 1(3)), were also covered by this.

[29] This time can be extended in some circumstances. See in particular the DMA Regulations 1999 (above n 25) reg 4; and DMA Regulations 2013, reg 6.

[30] Social Security Act 1998, s 9(1); DMA Regulations 2013, reg 5; and DMA Regulations 1999, reg 3.

[31] DMA Regulations 2013, reg 11(1); and DMA Regulations 1999, reg 3(4A).

[32] DMA Regulations 2013, regs 8–19; and DMA Regulations 1999, reg 3. Such revision can be initiated at any time. As to decisions that are not appealable, see DMA Regulations 2013, reg 50 and Sched 3; and DMA Regulations 1999, reg 27 and Sched 2; and see also above n 2.

[33] Social Security Act 1998, s 9(3).

[34] Department of Social Security (DSS), *Improving Decision-Making and Appeals in Social Security* (Cm 3328, 1996).

[35] Ibid, para 4.18.

[36] N Wikeley, 'Decision-Making and Appeals under the Social Security Act 1998' (1998) 5 *Journal of Social Security Law* 105, 107.

Claimants are effectively invited by the DWP to ask it to 'reconsider' decisions that they 'feel to be wrong'.[37]

This reconsideration process has become particularly important for cases hinging on health or disability questions, such as employment and support allowance (ESA)/universal credit (capability for work element(s)) or disability living allowance (DLA)/personal independence payment, since a claimant may have further medical evidence or other relevant information that was not taken into account when the initial decision was taken. Of course, this does mean that the onus is likely to be on claimants to realise the importance of this material and ensure that it is submitted. In the context of this broad category of cases, the Government announced an intention to 'incorporate a comprehensive reconsideration process as part of the initial assessment of any appeal to further reduce the number of appeals needing to progress to the tribunal' and to 'ensure that all new evidence is, wherever possible, included in the reconsideration process rather than at tribunal'.[38]

In its review of the reconsideration arrangements, the House of Commons Work and Pensions Committee, reporting in 2010, found that in a high proportion of DLA and attendance allowance cases, decisions were overturned following reconsideration: 51 per cent and 60 per cent of cases respectively in 2008–09.[39] Although this was considered to reflect badly on the quality of initial decision-making, error was attributed to the failure of claimants to carry out properly the self-assessment required by the claim forms.[40] The complexity of the DLA claim form was well known, although the Committee acknowledged the efforts being made to improve it.[41] Where ESA or incapacity benefit cases were concerned, the Committee was unable to obtain evidence on the numbers of decisions changed as a result of reconsideration, but it found anecdotal evidence that decisions were not being reviewed properly. The Committee also found that many claimants were 'deterred from an appeal by an unsuccessful request for a reconsideration'.[42] The Committee was particularly concerned that claimants may miss out on their entitlement due to a lack of thoroughness in the reconsideration process. Some evidence has, however, since emerged of reconsideration in ESA cases that have reached the tribunal administration and are waiting to be listed for a hearing. It was reported in 2011 that the DWP was running reconsideration pilots for such cases, in which the decision-maker would look at the case and consider

[37] See House of Commons Work and Pensions Committee, *Decision-Making and Appeals in the Benefits System* (2009–10, HC 313) Ev 113–19, para 22 (Memorandum submitted by HH Judge Robert Martin).

[38] Department for Work and Pensions, *A New Deal for Welfare: Empowering People to Work* (Cm 6730, 2006) ch 2, para 73.

[39] HC Work and Pensions Committee, *Decision-Making and Appeals in the Benefits System* (above n 37) 116–17.

[40] Ibid, paras 118–19.

[41] Ibid, 121.

[42] Ibid, 130.

whether the decision that had been reached was supportable; it found that in 13 per cent of cases, the decision was not supported and was therefore over-turned.[43] More generally, the President of the Social Entitlement Chamber of the First-tier Tribunal at the same time reported that 24 per cent of ESA appeals were being revised in favour of the appellant without a hearing, as the DWP has been making 'a more effective use of reconsideration'.[44]

The overall criticism of the reconsideration process by the Work and Pensions Committee was forthright. As then operating, the process repre-sented a 'missed opportunity' and did not function in claimants' best inter-ests.[45] In his memorandum to the Committee, HH Judge Robert Martin, the President of the Social Entitlement Chamber of the First-tier Tribunal, ques-tioned whether there was any advantage to a claimant in requesting a recon-sideration, since instituting an appeal was 'free, informal and involves scarcely more effort than writing in to ask for a reconsideration'.[46] Reconsideration, on the other hand, carried 'the risk of delay and further correspondence should the outcome be no improvement over the original decision'.[47] Nevertheless, the Welfare Reform Act 2012 contains amendments enabling regulations, which have now been made, to restrict the right of appeal to cases that have been through the reconsideration process.[48] The Government's change to what it terms 'mandatory reconsideration' (as part of an 'escalating dispute process'), in which the second look at the decision will 'whenever pos-sible' be undertaken by a 'different decision-maker' to the one who made the original decision, aims to increase the proportion of disputes resolved with-out an appeal, since in practice many claimants have simply been appealing rather than requesting reconsideration.[49] The reform has been criticised as 'a totally unnecessary measure, which will result in fewer people being able to

[43] Senior President of Tribunals, *Senior President of Tribunals' Annual Report* (London, Ministry of Justice, 2011) 10–11.

[44] Ibid, 40.

[45] HC Work and Pensions Committee, *Decision-Making and Appeals in the Benefits System* (above n 37) 131.

[46] Ibid, Ev 113–19, para 24.

[47] Ibid.

[48] Welfare Reform Act 2012, s 102 and Sched 11, amending the Social Security Act 1998, s 12; and the Child Support, Pensions and Social Security Act 2000, Sched 7. See the DMA Regulations 2013, reg 7, which also permits the Secretary of State to treat any purported appeal as an application for a revision. Parallel provision in relation to other social security benefit cases would be made as a result of draft amendment regulations (the draft Social Security, Child Support, Vaccine Damage and Other Payments (Decisions and Appeals) (Amendment) Regulations 2013), which were laid before Parliament in June 2013 and would amend (from 28 October 2013) the DMA Regulations 1999 (above n 25). Under these new provisions, it would be possible for an appeal to be treated as an application for revision.

[49] Department for Work and Pensions (DWP), *Explanatory Memorandum to the Social Security, Child Support, Vaccine Damage and Other Payments (Decisions and Appeals) (Amendment) Regulations 2013* (2013), www.legislation.gov.uk/ukdsi/2013/9780111540053/pdfs/ukdsiem_9780111540053_en.pdf, paras 7.6–7.7. See also the Welfare Reform Act 2012, Explanatory Notes (2012) para 497 and DWP, *Mandatory Consideration of revision before appeal* (2012).

challenge the decisions made about their entitlement to benefit'.[50] The concern is that it could deter claimants from appealing and increase the risk of would-be appellants missing the deadline for lodging an appeal. These problems may be ameliorated if reconsideration occurs fairly rapidly, but this has not been the case in practice. The Select Committee recommended that the DWP should adopt a target of five days for completion of the reconsideration process,[51] but the Government rejected it as impracticable.[52] The Government disclosed that in the DWP's Pensions, Disability and Carers Service, which administered DLA, attendance allowance and some other benefits, the target was 35 working days, but in the year to January 2010, its average clearance times were 30.3 days for DLA and 23.6 days for the attendance allowance.[53]

Revision is distinguishable from supersession, which is another mechanism for changing a decision.[54] A supersession of a decision generally has prospective effect, although as Wikeley has explained, the principle 'is subject to a number of exceptions in the complex regulations'.[55] Supersession may be applied for by a claimant or undertaken by an official.[56] As the regulations make clear, it is intended to deal with cases in which there has been a relevant change of circumstances affecting the claimant since the decision was made or in which the original decision was erroneous in point of law or made in ignorance of or on the basis of a mistake as to 'some material fact'.[57] Decisions by a tribunal (First-tier or the Upper Tribunal) may also be superseded on the grounds of ignorance/mistake in relation to material facts.[58]

A disadvantage to applying for supersession, as opposed to requesting revision or initiating the appeal process, arises from the fact that any arrears of benefit that are due are likely to be more limited, since the general rule is that supersession takes effect from the date it is applied for.[59] A decision to

---

[50] J Sanbach and V Pearlman, 'The Disappearing Right of Appeal' (2012) *Evidence* 4, 4.

[51] HC Work and Pensions Committee, *Decision-Making and Appeals in the Benefits System* (above n 37) para 114.

[52] House of Commons Work and Pensions Committee, *Decision-Making and Appeals in the Benefits System: Government Response to the Committee's Second Report of Session 2009–10* (2009–10, HC 523) paras 65 and 66. See also Department for Work and Pensions, *Mandatory Consideration of Revision before Appeal: Government Response to the Consultation* (September 2012), www.gov.uk/government/uploads/system/uploads/attachment_data/file/176976/mandatory-consideration-consultation-response.pdf.pdf, 7.

[53] HC Work and Pensions Committee, *Decision-Making and Appeals in the Benefits System: Government Response* (ibid) para 66.

[54] See Social Security Act 1998, s 10.

[55] N Wikeley, *Wikeley, Ogus and Barendt's Law of Social Security*, 5th edn (London, Butterworth Lexis Nexis, 2002) 186.

[56] Also, an application for a revision may be treated as an application for a supersession: DMA Regulations 2013, reg 33.

[57] DMA Regulations 2013, regs 22–31 (on decisions that may not be superseded, see reg 32); and DMA Regulations 1999, reg 6.

[58] DMA Regulations 2013, reg 31; and DMA Regulations 1999, reg 6(2)(c). See also the Social Security Act 1998, s 10(1).

[59] Social Security Act 1998, s 10(5) read with (6); DMA Regulations 2013, Pt 3, ch 3; DMA

supersede or not to supersede an earlier decision may in itself be appealed against, but in the case of a revised decision (above), an appeal may be made only against the original decision and not the revision.[60]

The complexity of the rules on revision and supersession may be contrasted with the previous arrangements – 'fairly straightforward rules of review which provided that a decision on benefit could be changed if it had been based on a mistake or there had been a subsequent change of circumstances'.[61] The concepts of revision and supersession themselves may make sense to professional decision-makers and adjudicators, although one cannot assume so in every case – indeed Nick Warren has commented, 'Very few DWP decision-makers understand these crucial concepts . . . and you cannot blame them.'[62] The concepts are in any case likely to be far from straightforward to claimants, certainly when compared with the basic idea of an appeal. As Mark Rowland and Robin White have noted, for the most part, the primary legislation gives 'no indication as to the circumstances in which a revision of a decision is more appropriate than a supersession or vice versa'.[63] Whilst the regulations, on the other hand, are more explicit, at least in relation to when a supersession may be needed (see above), they are not likely to be easily comprehensible to most claimants. Indeed, Rowland and White take comfort in the fact that 'an application for a supersession may be treated as an application for a revision and vice versa . . . so that it is not fatal if claimants or their advisors do not fully understand the difference when making the application'.[64] In fact, officials sometimes fail to issue a supersession or revision decision in the correct form, implying that some of them are indeed also confused about the distinction.[65] Yet it is a distinction that has important consequences for appeals, since, as noted above, an appeal post-revision will concern the original decision, whereas in the case of a supersession decision, it will be against that (later) decision.

Regulations 1999, Sched 3A; and the Child Benefit and Guardian's Allowance (Decisions and Appeals) Regulations 2003 (SI 2003/916), reg 16. As to the date from which the supersession of a decision is to take effect, see DMA Regulations 2013, regs 34–37 and Sch 1; and DMA Regulations 1999, reg 7, which now has 39 sub-paragraphs. 'It may well be necessary for the content of social security legislation to be complex but the machinery should be simpler and based on sound adjudication principles – so that decision-makers can understand it': N Warren, 'The Adjudication Gap: A Discussion Document' (2006) 13(2) *Journal of Social Security Law* 86, 116.

[60] Social Security Act 1998, s 12.
[61] See HC Work and Pensions Committee, *Decision-Making and Appeals in the Benefits System* (above n 37) Ev 113–19, para 41.
[62] Warren (above n 59) 115.
[63] M Rowland and R White, *Social Security Legislation 2012/13, Volume III: Administration, Adjudication and the European Dimension* (London, Sweet and Maxwell, 2012) 213.
[64] Ibid, 214, referring, inter alia, to DMA Regulations 1999, regs 3(1) and 6(5). And see now DMA Regulations 2013, reg 33(1).
[65] Rowland and White (above n 63) 214.

III. Alternative Dispute Resolution?

The present tribunal rules in Great Britain include a requirement that when an appeal is before it, the tribunal must seek, where appropriate, to bring the parties' attention to any appropriate alternative means of resolving the dispute and must, if the parties want to use this alternative means and provided that it is compatible with the 'overriding objective' per the tribunal rules,[66] facilitate its use.[67] This reflects the general governmental promotion of alternative dispute resolution (ADR) mechanisms, such as mediation.[68] Mediation is not, however, in use in this field nor in most other citizen-versus-state disputes, but in the field of special educational needs, it is well established, albeit under-utilised,[69] and the Government is shortly to give it a substantial push.[70] Mediation is, from an individual citizen's perspective, ostensibly less formal and perhaps more accessible than a formal appeal process.[71] But its appropriateness for cases involving questions of entitlement, such as will be involved in social security and tax credit cases, is considered doubtful, since in that context there is not considered to be any scope for negotiation or compromise:

> There is not an unlimited range of alternative outcomes that the parties can explore in order to 'resolve' a difference of view. Entitlement is based on the factual situation of the claimant in relation to the relevant regulation. The claimant may believe that her situation satisfies the requirements while the agency takes a different view. The role of the tribunal is to decide which view will prevail and award or deny the benefit on that basis.[72]

As the First-tier Tribunal (Social Entitlement Chamber) President has said, the DWP itself lacks the power to enter into a compromise over a claim.[73]

---

[66] The 'overriding objective' of the tribunal rules (ie, the Tribunal Procedure (First-tier Tribunal) (Social Entitlement Chamber) Rules 2008 (SI 2008/2685), r 2(1) and (2)) is to enable a tribunal to deal with a case 'fairly and justly', as explained more fully below.

[67] Ibid, r 3(1).

[68] Complaints processes, including ombudsman processes, are classed as alternative dispute resolution mechanisms. In this field, they offer a means by which aspects of the treatment of appellants by the system can be highlighted and in consequence addressed. However, they have little relevance to challenges to benefit decisions in individual cases and are considered to be insufficiently relevant to the present discussion.

[69] See further N Harris and S Riddell, *Resolving Disputes about Educational Provision: A Comparative Perspective on Special Educational Needs* (Farnham, Ashgate, 2011).

[70] In a prescribed case in which a person wishes to appeal against a special educational needs decision, he or she will be required first to receive information and advice on, and decide whether to utilise, mediation: Children and Families Bill 2013, cls 51.

[71] Harris and Riddell (above n 69) ch 3.

[72] Genn and Richardson (above n 23) 137.

[73] Senior President of Tribunals, *Annual Report* (2013) (above n 4) 30.

There is not the scope here to pursue the argument in detail, but even leaving aside the traditional concern about the inherent unfairness of mediation where it is conducted between greatly unequal parties, thereby giving rise to an imbalance of power,[74] there is also the serious ethical problem in enabling a claimant to 'settle' for a level of benefit that may not match his or her true entitlement.[75] There is also a strong case for ensuring a proper process for the 'vindication of individual rights'.[76] From an objective perspective, if, for example, a claimant believes he or she is entitled to the highest/higher rate of DLA/personal independence payment (PIP) because of his/her care needs, but the DWP disagrees, an accurate determination by an independent and expert judicial body is going to be preferable to a settlement between the parties that gives the claimant entitlement to the lower rate of the benefit. Of course, there is always the possibility in such a case that the tribunal may, rightly or otherwise, conclude that there is no entitlement at all to the benefit, but it would be wrong that the fear of such an outcome should create a potential injustice by compelling a claimant to settle for less than his or her potential entitlement. There is also a risk of inconsistency of result across identical cases, and consequential inequality, from the kind of individualised outcomes that result from mediation, which a nationally operated and judicialised appellate process is intended to prevent.

The justice concerns about mediation in general are important but cannot be fully analysed here.[77] However, we can note that in appeal cases, the primary function of the tribunal is to ensure that there is an outcome that is legally correct. The complexity of social security law makes that a task for an expert panel. Moreover, the appellate process functions in and serves the wider public interest by ensuring that decisions are rational as well as consistent. A mediator's role is generally envisaged to be one of brokering a solution, forging a compromise, which has more of a private character to it. While a combined role of the kind found in judicial mediation of social security disputes before the social and administrative courts in Bavaria may in theory be one way of ensuring that agreed outcomes are consistent with notions of substantive justice,[78] it is unlikely to be practicable in the United Kingdom, given the number of appeals in this field.

Another proposed measure is 'early neutral evaluation', which aims to identify appeal cases in which the likely outcome can easily be gleaned from

---

[74] Adler, 'Tribunal Reform' (above n 23) 977. See also R Hunter and A Leonard, 'Sex Discrimination and Alternative Dispute Resolution: British Proposals in the Light of International Experience' (1997) *Public Law* 298, 307.

[75] Adler, 'Tribunal Reform' (above n 23) 978.

[76] M Supperstone, D Stilitz and C Sheldon, 'ADR and Public Law' (2006) *Public Law* 299, 311.

[77] See in particular H Genn, *Judging Civil Justice* (Cambridge, Cambridge University Press, 2010); and Harris and Riddell (above n 69) ch 2.

[78] See U Becker and N Freidrich, 'Mediation in Bavarian Social Jurisdiction: Findings of a Model Project' in Max Planck Institute for Foreign and International Law (MPI), *Report 2008–2009* (Munich, MPI, 2010) 49–52.

the papers and to facilitate a declaration based on that prediction without the need for adjudication by the tribunal. It is therefore designed to limit the number of hopeless cases that go the tribunal and thereby avoid an unnecessary burden on claimants while at the same time reducing public costs and serving other claimants' interests by weeding out cases that contribute to overall delays. In pilot exercises in DLA cases (and employment cases), the process has involved a tribunal judge undertaking a prior review of an appeal case. If, for example, the judge identifies an appeal case as very weak or having no prospects of success at the tribunal, the judge would contact the likely unsuccessful party. If that party is the appellant, he or she would be able to make an informed decision about whether to proceed with the appeal (perhaps obtaining further evidence to bolster the case) or to withdraw it. If the likely loser of the appeal case is the Department, it could reconsider the matter having regard to the judge's recommendations. In practice, however, early neutral evaluation was found in the pilot exercises to offer mixed results. While conducive to the more proportionate resolution of cases, it did not bring down overall costs nor reduce the overall time for the resolution of disputes.[79] It has not been introduced in this field to date.

IV. Appeals in the First-tier Tribunal

Judicialisation of Appeal Tribunals

The social security appeal system has a long but not always illustrious history. It had its origins in the National Insurance (NI) scheme after 1911 and the unemployment assistance (UA) scheme in the 1930s. The separate NI and UA streams continued through later reforms, which, in the case of the latter, included the successor schemes of national assistance (from 1948) and then supplementary benefit (from 1966, later replaced by income support in 1987). The NI tribunals had greater independence and a more judicial character than their supplementary benefit counterparts, including a requirement that chairs be legally qualified.[80] The report on supplementary benefit appeal

---

[79] C Hay, K McKenna and T Buck, *Evaluation of Early Neutral Evaluation Alternative Dispute Resolution in the Social Security and Child Support Tribunal*, Ministry of Justice Research Series 2/10 (London, Ministry of Justice, 2010).

[80] See N Wikeley, 'Burying Bell: Managing the Judicialisation of Social Security Tribunals' (2000) 63(4) *Modern Law Review* 475. Their official name was 'National Insurance Local Tribunals' (NILTs).

tribunals by Professor Kathleen Bell, published in 1975[81] echoed the long-standing criticisms of these tribunals as the 'slums of the English Tribunals System'[82] due to: their procedural shortcomings; the unsuitable tribunal venues; their lack of independence; the absence of a requirement for legally qualified chairs; the lack of scrutiny by a second-tier appeal body, unlike national insurance tribunals, whose decisions could be appealed to the National Insurance Commissioners (renamed the Social Security Commissioners in 1980); and the unmet need for support for appellants to enable them exercise their appeal right effectively.[83] While Bell's proposed 'phased period of reconstruction' of the supplementary benefit appeal system was in part concerned with improving the quality of the tribunals themselves, a critical element was her recommendation of measures to assist appellants, through the provision of information, advice and assistance, by the exercise by tribunals of an 'enabling' role, and by a speeding up of the appeal process. The NI and supplementary benefit appeal bodies[84] were merged into a single social security appeal tribunal in the 1980s, under a central organisation.[85] This reform was designed to bring improved procedural and professional standards and greater independence.

Further advances in the judicialisation of tribunals within a unified system included the appointment of a national President and the phasing-in over five years of an exclusively legal chairmanship of tribunals.[86] It raised the prospect of improved standards of appeals adjudication. Yet concerns remained that Bell's central aims of making the system fairer to claimants as a whole had only partly been met.[87] In particular, the barriers to claimants' effective participation in the appeal process, arising from their lack of knowledge, experience (most of the appeals before the tribunal are the appellant's first[88]) and overall capacity, were not really addressed by the reforms. Consequently, Bell's aim that 'rights of appeal enshrined in statute law can be exercised effectively by ordinary people'[89] was largely unrealised.

---

[81] K Bell, *Research Study on Supplementary Benefit Appeal Tribunals: Review of Main Findings – Conclusions: Recommendations* (London, HMSO, 1975).

[82] H Rose, 'Who Can De-label the Claimant?' in M Adler and A Bradley (eds), *Justice, Discretion and Poverty* (Abingdon, Professional Books, 1976) 149–50.

[83] See, for example, M Herman, *Administrative Justice and Supplementary Benefits* (London, Bell, 1972); N Lewis, 'Supplementary Benefit Appeal Tribunals' (1973) *Public Law* 257; R Lister, *Justice for the Claimant*, Poverty Research Series No 4 (London, CPAG, 1974); and A Frost and C Howard, *Representation and Administrative Tribunals* (London, Routledge and Kegan Paul, 1977).

[84] NILTs and Supplementary Benefits Appeal Tribunals, noted above.

[85] Wikeley, 'Burying Bell' (above n 80).

[86] The Health and Social Services and Social Security Adjudication Act 1983. See J Mesher, 'The Merging of Social Security Tribunals' (1983) 10 *Journal of Law and Society* 135.

[87] See N Harris, 'The Reform of the Supplementary Benefit Appeals System' (1983) *Journal of Social Welfare Law* 212.

[88] J Baldwin, N Wikeley and R Young, *Judging Social Security: The Adjudication of Claims for Benefit in Britain* (Oxford, Clarendon Press, 1992) 156.

[89] Bell (above n 81) 19.

Some in fact argued that judicialisation would extend the barriers; for example, case law would now expand as a result of the new second-tier right of appeal in supplementary benefit cases and would be beyond the reach and understanding of most claimants, but probably not that of officials.[90] An exacerbating factor was the increasing legalism infusing social security, supplementary benefit in particular, through both the changes to first-tier adjudication within the administration, involving adjudication officers operating under the guidance of a Chief Adjudication Officer,[91] and the introduction of bright-line rules of growing complexity governing issues of entitlement, as noted above in chapter three. In addition, the call by Bell and others for recognition of the importance of ensuring that appellants had access to advice and representation, on whose benefits to appellants the evidence mounted,[92] went unheeded. Bell did not, however, consider that appellants needed representation in all cases. She had found that they 'were not completely incapable of coping – many did surprisingly well'.[93] Julian Fulbrook, however, considered that this conclusion 'underrated' the 'complexities' of the process.[94] However, if tribunals were able to play an effective enabling role, it could partly offset these difficulties. An empirical study published a few years after the commencement of the reforms found that the tribunal was in general making efforts 'to ensure that the appellant felt that he/she had been given an opportunity to put their case', although it was 'less certain that this view was taken by the appellant'; and appellant respondents had 'suggested that considerable scepticism remains on their part about the extent to which their contribution is likely to count'.[95]

A further and more comprehensive empirical study by John Baldwin, Nick Wikeley and Richard Young, published in 1992, provided strong evidence on the effects of the judicialisation from a variety of perspectives, including that of appellants.[96] The research revealed the continuing problems appellants experienced in engaging effectively with the appeal process, particularly if access to advice and representation was limited. For example, nearly a quarter of appellants in the survey by Baldwin, Wikeley and Young understood little or nothing that was in the appeal papers prepared by the department.[97] As this was a slightly higher proportion than that reported by Bell over a

[90] T Prosser, 'Poverty, Ideology and Legality: Supplementary Benefit Appeal Tribunals and their Predecessors' (1977) 4 *British Journal of Law and Society* 43.

[91] See R Sainsbury, 'The Social Security Chief Adjudication Officer: The First Four Years' (1989) *Public Law* 323.

[92] Eg, H Genn and Y Genn, *The Effectiveness of Representation at Tribunals* (London, Lord Chancellor's Department, 1989).

[93] Bell (above n 81) 18.

[94] J Fulbrook, *Administrative Justice and the Unemployed* (London, Mansell, 1978) 287.

[95] M P Jackson, H R Stewart and RE Bland, 'Appeal Tribunals on Supplementary Benefits' (1987) 21(1) *Social Policy and Administration* 58, 65.

[96] Baldwin, Wikeley and Young (above n 88).

[97] Ibid, 158

decade and a half earlier, it suggested that 'improvements in the layout of submissions over recent years have been outweighed by the increased complexity of the law involved'.[98] A subsequent study by Richard Berthoud and Alex Bryson found an even lower level of understanding by appellants, who were confused about the purposes of the department's written submissions.[99]

There has also long been an association between non-attendance at hearings and considerably reduced prospects of success. Baldwin, Wikeley and Young pointed out that a lack of understanding or clarity on the part of appellants could hamper their participation:[100] 'Confronted with a technically worded submission from an adjudication officer, it is no real surprise that a high proportion of claimants fail to attend the hearing.'[101] In 1979, unrepresented appellants who attended their hearings were four times more likely to win their appeals than unrepresented non-attending appellants.[102] As noted below, such a disparity was still in evidence in the 1990s.

Baldwin, Wikeley and Young also looked at appellants' experiences of the tribunal hearing. There was a high level of satisfaction among appellants, who felt they had had fair hearings; although at the same time, most appellants had found the hearings 'an ordeal', and some were observed to break down in tears during them.[103] Although the authors regarded the general satisfaction among appellants as suggestive of improved tribunal adjudication under the new President-led appeal system, they were cautious about it on the basis that appellants may not be the best judges of fairness.[104] Moreover, the researchers were 'often taken aback' by the views of the departmental presenting officers that '[p]roblems in making sense of the appeals papers were . . . hampering . . . appellants' ability to understand the hearing itself'.[105] The research by Baldwin, Wikeley and Young added also to the weight of evidence[106] confirming the importance of representation at the hearing: 'Given the essentially legalistic framework within which the tribunals operate and the complexity of the law they administer, the benefits of such representation seem to us to be almost self-evident.'[107] The authors were doubtful that, against this background of increasing legalism and legislative complexity, the adoption of an inquisitorial approach, in which the tribunal itself in effect acts for the appellant in adducing and examining evidence and testing whether the Department's

---

[98] Ibid.

[99] R Berthoud and A Bryson, 'Social Security Appeals: What Do Claimants Want?' (1997) 4(1) *Journal of Social Security Law* 17, 25 and 27.

[100] Baldwin, Wikeley and Young (above n 88) 161.

[101] Ibid, 179.

[102] Supplementary Benefits Commission, *Annual Report 1979* (London, HMSO, 1979) Table 13.1.

[103] Baldwin, Wikeley and Young (above n 88) 179.

[104] Ibid, 171.

[105] Ibid.

[106] See, for example, Frost and Howard (above n 83); and Genn and Genn (above n 92).

[107] Baldwin, Wikeley and Young (above n 88) 174.

case is consistent with the relevant legislation, could 'mask the need for a greater availability of advice and representation services'.[108]

Appeal figures for the year to 31 December 1997 confirm that this position continued. Although there was some variation in appeal success rates for appellants across different benefits (excluding housing benefit, which had a separate appeal/review system operated by local authorities, as discussed below), the overall rate was 35 per cent, but 45 per cent if only the representative and not the appellant attended the hearing, and 65 per cent if both attended. For appellants attending without a representative, the success rate was 48 per cent, while for those who did not attend and were not represented, it was only 12 per cent.[109] The different lay or legal backgrounds of representatives are not identified in these official statistics. However, it is known from other studies that there is no additional premium in this tribunal, in terms of achieving success, attached to legal representation as against representation by others.[110] Since this has been a field in which lawyers' involvement has always been very limited due to the lack of commercial profit attached to this area of work and the public funding limitations surrounding it, whether in relation to law centre grants or legal aid/advice for individual cases,[111] there has always been reliance on voluntary sector bodies such as citizens advice bureaux and welfare rights organisations – often very expert but themselves under increasing financial pressure. The department's figures for representation of appellants may in some instances also include friends, family members or support workers, who quite often accompany appellants to tribunal hearings. Despite their relative lack of expertise and experience, they can help claimants cope better with the experience of attending tribunals and in getting their points across. Whether representation at a hearing still carries the same 'premium' in terms of improved prospects of success is considered below.

The Social Security Act 1998 changed the structure of the social security tribunals, incorporating medical appeal tribunals (which dealt with industrial injuries cases), disability appeal tribunals, which were established in the early 1990s to deal with DLA/attendance allowance appeals, and child support appeal tribunals (established under the Child Support Act 1991) into the unified 'appeal tribunal'. Separate judicial and administrative arms of the appeal system were also established. The Independent Tribunal Service, as it had been known since 1991,[112] was renamed The Appeals Service, and a separate executive agency was created for the administration of appeals. The reforms

---

[108] Ibid, 211–12.

[109] Department of Social Security, *Social Security Statistics 1998* (Leeds, Corporate Document Services, 1998) Table H5.03.

[110] Genn and Genn (above n 92).

[111] See N Harris, *Quality and Effectiveness in Welfare Benefits and Related Work by Solicitors*, Research Study No 9 (Law Society, 1991); and the discussion of legal aid cutbacks following the Legal Aid, Sentencing and Punishment of Offenders Act 2012 below.

[112] Before then it was known as the Office of the President of Social Security Appeal Tribunals (OPSSAT).

also saw the abolition of lay members of tribunals, with the exception of specialist non-lawyer members to sit on panels in disability or child support cases. Medically qualified members also sat in disability cases. In incapacity benefit cases, a tribunal comprised a lawyer chair and a medical member only. These reforms resulted from regulations made under the power to prescribe the composition of tribunals,[113] although by statute, the chair had to have the requisite legal qualification.[114]

Wikeley has argued that the abolition of lay members, whose role on tribunals appeared to be generally favoured by appellants, along with the plan for certain kinds of case to be heard by legally qualified chairs alone,[115] may be regarded as consistent with the 'tendency on the part of governments to seek to increase efficiency in the judicial process, as measured by the throughput of cases'.[116] The concern, which continues, is that the absence of lay members might result in a lower degree of confidence in the process among appellants and limit appellants' capacity to engage effectively with it. Michael Adler, discussing the ending of lay membership, has cited as a widespread view that lay members 'are often more approachable than lawyers', as well as being able to bring 'wider experience to bear on the issues in dispute'; moreover, they tend to 'adopt a more "common sense" approach to decision-making'.[117] Their greater approachability probably stems from what Wikeley sees as their closer representativeness of the community at large compared to lawyers and medical members, who 'are usually drawn from a still narrower class base'.[118] Or as Adler has put it, 'Lay membership of administrative tribunals does give some assurance to an appellant that he is being judged by his peers.'[119]

Changes to Procedure

Another reform indicative of the mangerialist tendency was the removal of the provision for automatic oral hearings of appeals; appellants now had to indicate that they wanted such a hearing or, alternatively, have their case dealt with on the papers alone and in their absence. This requirement, introduced in 1996, has continued.[120] It soon resulted in a significant increase in cases in

[113] DMA Regulations 1999, reg 36, as amended.

[114] Social Security Act 1998, s 7.

[115] The cases heard by a chair alone are mainstream social security cases such as JSA, income support, housing benefit and council tax benefit. Some incapacity cases, such as sanctions for non-attendance at a medical examination, are also dealt with by chairs alone.

[116] Wikeley, 'Burying Bell' (above n 80) 492.

[117] M Adler, 'Lay Tribunal Members and Administrative Justice' (1999) *Public Law* 616, 624.

[118] Wikeley, 'Burying Bell' (above n 80) 492.

[119] Adler, 'Lay Tribunal Members and Administrative Justice' (above n 117) 624.

[120] Tribunal Procedure (First-tier Tribunal) (Social Entitlement Chamber) Rules 2008 (SI 2008/2685), r 27(1), which provides that an oral hearing must take place before a decision may be made, unless each party has consented to or not objected to a paper hearing, and provided the tribunal considers that it is 'able to decide the matter without a hearing'.

which the appeal was heard in the absence of the appellant.[121] By 2003, nearly one in four appeals cleared at hearing were decided on the papers alone.[122]

There are strong arguments favouring the use of an oral hearing as a 'transparent and structured opportunity for the parties to participate in the decision' and thus 'tied to the idea of democratic legitimacy'.[123] Paper hearings may, however, alleviate the stress and strain experienced by appellants through such participation.[124] This is particularly likely in respect of appellants who lack confidence or suffer from an anxiety disorder (although a domiciliary hearing is possible, if requested). When the Council on Tribunals consulted over the matter of oral hearings in tribunals, it found general support for them, particularly where there are complex issues of fact or law, either of which can occur in a social security appeal.[125] There is also a strong association between attendance at a hearing and an increased likelihood of success with the appeal, noted above, and the Department's leaflet on how to challenge its decisions even makes reference to it.[126] Recent research by Hazel Genn and Cheryl Thomas has examined the benefits of oral tribunal hearings.[127] Their research centred on a disability living allowance case simulation involving 66 different appeal panels in three regions (one from each part of Great Britain). The case concerned a 10-year-old child's entitlement to the allowance; his appointee was his mother. The researchers found, inter alia, that whilst appeals were more than two and a half times more likely to succeed if there were oral hearings rather than decisions on the papers alone, the disparity was considerably reduced if the paper cases were supplemented with the information that came to light at oral hearings. Therefore, it was the way that the oral hearing enabled further information to be accessible to the tribunal that was the telling factor rather than the presence of the appellant per se.[128] The research therefore indicated that better information should be elicited from claimants at the claim stage (discussed above in chapter four), so that more complete information will be in the papers before the tribunal at the appeal stage.

---

[121] R Sainsbury, 'Social Security Decision-Making and Appeals' in Harris et al (above n 10) Table 7.2.

[122] Department for Work and Pensions, *Work and Pension Statistics 2003* (2003) Table 3.

[123] Genn and Richardson (above n 23) 129 and 130.

[124] As noted by the Council on Tribunals, *The Use and Value of Oral Hearings in the Administrative Justice System* (September 2005).

[125] Council on Tribunals, *Consultation on the Use and Value of Oral Hearings in the Administrative Justice System* (2006) Summary of Responses, cited in Genn and Richardson (above n 23).

[126] Department for Work and Pensions, 'If You Think Our Decision Is Wrong', leaflet GL24 (February 2012).

[127] H Genn and C Thomas, *Tribunal Decision-Making: An Empirical Study* (London, UCL Judicial Institute, 2013), www.nuffieldfoundation.org/sites/default/files/files/Tribunal_decision_making_vFINAL.pdf.

[128] The appellant's attendance did, however, make a small positive different in her favour – one factor was that panel members found the mother more believable when able to see and hear from her at an oral hearing. The panel members were also more confident in their decision on the appeal where there had been an oral hearing.

Although there was acceptance within the system that an inquisitorial role should be adopted by the tribunal, the distancing of appellants through the reform measures threatened it.[129] The 1998 Act also stipulated[130] that a tribunal must not take account of issues that did not pertain at the date of the decision – that is, at the date of the decision against which the appeal was brought. This reform may have brought some clarity to a somewhat vexed issue facing tribunals, but it could, from the appellant's perspective, cause confusion and a sense of injustice, thereby reducing the perceived value of the tribunal,[131] as any new problems which he or she may have expected the tribunal would want to hear about would be ignored.[132]

Under the tightened-up appeal procedures, there was a reversion to a time limit of one month in which to lodge an appeal,[133] though it had stood at a more generous three months since 1986.[134] The one-month time limit (plus 14 days where an appellant has requested a written statement of reasons for the decision from the decision-maker[135]) for most types of case has continued, but a claimant may submit an appeal up to 12 months from the date of notice of the decision appealed against, provided the decision-maker or other respondent does not object.[136] Where an appellant submits a late appeal of this type to the tribunal, the tribunal may not (since April 2013) use its general discretion (to extend or shorten the time for complying with any rule) to

---

[129] Wikeley, 'Burying Bell' (above n 80) 495–98.

[130] Social Security Act 1998, s 12(8)(b).

[131] Sainsbury, 'Social Security Decision-Making and Appeals' (above n 121) 224.

[132] However, case law has since confirmed the need to consider changes of circumstances in some situations: see Rowland and White (above n 63) 236–39.

[133] DMA Regulations 1999, reg 31.

[134] Wikeley, *Wikeley, Ogus and Barendt's Law of Social Security* (above n 55) 195.

[135] Unless written reasons have already been provided, the claimant may, within one month of the notification to him/her of the decision, request a written statement of the reasons for the decision; where this is done, the Secretary of State or Board must provide the statement within 14 days of the receipt of the request 'or as soon as practicable afterwards': DMA Regulations 1999, reg 28(1)(b) and (2).

[136] Tribunal Procedure (First-tier Tribunal) (Social Entitlement Chamber) Rules 2008 (SI 2008/2685), r 22 and 23, as amended by the Tribunal Procedure (Amendment) Rules 2013 (SI 2013/477) (L 2). Currently, the Secretary of State is given a separate power to treat an appeal as made in time where it is in the interests of justice for various prescribed reasons, such as where the appellant's partner or dependant has died or suffered serious illness, and having regard to the principle that the greater the tardiness, 'the more compelling should be the special circumstances': Social Security and Child Support (Decisions and Appeals) Regulations 1999 (SI 1999/991), reg 32, which is set for revocation under the draft amendment regulations (see above n 48). Since April 2013, as a result of the amendment of rr 22 and 23 of the 2008 Rules by the (Amendment) Rules 2013, an appeal in a social security case is to be submitted to the tribunal rather than to the decision-maker unless, inter alia, the notice of the decision being challenged informs the appellant that any appeal must be sent to the decision-maker. See also the DMA Regulations 1999, reg 33 (notice of appeal to go to an office of the DWP), until its planed revocation in October 2013 under the draft amendment regulations (above n 48). The DWP has explained that this 'direct lodgement of appeals' will mean that once the mandatory consideration process has been completed, those who wish to appeal will make their appeal directly to the tribunal: DWP, 'Explanatory Memorandum: Amendments 2013' (above n 49) para 7.12.

extend the time for appealing by more than 12 months.[137] The time limit has been and remains a barrier for claimants, although written notice of the right of appeal must be provided by the Secretary of State or Her Majesty's Revenue and Customs (HMRC) when giving written notice of the decision on the claim.[138] Adding further complexity to the appeal process from an appellant's perspective was the requirement to return the enquiry form sent out by The Appeals Service (form TAS1), which asked, inter alia, whether he or she wished to have an oral hearing of the appeal. The appellant would be sent a second-class prepaid envelope in which to return the completed form. There was a power to strike out the appeal if the form was not returned within 14 days.[139]

The House of Commons Work and Pensions Committee highlighted the concerns of various organisations representing appellants that the tight deadlines could lead to the striking-out of appeals from claimants with physical or mental problems or from others with language or literacy problems, 'who might need time to understand the implications of the form and obtain assistance in completing it'.[140] While appeal clerks did not apply the time limit strictly, the Committee considered that reliance on them to take a 'relaxed view' of the time limit was 'not a satisfactory solution'.[141] When the procedural rules were changed in 2008 (see below), the provision for striking-out for non-return of the TAS1 within 14 days was dropped. Since then, it has been possible for an appeal to be struck out if the appellant fails to comply with a direction from a tribunal to return the form and if he or she has been warned of the possible striking-out on that ground;[142] however, in general, the appeal will simply proceed but be heard on the papers alone (since by not returning the form, the appellant has not opted for an oral hearing).[143] Before this change in the rules, 70,000 appeals each year were struck out for non-return of the enquiry form, although approximately 20,000 were subsequently reinstated when appellants showed appropriate cause for the failure, including that they did not understand the significance of the form or the fact that they were awaiting consultation with an advice agency.[144] The change can thus be regarded as beneficial for appellants.

---

[137] Tribunal Procedure (First-tier Tribunal) (Social Entitlement Chamber) Rules 2008 (SI 2008/2685), r 5(3)(a), read with r 22(8)(b), inserted by the Tribunal Procedure (Amendment) Rules 2013 (SI 2013/477) (L 2).

[138] DMA Regulations 2013, reg 51(2)(a); and DMA Regulations 1999, reg 28(1)(c).

[139] DMA Regulations 1999, reg 39.

[140] House of Commons Social Security Committee, *The Modernisation of Social Security Appeals* (1998–99, HC 581) para 45.

[141] Ibid, para 47.

[142] Tribunal Procedure (First-tier Tribunal) (Social Entitlement Chamber) Rules 2008 (SI 2008/2685), r 8.

[143] See also Rowland and White (above n 63) para 5.274.

[144] HC Work and Pensions Committee, *Decision-Making and Appeals in the Benefits System* (above n 37) para 139; and Senior President of Tribunals, *The Senior President of Tribunals' Annual Report: Tribunals Transformed* (London, Ministry of Justice, 2010), 27.

The Value of Representation

It was noted earlier that the judicialisation of tribunals after the merger of the 1980s may have resulted in greater procedural fairness for appellants at the hearing stage, but despite the emphasis on an enabling approach, it had not weakened the value of representation. Sir Andrew Leggatt had argued that tribunals were 'intended to provide a simple, accessible system of justice where users can represent themselves', but he found it 'discouraging to note the growing perception that they cannot'.[145] While the Report recommended that self-representation should be facilitated, it recognised that the 'factual or legal complexity of some cases' nevertheless made representation 'indispensable'.[146]

A study of self-representation by Adler was carried out shortly before the reforms that changed the structure of the tribunals under the Tribunals, Courts and Enforcement Act 2007 – reforms which were most certainly not intended to shift emphasis away from an enabling and more inquisitive approach in tribunals. The research showed that appellants in social security and child support tribunals who received effective advice prior to their hearings but were unrepresented fared almost as well, in terms of being 'wholly successful' in their appeals, as those who had merely had representation at their hearings.[147] But in cases where the appellant was '*partially or wholly*' successful, the position was reversed.[148] Adler also found a high level of activism on the part of chairs of these tribunals, which was only slightly higher again if the appellant was represented. Most tribunal chairs were found to preside in a 'helpful and enabling manner'[149] over hearings, the majority of which were inquisitorial in character.

The picture of hearings in which appellant involvement was facilitated by the tribunal mirrored that emerging from Hazel Genn et al's research a few years earlier in three tribunals, including social security/child support tribunals. Genn et al found that 'on the whole, with the assistance of tribunals, most users were able to present their cases reasonably well'.[150] Adler concluded from his research that the much reduced premium gained from having

---

[145] Leggatt (above n 20) 'Overview', para 7.

[146] Ibid, 'Main Report', paras 4.21–4.22.

[147] M Adler, 'Can Tribunals Deliver Justice in the Absence of Representation?', Legal Services Research Centre International Research Conference *Reaching Further: New Approaches to the Delivery of Legal Services* (21 November 2008), available at www.esrc.ac.uk/my-esrc/grants/RES-000-23-0853/outputs/read/490b00b3-af81-4136-8c8e-77aaf8822737, 10.

[148] Ibid, 11, emphasis added.

[149] Ibid, 14.

[150] H Genn et al, *Tribunals for Diverse Users*, DCA Research Series 1/06 (London, Department for Constitutional Affairs, 2006) 329. Genn et al (330) found that people's problems of access and participation in tribunals was related more to their educational background, language or cultural barriers than their ethnicity per se. Nevertheless, minority ethnic groups who were most likely to have regarded their hearing as unfair were less likely to consider it so if there was an ethnically diverse tribunal (332).

representation was attributable to the now embedded practices of tribunals in facilitating appellants' participation:

> The fact that the outcomes for those who represented themselves, particularly if they had received pre-hearing advice, compared so favourably with those who were represented at their hearing can, in my view, be attributed to the active, inter-ventionist and enabling procedures that many tribunals now adopt.[151]

Adler has expressed the view that the changes in tribunals have moved things in a positive direction and that in terms of serving the interests of justice, the policy is preferable to promoting 'agency' in the form of representation.[152]

Since Adler's research also confirmed the continuing value of pre-hearing advice, it can be seen as broadly consistent with Bell's conclusions some three decades earlier, since Bell had also strongly supported an enabling approach and an extension of access to advice. While Bell recognised the value of rep-resentation, she had considered that it was not needed in all cases. The President of the Social Entitlement Chamber of the First-tier Tribunal has similarly placed on an emphasis on the benefits of advice for appellants – on whether to appeal and in support of the preparation of the case – rather than representation.[153] Echoing Adler's findings, he has commented, 'At the hear-ing, the inquisitorial role of the tribunal may reduce the "added value" of being represented' and the 'scope for advocacy is circumscribed.'[154] Leggatt's vision was of an enabling approach 'supporting the parties in ways which give them confidence in their own abilities to participate in the process, and in the tribunal's capacity to compensate for appellants' lack of skills or knowledge'.[155] While Adler's research showed that the enabling approach was present and has arguably been obviating the need for representation in some cases, it has not confirmed how far it may be empowering appellants in the way that Leggatt envisaged.[156]

Legal Advice and Representation

There has long been a debate about whether legal representation has a role in these tribunals. The prevalent view maintains that while in social security cases tribunal representation should not be the sole preserve of lawyers, legal aid should be available in cases of particular complexity or difficulty when

---

[151]   Adler, 'Can Tribunals Deliver Justice?' (above n 147) 25.
[152]   Ibid.
[153]   See HC Work and Pensions Committee (above n 37) Ev 113–19, paras 41–44.
[154]   Ibid, para 44.
[155]   Leggatt (above n 20) para 7.5.
[156]   G McKeever, 'A Ladder of Legal Participation for Tribunal Users' [2013] *Public Law* 575, finds continuing barriers facing appellants.

legal skills could be advantageous to both claimant and the tribunal itself.[157] Bell was among those who argued that some cases might warrant the availability of legal advice and representation,[158] while the Royal Commission on Legal Services recommended the availability of legal aid for supplementary benefit cases involving cohabitation or dishonesty.[159] The Leggatt Report stated that while 'there will always be [in tribunals] a residual category of complex cases in which legal representation is imperative', it should be funded via financial support for voluntary and community bodies, and only via legal aid 'as a last resort'.[160]

Legal aid for representation has never been available for first-tier appeals in social security cases,[161] but access to publicly funded legal advice and assistance under the legal aid scheme has been.[162] This has meant, for example, that a solicitor (or perhaps more likely a legal executive or welfare rights adviser) could be funded to prepare a written submission on an appellant's behalf although not to appear for him or her at a hearing (save on a pro bono or cross-subsidised[163] basis).

Clearly some cases do involve evidence or legal questions upon which may turn issues of great financial significance for appellants, including, for example, overpayment cases in which an appellant may be appealing against a decision that £10,000 or more in benefit has been overpaid and is recoverable. In such cases, legal representation may well help to ensure that all issues are properly explored by the tribunal.[164] On the other hand, the involvement of the legal profession has traditionally been regarded as inconsistent with the informality and non-adversarial approach expected of administrative tribunals,[165] while a tribunal's legally qualified chair (now judge – see below) is expected to ensure that the law is correctly applied and to guide appellants through its application. As noted above, there is also evidence that, in terms of the outcome of appeals, legal representation is no more effective than that by laypersons. Adler concluded that concentrating on effective tribunal procedures 'may be a more appropriate way of enhancing justice for tribunal

[157] R Lister, *Justice for the Claimant* (London, CPAG, 1974) 66; H Street, *Justice in the Welfare State* (London, Stevens, 1975) 26.

[158] Bell (above n 81).

[159] Royal Commission on Legal Services, *Final Report* (Cmnd 7648, 1979) paras 15.24 and 15.25.

[160] Leggatt (above n 20), 'Overview', para 7.

[161] Moreover, while the Legal Aid Act 1979 provided for 'assistance by way of representation' to be made available in prescribed proceedings, first-tier social security cases were never included.

[162] N Harris, *Quality and Effectiveness in Welfare Benefits and Related Work by Solicitors*, Research Study No 9 (London, Law Society, 1991).

[163] Ie, that the fee income derived from the legal advice element of the work, with perhaps an extension of legal aid, is considered by the firm to be sufficient to subsidise the firm's attendance at the hearing.

[164] A view taken, for example, by Street (above n 157) 26.

[165] Eg, Frost and Howard (above n 83) 58; and J Fulbrook, *Administrative Justice and the Unemployed* (London, Mansell, 1978) 293.

applicants/appellants' than extending legal aid,[166] even assuming that public funds might be available for such a purpose. Nevertheless, there can be no denying the advantages to many appellants of receiving expert advice in connection with their appeals, including legal advice in appropriate cases. As HH Judge Robert Martin, the President of the Social Entitlement Chamber of the First-tier Tribunal, has commented, 'the ability of claimants to manage their appeals without support varies greatly', but the 'complexity of social security law defeats all but a few'.[167]

The availability of advice under the legal aid scheme has, however, become much restricted of late, despite the increasing lack of alternative sources due to reductions in public funding. In the Lord Chancellor's 2010 Legal Aid proposals,[168] the Government indicated a need to prioritise what it considered to be fundamental issues, concerning safety and liberty, and argued that social security issues were of 'lower objective importance (because they are essentially about financial entitlement)'.[169] In support of the argument, the Government contended that 'the accessible, inquisitorial, and user-friendly nature of the tribunal means that appellants can generally present their case without assistance'.[170] Appellants appealing to the First-tier Tribunal merely had to set out their argument 'in plain language'.[171] It was also argued that alternative sources of advice and information were available, including the relevant agency, the Benefits Enquiry Line and voluntary sector bodies.[172] The Government had therefore decided that social security matters should not have any civil legal aid funding at all.[173] The fact that a person may face losing his or her home as a result of a benefit decision was not even considered a sufficiently immediate risk to warrant funding legal aid, although it may be available in respect of repossession per se[174] (and see the scope for exceptional funding below). Judicial review cases would, however, be covered, although as the proposals indicated, they would mostly be confined to areas not covered by the right of appeal such as a decision to suspend benefit pending an investigation.[175] Access to legal aid in judicial review cases more generally was going to be markedly reduced, but the Government made a

---

[166] Adler , 'Can Tribunals Deliver Justice?' (above n 147) 25.

[167] See HC Work and Pensions Committee, *Decision-Making and Appeals in the Benefits System* (above n 37) Ev 113–19, para 41.

[168] Ministry of Justice (MoJ), *Proposals for the Reform of Legal Aid in England and Wales* (Cm 7967, 2010).

[169] Ibid, para 4.217.

[170] Ibid.

[171] Ibid.

[172] Ibid, paras 4.218 and 4.219.

[173] A similar conclusion was reached in relation to asylum support cases, which are considered straightforward and for which alternative sources of advice are said to be available: ibid, para 4.223.

[174] Ibid, paras 4.63, 4.76, 4.79 and 4.220.

[175] Ibid, para 4.224.

commitment partly to ease the restriction.[176] (Legal aid for judicial review applications currently faces a further restriction in relation to cases for which permission to apply is refused.[177])

Despite considerable opposition to the proposals concerning social security work, the Legal Aid, Sentencing and Punishment of Offenders Act 2012 excludes welfare benefits and tax credits cases from 'civil legal services' (namely legal advice, assistance and representation).[178] A government concession, however, resulted in an amendment to the Bill, to make legal advice and assistance available for appeals (on points of law) relating to welfare benefits to the Upper Tribunal and on to the appeal courts, as well as representation in the latter.[179]

A further concession, to be made via statutory instrument (amending the Act), would have involved making legal aid available in certain situations where the First-tier Tribunal reviews its own decision;[180] but it would have been relevant to relatively few cases,[181] and the concession, which was rejected

[176] Under the draft Civil Legal Aid (Merits Criteria) Regulations 2012, reg 53(b), legal aid would only have been available where, inter alia, the act, omission, etc appeared susceptible to challenge and '[t]he individual has exhausted all administrative appeals and other alternative procedures which are available to challenge [it] . . . before bringing a public law claim.' In the House of Lords, Lord Pannick argued that this restriction constituted an absolute bar, giving no discretion to the legal aid authorities. He argued that, for example, it could take considerable time to try other remedies first and that in the High Court, although access to judicial review was also limited to cases where there were no alternative remedies which had not been exhausted, the court could grant exception if those remedies were insufficiently effective or were less convenient: HL Deb 3 December 2012, vol 741, cols 468–70. He had considerable support from other members, and the Minister gave an assurance that the proposed regulations would be amended to ensure the that the director of legal aid case work was empowered to make an award notwithstanding the non-exhaustion of alternative remedies, in a case where those alternatives would not be effective in providing the necessary remedy sought by the individual concerned: col 484 (Lord McNally). The Civil Legal Aid (Merits Criteria) Regulations 2013 (SI 2013/104), reg 53 adopts the same wording as the draft, but amendment regulations seek to give effect to the Government's commitment by providing that legal aid will not be available for judicial review unless 'there are no alternative proceedings before a court or tribunal which are available to challenge the act, omission or other matter, *except where the Director considers that such proceedings would not be effective in providing the remedy that the individual requires*' (emphasis added). (See also reg 39 of the 2013 Merit Criteria Regulations above, referring to exhaustion of alternatives to bringing proceedings.)

[177] Ministry of Justice, *Transforming Legal Aid: Delivering a More Credible and Efficient System*, Consultation Paper 14/2013 (2013) paras 3.69–71. It is proposed that legal aid for such work will not be provided if permission in the case is not granted. However, it will be available for advice on the strength of a potential claim for pre-action correspondence.

[178] Legal Aid, Sentencing and Punishment of Offenders Act 2012, Sched 1, para 8, read with s 8 (meaning of 'civil legal services').

[179] Ibid, Sched 1, para 8.

[180] Ie, (i) where it invites representation from the appellant or (ii) has taken action on the decision following such a review without having first given the appellant and respondent an opportunity to make representations and there is an application to set aside the decision and review it again: Legal Aid, Sentencing and Punishment of Offenders Act 2012, Sched 1, para 7A, which would have been inserted by the Legal Aid, Sentencing and Punishment of Offenders Act 2012 (Amendment of Schedule 1) Order 2012 (draft).

[181] Estimated by the Government to be 696 cases: cited by Baroness Doocey, HL Deb 3 December 2012, vol 741, col 476.

by the House of Lords,[182] was criticised for falling short of an apparent commitment given by the Government in the final stages of the Bill to make legal aid available for appeals in the First-tier Tribunal based on points of law.[183] Lord Bach, for example, questioned how appellants in the minority of cases involving a point of law, many of whom are in fact disabled, could be 'expected to know or understand the legal points that arise in their case'.[184] Baroness Doocey commented that what exacerbated the situation was 'that the Government are in the middle of a major overhaul of the welfare benefits system'; and, as millions of claimants would during the transition phase be 'be reassessed and moved on to different benefits', they would need access to legal help 'to challenge inaccurate decisions about their benefits'.[185] Lord Phillips of Sudbury said that across all the various areas of law, there was 'nowhere more complex than the forest of social welfare legislation', and it was 'utterly futile to pretend that the ordinary bloke can begin to put together the grounds . . . to ask for support to launch an appeal if he or she has got to understand the legal background and legal prospects'.[186] When a new draft statutory instrument was subsequently introduced in place of the defeated one, it did not contain this provision but added appeals relating to council tax reduction schemes to the scope of the legal aid concession concerning second-tier and higher level appeals.[187]

One idea that had support in the Lords debate involved giving tribunal judges power to certify individual cases as warranting the award of legal aid, which echoed similar suggestions made in the 1970s.[188] The minister, however, asserted, 'If the judiciary had to consider up to 135,000 interlocutory applications for legal aid' (that being the number of welfare benefit cases where legal advice and assistance was funded in 2009–10), 'the impact on the tribunal service would be severe, and it could lead to serious delays in the resolution of other cases'.[189] He also argued that if the legal aid authorities had a similar burden, it would give rise to costs which the Government was not prepared to meet in the current economic climate.[190] Thus, ultimately, the matter was one of resource allocation, and it provides another example of the burden of expenditure restraint that is presently being carried by poorer citizens.

---

[182] The Minister subsequently announced that the provision would not be reintroduced: HL Deb 8 January 2013, vol 742, cols 13–15 (Lord McNally).

[183] See HL Deb 3 December 2012, vol 741, cols 471–73 (Lord Bach).

[184] Ibid, col 473.

[185] Ibid, col 476.

[186] Ibid, col 480.

[187] See now the Legal Aid, Sentencing and Punishment of Offenders Act 2012 (Amendment of Schedule 1) Order 2013 (SI 2013/748), inserting (from 1 April 2013) Sched 1, para 8A into the 2012 Act (above n 178). These appeals in relation to a council tax reduction scheme lie on a point of law to the High Court. Further appeals to the Court of Appeal and UK Supreme Court are also covered.

[188] Street (above n 157) 26; and Phillips (above n 157).

[189] See HL Deb 3 December 2012, vol 741, col 486.

[190] Ibid, col 487.

The legal aid changes came into force in April 2013, although interim measures will provide some continuation of support for welfare benefits work until the Legal Services Commission issues new contracts from October 2013.[191] Meanwhile, various voluntary sector bodies have sponsored the establishment of the Low Commission on the Future of Advice and Legal Support in the field of social welfare law. The Commission aims to develop a realistic strategy for meeting the needs of the public, particularly the 'poor and marginalised', via 'good quality independent legal advice' and to use it and evidence on the effects of funding changes to influence political thinking in the run-up to the next general election.[192] The Low Commission is hoping to report by December 2013.

As to whether the legal advice and legal aid restrictions could be success-fully challenged under the Human Rights Act 1998 for incompatibility with Article 6(1) of the European Convention on Human Rights (ECHR)[193] – on the basis of prejudicing the determination of a claimant's civil rights via a fair hearing – this must be open to question. Due to the 1979 Court of Human Rights' decision in *Airey v Ireland*, it would have to be shown that the assist-ance of a legal representative is 'indispensable' in view of the 'complexity of the procedure or the case'.[194] Moreover, the Court considered that states have a free choice of how to support effective access to justice, including 'simplifi-cation of procedure'.[195] Many social security cases are indeed complex, and the threat to an 'equality of arms' that Strasbourg case law indicates Article 6(1) is concerned with[196] is pronounced in citizen-versus-state disputes of the kind at issue. Yet the need for legal representation in the First-tier Tribunal is contested, particularly in a tribunal system with active judicial support for appellants and an 'enabling' ethos, as well as in the light of evidence that lay representation may be equally effective. However, in those social security appeal cases where particularly complex points of law are at issue, expert legal representation may assist the tribunal as much as the appellant, while state funding will also help to ensure that the legal profession as a whole is able to retain an involvement in this publicly important field of law.

In *McVicar v United Kingdom*, the Court of Human Rights did not con-sider that Article 6(1) necessarily required legal aid to be available even for High Court libel proceedings to be determined before a judge and jury.[197] But

---

[191] See the announcement by the Legal Services Commission at http://ftp.legalservices.gov.uk/civil/cls_news_14190.asp?page=2.

[192] See the Low Commission website, www.lowcommission.org.uk/About (as at 18 February 2013).

[193] Art 6(1) is applicable to social security cases: see in particular *Schuler-Zgraggen v Switzerland* (1993) 16 EHRR 405; and *Salesi v Italy* (1993) Series A No 257-E.

[194] *Airey v Ireland* (1979) 2 EHRR 305 [26].

[195] Ibid.

[196] See, eg, *Bombo Beheer BV v The Netherlands* (1994) 18 EHRR 213 [33]; and *Steel and Morris v United Kingdom* [2005] ECHR 103 (15 February 2005), Application No 68416/01, 72.

[197] *McVicar v United Kingdom* [2002] ECHR 436 (7 May 2002) Application No 46311/99.

Human Rights and the Welfare State

the Court took account of the fact that the complainant was 'a well-educated and experienced journalist who would have been capable of formulating cogent argument', and it did not consider that the law of defamation was 'sufficiently complex to require a person in the applicant's position to have legal assistance under Article 6 § 1.'[198] As we have seen, many claimants of social security benefits are neither well-educated nor capable of understanding the law. Moreover, in *McVicar*, the Court specifically contrasted the applicant's capacity with that of the applicant in *Airey*,[199] who had started work as a shop assistant at a young age prior to marrying and having four children, came from a 'humble family background' and had been on unemployment benefit.[200]

In a subsequent Strasbourg case arising out of the so-called 'McLibel' litigation, the libel action in question was considered by the Grand Chamber of the court to be of sufficient complexity to warrant the provision of legal aid:

> [N]either the sporadic help given by the volunteer lawyers nor the extensive judicial assistance and latitude granted to the applicants as litigants in person, was any substitute for competent and sustained representation by an experienced lawyer familiar with the case and with the law of libel.[201]

Yet in social security cases, a reasonably accessible appeal process is available, and while appeal papers can sometimes run to 200 pages, they do not come close to the 40,000 pages (and 130 oral witnesses) that were involved in the 'McLibel' action.

The Legal Aid, Sentencing and Punishment of Offenders Act 2012 recognises the possibility that the unavailability of civil legal aid may in some cases give rise to a potential breach of Article 6(1) through its provision for exceptional funding via an 'exceptional case determination' (by the Director of Legal Aid Casework).[202] This is a determination that it is 'necessary' to make civil legal services not otherwise covered by funding under the Act available to an individual on the basis that otherwise there would be a breach of the individual's rights under the ECHR (or any rights to the provision of legal services that are enforceable EU rights[203]).

The Lord Chancellor's guidance on this exceptional funding emphasises that on the assumption that the proceedings in question involve the determination of a civil right (its view being that cases about 'discretionary' welfare benefit do not – a view supported by judicial authority[204]), the grant of excep-

---

[198]   Ibid, [53] and [55].
[199]   Ibid, [53].
[200]   See *Airey v Ireland* (above n 194) [8].
[201]   *Steel and Morris v UK* (above n 196) 69.
[202]   Legal Aid, Sentencing and Punishment of Offenders Act 2012, s 10(2) and (3).
[203]   See Art 47 of the Charter of Fundamental Rights of the European Union.
[204]   The guidance cites the UK Supreme Court decisions in *Tomlinson v Birmingham City Council* [2010] UKSC 8; and *R (A) v London Borough of Croydon* [2009] UKSC 8. In *A*, in each of the two substantive judgments, by Lady Hale and Lord Hope, the decision in *Tsfayo v United Kingdom* (2009) 48 EHRR 18 was cited. *Tsfayo* concerned a housing review board decision on

tional funding will hinge on whether the withholding of legal aid 'would make the assertion of the claim *practically impossible* or lead to an *obvious fairness* in proceedings . . . a *very high threshold*'.[205] The criteria that the guidance indicates should be taken into account reflect the court's approach in Article 6(1) cases such as *Airey*: the importance or seriousness of what is at stake in the proceedings; the complexity of the procedure, area of the law or evidence in question; and the capacity of the applicant to present his or her case effectively. The guidance also indicates, with regard to cases specifically concerning entitlement to welfare benefits, that the issues to be considered in applying the test of impossibility or unfairness should include: whether the case concerns 'complex legal issues about the interaction of EU and domestic law or complex immigration matters'; whether the benefits at stake might affect the claimant's right to stay in his or her home or be evicted; and the extent of the claimant's ability to present his or her case (with reference to disability, vulnerability, learning difficulties and so on). Quite a number of social security cases might meet at least the factors relating to the importance of the issues at stake or the capacity of the claimant, but this exceptional funding is, as the guidance indicates, intended for 'rare cases'[206] and is in any event subject to the relatively restrictive merits criteria for legal aid funding, such as the exhaustion of reasonable alternatives to bringing proceedings and the likelihood of success.[207]

Structure, Procedure and the Interests of Users

The First-tier Tribunal and the Upper Tribunal were established under the Tribunals, Courts and Enforcement Act 2007 on 3 November 2008. The new

---

housing benefit and thus involved neither discretion nor professional judgment; nor did it hinge on the application of Government policy per se but rather concerned statutory entitlement and was in turn accepted to concern a 'civil right' (an approach consistent with the decisions in *Salesi v Italy* (1998) 26 EHRR 187 and *Mennitto v Italy* (2002) 34 EHRR 48). In *A*, the decision at issue was that of determining a person's age for the purposes of the Children Act 1989, s 20(1) duty of a local authority to provide accommodation for a 'child'. Lady Hale noted that it depended upon 'evaluation of some very "soft" criteria rather than specific rules', and if the right was a civil right for Art 6(1) purposes, 'it must lie close to the boundary of the concept' (para 40). The Court effectively left open the question whether the decision in question in *A* was of a kind covered by Art 6(1). In *Tomlinson*, the UK Supreme Court held unanimously that an appeal to the county court after a local authority review process for homelessness decisions was not covered by Art 6(1). Lord Dyson said that the statutory duty at issue lacked precision and did not concern a right to particular accommodation, and those factors, 'together with the essentially public nature of the duty, mean that the duty does not give rise to an individual economic right' (73). Lord Kerr was influenced by, inter alia, 'the dependence on discretionary judgments not only to establish entitlement but also to discharge the state's obligation'.

[205] Ministry of Justice, *Lord Chancellor's Exceptional Funding Guidance (Non-Inquests)* (2013), www.justice.gov.uk/downloads/legal-aid/funding-code/chancellors-guide-exceptional-funding-non-inquests.pdf, para 18 (original emphasis).

[206] Ibid, para 6.

[207] See the Legal Aid, Sentencing and Punishment of Offenders Act 2012, s 11; and the Civil Legal Aid (Merits Criteria) Regulations 2013 (SI 2013/104), regs 39, 43 and 49.

system as a whole was designed to provide a coherent judicial structure, under a Senior President of Tribunals and with a procedural framework guided by a Tribunals Procedure Committee,[208] covering administrative tribunals in Great Britain.[209] The First-tier Tribunal's Social Entitlement Chamber, under its own President and Regional Judges, is one of the Tribunal's six chambers and has jurisdiction over tax credit appeals and social security appeals. The latter have included housing benefit cases, which until 2001 were governed by a process of review, not appeal, and were heard by locally administered and much criticised housing benefit review boards[210] before being transferred into the jurisdiction of the social security appeal system.[211] Tribunal chairs have become tribunal judges, but otherwise, the membership and composition of tribunals is unaltered, although the legal framework itself has changed.

In a sense, so far as social security appeals are concerned, the 2007 Act has consolidated the judicialisation of the system. But at the same time, the needs of appellants to be assisted in this leg of their complex journeys to possible entitlement, which takes them outside the welfare system and into the judicial system, have not been overlooked. The Act contains a number of measures designed to ensure that tribunals operate in the interests of their users, not merely as a result of the tribunals having greater independence and being required to adopt fair procedures. For example, the Senior President of Tribunals has a duty to have regard to 'the need for tribunals to be accessible'.[212] Also, the power to make rules of procedure for tribunals must be exercised with a view to securing that 'the tribunal system is accessible and fair', that 'the rules are both simple and simply expressed' and that tribunal members are given 'responsibility for ensuring that proceedings before the tribunal are handled quickly and efficiently'.[213]

---

[208] Tribunals, Courts and Enforcement Act 2007, Sched 5. The committee's role includes developing rules of procedure for tribunals: see further below in this section.

[209] On Northern Ireland, see G McKeever, 'Reforming Social Security Appeal Tribunals in Northern Ireland: Parity whether we Leggatt or not?' (2010) 17 *Journal of Social Security Law* 71.

[210] Criticism centred on their procedural shortcomings, weak independence and lack of expertise and training among members: see N Wikeley, 'Housing Benefit Review Boards: The New Slum?' (1986) *Civil Justice Quarterly* 18; R Sainsbury and T Eardley, 'Housing Benefit Review Boards: A Case for Slum Clearance?' (1992) *Public Law* 551; and R Sainsbury and T Eardley, *Housing Benefit Reviews: An Evaluation of the Effectiveness of the Review System in Responding to Claimants Dissatisfied with Housing Benefit Decisions*, Department of Social Security Research Report No 3 (London, HMSO, 1991).

[211] Child Support, Pensions and Social Security Administration Act 2000, s 68 and Sched 7. Council tax benefit cases were also transferred to the appeal tribunal. Rahilly commented that tribunal members having to grapple with housing benefit cases 'will be faced with a benefit with complex rules, to which successive governments have been prone to making constant changes; transitional arrangements are commonplace, and dates can be critical. The period of transition [to the new system] will add an additional layer of complexity . . .' See S Rahilly, 'Housing Benefit Appeals: From Housing Benefit Review Boards to the Appeals Service' (2001) 8 *Journal of Social Security Law* 57.

[212] Tribunals, Courts and Enforcement Act 2007, s 1(3)(a).

[213] Ibid, s 22(4)(b) and (d).

Ensuring that the appeal process is as accessible as possible is clearly very important, as there remain significant barriers for some claimants. For example, recent research that examined ESA claimants' reasons for not bringing appeals found that typical reasons included a feeling that it was pointless either because they had been advised after discussing the matter with a third party such as a Pathways adviser that they were unlikely to be successful or because 'they felt "powerless in the face of officialdom" '.[214] Another factor was a feeling of discomfort about bringing an appeal, in particular that it was not in their nature to appeal.[215] Some claimants had other priorities or concerns at the time, such as health, housing or family difficulties, which distracted them from bringing appeals. For some, bringing an appeal carried a perceived risk of having to do without benefit income, a perception that was erroneous since benefit would continue to be paid (at the basic pre-assessment rate) until the appeal decision; this misconception has deterred some from appealing.[216] With hindsight, some regretted not having appealed because they realised they may have been successful.[217]

Given that the history of social security appeals has seen procedural regulations become 'increasingly complex and formalistic, borrowing from the courts concepts such as striking-out and tighter time limits',[218] and in the light of appellant difficulties in following 'the ins and outs' of procedures,[219] the above statutory commitments are attractive. Yet there are formal procedural elements in the current rules, including case management powers (such as giving directions to the parties on various matters), that were introduced when the new tribunals structure was brought in. Those relevant to social security cases are in the Tribunal Procedure (First-tier Tribunal) (Social Entitlement Chamber) Rules 2008, as amended.[220] There is evidence from the above survey of ESA appellants that procedural requirements are sometimes perceived as barriers. Even the need to respond to a letter from a tribunal asking for the completion and return of a form deters some from proceeding to a hearing of their appeal.[221] However, as noted earlier the rules at least no longer provide for an administrative power to strike out an appeal when the appellant fails to return the form – a power that, as we saw above, was applied in around 70,000 appeals each year (although as was also noted, just under one third were subsequently reinstated when an appropriate cause for the failure was shown). Also, appellants now receive a welcoming leaflet, a reminder

---

[214] H Barnes et al, *Unsuccessful Employment and Support Allowance Claims: Qualitative Research*, DWP Research Report No 762 (2011) 19.

[215] Ibid.

[216] Ibid, 20.

[217] Ibid

[218] See Wikeley, 'Burying Bell' (above n 80) 496.

[219] Berthoud and Bryson (above n 99) 37.

[220] SI 2008/2685, as amended by the Tribunal Procedure (Amendment) Rules 2013 (SI 2013/477) (L 2). For the time limit for appeals, see above nn 136 and 137 and linked text.

[221] Barnes et al (above n 214) 21.

letter and an offer to speak to someone on the telephone; and if they still fail to respond, the matter is passed to a tribunal judge for a decision on how to proceed.

The Senior President of Tribunals has commented, 'Bearing in mind that surveys have shown that one half of Social Security appellants lack confidence to deal with official forms, the enquiry form strike-out process proved a substantial hindrance to justice.'[222] Indeed, a few months into the operation of the new rules, some 1,200 appellants whose appeals would have been struck out under the old rules had their appeals heard and upheld.[223] Nevertheless, some of the above ESA appellants who withdrew an appeal[224] had 'decided they could no longer carry on with it as it entailed several stages and an increasing amount of paperwork'.[225] One of the requirements under the rules is, for example, that when a decision-maker sends in his/her response to an appeal,[226] any submission or further documents the appellant wishes to have considered by the tribunal must be provided to the tribunal within one month.[227] In practice, however, tribunals have 'always been at pains to exercise . . . discretion to extend the time limit'.[228] In any event, the rules also specify as their 'overriding objective' that tribunals are to deal with cases 'fairly and justly', which specifically includes avoiding unnecessary formality; seeking 'flexibility in the proceedings'; 'ensuring, so far as practicable, that the parties are able to participate fully in the proceedings'; 'avoiding delay, so far as is compatible with proper consideration of the issues'; and 'dealing with the case in ways which are proportionate to the importance of the case, the complexity of the issues, the anticipated costs and the resources of the

---

[222] Senior President of Tribunals (above n 144) 27.

[223] Ibid, 28.

[224] Prior to the amendment of the rules in April 2013, withdrawal of an appeal was a right that could be exercised: (i) in writing at any time before either a hearing or a determination of the appeal on the papers; or (ii) with the tribunal's permission, orally at the hearing: Tribunal Procedure (First-tier Tribunal) (Social Entitlement Chamber) Rules 2008 (SI 2008/2685), r 17. This rule, as amended the Tribunal Procedure (Amendment) Rules 2013 (SI 2013/477) (L 2), seems not now to require the tribunal's permission for a withdrawal of an appeal orally at the hearing. It is also now provided that a tribunal may direct that a written notice of withdrawal may only take effect with the tribunal's consent. Withdrawal prior to the hearing occurred in 6.4% of cases around 2010–11: Senior President of Tribunals, *The Senior President of Tribunals' Annual Report* (London, Ministry of Justice, 2011) 40. This withdrawal rate had increased from 1% of cases, an increase attributed to improvements in the information supplied to appellants and to increased contact between them and clerks to the tribunal.

[225] Barnes et al (above n 214) 3.

[226] The decision-maker is required to do this, although rather than being bound by a fixed time limit, he or she must respond 'as soon as reasonably practicable': Tribunal Procedure (First-tier Tribunal) (Social Entitlement Chamber) Rules 2008 (SI 2008/2685), r 24(1). In practice, the average response time in 2009–10 was 63 days: see HC Work and Pensions Committee, *Decision-Making and Appeals in the Benefits System* (above n 37) Oral Evidence Q76 (Tom Levitt MP).

[227] Tribunal Procedure (First-tier Tribunal) (Social Entitlement Chamber) Rules 2008 (SI 2008/2685), r 24(7).

[228] See HC Work and Pensions Committee, *Decision-Making and Appeals in the Benefits System* (above n 37) Oral Evidence, Q74 (HH Judge Robert Martin).

parties'.[229] The parties to an appeal are charged with helping the tribunal to further the overriding objective and must co-operate with the tribunal generally.[230] The power of the Senior President of Tribunals and of the Chamber Presidents to give directions on practice and procedure could also be used to facilitate participation in hearings by appellants. Those practice directions made to date have included one that facilitates the use of the Welsh language in Wales and another that deals with the attendance and giving of evidence by children, vulnerable adults and 'sensitive witnesses'.[231]

The role of presenting officers (POs) from the relevant agency has been another issue of concern. It is unclear whether the absence of any PO (which is likely when a PO's agency is the DWP or HMRC) makes the experience before the tribunal an easier one for an appellant. Currently, POs attend on average around one in six hearings, a decline from two in five hearings in 2000–01.[232] According to DWP policy, a PO should attend a First-tier Tribunal hearing if it is so directed by a tribunal judge or if: a) the law or facts are 'considered to be complex, for example, where complex legal arguments have been raised or contentious case law has been referred to'; or b) the case involves new legislation that is still in a period of bedding-in (a period whose length 'will be determined by the complexity of the legislation').[233]

In the past, there were concerns that some presenting officers, especially prior to the merger of supplementary and national adjudication, acted as advocates for the department in a way that could be intimidating to appellants rather than as amicus curiae assisting tribunals to get the facts straight and elaborating the decision-maker's reasons for the benefit of appellants and tribunals.[234] Wikeley and Young, writing in 1991, concluded from empirical research that POs were only rarely taking on a 'crude adversarial position', but the adoption of an amicus curiae role was 'far from the norm', since most often POs were either passive or reactive during hearings and failed to take the initiative by either advancing points supportive of the appellant's position

---

[229] Tribunal Procedure (First-tier Tribunal) (Social Entitlement Chamber) Rules 2008 (SI 2008/2685), r 2. The tribunal is under a duty to seek to give effect to the overriding objective when exercising any power under the rules or in interpreting any rule or practice direction.

[230] Ibid.

[231] Senior President of Tribunals, 'Practice Direction (First-tier and Upper Tribunals: Use of the Welsh Language in Tribunals in Wales)' (30 October 2008); and Senior President of Tribunals, 'Practice Direction (First-tier and Upper Tribunals: Child, Vulnerable Adult and Sensitive Witnesses)' (30 October 2008).

[232] HC Work and Pensions Committee, *Decision-Making and Appeals in the Benefits System* (above n 37) para 164.

[233] Ibid, Written Evidence, Ev 125–33, para 10.2 (Memorandum submitted by the Department for Work and Pensions (DM 29)).

[234] See Frost and Howard (above n 83) 45–46; and J Fulbrook, *Administrative Justice and the Unemployed* (London, Mansell, 1978) 238–39. Fulbrook found that in insurance benefit cases, officers protected their independence and did act as amicus curiae, in contrast to supplementary benefit presenting officers, who tended to act as advocates for the Department. Bell (above n 81), however, found 'few examples of hostility towards appellants although there were one or two incidents where a PO found it difficult to suppress his feelings' (11).

or different legal interpretations to those of the first-instance decision-makers.[235] Those authors concluded, 'The concept of amicus curiae to some extent legitimises and disguises the weak position in which appellants find themselves before social security appeal tribunals.'[236] While this view may have some validity in the present context as well, the amicus curiae role does now appear to be better recognised within the Department. The DWP has stated that a PO is meant to 'help the tribunal to reach the correct decision based on all the facts and the application of the law', and 'although the PO presents the Secretary of State's/Local Authority's case, they should also assist the appellant, where possible'.[237]

The greater problem now perhaps is that the absence of a PO may compromise a tribunal's neutrality in the mind of an appellant[238] and weaken the tribunal's judicial character.[239] As the President of the Social Entitlement Chamber has commented, where a tribunal is exercising its enabling role and the PO is absent, the appellant may wonder why the tribunal, 'which is supposed to be impartial, is explaining the case of the Department'.[240] However, the Government has rejected the argument that a tribunal's independence is undermined by the absence of a PO.[241] A further disadvantage is that appellants, as well as the tribunals themselves, are deprived of the opportunity to challenge the relevant body's arguments through oral questions.[242] There is, however, no Government commitment to increase POs' attendance rates. The previous Government implied in 2010 that for that to happen, staffing resources would have to be reallocated away from decision-making, and '[i]t would not be in customers' interests if making more presenting officers available resulted in longer claims clearance times'.[243]

The Wait for a Hearing

The time it takes for an appeal to reach a hearing has also been a problem. The speed with which appeals are heard was identified in the 1996 Green

---

[235] N Wikeley and R Young, 'Presenting Officers in Social Security Tribunals: The Theory and Practice of the Curious *Amici*' (1991) 18(4) *Journal of Law and Society* 464, 471.

[236] Ibid, 472.

[237] HC Work and Pensions Committee, *Decision-Making and Appeals in the Benefits System* (above n 37) Ev 125–33, para 10.1 (Memorandum submitted by the Department for Work and Pensions (DM 29)).

[238] The House of Commons Work and Pensions Committee has expressed concern about this: ibid, para 165.

[239] See N Harris and N Wikeley, 'Amicus Curiae: In Absentia' (2002) 9(2) *Journal of Social Security Law* 51–54.

[240] HC Work and Pensions Committee, *Decision-Making and Appeals in the Benefits System* (above n 37) Oral Evidence, Q84 (HH Judge Robert Martin).

[241] HC Work and Pensions Committee, *Decision-Making and Appeals: Government Response* (above n 52) para 94.

[242] Harris and Wikeley (above n 239) 52.

[243] HC Work and Pensions Committee, *Decision-Making and Appeals: Government Response* (above n 52) para 94.

Paper as a benchmark of the quality of service provided by the appeal system.[244] Yet over the years, the waiting period has lengthened, despite efforts by the appeals administration to reduce it. Regarding the main social security tribunals, the average clearance times for appeals lengthened between 1995–96 and 1998–99 to nearly 28 weeks in the case of social security appeal tribunals and nearly 39 weeks in the case of medical appeal/vaccine damage and disability appeal tribunals.[245]

The House of Commons Social Security Committee highlighted the psychological and in some cases financial difficulties that such long delays could cause appellants, along with the greater likelihood that an appellant's circumstances will have changed since the original decision.[246] The Committee attributed the delays to, first, the substantial rise in the number of appeals (a 51 per cent rise between 1995–96 and 1997–98, when approximately 346,000 appeals were received).[247] In 1998–99, despite a fall in the number of appeals received, a record 360,000 social security appeals were cleared – 370,000, if child support appeals are included.[248] Secondly, there was the impact of budgetary constraints on human resource levels in the administration and among the judiciary. Running cost allocations had remained static, and there had been 'no increase in staffing levels concomitant with the substantial rise in workloads'.[249] The Committee considered that the managerial emphasis in the reforms under the 1998 Act and the oral/paper hearings option change in 1996 had been to tackle 'unacceptable delays' in the hearing of appeals, and the success or failure of those reforms 'will be largely judged by their success in achieving this object'.[250]

Clearance times have fluctuated somewhat since then but rose substantially between 2007–08 and 2009–10, after the introduction of ESA, putting 'a considerable strain on the Tribunals Service's resources'.[251] The Tribunals Service (which since 2010 has been part of HM Courts and Tribunals Service) had a performance target of hearing 75 per cent of appeals within 14 weeks of receipt. Whereas this was exceeded in 2007–08, when 87 per cent of appeals were heard within that timescale, it declined to 78 per cent the following year and to 59 per cent in 2009–10.[252] There appears to have been a further fall in 2011–12, when approximately 40 per cent of appeals were cleared within

---

[244] DSS, *Improving Decision-Making and Appeals* (above n 34) para 6.10.

[245] HC Social Security Committee, *The Modernisation of Social Security Appeals* (above n 140) Table 1.

[246] Ibid, para 7 and Table 2.

[247] Ibid, para 8 and Table 2.

[248] Ibid, Table 2.

[249] Ibid, paras 9 and 10.

[250] Ibid, para 13.

[251] HC Work and Pensions Committee, *Decision-Making and Appeals in the Benefits System* (above n 37) para 162.

[252] Ibid, para 160; and Tribunals Service, *Tribunals Service Annual Report and Accounts, 2010–11* (HC 1245, 2011) Table B.

14 weeks.[253] A total of 380,000 social security appeals and child support appeals (the former representing well over 90 per cent of the total) were cleared in 2010–11 (up from 279,000 in 2009–10 and 245,500 in 2008–09), while 418,500 appeals were received (174,000 more than in 2008–09).[254] The forecast trend has been for a continuing growth in appeal numbers, from a reduced intake of 370,800 in 2011–12 (attributed to 'a temporary constriction in benefit processing by [the] DWP') to escalating projected annual totals peaking at 807,000 in 2015–16 before falling back to 646,000 in 2016–17.[255] The increased caseload after 2008 was largely due to a surge in ESA cases[256] (which represented 50 per cent of appeals in 2011–12[257]) and is expected, after 2013, to be contributed to by the reassessments consequent on the transition from DLA to PIP[258] and the introduction of universal credit, which will affect around 12 million claimants.[259] Despite the fall in numbers in 2011–12, the overall total was still significantly higher than it was in 2008–09. Moreover, appeals disposed of in 2011–12 were 14 per cent greater than in the previous year, rising to 433,600, including 340,400 that were heard.[260]

At a time of austerity in the public sector, the high numbers of appeals have clearly made a reduction in the average timescale for the clearance of an individual appeal impossible. Despite the fall in appeals received in 2011–12, the impression is of a system under considerable strain and in which significant reductions in delay are unlikely to be realisable.

Post-hearing

Following a hearing and after a tribunal's decision disposing of all the issues in the proceedings, the appellant must be provided 'as soon as reasonably practicable' with a decision notice and notification of the right to apply for a written statement of the reasons for the decision.[261] Appellants were successful[262] in 35 per cent of appeals heard in 2011–12.[263] Appellants must also be

---

[253] Ministry of Justice (MoJ), *Annual Tribunals Statistics, 2011–12* (28 June 2012), www.justice.gov.uk/downloads/statistics/tribs-stats/ts-annual-stats-2011-12.pdf, Fig7.

[254] Tribunals Service (above n 252) 8 and Table A.

[255] Senior President of Tribunals, *Annual Report* (2013) (above n 4) 29–30.

[256] Senior President of Tribunals, *Annual Report: Tribunals Transformed* (2010) (above n 144) 13.

[257] MoJ, *Annual Tribunals Statistics, 2011–12* (above n 253) 7, also noting that 24% of appeals concerned DLA/attendance allowance and 12% JSA.

[258] Senior President of Tribunals, *The Senior President of Tribunals' Annual Report* (London, Ministry of Justice, 2012) 24.

[259] Senior President of Tribunals, *Annual Report* (2013) (above n 4) 30.

[260] Ibid, 10 and 12.

[261] Tribunal Procedure [etc] Rules 2008 (SI 2008/2685) above n 226, r 33, as amended by the Tribunal Procedure (Amendment) Rules 2013 (SI 2013/477) (L 2). Including brief reasons in ESA appeal decision notices is being piloted in some areas.

[262] In the sense that the tribunal did not uphold the original decision.

[263] MoJ, *Annual Tribunals Statistics, 2011–12* (above n 253) 12.

informed of their further right of appeal (to the Upper Tribunal) and the time within which it must be exercised.[264] Appellants have one month from the date on which they were sent or otherwise provided with a decision notice in which to request the written statement of reasons.[265]

If an appellant wishes to seek permission to appeal to the Upper Tribunal, he or she must apply to the First-tier Tribunal[266] within one month of the latest of the dates on which he or she is sent by the tribunal: a) the decision notice; b) the statement of reasons; c) notification of any amended reasons for or corrected decision following a review by the tribunal;[267] or d) notification that an application to set aside the tribunal's decision[268] (for example, on the grounds that the appellant was unable to attend the hearing) was refused. If the First-tier Tribunal refuses permission to appeal, it must notify the appellant of its reasons and of his/her right to apply to the Upper Tribunal for permission to appeal and the time within which they must apply.[269] The appellant therefore has two opportunities to seek permission to appeal. The above time limits may appear restrictive, but the rules permit the First-tier Tribunal to extend them under its case management powers.[270]

V. The Upper Tribunal and Beyond

As noted above, appeals against decisions of the First-tier Tribunal in social security and tax credit cases lie, with permission, to the Upper Tribunal (Administrative Appeals Chamber) (AAC), one of four Chambers established

---

[264] Tribunal Procedure (First-tier Tribunal) (Social Entitlement Chamber) Rules 2008 (SI 2008/2685), r 33, as amended by the Tribunal Procedure (Amendment) Rules 2013 (SI 2013/477) (L 2).

[265] Ibid, r 34 (2008 rules, as amended by the Amendment Rules 2013).

[266] Ibid, r 38 (2008 rules, as amended by the Amendment Rules 2013).

[267] If permission to appeal is applied for, the tribunal must, having regard to the 'overriding objective' in r 2 (discussed earlier above), consider whether to review its decision: Tribunal Procedure (First-tier Tribunal) (Social Entitlement Chamber) Rules 2008 (SI 2008/2685), r 39(1). On reviews, see r 40.

[268] Covered by r 37. The grounds for the tribunal's setting aside of its decision are that it is in the interest of justice to do so and one or more of various prescribed conditions apply (eg, a party or his/her representative did not attend or did not receive a document relating to the proceedings).

[269] The Tribunal Procedure (Upper Tribunal) Rules 2008 (SI 2008/2698), r 21. The time limit in social security and tax credit cases is one month after being sent notice of the First-tier Tribunal's refusal to grant permission to appeal: r 21(3)(b). The case management powers in the rules contain general provision for extending time: r 5(3)(a).

[270] Tribunal Procedure (First-tier Tribunal) (Social Entitlement Chamber) Rules 2008 (SI 2008/2685), r 5(3)(a).

following the creation of the Upper Tribunal under the Tribunals, Courts and Enforcement Act 2007.[271] The Upper Tribunal also has a judicial review jurisdiction.[272] Its decisions may themselves be amenable to judicial review,[273] although most challenges to its rulings would be expected to take the route of an appeal on a point of law to the Court of Appeal.[274]

Irrespective of the overall anticipated position of the Upper Tribunal as 'at least equivalent to that of the Administrative Court in England and Wales', with an authority derived from 'its specialist skills, and its status as a superior court of record, with judicial review powers, presided over by a Senior President',[275] its place in the social security appellate structure (see Figure 4 below), its status therein and its role in the development of case law in this field are little different from those of the Social Security and Child Support Commissioners, whose jurisdiction in this field it has replaced. Indeed, the President of the AAC has commented, 'The new procedural rules have made very few differences to the way [social security and child support] cases need to be handled, and so it has been possible to provide users with a seamless transition into the new tribunal system.'[276]

There has nevertheless been an overall fall over the years in the number of social security and child support (SSCS) cases that have come before the second-tier tribunal for decisions – such cases currently represent around one in

---

[271]   See the First-tier Tribunal and Upper Tribunal (Chambers) Order 2008 (SI 2008/2684). See N Wikeley, 'The Role of the Upper Tribunal (AAC)' (2011) *Family Law* 1255–58.

[272]   Tribunals, Courts and Enforcement Act 2007, ss 15–19; and the Senior Courts Act 1981 (formerly Supreme Court Act 1981), s 31A. By direction of the Lord Chief Justice, certain types of judicial review case have been transferred to the jurisdiction of the Upper Tribunal, of which the most significant for social security is challenges to the First-tier Tribunal's decision over matters that are excluded from a right of appeal: see *Practice Direction (Upper Tribunal: Judicial Review Jurisdiction)* [2009] 1 WLR 327. See also Senior President of Tribunals, *Annual Report: Tribunals Transformed* (2010) (above n 144) para 49.

[273]   See *R (Cart) v Upper Tribunal* [2011] UKSC 28. Amenability to judicial review here will depend on the case involving an important point of principle or practice or where there is a compelling reason to justify the superior's court's review: see paras 52–57. See further E Laurie, 'Assessing the Upper Tribunal's Potential to Deliver Administrative Justice' (2012) *Public Law* 288. The courts' capacity to supervise this specialist tribunal via judicial review has some constitutional significance: see Laurie (above); and M Elliott and R Thomas, 'Tribunal Justice and Proportionate Dispute Resolution' (2012) 71(2) *Cambridge Law Journal* 297.

[274]   Not least because in practice, challenges to most interlocutory decisions of the First-tier Tribunal, which might have been expected to require a challenge to be brought via judicial review, have been found to be appealable: Senior President of Tribunals, *Annual Report: Tribunals Transformed* (2010) (above n 144) para 126. On making an application for permission to appeal a decision of the Upper Tribunal, see, inter alia, the Tribunal Procedure (Upper Tribunal) Rules 2008 (SI 2008/2698), rr 43 and 44. The Upper Tribunal may review its decision on certain grounds if an application for permission to appeal is made: r 46. Laurie has pointed out that despite the courts' general deference to or at least respect for specialist tribunals, the Court of Appeal upheld 44% of the appeals it heard from decisions of the Social Security Commissioners in 2000–08 (above n 273, 293–96).

[275]   Senior President of Tribunals, *Annual Report: Tribunals Transformed* (above n 144) para 27.

[276]   Senior President of Tribunals, *Annual Report: Tribunals Transformed* (2010) (above n 144) para 127.

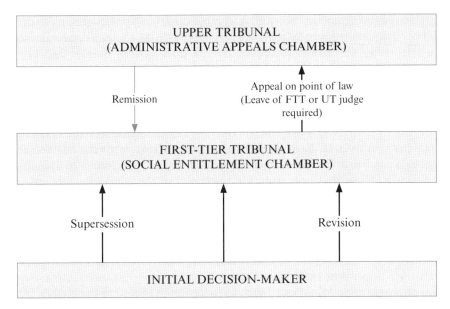

Figure 4: First-Tier and Second-Tier Appellate Routes for Social Security Cases

three of those that started out as applications to it. In 2003 there were 2,227 appeals which came before the Social Security and Child Support Commissioners,[277] but in 2008–09 there were only 1,762 appeals received by the Upper Tribunal (AAC),[278] the overwhelming majority of which were SSCS cases. Between 2009–10 and 2010–11, the number of such appeals fell further from 1,308 to 1,212 and, represented as a percentage of First-tier Tribunal decisions, went down from 0.47 per cent to 0.32 per cent.[279] No official reason has been given for the reductions in cases during this period, and one has in any event to take account of past criticism regarding the quality of statistical information in this sphere.[280] The overall number of applications to the Upper Tribunal (AAC) actually *increased* by 10 per cent between 2009–10 and 2010–11,[281] although the run-in time for Upper Tribunal social security appeal disposals makes comparison problematic. Furthermore, in 2012 the number of SSCS appeals alone coming before the Upper Tribunal increased to over 1,500.[282]

[277] Cited in T Buck, D Bonner and R Sainsbury, *Making Social Security Law: The Role and Work of the Social Security and Child Support Commissioners* (Aldershot, Ashgate, 2005) 48.
[278] See ajtc.justice.gov.uk/stats/186.htm.
[279] Senior President of Tribunals, *Annual Report* (2012) (above n 258) 26.
[280] Buck, Bonner and Sainsbury (above n 277) 201–3.
[281] Tribunals Service (above n 252) Table A.
[282] Upper Tribunal internal statistics for England and Wales for the calendar years 2010, 2011

One question that may be asked is whether the fall in appeals coming to the Upper Tribunal prior to 2012 was contributed to by an increased refusal rate in relation to permission to appeal. Trevor Buck, David Bonner and Roy Sainsbury have noted that the Commissioners indicated in 2004 that they were adopting a more robust approach to leave applications in cases of little merit.[283] Recent figures show a fluctuating pattern. The proportion of applications to the Upper Tribunal for permission which succeeded fell from 38.6 per cent in 2010 to 32.4 per cent in 2011.[284] The permission rate increased to 38.8 per cent in 2012, however, although the main reason for the increase in appeals coming before the Upper Tribunal that year was a surge in applications, which rose by 15 per cent (although part of the reason for this was a concomitant fall in permissions granted by the First-tier Tribunal).[285] Buck, Bonner and Sainsbury have concluded that the fall in appeals in the four years to 2004–05 was also contributed to by the review and setting aside powers of the appeal tribunal introduced under the Social Security Act 1998, which may have increased the number of earlier resolutions in claimants' favour.[286] It seems unlikely – and there is no evidence – that such factors may have become more pronounced such as to have contributed to the further fall in appeals in recent years.

For appellants, it is clear that a degree of patience is needed in bringing an appeal, since the process does not operate quickly. In terms of the time from application to disposal of appeal, trends are difficult to identify since there were changes in reporting in 2010–11, reflecting new and tighter targets. What we can see is that in that year, 53 per cent of appeals were disposed of within 20 weeks of receipt, as against the target rate of 75 per cent; and 57 per cent of applications for permission to appeal were disposed of within 10 weeks of receipt, for which the target was also 75 per cent.[287] Nevertheless, while statistical comparison is difficult, these figures appear to suggest a considerable reduction in the waiting time as against the late 1990s. The average time waiting time in 1998, for example, was over 64 weeks, although it had fallen in the first nine months of 1999 to 50.9 weeks,[288] and the House of Commons Social Security Committee expressed considerable concern at its length and to a 'culture of delay' surrounding the Social Security Commissioners.[289] The 'overriding objective' of dealing with a case 'justly and fairly' to which the Upper Tribunal must 'seek to give effect' mirrors that applicable to the First-tier Tribunal and similarly includes 'avoiding delay, so far as is compatible

and 2012 (to 7 December 2012) approved for inclusion here via private communication.

[283] Buck, Bonner and Sainsbury (above n 277).
[284] See above n 282.
[285] Ibid.
[286] Buck, Bonner and Sainsbury (above n 277) 103 and 108.
[287] Tribunals Service (above n 252) Table B.
[288] HC Deb 9 November 1999 vol 337, col 503W (J Kennedy).
[289] House of Commons Select Committee on Social Security, *Social Security and Child Support Commissioners* (1999–2000, HC 263) para 10.

with proper consideration of the issues'.[290] Notwithstanding the complexity of some cases, however, many appellants face a likely overall wait of more than six months before the appeal process is concluded.

The time an appeal takes is, however, but one element of the experience facing those who undertake this leg of the journey to potential entitlement. Buck, Bonner and Sainsbury found in their study of the Social Security and Child Support Commissioners that appellants' 'perception of an appeal to the Commissioners is one marked out by complexity and remoteness'.[291] For example, the Commissioners' necessary focus on points of law in the context of the 'increasing complexity of social security legislation' was inconsistent with what appellants were looking for.[292] What some appellants wanted was the righting of 'a failure in the rational process of decision-making' which had been caused by a breaking down of the 'correct process of applying social security law to the facts of the appellant's circumstances' due to the flaws in the 'evidence from which the "facts" were derived'.[293] Others were looking for a closer focus on their needs, while a further motivating factor behind an appeal was a 'sense of their own "deservingness" to the benefit in question'.[294] All these appellants had a sense of grievance, but the researchers also identified grievances connected to the way the First-tier Tribunal hearing was conducted or with the fairness of the law, that the Commissioners were powerless, at least in the latter case, to address.[295] A mismatch between appellant expectations and the reality of adjudication by the Upper Tribunal can perhaps be countered to a degree through the provision of information to appellants or through advice and assistance, including representation. This is part of a wider point about the need for such provision at this level of adjudication, which is discussed below.

An appellant whose case is before the Upper Tribunal has already had to cope with the burden of seeking permission to appeal. If that permission had to be sought from the Upper Tribunal itself, the appellant will have had to state in the application the grounds of appeal and to provide a copy of any written record of the decision that he or she is challenging, as well as any separate written statement of reasons that was provided following that decision.[296] The appellant also has to state whether he or she wishes the application for permission to be dealt with at a hearing.[297] If permission to appeal

---

[290] Tribunal Procedure (Upper Tribunal) Rules 2008 (SI 2008/2698), r 2. Like the First-tier Tribunal, the Upper Tribunal is also expected to seek bring the parties' attention, where appropriate to do so, to the availability of alternative procedures for the resolution of the dispute and, if it is compatible with the overriding objective to do so, to facilitate its use: r 3.

[291] Buck, Bonner and Sainsbury (above n 277) 209.

[292] Ibid, 210.

[293] Ibid, 114.

[294] Ibid, 115.

[295] Ibid, 116.

[296] Tribunal Procedure (Upper Tribunal) Rules 2008 (SI 2008/2698), r 21(4)(e) and (5).

[297] Ibid, r 21(4)(f).

has been granted by the Upper Tribunal, the application for permission is to be treated as the notice of appeal, and the Upper Tribunal must send the respondent(s) a copy of it and any other documents submitted by the appellant.[298] If, on the other hand, the First-tier Tribunal has granted permission to appeal, the appellant has to provide a notice of appeal to the Upper Tribunal within one month after being sent the permission[299] and include in it the grounds on which he or she is relying.[300] The appellant would also have to provide a copy of the written record of the decision appealed against, any separate written statement of reasons for that decision, and the notice of permission to appeal.[301] Although the respondent is able to submit a response to the appeal, it is not mandatory; and if both/all parties consent, the appeal can be determined without it.[302] If a response is made, it must be in writing and state whether the appeal is opposed and, if so, on what grounds.[303] The appellant is permitted to provide within one month a written reply to the respondent's response to the appeal.[304] The Upper Tribunal's range of case management powers includes that of giving directions to the parties and of disposing of the proceedings at any time.[305]

Despite the information on the procedure that is made available to appellants by the Upper Tribunal, the process may not be an easy one to navigate. While the Upper Tribunal's power to 'take such action as it considers just' if a party fails to comply with any of the requirements in the rules includes 'waiving the requirement', it also includes striking-out the party's case.[306]

There is no fee for appealing to the Upper Tribunal, and an appellant does not face the possibility of an award of costs against him or her if unsuccessful.[307] Furthermore, an appellant can be – and in practice is – paid travel expenses (oral hearings are arranged in a number of centres around the country, although video-conferencing is now also in use) and 'compensation for loss of any remunerative time' for attending a hearing.[308] The appellant is in fact unlikely to have to face an oral hearing of his or her appeal unless he or she wants one. Even if a request for one is made, the Upper Tribunal has discretion to decide a case without a hearing, although it must have regard to the view of any party before deciding the matter.[309] In practice, the overwhelming majority

---

[298] Ibid, r 22(2)(b).
[299] Ibid, r 23(2), but note the possibility of extension of time under r 5(3)(a).
[300] Ibid, r 23(3) and (4).
[301] Ibid, r 23(4).
[302] Ibid, r 22(2)(c).
[303] Ibid, r 24.
[304] Ibid, r 25.
[305] Ibid, r 5. On the procedure for giving directions, see r 6.
[306] Ibid, r 7. The power to strike out the case is in r 8.
[307] See ibid, r 10.
[308] Ibid, r 21.
[309] Ibid, r 34. Rowland and White have discussed the case law indicating that an oral hearing by a second-tier appeal body such as the Upper Tribunal is not necessary under the European Convention on Human Rights: Rowland and White (above n 63) 1478.

of cases have paper hearings.[310] This seems to be mostly because few appellants request an oral hearing rather than many being refused one.[311] As the appeal is concerned with a point or points of law and is generally based on evidence which was before the First-tier Tribunal, a determination on the papers may be entirely appropriate. It also means that the appellant is spared the strain and expense in attending an oral hearing, particularly given the probable need to travel some distance. On the other hand, the lack of a hearing can accentuate the 'remoteness' of the process as so described by Buck, Bonner and Sainsbury (above), and some appellants may want to explain matters to the tribunal in person and 'see' justice done. If there is a hearing, both parties must be given notice of it and (unless the Upper Tribunal has directed their exclusion on specific grounds) will have a right to attend it.[312] Such a hearing must be held in public, although the Upper Tribunal may direct that it be held in private.[313] As is the case in the First-tier Tribunal, if a party does not attend, the appeal may be determined in his or her absence,[314] although there is a possibility of the Upper Tribunal's power to set aside its decision being exercised 'in the interests of justice' if there was a good reason for the absence.[315]

Statistics on the outcome of appeals to the Upper Tribunal (AAC) in social security and tax credit cases are not available. Figures for Social Security and Child Support Commissioners in the late 1990s revealed a success rate for appellants of nearly 75 per cent but did not distinguish between full and partial success nor identify whether the appellants were claimants or the relevant agencies.[316] If the Upper Tribunal concludes that a First-tier Tribunal's (FTT's) decision evinces an error on point of law, the Upper Tribunal may (not must) set aside that decision, and if it does so, it must either: (i) remit the case to the FTT with directions for its reconsideration or (ii) remake the decision (in which case it may make any decision that the FTT could make if the FTT were remaking the decision) and make any findings of fact which it considers appropriate.[317]

---

[310] An estimated 96% of Social Security and Child Support Commissioner hearings involved hearings on the papers, according to Buck, Bonner and Sainsbury (above n 277) 85. Figures for 1998 show that 4,317 appeals were determined by the Social Security and Child Support Commissioners, and there were 254 oral hearings, indicating that 94% were decided on the papers: HC Deb 9 November 1999 vol 337, col 503W (J Kennedy).

[311] Buck, Bonner and Sainsbury (above n 277) 85.

[312] Tribunal Procedure (Upper Tribunal) Rules 2008 (SI 2008/2698), r 35.

[313] Ibid, r 37(1) and (2).

[314] Ibid, r 38.

[315] See ibid, r 43. Other grounds for setting aside include non-receipt of a document relating to the proceedings or the absence of a representative.

[316] HC Deb, 9 November 1999 vol 337, col 504W (J Kennedy).

[317] Tribunals, Courts and Enforcement Act 2007, s 12. If it chooses (i), the Upper Tribunal may also direct that the FTT be differently constituted (ie, have members who are different from those who decided the appeal the first time) and give any procedural directions with regard to the reconsideration by the FTT: s 12(3).

Either party may appoint a legal or lay representative for an Upper Tribunal hearing.[318] Given the nature of appeals to the Upper Tribunal, the case for appellants having representation as opposed to assistance for preparation of their appeals, such as in setting out the grounds in writing and managing the interlocutory process, may on the face of it appear not to be strong. Buck, Bonner and Sainsbury were, however, clear that their study 'rejects the "do-it-yourself" representation implied by Leggatt', and they argue that 'there is a clear and pressing need for the public financing of quality representation for cases at Commissioner level'.[319] They found that good representation was valued by the Commissioners, particularly 'technical competence in presenting legal argument' (not necessarily by solicitors – indeed, welfare rights bodies such as CPAG have a technical grasp which private practitioners often lack); but appellants for whom 'the processes and language of legal argument were effectively beyond their grasp' also appreciated greatly a representative's capacity in these areas as well as deriving moral support and reassurance from their involvement.[320] Those appellants who had the confidence and competence to pursue an appeal to the Commissioners on their own were 'a rare breed'.[321] The Social Security Select Committee recommended in 2000 that legal aid should be made available for 'complex cases' before the Social Security and Child Support Commissioners.[322] As noted above, funded legal advice and assistance in preparation for appeals (on points of law) to the Upper Tribunal is available, but legal aid has not been extended to appeals to the Upper Tribunal in social security cases and is available only for representation in the Court of Appeal or UK Supreme Court.

While the procedural framework for second-tier appeals has changed since the 2007 Act, the general judicial character and process features have not. There have been efforts to reinforce the enabling role played by Upper Tribunal judges under this new system, as part of the wider effort to promote attention to the user's perspective – for example, as noted above, through the 'overriding objective' of dealing with cases 'fairly and justly', which includes 'ensuring, so far as practicable, that the parties are able to participate fully in the proceedings'.[323] But it is difficult for such a system in itself to counter the 'feeling of powerlessness' that Buck, Bonner and Sainsbury documented among many of those appealing to the predecessor body.[324] Those authors were firm in their conclusion that, at this tier at least, assistance for appellants, particularly in the form of representation, is needed. Their research therefore strengthens the case for expanding assistance, through public funds as necessary, beyond the current reliance on voluntary advice bodies and pro

---

[318] Tribunal Procedure (Upper Tribunal) Rules 2008 (SI 2008/2698), r 11.
[319] Buck, Bonner and Sainsbury (above n 277) 209.
[320] Ibid, 127–28 and 130.
[321] Ibid, 135.
[322] HC Select Committee on Social Security (above n 289), para 21.
[323] Tribunal Procedure (Upper Tribunal) Rules 2008 (SI 2008/2698), r 2(1) and (2)(c).
[324] Buck, Bonner and Sainsbury (above n 277) 135.

bono assistance provided by the small number of lawyers who have the requisite specialist knowledge and commitment to this field.

VI. Conclusion

While the complex powers and procedures through which frontline agencies may change erroneous decisions have been reinforced and their use promoted, the right to appeal against decisions on social security, which has been discussed at some length, represents the principal independent means by which injustices that result from various interactions between claimants and the relevant state agencies can be corrected. The process of reform, marked by judicialisation, has resulted in a First-tier Tribunal and an Upper Tribunal well equipped to manage the legal complexity surrounding social security and tax credits. Even so, the challenges that the law poses for them are perhaps not as well recognised publicly as they should be. At the same time, from a claimant's perspective, the process of appealing is not straightforward, and the tribunals judiciary appears to acknowledge this.

Since it may be said that 'redressing grievances is a constitutional activity – it conditions the relationship between citizens and the state',[325] it is important that appeal and other redress mechanisms can operate in a way that offers a guarantee of the rights of citizens to receive their correct entitlement. Yet judicial bodies such as tribunals obviously cannot fulfil their constitutional function of scrutinising and correcting erroneous decisions by the executive agencies without the actions of citizens in invoking their procedures. Furthermore, even if an appeal process is utilised, the active and meaningful participation of appellants is needed to maximise its effectiveness. Tribunals seem to have adjusted very successfully to the inquisitorial and enabling role which best serves the social security appellants' interests and is widely regarded as highly conducive to the maximisation of access to justice. But to many claimants, entry to the appeal system is merely the final stage of the complex journey that may be needed to secure entitlement. The proposal in the Ministry of Justice's Strategic Work Programme 2013–16 to make the services of tribunals 'digital by default' – that is, 'delivered through digital channels rather than face to face, post or phone'[326] – in order to improve their

---

[325] V Bondy and A Le Sueur, *Designing Redress: A Study about Grievances against Public Bodies* (London, Public Law Project, 2012) 37.

[326] Ministry of Justice, *Administrative Justice and Tribunals: A Strategic Work Programme (2013–16)* (December 2012) paras 79 and 83.

quality and efficiency must in that regard be viewed with caution in view of concerns about claimant access to and use of information technology (IT).[327]

Leaving aside the issue of IT, the character of the appeal process arguably reflects the complex role it plays in having to adduce often quite detailed evidence and interpret and apply technical rules in relation to an agency's decision. Of course, there is inevitably a trade-off in how the system functions, since a redress system has to be managed in a way that meets efficiency goals as well as justice aims.[328] Procedural rules may need to serve both ends and in that regard involve a complex framework of case management powers, time limits and so on. Such formalities are not the normal procedural territory of ordinary citizens. Although it may have its limits as a mode of empowerment, assisting citizens to cope with these complexities is recognised as part of a tribunal's functions, at least at the hearing stage. Such assistance may also help to engender trust in the appeal system. Maintaining such trust is now rightly regarded as a key requirement of the social security appeal system and is rendered all the more so by the distancing or alienating effects of complexity, conditionality and biting austerity measures on the citizen in his or her relationship with the welfare state.

As we have seen, some appellants mount appeals out of a general sense of deservingness to a benefit. While a tribunal's role in overturning incorrect decisions may serve to legitimise the harsh policies and limiting rules which restrict entitlement,[329] from a constitutional perspective, the tribunal is powerless to countermand and will be instinctively deferential to government policy enshrined in often highly prescriptive legislation.[330] Accordingly, 'the appeal system fails to identify "deservingness"'.[331] The complex and detailed rules that drive the bureaucratic rationality governing frontline decisions[332] are unable to be tempered by the goals of fairness or justice[333] that are associated with courts and tribunals as neutral decision makers.[334] This plays into the idea that appeal bodies with jurisdiction over a highly policy-driven area of governance may in fact be an instrument of the policy's implementation.[335]

---

[327] See above ch 2.

[328] See R Thomas, *Administrative Justice & Asylum Appeals: A Study of Tribunal Adjudication* (Oxford, Hart Publishing, 2011).

[329] P Cane, *Administrative Tribunals and Adjudication* (Oxford, Hart Publishing, 2009) 215.

[330] See the discussion above ch 3, s II.

[331] Buck, Bonner and Sainsbury (above n 277) 220.

[332] See J Mashaw, *Bureaucratic Justice* (New Haven, Yale University Press, 1983); and above ch 3, s II.

[333] See Baldwin, Wikeley and Young (above n 88) 212, who comment that tribunals must determine whether the rules have been applied correctly 'not whether justice has been done in the individual case'.

[334] Reflected in the third of Mashaw's models, the 'moral judgment' model of administrative justice: Mashaw (above n 332) 29–31 (also noted above ch 3). This model's primary goal is conflict resolution, and it has a legitimating value of fairness. See further M Adler (ed), *Administrative Justice in Context* (Oxford, Hart Publishing, 2010).

[335] Thomas (above n 328) 285–86.

6

Obligations of Benefit Recipients

I. Introduction

This chapter considers the impact of complexity on the relationship between benefit recipients and the state with particular reference to the obligations which condition entitlement to welfare support. The obligations in question essentially fall into three main categories. First, as was discussed in chapter two, there is the duty of recipients to notify the authorities of any change in their circumstances that may affect their eligibility for or level of entitlement to benefit. Failure to meet this obligation could in some circumstances amount to fraud but in any event may well give rise to an overpayment of benefit, which could be recoverable. As we saw, complexity may contribute to such a failure. Secondly, there are obligations concerning attendance and participation in relevant interviews, such as mandatory interviews with personal advisors for unemployed claimants, which are scheduled on a regular basis at Jobcentre Plus, and the undergoing of assessments such as the medically-based work capability assessment, which is designed to inform decisions on entitlement to employment and support allowance (ESA) or the equivalent capability-for-work elements of universal credit. The obligations in this second category, also discussed in chapter two, provide a foundation for the measures evident within the third category, where the claimant's entitlement to benefit is subject to requirements concerning work search, work preparation or, if suitable work is offered, the acceptance of work. They are obligations that, where applicable, are enforceable through the threat of termination of benefit entitlement in the case of non-compliance. Other sanctions of fixed or discretionary length may also be imposed for failing to meet the prescribed conditions. What we see is a complex set of arrangements designed to enforce strict conditions tied to the award of benefit and based around a policy of 'activating' claimants towards entry to employment and, with it, the prospect of at least a degree of self-sufficiency.

II. The Relationship between a Benefit Recipient and the State

The award of benefit by the state establishes an ongoing relationship between it and the claimant. It is a relationship that can perhaps be viewed at two separate levels, distinguished by the extent of the citizen's active engagement with the welfare system in the sense of drawing financial support from it. At one level are those who have claimed entitlement and receive benefits from the state, and at the other are those who do not depend on welfare and are not engaged in seeking it but nevertheless retain an inherent right to support if or when particular circumstances arise.

In both cases, the rights are attached to a person's status in terms of citizenship. In this context, the rights will be strongest where institutions or provision accessible on a basis of universality are concerned, since they reinforce 'the common bonds of citizenship'.[1] This perspective accords with the Marshallian notion of citizenship rights (noted in chapter one), a set of interconnected rights: political, civil and social.[2] But at the same time, a self-sufficient person may nevertheless, as an employee, have obligations to pay National Insurance contributions in order to satisfy the relevant conditions attached to contributory benefits, including an entry condition for entitlement to the state retirement pension. This emphasises the reciprocal element in the state–citizenship relationship, which can seem to place it on a quasi-contractual footing, as discussed below. Yet it essentially reflects a solidaristic, collectivist model of citizenship which is based around the idea that individual citizens derive protection and support through their rights as members of society.[3] This model is still evident in the UK welfare system, but as has been widely analysed, government

---

[1] R Lister, 'The Age of Responsibility: Social Policy and Citizenship in the Early 21st Century' in C Holden, M Kilkey and G Ramia (eds), *Social Policy Review 23: Analysis and Debate in Social Policy, 2011* (Bristol, Policy Press, 2011) 76.

[2] TH Marshall, 'Citizenship and Social Class' in TH Marshall and T Bottomore (eds), *Citizenship and Social Class* (London, Pluto, 1992) 3–51.

[3] H Dean, *Welfare Rights and Social Policy* (Harlow, Pearson Education, 2002) 187–88 and 202.

policy since the 1980s has constantly sought to rebalance the relationship by building on the contractual notion reflected in the insurance basis to social security, with its 'ethic of mutuality',[4] whilst at the same time emphasising the responsibilities of citizenship more strongly. This has been the case irrespective of the political colour of the government of the day.

The policy preoccupation with individual responsibility has been most clearly evident in the United Kingdom in the area of benefits for the unemployed.[5] Here a claimant's entitlement to state support has been increasingly based, to a highly significant degree, on satisfaction of a range of reciprocal obligations or conditions which in many cases are enforced by various sanctions, including the potential loss, in cases of default, of entitlement to the benefit in question. At the same time, a policy emerged in the 1980s that attempted to make public services more efficient and accountable through the introduction of private market mechanisms of competition, choice, and customer focus (including the use of customer 'charters' for particular services); the trend has shifted the paradigm from citizenship per se to the 'consumer-citizen'.[6] In the case of social security, this implies that 'users of social security . . . have an individualised and market-like nexus within service provision' even though they 'do not exercise the sort of "consumer sovereignty" characteristic of competitive markets'.[7] It reflects a more contractarian view of citizenship whereby each individual pursues his or her own interests but in a way that brings wider public benefits through improved accountability and increased effectiveness of the services on which many depend.[8] This should not, however, be viewed as involving a meaningful re-allocation of power, despite the frequent political references to the 'empowerment' of users of public services. Certainly, where the welfare state is concerned, the rhetoric bears little relationship to the reality of citizen power, which is located in increasingly conditional substantive rights in respect of the key area of benefit provision.[9]

Some of the characteristics that underpin such conceptions of the relationship between the state and welfare recipients were evident in the earlier decades of the modern welfare state's history, but what has substantially changed is the active involvement demanded of claimants, who can no longer be considered

---

[4] Commission on Social Justice, *Social Justice: Strategies for National Renewal* (London, Vintage, 1994) 232.

[5] See, eg, P M Larkin, 'The Legislative Arrival and Future of Workfare: The Welfare Reform Act 2009' (2011) 18(1) *Journal of Social Security Law* 11.

[6] See, eg, E Vidler and J Clarke, 'Creating Consumer-Citizens: New Labour and the Remaking of Public Services' (2005) 20(2) *Public Policy and Administration* 19.

[7] B Stafford, 'Service Delivery and the User' in J Millar (ed), *Understanding Social Security: Issues for Policy and Practice* (Bristol, Policy Press, 2009) 256.

[8] Dean (above n 3) 188 and 202.

[9] See JF Handler, 'Poverty, Dependency, and Social Welfare: Procedural Justice for the Poor' in BG Garth and A Sarat (eds), *Justice and Power in Socio-Legal Studies* (Evanston, Northwestern University Press, 1998) 150.

the 'passive recipient[s] of public largesse'.[10] The conditions or obligations surrounding this active engagement, representing the terms on which the state undertakes to provide support to individuals, emphasise its contractual character,[11] which is further reinforced by the terminology and structures that have been adopted. Thus, unemployment benefit became 'jobseeker's allowance' (JSA) in 1996, and as noted in chapter two, a condition of entitlement was the entry into a 'jobseeker's agreement'. Furthermore, in promoting its reforms, New Labour advanced the underpinning notion of the 'welfare contract': 'At the heart of the modern welfare state will be a new contract between the citizen and the Government, based on rights and responsibilities'.[12] The state's obligation to support people with various kinds of need while at the same time assisting and encouraging the take-up of work would be complemented by individuals' responsibility to seek work and training, support themselves and their families where able to do so, save for retirement and be open and honest about their personal circumstances and any changes in them. The language of contract was also evident in the training and work preparation schemes in which some claimants were expected to participate, notably the various 'New Deal' programmes.[13]

In some respects, the contractual ideal can in fact be regarded as having been built on the basic bilateral relationship between welfare recipient and state that is traceable back to the Beveridge Report.[14] Indeed, in the 2008 Green Paper on 'welfare to work', the Government reminded us that William Beveridge had advanced the principle that 'social security must be achieved by co-operation between the State and the individual', and the state should 'offer security for service and contribution'.[15] However, the Government outlined various ways in which its ' "something for something" approach' would require claimants to shoulder 'more responsibility' in terms of personal obligations to improve their employability and demonstrate a progression towards work.[16]

Within the framework of the 'Flexible New Deal', introduced in the previous Labour Government's final term, more personalised support was promised for the unemployed, but the screws were tightened on the long-term

---

[10] D Oliver, *Government in the United Kingdom: The Search for Accountability, Effectiveness and Citizenship* (Milton Keynes, Open University Press, 1991) 32.

[11] A Paz-Fuchs, *Welfare to Work: Conditional Rights in Social Policy* (Oxford, Oxford University Press, 2008).

[12] Department of Social Security (DSS), *New Ambitions for Our Country: A New Contract for Welfare* (Cm 3805, 1998) ch 11, para 5.

[13] Such as those for disabled people, young people, lone parents and people aged 50 or over, participation in which had been a condition for many claimants of JSA.

[14] WH (Lord) Beveridge (Inter-departmental Committee on Social Insurance and Allied Services), *Social Insurance and Allied Services* (Cmnd 6404, 1942).

[15] Cited in Department for Work and Pensions (DWP), *No One Written Off: Reforming Welfare to Reward Responsibility* (Cm 7363, 2008) 7.

[16] Ibid, 12.

unemployed in particular, who faced 'escalating conditionality'.[17] Under the Flexible New Deal, claimants faced as a condition of entitlement a requirement to participate in work experience if they had been on the programme for 12 months or more. Additionally, more lone parents were brought within the welfare-to-work regime, and there was even the prospect of 'problem drug users' being subjected to special measures designed to pressurise them into tackling their drug use or addiction with a view to improving their employability.[18] Even 'work for your benefit' schemes were in prospect; legislative provision for them to be piloted was made in the Welfare Reform Act 2009,[19] and regulations have been introduced by the Coalition Government,[20] whose Work Programme places the same emphasis on claimant responsibility as its predecessors' schemes. Indeed, the Coalition Government has adopted New Labour's 'responsible citizenship' mantra across this field of policy.[21] It has underpinned the Coalition's reforms to welfare, including, as was the case under the Labour Government, its legislative measures on the entitlement of those with an incapacity for work.

III. Managing the Relationship: Incapacity for Work

The treatment of incapacity for work provides a pertinent case study of how increases in conditionality and the obligations of benefit recipients have contributed to the complexity of the law, structures and processes affecting the ongoing engagement of recipients with the welfare system.

The Obligations of Recipients of ESA (or Work Capability Elements of Universal Credit)

Those classed in the United Kingdom as having an incapacity for work due to sickness or disability and who in consequence were receiving ESA or incapacity

---

[17] Department for Work and Pensions (DWP), *In Work, Better Off: Next Steps to Full Employment* (Cm 7130, 2007) para 49.

[18] See the last part of s III below.

[19] Welfare Reform Act 2009, s 1.

[20] Jobseeker's Allowance (Employment, Skills and Enterprise Scheme) Regulations 2011 (SI 2011/917). But as discussed above in ch 3, parts of them were declared ultra vires, leading to new legislation – the Jobseeker's Allowance (Schemes for Assisting Persons to Obtain Employment) Regulations 2013 (SI 2013/276) and the Jobseekers (Back to Work Schemes) Act 2013. See above ch 3, s II.

[21] See, eg, Department for Work and Pensions (DWP), *21st Century Welfare* (Cm 7913, 2010) ch 6, paras 7 and 9.

benefit comprised in August 2012 a total of approximately 2.3 million people.[22] Prior to the introduction of incapacity benefit in 1995, claimants of long-term sickness benefits could expect an unlimited period in receipt of benefit (then 'invalidity benefit') with no specific attendance or signing-on requirements. Benefit would continue for as long as their illness or disability (generally confirmed by a doctor's sickness note) continued. Although more rigorous assessment of a person's incapacity was brought in with the introduction of incapacity benefit,[23] with the possibility of periodic reassessment (although fairly infrequently invoked), the ongoing receipt of benefit was at first more or less unconditional. The implicit premise was that a claimant's return to work was a matter not for the benefit authorities but rather for the claimant him/herself and his or her doctor. However, as a welfare-to-work strategy based around the idea of a single gateway to work was developed by New Labour after 1997, it was extended to recipients of incapacity benefit. The Government referred to a 'legacy of lack of action to help people with long-term illness or disability retain and regain their links with the labour market'.[24] The new single gateway aimed to 'enable people to access information on work, benefits and government services in one place' and included people with a long-term illness or disability.[25] The policy involved assigning each new claimant of incapacity benefit to a 'personal adviser', who would conduct an interview at an early stage to provide the claimant with 'the opportunity to discuss what they may be capable of doing' and support progression towards becoming (financially) independent.[26]

The move into a more conditional regime, of the same kind as that facing JSA recipients, was confirmed by the proposed introduction in April 2000, initially in pilot areas, of new legislation to make participation in such an interview a condition of receiving incapacity benefit.[27] This approach was carried forward into a new 'Pathways to Work' initiative, which started out in seven pilot areas in 2003. Under Pathways, each claimant was required to attend a 'work-focused interview' (WFI)[28] in week 8 of his or her claim, followed by five

---

[22] See the DWP statistics at 83.244.183.180/100pc/esa/payment_type/ccsex/a_carate_r_payment_type_c_ccsex_aug12.html and at 83.244.183.180/100pc/ib/ccsex/cnage/a_carate_r_ccsex_c_cnage_aug12.html.

[23] See D Bonner, 'Incapacity for Work: A New Benefit and New Tests' (1995) 2 *Journal of Social Security Law* 86; and R Berthoud, 'The "Medical" Assessment of Incapacity: A Case Study of Research and Policy' (1995) 2 *Journal of Social Security Law* 61.

[24] Department of Social Security, *A New Contract for Welfare: Support for Disabled People* (Cm 4103, 1998) ch 2, para 1.

[25] Ibid, para 11.

[26] Ibid, para 12.

[27] Ibid, para 15. See further the Social Security (Work-Focused Interviews) Regulations 2000 (SI 2000/897).

[28] The definition of a WFI in the Social Security (Work-Focused Interviews) Regulations 2000 (SI 2000/897), reg 3 was an interview with a relevant person for the purposes of any or all of (a) assessing the claimant's work prospects (whether paid or voluntary); (b) assisting or encouraging them to enhance their employment prospects; (c) identifying activities which could strengthen those prospects; (d) identifying current or future employment or training opportunities; and (e) identifying relevant educational opportunities.

further monthly interviews. The requirement was enforced through sanctions for non-cooperation, in the form of loss of benefit, imposed by Jobcentre Plus.

In October 2008, under reforms introduced by the Welfare Reform Act 2007, ESA began to replace incapacity benefit, starting with new claims and then including existing claimants when subjected to reassessment of work capacity. This reform was intended to shift the emphasis in this part of the benefit system away from the notion of work incapacity per se and towards the idea of helping and guiding people back into work wherever possible.[29] People who were in receipt of incapacity benefit remained entitled to it for a time but have been progressively migrated onto ESA.[30] However, the reassessments which have taken place have resulted in some potential transferees failing to qualify for ESA, which has a higher threshold of work incapacity,[31] based on an assessment of the extent of a claimant's 'limited capability for work' resulting from a physical or mental condition, which limitation is such that 'it is not reasonable to require him [or her] to work'.[32] The ESA scheme provides for contributory ESA for those meeting the contribution conditions, as noted in chapter two. Since May 2012, entitlement to this contributory ESA can only normally be enjoyed for a maximum period of 365 days.[33] Beyond that period, or for those not meeting the contribution conditions, there has been the alternative of income-based ESA, which, in due course, will be subsumed within universal credit[34] in the form of the capability-for-work elements of the credit.[35] ESA is therefore continuing in its contributory form only, governed by new regulations.[36] As a result, there are now two entirely separate legislative frameworks governing benefit for people with work incapacity, working against the simplification that was promised by the more unified benefit structure of universal credit.

---

[29] Department for Work and Pensions (DWP), *A New Deal for Welfare: Empowering People to Work* (Cm 6730, 2006).

[30] People who did not meet the contribution conditions for incapacity benefit but who received income support on the basis of incapacity for work have also been migrated onto ESA.

[31] See generally N Harris and S Rahilly, 'Extra Capacity in the Labour Market? ESA and the Activation of the Sick and Disabled in the UK' in S Devetzi and S Stendahl (eds), *Too Sick to Work? Social Security Reforms in Europe for Persons with Reduced Earnings Capacity* (Alphen aan den Rijn, Wolters Kluwer, 2011) 43–75.

[32] Welfare Reform Act 2007, s 1(3)(a) and (4).

[33] Ibid, s 1A, inserted by the Welfare Reform Act 2012, s 51. Any days on which the claimant qualifies for ESA as a member of the 'support group' (see below) do not count towards the prescribed period of 365 days. Claimants can qualify again for contribution-based ESA after a further period of contribution accumulation: see s 1A(3). Also, a person whose 365 days has expired but who has continued to have a limited capability for work and to meet the basic conditions for ESA may, if he or she falls within the support group and for so long as he or she is in that group, receive contributory ESA: s 1B, inserted by the 2012 Act, s 52. The Secretary of State is given a power by s 1A to increase the prescribed period (the negative resolution procedure is specified).

[34] See the Universal Credit Regulations 2013 (SI 2013/376), Pts 4 and 5.

[35] But note the earlier introduction of the new credit (in April or July 2013) in a small number of pilot areas and the limited further roll out in October 2013: see above ch 2.

[36] Employment and Support Allowance Regulations 2013 (SI 2013/379) (hereafter 'ESA Regulations 2013').

In proposing ESA, the Labour Government had stressed that the allowance's framework of rights and responsibilities would include obligations for claimants other than those with 'the most severe disabilities and health conditions' to 'participate in work-focused interviews, produce action plans and engage in work-related activity, or see their benefit level reduced'.[37] Thus, for example, the WFI regime that has operated under ESA[38] has covered recipients of the benefit who have been placed in the 'work-related activity group' (WRAG) of claimants classed as not having a limited capability for work-related activity. The regime has not applied to those placed in the 'support group', comprising persons who have limited capability both for work and for work-related activity.[39] (Support group members only have to attend an initial meeting with an adviser.)

Figures indicated that for all new ESA claims assessed from the introduction of the benefit in October 2008 until February 2011, 62 per cent of claimants were found fit for work; 27 per cent were placed in the WRAG; and 11 per cent were placed in the support group.[40] More recent statistics, however, have revealed a shift in the figures. They show that for claims between December 2011 and February 2012, completed initial assessments found 54 per cent of claimants fit for work; and the 46 per cent of claimants who were entitled to ESA were made up of 26 per cent in the support group and 20 per cent in the WRAG.[41] From June to August 2012, even fewer (51 per cent of claimants) were found fit for work, and of the 49 per cent who were entitled to ESA, 26 per cent went into the support group and 23 per cent into the WRAG[42] – although as with the earlier figures, these do not include claimants whose work incapacity is confirmed only via appeal. (Approximately 40 per cent of appeals have such an outcome: see below section III.[43])

The legislation governing ESA imposes on some claimants 'work-related requirements', set out in sections 11–11I of the Welfare Reform Act 2007,

[37] DWP, *A New Deal for Welfare* (above n 29) 6.

[38] On the requirement to take part in a WFI, see the Employment and Support Allowance Regulations 2008 (SI 2008/794) (hereafter 'ESA Regulations 2008'), reg 54. The ESA definition of the WFI is very similar to that under the previous regime but includes a focus on activities, training, education or 'rehabilitation' that make it 'more likely' that the claimant will secure or remain in work: see below nn 47 and 48.

[39] Ibid, reg 34 and Sched 3.

[40] Department for Work and Pensions, *Employment and Support Allowance: Work Capability Assessment by Health Condition and Functional Impairment – Official Statistics* (October 2011), statistics.dwp.gov.uk/asd/workingage/esa_wca/esa_wca_25102011.pdf, 3.2.1. Note that a further 2% of cases were still in the process of assessment.

[41] Department for Work and Pensions (DWP), *Employment and Support Allowance: Outcome of Work Capability Assessments, Great Britain – New Claims*, quarterly statistics bulletin (23 October 2012), research.dwp.gov.uk/asd/workingage/esa_wca/esa_wca_oct2012.pdf.

[42] Department for Work and Pensions, *Employment and Support Allowance: Outcome of Work Capability Assessments, Great Britain – New Claims*, quarterly statistics bulletin (22 January 2013), research.dwp.gov.uk/asd/workingage/esa_wca/esa_wca_jan2013.pdf, 7–8.

[43] Department for Work and Pensions, *ESA: Work Capability Assessment Statistical Release* (January 2013) Tables, research.dwp.gov.uk/asd/workingage/esa_wca/esa_wca_jan2013_tables. xls, Table 3. On appeals, see above ch 5.

which were inserted by section 57 of the Welfare Reform Act 2012 for the period after universal credit is in force. Similar provisions covering universal credit itself are found in Part 1 of the 2012 Act,[44] although they also include work search and work availability requirements that are not applicable to those with limited capability for work.[45]

The ESA work-related requirements, from which certain victims of domestic violence are exempt for a 13-week period,[46] fall into two categories: a 'work-focused interview requirement' and a 'work preparation requirement'. The former is defined in simple terms as a requirement to attend one or more WFIs – defined as interviews 'for prescribed purposes relating to work preparation'.[47] The purposes for which WFIs may be prescribed 'include in particular that of making it more likely in the opinion of the Secretary of State that the person will obtain paid work (or more paid work or better-paid work)'.[48] The 'work preparation requirement' is discussed below. Some claimants will be subject to the work-focused interview requirement only,[49] some to both categories of requirement[50] and some to neither.[51] Note that a claimant may also be required to participate in an interview for any purpose related to the imposition of a work-related requirement or for verifying or assisting with his or her compliance with such a requirement.[52] The work-related requirements applicable to a particular claimant will be among the matters included in his or her 'claimant commitment', which sets out his or her responsibilities as a recipient of an award of ESA.[53]

---

[44] Welfare Reform Act 2012, ss 15–25.

[45] Ibid, esp ss 17 and 18.

[46] Welfare Reform Act 2007, s 11H(5) and (6), inserted by the Welfare Reform Act 2012, s 57. A person is a 'victim' of domestic violence if it has been inflicted on him or her or threatened. 'Recently' and 'domestic violence' are to be defined by regulations, which will also specify the circumstances in which the domestic violence exemption will apply. See the ESA Regulations 2013 (above n 36), reg 49.

[47] Welfare Reform Act 2007, s 11B, as inserted by the Welfare Reform Act 2012, s 57.

[48] Welfare Reform Act 2007. The purposes are defined in the ESA Regulations 2013 (above n 36), reg 46 and include assessing the claimant's work prospects, assisting or encouraging him or her to remain in or obtain work, and identifying training/educational/rehabilitative opportunities which may enhance work retention or capacity.

[49] Welfare Reform Act 2007, s 11E, as inserted by the Welfare Reform Act 2012, s 57. This covers a person with a child aged at least one but under a prescribed age to be set at three or over (the age of five has been prescribed by the ESA Regulations 2013 (above n 36), reg 48(1)) and others prescribed by the regulations (reg 48(2) and (3) – includes certain foster parents or carers of children).

[50] Welfare Reform Act 2007, s 11F, as inserted by the Welfare Reform Act 2012, s 57. A person falls in this category if he or she does not fall into one of the other two.

[51] A claimant will not be subject to a work-related requirement if he or she has both a limited capability for work *and* a limited capability for a work-related activity, or regular and substantial caring responsibilities for a severely disabled person (see further ESA Regulations 2013 (above n 36), reg 30); or is a single person responsible for a child under the age of one year; or is a person of a prescribed description: Welfare Reform Act 2007, s 11D, as inserted by the Welfare Reform Act 2012, s 57.

[52] Welfare Reform Act 2007, s 11G, as inserted by the Welfare Reform Act 2012, s 57.

[53] Welfare Reform Act 2007, s 11A, as inserted by the Welfare Reform Act 2012, s 57.

The claimant commitment, prepared by the Secretary of State, is a feature of both ESA and universal credit. The potential broadness of the commitment suggests it could be used to extend conditionality in a wide variety of ways, although it may not perhaps be intended to go beyond a claimant's obligations under the standard legislative provisions.[54] Yet on the other hand, the expectation of the Department for Work and Pensions (DWP) that 'a personalised Claimant Commitment will be drawn up by their personal adviser during a face-to face discussion' implies individualised arrangements more akin to a jobseeker's agreement.[55] Indeed, the White Paper indicated that the intention was to 'clearly set out what is expected of each recipient. We will raise the requirements placed on some individuals and will introduce tougher sanctions to ensure recipients meet their responsibilities'.[56] The second sentence could also suggest a more individualised commitment, although it is perhaps ambiguous. Under the Welfare Reform Act 2012, the claimant commitment is defined as a 'record of the claimant's responsibilities in relation to an award' either of universal credit[57] or ESA.[58] The contractual element is reinforced by a stipulation that the claimant 'must accept a claimant commitment' – either electronically, by telephone or in writing.[59]

For the most part, recipients of ESA other than those falling within the support group are expected to attend up to six WFIs during the first 12 months of their claims. If a claimant does not attend a WFI and has not, within five working days of the date on which the Secretary of State notified him or her of the failure to attend, shown 'good cause' for the non-attendance, this constitutes a breach of what is now known as a 'compliance condition', and a sanction will be imposed. The onus is therefore on the claimant show 'good cause'. 'Good cause' is not defined for this purpose, but until December 2012, the Secretary of State was under a duty to take account of all the circumstances of a case including the claimant's physical or mental health or condition. However, that duty has been revoked,[60] and from that date, the matter has been covered by guidance only, which indicates that 'all matters relevant to the claimant should be considered' in determining whether there was good cause.[61] A claimant may at any point during a claim also be required

---

[54] See, eg, Department for Work and Pensions (DWP), *Universal Credit: Welfare that Works* (Cm 7957, 2010) ch 3 para 12.

[55] Department for Work and Pensions, *Explanatory Memorandum for the Social Security Advisory Committee* (2012) para 211.

[56] DWP, *Welfare that Works* (above n 54) ch 3, preamble.

[57] Welfare Reform Act 2012, s 14(1).

[58] Welfare Reform Act 2007, ss 1C(1) (applicable only before the introduction of universal credit) and 11A, as inserted by the Welfare Reform Act 2012, ss 54 and 57 respectively.

[59] ESA Regulations 2013 (above n 36), reg 44; and Universal Credit Regulations 2013 (above n 34), reg 15.

[60] By the Employment and Support Allowance (Sanctions) (Amendment) Regulations 2012 (SI 2012/2756), reg 3.

[61] Ibid, Explanatory Note.

by the Secretary of State[62] to complete a questionnaire giving information relevant to his or her capacity to perform the activities that are relevant to the assessment of whether he or she has a limited capability for work,[63] which is also an entry condition for the 'limited capability for work element' of universal credit.[64] This will in any event normally happen at the start of a claim.

A claimant required to undergo the limited capability for work assessment[65] may also be required to attend a medical examination conducted by a health care professional to determine the extent of his or her capability for work.[66] The assessment is based around the claimant's capacity to undertake various activities prescribed by the regulations.[67] It is conducted within the first 13 weeks of the claim, known as the 'assessment period'.[68] Prior to the limited capability for work assessment, entitlement will be based on medical certificates submitted by the claimant. In particular, there will be a note signed by his or her general practitioner, known as a 'fit note'. If the claimant is found to have a limited capability for work, he or she will be allocated to a particular group, either the WRAG or support group, or the equivalent under universal credit.[69] A claimant who fails without 'good cause' either to provide

[62] ESA Regulations 2008 (above n 38), reg 21, but note that there are exceptions (in reg 21(3)); and ESA Regulations 2013 (above n 36), reg 17.

[63] Ibid (both 2008 and 2013 Regulations), Sched 2; and the Universal Credit Regulations 2013 (above n 34), Sched 6.

[64] Welfare Reform Act 2012, s 12; and the Universal Credit Regulations 2013 (above n 34), regs 27, 39 and 40.

[65] Some claimants fall to be treated as having a limited capability for work: see ESA Regulations 2008 (above n 38), reg 20; ESA Regulations 2013 (above n 36) reg 16; and the Universal Credit Regulations 2013 (above n 34), reg 39(6) and Sched 8.

[66] ESA Regulations 2013 (above n 36), reg 19; and the Universal Credit Regulations 2013 (above n 34), reg 44. The latter also contains a requirement to attend a medical examination to determine whether the claimant has a limited capability for a work-related activity when called to do so; there is equivalent provision in the ESA scheme under the ESA Regulations 2013, reg 35.

[67] The activities are prescribed in the ESA Regulations 2013 (above n 36), Sched 2. See also reg 15. (In the case of universal credit, see the Universal Credit Regulations 2013 (above n 34), reg 39 and Sched 6.) For each activity (whether related to physical disability (covered by Pt 1 of the schedule) or to mental, cognitive and intellectual capacity (covered by Pt 2)), there are descriptors referring to different levels of capacity; prescribed numbers of points are scored for each, with a higher number of points awarded the greater the lack of capability (only one descriptor per activity may score in any individual case). The threshold for being assessed as having a limited capability for work is a total of 15 points scored for on one or more activity. A claimant who, for example, cannot pick up a £1 coin or equivalent with either hand would score 15 points, while someone who frequently, due to impaired mental function, 'cannot reliably initiate or complete at least two sequential personal actions' would score 6 points.

[68] The assessment phase can sometimes be longer than this, for example, if the limited capability for work assessment is not conducted within the first 13 weeks.

[69] To be placed in the support group, the claimant must satisfy one or more descriptor in Sched 3 of the ESA Regulations 2013 (above n 36) (this time there is no points calculation) and have a limited capability for work-related activity such that he or she cannot reasonably be expected to undertake such activity: reg 30. In the case of universal credit, the award would include both the limited capability for work and the limited capability for undertaking a work-related activity elements, provided that the claimant has a limitation for such activities, one or more relevant descriptor (this time in Sched 7 of the Universal Credit Regulations 2013 (above n 34)) applicable and the claimant's limitation such that it is not reasonable to require that claimant to undertake the activity (Universal Credit Regulations 2013 reg 40(2)).

the requested information (which will include responses to a questionnaire issued by the Department[70]) within a prescribed period of time or to attend and submit for a medical examination for which the required period of advance notice was given is to be treated as not having a limited capability for work.[71] Under universal credit, the same consequence is to follow from such a failure, save that the defence is based on having a 'good reason' for the failure.[72]

Elements of the work capability assessment/limited capability for work assessment have had to be adjusted several times following reviews of the physical and especially mental disability descriptors on which the assessment is based.[73] Indeed, the particular problems faced by claimants with mental health problems in the assessment process have been highlighted in a recent judicial review undertaken by the Upper Tribunal.[74] It concerned two claimants, MM and DM, both of whom had mental health problems. MM and DM argued that claimants with mental health problems are, by virtue of their problems, at a particular disadvantage in the application of the ESA assessment process. They asserted that in response to this disadvantage, the DWP has a duty to make reasonable adjustments by ensuring that further medical evidence is sought at an early stage. In the case of these claimants, they believed there was a failure in that duty, giving rise to discrimination under the Equality Act 2010.

The Upper Tribunal found that the DWP was aware that claimants with mental health problems may have 'particular difficulties . . . in completing the questionnaire'.[75] Moreover, where a face-to-face examination of such a claimant was considered necessary, 'special provision' was generally made on account of these difficulties and of the claimant's 'vulnerability'; this provision included encouraging the claimant to bring a friend or advocate to the examination.[76] The complaint was that, nonetheless, the Department did not have a practice of ensuring that further medical evidence was sought on a more routine basis, which meant that it was flying in the face of the recommendations by Malcolm Harrington.[77] Harrington's view was that decision-makers should actively seek further documentary evidence in every

[70] ESA Regulations 2013 (above n 36) reg 17(1)(a); and ESA Regulations 2008 (above n 38) reg 21(1)(b). The questionnaire is known as form ESA 50.

[71] ESA Regulations 2008 (above n 38), regs 22–24; and ESA Regulations 2013 (above n 36), regs 18–20. Under both sets of provisions, the prescribed matters to be taken into account in determining 'good cause' are whether the claimant was outside Great Britain at the relevant time, the claimant's state of health and the nature of any disability he or she may have.

[72] Universal Credit Regulations 2013 (above n 34), regs 43 and 44. No specific factors are prescribed to be taken into account in determining whether there was 'good reason' for this purpose.

[73] See Harris and Rahilly (above n 31).

[74] MM and DM v Secretary of State for Work and Pensions [2013] UKUT 0260 (AAC).

[75] Ibid, [38].

[76] Ibid, [45].

[77] M Harrington, An Independent Review of the Work Capability Assessment: Year Three (London, Stationary Office, 2012).

claimant's case, and in view of 'the unique circumstances of their condition, particular care should be taken when the claimant has a mental, intellectual or cognitive condition, as these individuals may lack insight into the effects of their condition on their day-to-day functioning'.[78] The Upper Tribunal found that the DWP was not doing enough for it be regarded as taking reasonable steps to avoid the substantial disadvantages that claimants with mental health problems face, although the judges felt that they had insufficient evidence to determine what steps would be reasonable for the Department to take in that regard. The Department was therefore directed by the Upper Tribunal to investigate what changes in practice were needed.

Among claimants in general, many have complained that the limited capability for work assessment does not take proper account of their symptoms or of particular aspects of their conditions.[79] While, as Harrington has pointed out, theirs is clearly a subjective viewpoint, it perhaps shows that some claimants do not fully understand the basis for the assessment, and this is compounded by the failure of the DWP in a majority of cases to provide an explanation of how a decision was reached.[80] Claimants are meant to receive a 'decision assurance' phone call from the Department that enables them to discuss the decision and whether any further documentary evidence is available, although only one in three calls gets through.[81] Decision-makers are also now producing 'decision-maker's reasoning' for decisions. On the basis of a very small sample of cases cited by Harrington, in which 75 per cent of claimants stated they could 'recognise themselves' in such accounts of the decision-maker's reasoning, this appears to be better at explaining the complex basis for decisions.[82]

Under the initial ESA scheme, claimants in the WRAG could also be required to undergo additional assessment known as 'work-focused health-related assessment' by health care professionals in order to determine the existence and extent of any changes in their capability for work. This assessment was abolished in June 2011[83] but appears to have been revived as a possible work preparation requirement (see below).

Aside from interview and assessment requirements, claimants other than those in the support group faced (from June 2011) the possibility of being subjected to a requirement to undertake a work-related activity, provided: first, they were not in one of the few exceptional categories;[84] secondly, that the requirement was 'reasonable' having regard to their circumstances; and thirdly,

---

[78] Ibid, ch 2, paras 40 and 41.

[79] See, eg, ibid, ch 6, para 24.

[80] Ibid.

[81] Ibid, ch 2, para 13.

[82] Ibid, para 68.

[83] See the Employment and Support Allowance (Work-Related Activity) Regulations 2011 (SI 2011/1349).

[84] Comprising lone parents of children under 5 years of age or claimants entitled to a carer's allowance or an ESA carer premium.

the requirement did not involve applying for a job or undergoing medical treatment.[85] In the case of a lone parent of a child under age 13, the activity had to be limited to normal school hours.[86] The claimant would be given a written action plan dealing with the route towards a return to employment and specifying the work-related activity that he or she was expected to carry out.[87] Failing to carry out the work-related activity in question amounted to breach of a compliance condition, as noted above, thereby attracting the same sanction, and on the same basis (ie, absence of 'good cause'), as a failure to attend a WFI noted above.[88] However, the sanction would cease if the claimant were no longer subject to a requirement to undertake a work-related activity or if the Secretary of State considered it was no longer appropriate for the claimant to be required to undertake such an activity.[89]

Under the new ESA legislation, there is reference instead to a 'work preparation requirement', as noted above. This is defined as

> . . . a requirement that a person take particular action specified by the Secretary of State for the purpose of making it more likely in the opinion of the Secretary of State that the person will obtain paid work (or more paid work or better-paid work).[90]

The Secretary of State may also specify the amount of time to be devoted to any particular action to be taken by a claimant.[91] The kinds of action which a claimant could be expected to take may include attending skills assessment, 'improving personal presentation', participation in training and/or an employment programme, undertaking work experience or a work placement, 'developing a business plan' and any other form of action that is prescribed for this purpose by the Secretary of State.[92] Action that could be prescribed is that of undergoing a 'work-focused health-related assessment',[93] as defined.[94] Parallel provision governing work pre-

---

[85] Welfare Reform Act 2007, s 13; and the Employment and Support Allowance (Work-Related Activity) Regulations 2011 (SI 2011/1349), reg 3.

[86] Employment and Support Allowance (Work-Related Activity) Regulations 2011 (ibid).

[87] Ibid, regs 4–6; and the Welfare Reform Act 2007, s 14.

[88] Employment and Support Allowance (Work-Related Activity) Regulations 2011 (SI 2011/1349), reg 8; and the ESA Regulations 2008 (above n 38), reg 63 (both as amended by the Employment and Support Allowance (Sanctions) (Amendment) Regulations 2012 (SI 2012/2756), reg 4).

[89] ESA Regulations 2008 (above n 38), reg 64, as amended by Employment and Support Allowance (Sanctions) (Amendment) Regulations 2012 (SI 2012/2756), reg 5.

[90] Welfare Reform Act 2007, s 11C(1), inserted by the Welfare Reform Act 2012, s 57. The specified purpose is the same as that in the purpose which may be prescribed for a WFI, noted above.

[91] Welfare Reform Act 2007, s 11C(2).

[92] Ibid, s 11C(3).

[93] Ibid, s 11C(4).

[94] Ibid, s 11C(5) – an assessment carried out by a health care professional (as defined in s 11C(6)) approved by the Secretary of State for the purposes of 'assessing (a) the extent to which the person's capability for work may be improved by taking steps in relation to their physical or mental condition, and (b) such other matters relating to their physical or mental condition

paration requirements is made, in the same terms, in relation to universal credit.[95]

Sanctions

The range of complex and strict conditionality requirements facing ESA recipients has been reinforced by detailed sanction provisions. The sanctions are themselves governed by complex rules, and as was noted in chapter two, complexity is one of the reasons that benefit sanctions are not well understood by claimants. Under the pre-universal-credit ESA scheme, a claimant who failed without good cause to attend a medical examination for the purpose of assessing whether he or she had a limited capability for work faced a loss of entitlement.[96] The same outcome could result from a failure without good cause to comply with a request for information in a questionnaire (unless the Secretary of State considered there was sufficient information without it) or for any additional information.[97] The position is the same under the post-universal-credit ESA scheme in respect of both of these kinds of failures, if occurring without good cause.[98] Also under the pre-universal-credit ESA scheme, a failure without good cause to attend a WFI or (until its abolition) work-focused health-related assessment or to undertake a required work-related activity could lead to a reduction in the WRAG component of benefit by 50 per cent for four weeks and, for so long as the failure continued, by 100 per cent for each further week.[99]

There were 11,130 conditionality sanctions imposed on ESA claimants in the year to 31 May 2012; 343,480 claimants were eligible to receive such a sanction, so the overall sanction rate was 2.7 per cent; and the average duration of a sanction was 7 weeks.[100] Just over two thirds of those sanctioned received a 50 per cent reduction in the WRAG component, the rest a 100 per cent reduction.[101] (The figures do not distinguish between the different grounds for their imposition.) The rules governing the sanction to be imposed for breach of what was referred to as 'a compliance condition' (relating to WFI participation or undertaking a work-related activity) were amended

and the likelihood of their obtaining or remaining in work or being able to do so as may be prescribed'.

[95] Welfare Reform Act 2012, s 15. See also s 21 as regards the imposition of a work preparation requirement on a universal credit claimant.

[96] ESA Regulations 2008 (above n 38), regs 23 and 24.

[97] Ibid, regs 21, 22 and 24

[98] ESA Regulations 2013 (above n 36), regs 18–20.

[99] ESA Regulations 2008 (above n 38), regs 61 and 63 (both as amended).

[100] DWP Labour Market Interventions Strategy Division, *ESA Sanctions Official Statistics, August 2012* (August 2012), statistics.dwp.gov.uk/asd/workingage/esa_sanc/esa_sanc_aug12.pdf

[101] Ibid.

with effect from 3 December 2012. As from that date,[102] (i) the amount of the reduction will be 100 per cent from the start of the sanction period; and (ii) the duration of the reduction will be 'one week for each 7-day period during which the claimant fails to meet a compliance condition' and thereafter a further fixed period of one, two or four weeks, determined with reference to whether there have been previous failures at least two weeks but not more than 52 weeks before the current period.

Section 11J of the Welfare Reform Act 2012, in combination with the ESA Regulations 2013 and the Universal Credit Regulations 2013, has now set in place a complex new framework of sanctions for breach of compliance conditions. (There is also the continuing longstanding sanction of disqualification from receipt of ESA for up to six weeks for claimants whose limited capability for work results from their own misconduct or failure without good cause to follow medical advice or who without good cause have failed to observe any prescribed rules of behaviour;[103] but this issue lies outside the scope of the present discussion.) Note that the compliance-related sanctions applicable to universal credit are intended to form part of a unified sanctioning framework under the new regulations.

The ESA sanctions being discussed here correspond with the 'low' and 'lowest' levels of sanction under the rules governing universal credit[104] (which of course will also apply to universal credit claimants in the equivalent of the WRAG category applicable to ESA).[105] The 'low' level is applicable to a failure to meet a work-related requirement on the part of someone subject to both WFI participation and work preparation requirements,[106] while the 'lowest' level concerns a failure to attend a WFI by someone who is subject only to a WFI participation requirement (see above).[107] The sanction will involve a reduction in the amount of an award of ESA where there is a 'sanctionable' failure in the form of failing 'for no good reason' to comply with the relevant work-related requirement[108] or a connected requirement to attend an interview for any purpose relating to: the imposition of a work-related requirement; verifying the claimant's compliance with such a requirement; or assisting him or her to comply with such a requirement.[109] 'Good reason' is

---

[102] See ESA Regulations 2008 (above n 38), regs 61 and 63, as amended by Employment and Support Allowance (Sanctions) (Amendment) Regulations 2012 (SI 2012/2756), regs 3 and 4; and see the ESA Regulations 2013 (above n 36), regs 52 and 53.

[103] See the Welfare Reform Act 2007, s 18; and the ESA Regulations 2013 (above n 36), reg 93.

[104] 'Higher-level sanctions' in universal credit relate to voluntary leaving or misconduct causing a loss of employment; failure to undertake a work placement as a work preparation requirement; failure to apply for a vacancy for paid work; or failure to take up an offer of paid work. See Welfare Reform Act 2012, s 26. Provision is made for hardship payments in some circumstances: s 28. There is also a 'medium-level' sanction for not meeting a work availability or work search requirement: Universal Credit Regulations 2013 (above n 34), reg 103.

[105] See the Universal Credit Regulations 2013 (above n 34), regs 104 and 105.

[106] See above n 50. It is also low level for failure in a 'connected requirement' (below).

[107] See above n 49 and ESA Regulations 2013 (above n 36) reg 50.

[108] Welfare Reform Act 2007, s 11(2), noted above.

[109] Ibid, ss 11J(1)–(3) and 11G, inserted by the Welfare Reform Act 2012, s 57.

not defined, unlike 'good cause' applicable to the medical examination or information provision sanctions above.

In the case of a low-level sanction, the rules provide for the sanction period to be seven days. However, it will be 14 days if, in the 365 days preceding the failure in question, there was a separate ESA sanctionable failure giving rise to a low-level sanction for which a seven-day sanction applied or an equivalent sanction in respect of JSA or universal credit. The applicable ESA reduction period will be 28 days if there has been, within the previous 365 days, a previous sanction of 14 or 28 days in respect of any of these benefits.[110] The sanction could continue if, in particular, a specified compliance condition remains unmet, but although sanction periods run concurrently, they must not continue beyond a total period of 1095 days.[111] Moreover, if a claimant has been in paid work for at least 26 weeks since the date of the most recent sanctionable failure that gave rise to a benefit reduction, the reduction must terminate.[112]

Where a lowest-level sanction is concerned, the reduction period runs from the date of the sanctionable failure until the soonest of: the day before the specified compliance condition is met; the day before the claimant becomes someone not subject to any work-related requirements;[113] or the date the claimant's ESA award is terminated.[114] If the reduction period has not expired when the claimant's award of ESA has terminated, the sanction period will continue to run, so that if the claimant re-qualifies for and claims ESA while that period is still running, the new award will be reduced in accordance with the sanction until the sanction period has ended.[115] The rules about the 1095-day maximum total duration of sanction periods and the termination of a reduction once the claimant has worked for 26 weeks noted in relation to the low-level sanction (above) apply also to the lowest-level sanction.

For both low-level and lowest-level sanctions, there is a fairly complex formula for calculating the amount of reduction for each benefit week.[116] The

---

[110] ESA Regulations 2013 (above n 36), reg 52.

[111] Ibid, reg 51(3).

[112] Ibid, reg 57.

[113] See above n 51.

[114] ESA Regulations 2013 (above n 36), reg 53.

[115] Ibid, reg 55.

[116] Ibid, regs 58–60. The calculation is set out in three steps: (1) take the number of days in the benefit week or, if lower, in the total outstanding reduction period, less in either case any number of days during which the reduction is suspended (Suspension could occur where a fraud sanction is applicable: reg 56); (2) multiply the number of days calculated in (1) by the 'daily reduction rate'; and (3) deduct the amount calculated in (2) from the amount of the claimant's award of ESA for the benefit week. The daily reduction rate referred to in (2) will normally be the relevant basic rate of ESA (currently £71.70 or, during the assessment phase in the case of someone under 25, £56.80) multiplied by 52 and divided by 365. The benefit week is defined as a seven-day period (reg 2). (Note also reg 61, which prescribes the level of reduction to be applied when a claimant subject to a universal credit sanction qualifies for ESA.) On the amount of the reduction applicable in the case of universal credit, see the Universal Credit Regulations 2013 (above n 34), regs 110 and 111.

overall effect of this calculation should be more or less a weekly reduction close to the basic rate of ESA but apportioned where the reduction applies only to part of a benefit week. However, the daily reduction rate used in the calculation will be much lower in certain cases, including in the case of persons subject to the WFI requirement only or in the case of those who are lone parents of a child aged under one.[117] If a claimant with a benefit sanction ceases to be subject to a work-related requirement by the end of the benefit week in question, his or her daily reduction rate for that week is nil.

Contracting

The involvement of private and voluntary sector bodies in parts of the welfare system was discussed in chapter two and, as was noted there, has brought additional complexity to the system. Such involvement has been occurring in this sphere since the Secretary of State was given the power to authorise such bodies to conduct WFIs (although a claimant's first WFI is conducted by Jobcentre Plus), set in place a claimant's action plan, and make a direction to a claimant regarding work-related activity.[118] Provision was also made for other functions, including the revision of a decision that affects entitlement, to be extended to such bodies via regulations, although not a power to impose a benefit sanction.[119] Delegation and contracting-out of functions are now covered by a loose framework introduced under the Welfare Reform Act 2012, covering all those relating to work-related activity requirements within sections 11–11I of the 2007 Act outlined above but therefore excluding those concerning sanctions per section 11J. The Secretary of State has a broad power to authorise a person and his or her employees to exercise, wholly or to a limited extent and for such period as he or she determines, a function covered by sections 11–11I, although anything done or purported to be done by them must generally be treated for all purposes as done by the Secretary of State or an officer of him/her.[120] Parallel provisions are in place covering the work-related requirements under the universal credit scheme, again excluding the imposition of sanctions.[121]

The progression to work activities managed by contractors under the Pathways programme are now being undertaken under the Coalition

---

[117] It will be only 40% of the standard rate calculated via the method described in n 116 above.

[118] Welfare Reform Act 2007, ss 12, 14 and 15; and the Employment and Support Allowance (Work-Related Activity) Regulations 2011 (SI 2011/1349), reg 9, as amended (contracting out).

[119] Welfare Reform Act 2007, s 16.

[120] Ibid, s 11K(1)–(4). But not, for example, for the purpose of any criminal proceedings arising out of any such action or an omission: s 11K(5).

[121] Welfare Reform Act 2012, s 29, referring to the functions in ss 13–25. The administration of hardship payments (see s 28) is also outside the scope of the delegation and contracting powers.

Government's Work Programme, which has also replaced the Flexible New Deal for jobseekers and is reinforced by the levering up of the level of conditionality attached to out-of-work benefits.[122] The performance of Pathways to Work was subject of some criticism. The arrangements were considered to offer poor value for money[123] and to have achieved a below-expected level of success in moving people off benefit and into work.[124] The operation of the Work Programme also involves contractors, who are engaged via a complex contracting regime,[125] as noted in chapter two.[126] In addition, as was also explained in that chapter, the assessments to determine whether there is limited capability for work and limited capability for undertaking a work-related activity for the purposes of ESA (or, in due course, universal credit) are conducted by Atos healthcare professionals. As Ruth Lister has explained, these contracting-out arrangements are another facet of the 'welfare contract' that has featured in both New Labour and Conservative policy frameworks – a facet that is separate from the state's 'contract' with citizens.[127]

Conditionality and Complexity

Further extension of conditionality for recipients of ESA or the capability-for-work elements of universal credit may occur as the result of the continuing pursuit of the responsibility agenda. The Welfare Reform Act 2009 contained measures enabling conditions to be applied to 'problem drug users' receiving ESA (or JSA), as noted above. They included conditions about answering prescribed questions about drug use or undergoing 'substance-related assessment' and 'drugs interviews'. There was provision in the 2009 Act that failure to participate could result in a requirement to undergo testing for drugs.[128] In some instances, sanctions in the form of loss of benefit could be incurred. There was also the prospect of being required to agree a

---

[122] DWP, *Welfare that Works* (above n 54); and DWP, *21st Century Welfare* (above n 21).

[123] National Audit Office, *Support to Incapacity Benefit Claimants through Pathways to Work* (2010–11, HC 21).

[124] House of Commons Committee of Public Accounts, *Support to Incapacity Benefit Claimants through Pathways to Work* (2010–11, HC 404) paras 2.15 and 2.16.

[125] House of Commons Work and Pensions Committee, *Work Programme: Providers and Contracting Arrangements* (2010–12, HC 718).

[126] See further See D Finn, 'Welfare to Work after the Recession: From the New Deals to the Work Programme' in Holden, Kilkey and Ramia (eds) (above n 1) 127–45; and N Harris, 'Welfare's Mixed Economy in the UK: Public Rights and Private Actors' in F Pennings, T Erhag and S Stendahl (eds), *Non-public Partners in Social Security* (Alphen aan den Rijn, Wolters Klewer, forthcoming).

[127] Lister (above n 1) 65.

[128] These measures, which also applied to JSA, were set out in the Welfare Reform Act 2009, s 11 and Sched 3. For a critical review of these provisions, see N Harris, 'Conditional Rights, Benefit Reform, and Drug Users: Reducing Dependency?' (2010) 37(2) *Journal of Law and Society* 233.

'rehabilitation plan' with a specialist employment adviser. Although these measures were not implemented and have now been repealed under the Welfare Reform Act 2012,[129] the Government is reported to be proposing to pilot arrangements under which problem drug users and alcoholics could be denied benefit for failing to be treated.[130] This would go further than the previous measures, which contained no provision for requiring drug users to undergo treatment and did not in themselves apply to alcoholism, although there was a statutory power to extend the regime to people with alcohol dependency.[131]

Even without such reform, it is clear that the conditionality regime operating under ESA, which is also rolling forward into the relevant part of the universal credit system, has given greater complexity to the relationship between sick/disabled claimants and the state. Indeed, claimants already receiving income-based ESA when universal credit is introduced will face a further twist and turn to their journey as they are moved into the new system, although the Government has given an undertaking that they will not be worse off under it. Under both ESA and universal credit, the conditionality regime is a strict one. In an attempt to constrain various kinds of behaviour deemed inconsistent with responsibilities attached to being a client of the welfare state, considerable burdens have been placed on claimants. This is despite the fact that claimants would not be in the work-related activity group if they did not have physical or mental disabilities (for approx 40 per cent of those initially assessed as falling within this group, the main cause of a limited capacity for work is a mental/behavioural disorder[132]), even if their difficulties are less severe than those of their counterparts in the support group, who are mostly spared any conditionality.

The conditionality regime also places burdens on the system's administrative authorities and those delegated to carry out non-sanctioning functions. Those burdens are increased due to the high likelihood of appeal (under arrangements discussed in the previous chapter). Between October 2008 and August 2010, almost 182,000 appeals were heard regarding decisions that the claimants were fit for work, meaning that at least 40 per cent of unsuccessful claimants appealed.[133] The overall success rate for appellants over this period was 38 per cent,[134] but probably as a result of the tightening-up of the work capability assessment following reviews of the assessment process and

---

[129] Welfare Reform Act 2012, s 60 and Sched 14, pt 6.

[130] C Hope, 'Clampdown on Benefits for Addicts', *Daily Telegraph* (6 November 2012) 2.

[131] Welfare Reform Act 2009, s 11(2) and para 10 of the new schedules, inserted into the Jobseekers Act 1995 and Welfare Reform Act 2007, respectively, by the 2009 Act, Sched 3.

[132] DWP, *Employment and Support Allowance: Official Statistics* (October 2011) (above n 40) Table 7.

[133] Ibid, Table 3. 'At least', because a small number of appeals may have been withdrawn by claimants and thus not heard.

[134] Ibid.

criteria[135] and amendments to the regulations in March 2011,[136] the success rate has progressively fallen. In the quarter to the end of August 2011 (the most recent known at the time of writing), 31 per cent of appeals were upheld.[137]

IV. Conclusion

This and the previous two chapters have attempted to show how the complexity of the UK social security system and its legal framework clearly affects the claimant's experience of the journey to entitlement and his or her ongoing relationship with the welfare state. We have seen ample evidence of the deleterious impact of complexity on citizens and, often, on those responsible for the administration of the system, throughout all stages of the journey. Chapter four, for example, highlighted the link between complexity and the rates of benefit take-up – critical to the proper enjoyment of social rights – as well as the link between complexity and errors in decision-making. In this chapter, we have seen the complicated arrangements governing engagement with ESA, which, as carried through into universal credit in the case of income-based entitlement, will continue to be covered by highly technical legislative measures that reflect the continued harnessing of the benefit system, including the rules on incapacity benefits, to advance a form of 'positive' or responsible citizenship.[138] Yet the regime of conditionality and support such as the ESA scheme represents was regarded by the influential Gregg Review as being 'not . . . as effective as it could be whilst there is still a complex, frequently confusing and administratively expensive benefits structure overlaying it'.[139]

---

[135] J Bolton, *Work Capability Assessment Internal Review: Report of the Working Group* (DWP, October 2009), webarchive.nationalarchives.gov.uk/+/http://www.dwp.gov.uk/docs/work-capability-assessment-review.pdf; and M Harrington, *An Independent Review of the Work Capability Assessment* (London, Stationery Office, 2010). See also Secretary of State for Work and Pensions, *Government's Response to Professor Malcolm Harrington's Independent Review of the Work Capability Assessment* (Cm 7977, 2010); and M Harrington, *An Independent Review of the Work Capability Assessment: Year Two* (London, Stationary Office, 2011), to which the Government has again responded: Secretary of State for Work and Pensions, *Government's Response to Professor Malcolm Harrington's Second Independent Review of the Work Capability Assessment* (Cm 8229, 2010). For Harrington's *Year Three* review, see above n 77.

[136] Employment and Support Allowance (Limited Capability for Work and Limited Capability for Work-Related Activity) (Amendment) Regulations 2011 (SI 2011/228).

[137] DWP, *Employment and Support Allowance: New Claims* (above n 41) Figure E.

[138] See P Larkin, 'Incapacity, the Labour Market and Social Security: Coercion into "Positive" Citizenship' (2011) 74(3) *Modern Law Review* 385, 405.

[139] P Gregg, *Realising Potential: A Vision for Personalised Conditionality and Support* (London, Stationery Office, 2008) 97.

At each stage of the journey, whether in the context of identifying his or her rights, validly claiming a benefit or credit, complying with the conditions and requirements specified for securing or retaining entitlement to benefits or credits, or challenging a benefit or credit decision, a claimant's position is affected by a complex set of rules and processes. As we have seen, the introduction of universal credit may ease the experience in some respects, such as through a unified claims process and administration, but it would be wrong to assume that for new claimants, the experience will be a simple one. The need for assistance in coping with complexity, which is generally acknowledged, will continue but is likely to remain not fully met. Of course, not all claimants will experience the same degree of difficulty: the social/educational background of some may better equip them to navigate the system, while others will have to undertake more arduous journeys because of their specific circumstances. As the National Audit Office has explained, some people's dealings with the system 'are uncomplicated and their needs and circumstances are straightforward', while 'for many others, the benefits system is seen as highly complex and problematic'.[140] For those whose relationship with the system must be an active one – notably those who are within the welfare-to-work and conditionality regime applicable to out-of-work benefits – the burdens can be considerable.

---

[140] National Audit Office, *Department for Work and Pensions: Dealing with the Complexity of the Benefits System* (2005–06, HC 592) 6.

7

Welfare Complexity in the International Context

I. Introduction

Over the past couple of decades, there has been considerable common ground to key aspects of social security policy across industrialised nations. This is not surprising, given that these states have been faced with similar social and economic conditions, including widening budgetary deficits and weakening markets. The pursuit of economic and political imperatives along with underlying ideological goals has included a common focus on reducing the state's commitment of resources, limiting welfare dependency and strengthening citizen responsibilities. There has been a reinforcement of what was already a dominant policy trend not only in the United Kingdom, as noted in previous chapters, but also across a wide range of states, in the form of welfare-to-work policies based around increasing conditionality and the activation of the unemployed.[1] Another common policy direction has been towards reform of state pension provision through, inter alia, a raising of the retirement age – a response to the issue of ageing populations and increased longevity

---

[1] See, eg, P Van Aerschot, *Activation Policies and the Protection of Individual Rights: A Critical Assessment of the Situation in Denmark, Finland and Sweden* (Farnham, Ashgate, 2011); T Carney, 'Australian Social Security Welfare-to-Work: Avoiding Freudian Slips' (2008) 15 *Journal of Social Security Law* 51; T Carney, 'Not the Old Way, Not the Third Way, but the OECD/US Way? Welfare Sanctions and Active Welfare in Australia' (2005) 12 *Journal of Social Security Law* 57; JM Dorstal, 'The Workfare Illusion: Re-examining the Concept and the British Case' (2008) 42(1) *Social Policy and Administration* 19; S Stendahl, T Erhag and S Devetzi (eds), *A European Work-First Welfare State* (Gothenburg, Centre for European Research, 2008); and A Paz-Fuchs, *Welfare to Work: Conditional Rights in Social Policy* (Oxford, Oxford University Press, 2008).

combined with concern about the consequent long-term affordability of pension provision.[2]

One should not, however, over-emphasise the degree of common ground between individual states' policies in these areas. For example, the Organisation for Economic Co-operation and Development (OECD) has reported that the extent to which retirement pensioners are being insulated from the general retrenchment of welfare provision by protective redistribution of income varies internationally.[3] Nevertheless, not merely within the European Union,[4] but also more broadly,[5] there has been an increasing convergence of policy in some areas. Even so, there is a continuation of the core defining characteristics of the different models of welfare state associated with individual nations' systems.[6]

The complexity of welfare systems and their governing legislation is recognised as one of the areas of common ground between nation states. This is particularly so with regard to social assistance schemes designed to provide support to citizens on a systematic but, to a certain extent, individualized basis related to need.[7] As we have seen in earlier chapters, means-tested provision through such schemes is particularly associated with complexity, arising as it does from the goal of targeting support and responding in a consistent and yet adaptive way to a wide diversity of individual circumstances. Complexity, however, extends beyond the area of social assistance and is a general feature of social security schemes across the world, even though its degree varies between states.[8] The technicality and intricacy of social security law is widely acknowledged internationally.[9]

---

[2] See, eg, OECD, *Pensions at a Glance (2011): Retirement-Income Systems in OECD and G20 Countries* (2011), dx.doi.org/10.1787/pension_glance-2011-en, which notes that 'half of OECD are already increasing statutory pension ages or will do so in the coming decades' (9).

[3] Ibid, 10.

[4] See, eg, S Devetzi, 'Reforms of Incapacity Benefits Systems in Europe' in S Devetzi and S Stendahl (eds), *Too Sick to Work? Social Security Reforms in Europe for Persons with Reduced Earnings Capacity* (Alphen aan den Rijn, Wolters Kluwer, 2011).

[5] See, eg, C Prinz and W Tompson, 'Sickness and Disability Benefit Programmes: What Is Driving Policy Convergence?' (2009) 62(4) *International Social Security Review* 41.

[6] See above ch 1, n 21 (discussing G Esping-Andersen, *The Three Worlds of Welfare Capitalism* (Cambridge, Polity Press, 1990)).

[7] T Eardley et al, *Social Assistance in OECD Countries: Synthesis Report*, Department of Social Security Research Report No 46 (1996) para.4.12.

[8] J Kvist, 'Complexities in Assessing Unemployment Benefits and Policies' (2008) 51(4) *International Social Security Review* 33, 36.

[9] F Bates, 'Social Security Law and Children with Disabilities: Change and Decay in Australian Statute Law' (1997) 18(3) *Statute Law Review* 215; PA Kemp, 'The Role and Design of Income-Related Housing Allowances' (2000) 5(3) *International Social Security Review* 43; A O'Neill, 'Plain English and the 1991 Social Security Act' in J Disney (ed), *Current Issues in Social Security Law* (Canberra, Centre for International and Public Law, Australian National University, 1994); D Pieters, *Systems of the Member States of the European Union* (Antwerp, Intersentia, 2002); D Pieters, *The Social Security Systems of the States Applying for Membership of the European Union* (Antwerp, Intersentia, 2003); B Schulte, 'Social Rights under International and National Law: Access to Social Security – A Discussion Paper for the ISSA' (2002), www.issa.int/pdf/initiative/reports/2Schulte.pdf; and RA White, *EC Social Security Law* (Harlow, Longman, 1999).

Over the past couple of decades, not only has there been a collective strategy in terms of the European Union's rolling programme of simplification of its social security provisions, which was discussed in chapters one and two, but also a number of individual states have made attempts to simplify the structure, administration and legislative basis to their social security systems. At a time when there is within the United Kingdom a coherent attempt by government to effect simplification in this field, it is therefore instructive to examine the experience of other states. The analysis in this chapter is focused on states where the most significant developments have occurred. Perhaps the most interesting are Australia and New Zealand, where some of the social security benefits are very similar to those in the United Kingdom in terms of structure and where welfare policies are close to those being applied in the United Kingdom in recent years – and indeed have influenced the latter policies in various ways. Developments in Germany and Sweden also warrant examination, because the codification of much of their social security legislation has been part of an effort to increase the accessibility of the law. The discussion in each case will focus on relevant reforms rather than attempt to provide a complete description of national welfare systems, although where considered helpful, a brief overview will be included to aid understanding of a particular state's attempts to address complexity.

II. 'A Maze of Provisions . . .': Social Security Law and Welfare Provision in Australia

Social security in Australia is administered by the Department of Human Services (DHS) through an agency known as Centrelink. The main benefits are governed by the Social Security Act 1991 (Commonwealth).[10] None of the benefits are insurance-based, including Newstart Allowance, which is the principal unemployment benefit. Newstart Allowance is a means-tested benefit. People aged 22 or over and under pensionable age are eligible for this allowance if unemployed and looking for work. It is therefore equivalent to JSA (and the equivalent form of universal credit) in the United Kingdom. Indeed, as in the United Kingdom, the term 'jobseeker' is used in the Australian system, such as in the 'Job Seeker Diary', which may be issued to claimants to record their efforts to find work, including attending interviews. 'Working credit' is also available in some cases for those who take up work.

---

[10] Also the Social Security (Administration) Act 1999 (Cth).

For young people under the age of 22 or for those who are full-time students or apprentices there is a youth allowance (or for older students, support known as 'Austudy'). These are quite complex schemes. For example, in the case of a person who is not classed as independent and seeks the youth allowance, a parental means test is applied, comprising a parental income test, a family assets test and a 'family actual means test'. Newstart and youth allowance give rise to eligibility for passported benefits such as a health care card providing access to free prescriptions.

Other benefits are also aimed at providing income support (in the broad sense) but with no work search activity conditions attached: age pension;[11] carer payment;[12] disability support pension;[13] and parenting payment.[14] Pensions, including disability support pension, have undergone some reform in recent years following a Pension Review, which reported in 2009.[15] There is also sickness allowance for people who are temporarily unable to work due to illness, disability or injury. All these benefits are means-tested. So is another important benefit, Family Tax Benefit (FTB). Indeed, Australia has been described as having 'the most progressive benefit structure in the OECD by an extremely wide mile' as a result of its reliance on means-testing.[16]

FTB is governed by a statute named A New Tax System (Family Assistance Act) 1999 (Cth) and is comprised of two parts.[17] Part A is designed to help with the cost of rearing children and young people up the age of 22 (if in education), whilst Part B is designed to provide extra help with such costs (up to the end of the year in which the child/young person turns 18) for lone parents or those in families with only one main income. In some cases, this benefit can be claimed as a single lump sum, but it is an indication of the complexity of the Australian system that the form for claiming it is 47 pages long.[18]

---

[11] Australia is one of the many countries whose pension age is rising. Women's pension age will progressively rise to men's retirement age of 65 by 2017. Subsequently, the retirement age for both men and women will progressively increase to 67 by 2023.

[12] For people providing full-time care on a daily basis for another person who needs such care. In some cases, a separate non-means-tested 'carer allowance' may also be payable.

[13] A disability benefit for people whose disability prevents them from working or being able to take up work (with training, etc) within two years.

[14] This is a payment made fortnightly to a single person caring for a child aged below 8 years or to a member of a couple (but only one member) caring for a child aged under 6. Grandparents can also qualify for a payment.

[15] Department of Families, Community Services and Indigenous Affairs, *Pension Review Report* (the 'Harmer Report') (27 February 2009), www.fahcsia.gov.au/sites/default/files/docume nts/05_2012/pensionreviewreport.pdf, 142 and 144–47. Increases in pension ages were initiated via the Social Security and Other Legislation Amendment (Pension Reform and Other 2009 Budget Measures) Act 2009. Disability support pensioners can now work for up to 30 hours per week and still be eligible for their disability support pension: Social Security Act 1991 (Cth), s 96.

[16] P Whiteford, 'The Henry Review and the Social Security System' (2010) 43(4) *Australian Economic Review* 429, 430.

[17] It is also covered by A New Tax System (Family Assistance Act) (Administration) Act 1999 (Cth).

[18] See the form for the 2011–12 financial year: www.humanservices.gov.au/spw/customer/forms/resources/fa048-1207en.pdf.

The claim form for parenting payment runs to 31 pages,[19] and that for disability support pension or sickness allowance to 27 pages.[20] Australia has, however, already instituted online claiming for some benefits – for example, youth allowance must normally be claimed this way. As we saw in chapter four, this will become the standard method for claiming universal credit in the United Kingdom. For Newstart Allowance, a claimant must register an 'intent' to claim, either online, by phone or by attending the nearest DHS service centre and will then be interviewed, which mirrors arrangements for claiming JSA in the United Kingdom. Social security claimants have a right to request a review of a decision with which they disagree by an officer other than the decision-maker. If dissatisfied with the outcome of the review, there is a right of appeal to the independent social security appeal tribunal and thereafter to the Administrative Appeals Tribunal.

The legislation governing the above and the various other benefits in Australia's social security system is considered to be very complex, despite the legislative reforms (discussed below) that were intended to make it easier to understand.[21] To aid their comprehension decision-makers are guided by two official documents published by the Department of Families, Community Services and Indigenous Affairs (FaCSIA), the *Guide to Social Security Law* and the *Family Assistance Guide*,[22] which are updated on a monthly basis. Their content is not legally binding,[23] but on the basis of case law, it is considered to be legitimate for decision-makers to have regard to the guides and to follow them unless there is good reason for not doing so.[24] The principal statute, the Social Security Act 1991, has been amended numerous times.[25] The Act represented a codification of the legislation and sought to modernise the language used. In replacing the Social Security Act 1947, the 1991 Act constituted a rewriting of social security law into what was intended to be a more usable and intelligible form. As the Minister, speaking in 1990, indicated, an aim was to set in place 'a more accessible piece of legislation that ordinary Australians can reasonably be expected to understand'.[26] The 1991 Act also sought to make provisions governing specific parts of the system self-contained regardless of the repetition that served to increase the statute's length.

[19] See www.humanservices.gov.au/spw/customer/forms/resources/sc277-1301en.pdf (as at 10 June 2013).

[20] See www.humanservices.gov.au/spw/customer/forms/resources/sa317b-1207en.pdf.

[21] Bates (above n 9); and O'Neill (above n 9).

[22] The guides are published at guidesacts.fahcsia.gov.au/guides_acts.

[23] *Stevens v Secretary, Department of Family and Community Services* [2004] AATA 1137 [51].

[24] In particular, the dictum: 'Although the Tribunal ought not, indeed cannot, deprive itself of its freedom to give no weight to a Minister's policy in a particular case, there are substantial reasons which favour only cautious and sparing departures from Ministerial policy . . .'. See *Re Drake and the Minister for Immigration and Ethic Affairs* [1979] AATA 179 (per Brennan J).

[25] Amendments are listed at www.comlaw.gov.au/Details/C2012C00298/Html/Volume_4. Writing in 1994, O'Neill reported that 'Between 1 July 1991 and October 1993 there were 12 Acts amending the Social Security Act 1991. The 1992 and 1993 Commonwealth budgets alone led to 175 changes': O'Neill (above n 9) 157.

[26] Cited in *Re Blunn v Cleaver* (1993) 47 FCR 111, 121.

In 1993, the Full Court of the Federal Court expressed forcibly its view that the 1991 Act had not succeeded in reducing complexity to the intended degree:

> The Act in its current form contains more than 1,364 sections. We have not counted the precise number. To do so would involve taking account of a number of sections which are identified by letters as well as numbers. These have been added to the Act in the short period of two years in which it has been in force. The Act, including the notes to it, occupies 1,471 pages of the Commonwealth Statutes . . . The professed aim of the drafting of the Act is to make it more accessible to persons without legal training. It is necessary to say 'more accessible' . . . because no one seriously believes the layman can master the Act unaided . . . [A]n Act that is two or three times as long is not necessarily easy to read because some technical expressions (which once understood were succinct) have been replaced by wordier ones . . . [T]he increasingly complex society in which we all live very often demands that legislation be expressed in a complex form. That is the factor which will so often operate to prevent simplicity in legislative drafting. The area of social services legislation is a complex one . . . That is what the draftsman of this legislation may have sought to overcome. Regrettably, the replacement consists of a maze of provisions made the more complex by prolix definitions, provisos and exceptions. Both those who claim entitlements under it and those responsible for its administration will not always find it easy to discover whether or not a benefit is payable.[27]

In 1999, Weinburg J, in a lengthy judgment in the Federal Court concerning a decision by Centrelink to take into account a man's disposal of an asset to a trust when calculating both his entitlement to Newstart Allowance and his wife's eligibility for a parenting allowance, commented that the 1991 Act was 'drafted in a manner which is both prolix and obscure'.[28] Four years later, Jones J, also in the Federal Court, found the Act 'notoriously complex and difficult to interpret',[29] while the following year, Weinberg J reflected, 'Regrettably, as each year goes by, the Social Security Act becomes still more complex, and less accessible to those who most need to understand it . . .'[30] Plainly, when the Act was put to the test in practice, it was shown to have patently failed in its objective of making the legislation more straightforward and intelligible.[31]

Separate legislation, the Social Security (Administration) Act 1999, focused on the system's administrative framework and aimed to make the arrangements simpler and more coherent. As a result of the Act, the law governing the administration of social security benefits was taken out of the 1991 Act.

---

[27]   Ibid, 127–28.

[28]   *Anstis v Secretary, Department of Social Security* [1999] FCA 1176 [11].

[29]   *Secretary, Department of Family & Community Services v Draper* [2003] FCA 1409 [24] (Jones J).

[30]   *Secretary, Department of Family and Community Services v Geeves* [2004] FCAFC 166 [37] and [38].

[31]   See also O'Neill (above n 9), who notes that the Social Security Act 1991 is 'sophisticated and complex, and is daunting to anyone not fully familiar with its structure and operations . . . [T]he structure, language and design of the Act also limit its accessibility' (158), even though some parts are set out in plainer English.

The 1999 Act did not seek to change the basic framework of entitlement under the 1991 Act, although some of its provisions seemed to have that effect. The Australian Government considered that the rules as a whole would be shorter and more comprehensible if there was a departure from the self-contained approach reflected in the different parts of the 1991 Act as drafted. The element of consolidation resulted in a need to read across provisions in a way that would be familiar to those who make reference to and utilise social security legislation in the United Kingdom.

Following these two significant attempts at reform, the complexity of Australian social security law as a whole nevertheless remained problematic. One of the reasons for its complexity was that the structure of benefits was also complex. With a view to clarification and simplification, two specific initiatives were undertaken between 2001 and 2003. First, in February 2001, a Rules Simplification Task Force was established. It comprised members of the FaCSIA and Centrelink. It was expected to find ways to simplify the rules governing the age pension and the Newstart Allowance. A means was, for example, identified of streamlining the process for re-claiming benefit within 12 months of having received it. Also, there were improvements in the assessment of new claims for age pension after the Minister had ordered a simplification of the rules.[32] Plans for further legislative simplification were announced in the 2003–04 budget,[33] including measures to reduce unnecessary duplication and alter the numbering format of the 1991 Act, although there were no proposals for comprehensive reform.

Secondly, in December 2002, the Australian Government published a policy document entitled *Building a Simpler System to Help Jobless Families and Individuals*[34] in which it proposed a modernisation of the system. It was observed, 'As the system has evolved over the years, more payment types have been added and rules and payments changed. This has created an unnecessarily complex system that people can find hard to navigate'.[35] Moreover, some of the disparities in the levels of support provided to diverse groups were considered to be difficult to justify.[36] The principles identified for the design of a reformed system of working-age benefits included 'simplicity and fairness' – with, for example, parity of obligations among people with a similar capacity for work – and an administrative structure that is 'transparent, easy to navigate and cost-effective'.[37] There was no conclusion on whether reform

---

[32] Commonwealth of Australia Parliamentary Debates, House of Representatives, 26 June 2002, 4467.

[33] Available at www.budget.gov.au/2003-04/.

[34] Commonwealth Department of Family and Community Services, *Building a Simpler System to Help Jobless Families and Individuals* (2002), www.airc.gov.au/safetynet_review/aig/AiGsubmission_AnnexureI.pdf.

[35] Ibid, para 15.

[36] Ibid, paras 36 and 37.

[37] Ibid, para 47.

should be incremental (through selective simplification[38]) or comprehensive (involving a complete redesign).[39] In addition to simplification, there was also perceived to be a need to incentivise working, increase social participation and improve the interface between tax and benefits.

There has been criticism that the post-2000 reforms 'failed to grapple with the problems of complexity and disincentives'.[40] The failure by the Australian Government to realise its goal of a simpler system, in particular one based on a structural reform involving the introduction of a single base rate of benefit with additional elements related to disability, children and other factors, was regarded as reflecting a lack of commitment to the approach evinced in *Building a Simpler System*.[41] Only piecemeal reform has occurred, against a background of policy preoccupation with welfare-to-work (as reflected in a tightening-up of jobseekers' obligations).[42] As in the United Kingdom, the complexity of the social security system has been identified as a major barrier to the take-up of employment, but as the Australian Law Commission stated recently, 'Without large-scale reform of the social security system . . . this complexity will remain.'[43]

An opportunity for reform has been provided by the report of the Henry Review of the tax system and the 'transfer' system – the latter refers predominantly to social security benefits – which was published in 2010.[44] It stated that the transfer system 'is overly complex, can treat people of similar means differently and can result in people making choices that potentially undermine lifetime wellbeing'.[45] It recommended, inter alia, a rationalised framework of income support intended to counter the 'currently large differences in rates and conditions for payment, especially for people of working age, which produce very different outcomes for people with a similar ability to work', differences which 'create disincentives to work or incentives to move to higher payments'.[46] It argued that '[s]treamlining payment types and applying a comprehensive means test base would ensure a more consistent treatment of payment recipients'.[47] The Henry Report also called for a more comprehensive definition of means. Noting that 'means testing can increase the complexity a

---

[38] Ibid, paras 51–53.

[39] Ibid, paras 54–58. 'Income support' is used here to refer to benefit support in general.

[40] P Saunders, *Disability, Living Standards and Welfare Dependency in Australia*, SPRC Discussion Paper No 145 (University of New South Wales, 2005) 2.

[41] See Commonwealth of Australia Senate (Community Affairs Legislation Committee) Report, 21 November 2005, CA 37.

[42] See the two articles by Carney (above n 1).

[43] Australian Law Reform Commission, *Grey Areas: Age Barriers to Work in Commonwealth Laws (DP78)*, Discussion Paper No 78 (2012), www.alrc.gov.au/publications/grey-areas%E2%80%94age-barriers-work-commonwealth-laws-dp-78, para 5.28.

[44] Henry Committee, *Australia's Future Tax System: Report to the Treasurer (December 2009) – Part 1, Overview* (the 'Henry Report') (2010), www.taxreview.treasury.gov.au/content/downloads/final_report_part_1/00_AFTS_final_report_consolidated.pdf.

[45] Ibid, 59.

[46] Ibid, 61.

[47] Ibid, 59.

person faces in interacting with the tax and transfer system', the report proposed a 'comprehensive means test base that determined access to all income support payments, including Newstart Allowance and the Age Pension' in place of the two-part means test comprised of an income test and an assets test.[48] The report also called for better targeted family-related payments,[49] with a single family payment in place of existing and 'unnecessarily complex' family benefits, including Family Tax Benefits Parts A and B,[50] and for the integration of child care benefit and the child care rebate.[51] It also sought to deal with the problem that people's interactions with the system 'tend to be complex and fragmented', advocating 'citizen-centric design' based around the use of technology and better co-ordination and management to facilitate 'transformation of the client experience'.[52]

One can see clear policy parallels with the United Kingdom, especially in the context of universal credit, not least in the emphasis on 'a reduction in the compliance costs of interacting with government'.[53] Another policy proposal that is also attracting government interest in the United Kingdom is 'tied transfers' linked to specific goods and services, as an alternative to cash payments.[54]

The Henry Report's review of the social security schemes is detailed and extensive, but there is little sign that the Australian Government wants to capitalise on it and adopt its recommendations. Peter Whiteford considers that the review recommendations 'go in the right directions' but that there appears to be an unwillingness on the Australian Government's part to debate these or the review's analysis.[55] Indeed, the Australian Government's recent *Tax Reform Road Map*[56] eschews wide-ranging reforms to social security, such as the restructuring of family benefits and income support recommended by the Henry Report. Meanwhile, the Henry Report itself illustrates the emphasis now being placed on the structure of the benefits framework as the key issue so far as increasing simplification and tackling complexity are concerned. Significant reduction in legal complexity per se has seemingly been receiving increasingly less emphasis in policy debate in recent years despite on-going problems. The 'maze of provisions' continues.

---

[48] Ibid, 62.

[49] Ibid, 63–65.

[50] Henry Committee, *Australia's Future Tax System: Report to the Treasurer – Part 2, Detailed Analysis (Volume 2)* (December 2009), www.taxreview.treasury.gov.au/content/downloads/final_report_part_2/AFTS_Final_Report_Part_2_Vol_2_Consolidated.pdf, 565 and 576.

[51] Henry Committee, *Australia's Future Tax System – Part 1, Overview* (above n 44) 65. Child care benefit is a means-tested per hour rate of assistance payment, whereas the rebate is not means-tested and covers 50% of out-of-pocket costs.

[52] Ibid, 71.

[53] Ibid.

[54] Henry Committee, *Australia's Future Tax System – Part 2 (Volume 2)* (above n 50) 617–18.

[55] Whiteford (above n 16) 435.

[56] Australian Government, *Tax Reform Road Map* (May 2012), www.budget.gov.au/2012-13/content/glossy/tax_reform/download/tax_overview.pdf.

III. New Zealand's Major Welfare Reform Programme

As the United Kingdom embarks on the most significant reform of welfare since the Beveridge Report, New Zealand's social security system, which like that of Australia, is based almost entirely on means-tested support, is undergoing a similar process of transformation. The changes are being introduced by the National Party Government, which was elected to office in 2008. The previous administration was led by the Labour Party and had plans to introduce[57] a single core benefit with work-ready and work-exempt categories in place of out-of-work and sickness benefits – a reform 'justified partly to overcome the complexity of the benefit system' although also to 'assist in the work-focused objective of social security'.[58] Yet progress in developing the single core benefit, which attracted much interest in the United Kingdom,[59] was 'very slow', in part because it had to take place in the context of wider welfare policy development in New Zealand and would involve 'a total rewrite' of the main social security statute, the Social Security Act 1964.[60] This Act covers all main aspects of social security in New Zealand. It also sets out the right of appeal against decisions on social security to the Social Security Appeal Authority and from there, on a point of law, to the High Court.[61]

The proposal for a single core benefit emerged from the Labour-coalition Government's policy paper *Pathways to Opportunity: From Social Welfare to Social Development*, published in 2001.[62] Aside from its commitment to a welfare-to-work agenda, while also seeking to address citizen needs, the

---

[57] Originally this reform was planned for 2008 or 2009, according to the New Zealand Ministry of Social Development (cited in R Sainsbury and K Stanley, *One for All: Active Welfare and the Single Working-Age Benefit* (London, IPPR, 2007) 14). However, the UK House of Commons Work and Pensions Committee stated that it was planned for 2010: HC Work and Pensions Committee, *Benefits Simplification* (2006–07, HC 463-I) para 347.

[58] R Sainsbury and R Stephens, 'A Single Core Benefit: Lessons from New Zealand' (2009) 16(1) *Journal of Social Security Law* 12, 19.

[59] See, eg, House of Commons Work and Pensions Committee, *The Government's Employment Strategy* (2006–07, HC 63-I) para 347.

[60] Sainsbury and Stephens (above n 58) 20.

[61] Social Security Act 1964, ss 12A–12C, 12I, 12J and 12Q. In addition, a Special Social Security Appeal Authority may be appointed from time to time by the Governor General: s 12D. From the High Court there is a right of further appeal to the Court of Appeal: s 12R. As in the UK, there is a final appeal, with leave, to the Supreme Court – either via the Court of Appeal or direct from the High Court: see s 12S.

[62] Ministry of Social Development, *Pathways to Opportunity: From Social Welfare to Social Development* (Wellington, Ministry of Social Development, 2001).

Government acknowledged the complexity of the benefit system and the resultant problems for claimants in terms of their understanding of benefits and having their needs properly addressed. The Government undertook to work towards the progressive removal of unnecessary complexity from the system. It focused in particular on the existence of five separate benefits for people of working age.[63] *Pathways* proposed as one option the idea of a '"universal" benefit with standardized eligibility rules and conditions that would greatly simplify the system for both the beneficiary and administration'.[64] There could be 'add-ons' to reflect particular circumstances, such child care responsibilities or disability. Thus, as Roy Sainsbury and Robert Stephens have explained, the proposed single core benefit, which was announced in 2005, would represent the first tier of support, and there would also be a second tier comprising a portable (ie, payable to persons whether in or out of work) additional element in respect of, for example, disability or caring responsibilities.[65]

Although the single core benefit did not materialise, the Labour-led administration established, via the Social Security Administration Act 2007, a framework for managing a welfare-to-work regime (similar to that operating in the United Kingdom under the JSA scheme), although an opportunity was also taken for the alignment of various rules on income-related benefits. Some other small-scale simplifications were also effected (see below). The next phase of reform would have involved replacing the working age benefits with the single core benefit. Under the single benefit there would be three streams. The first would be a 'rapid return to full-time work' stream, or a 'work support' group, placement in which would represent the standard position for claimants. The second would comprise a 'development' stream – 'work development support' – for those who could not immediately undertake employment, such as those who had child care responsibilities. They would be provided with assistance to plan for work in the future, including the development of work-related skills. The third stream would cover a 'community support' group comprising those who would be the most detached from work, such as some recipients of invalids benefit or people with responsibility for caring for someone who was infirm.[66] Despite the apparent simplification that a single core benefit would represent, there was a concern that provision for variable elements to take account of disability or the size of families would mean the replacement of 'one hopelessly complex system with another'.[67] Overall, gains in terms of simplification might therefore have been somewhat limited.

[63] The benefits in question were unemployment, sickness, invalid's, widows' and 'domestic purposes' benefits.

[64] Ministry of Social Development, *Pathways to Opportunity* (above n 62) 6.

[65] Sainsbury and Stephens (above n 58) 21.

[66] Ministry of Social Development, 'Working New Zealand, Phase Two: A Core Benefit Approach', press release (July 2008), cited in Sainsbury and Stephens (above n 58) fn 14.

[67] Child Poverty Action Group (New Zealand), *Submission on the Single Core Benefit Proposal* (Auckland, CPAG (NZ), 2005) para 5.

There were, however, some small-scale simplifications under the 2007 Act such as to the residence requirements applicable to various benefits. Nevertheless, a close examination of the legislation reveals that purported simplification may not have greatly improved the intelligibility of the law. For example, section 120(1) of the Social Security Act 1964 provides for the loss of benefit for a couple in a situation where there has been imposed on one member a work test sanction comprising the suspension or cancellation of benefit.[68] The 1964 Act had provided that where this sanction was imposed:

(a) it only applies to one half the applicable rate of the benefit before any abatement on account of income; and
(b) the other spouse or partner is entitled to receive half of that rate (and the appropriate Income Test applies to that rate, but at half the abatement rate in that test).

As amended by the 2007 Act, section 120(1) not only refers to members of civil unions as well as married couples but also provides that where the above sanction is imposed:

(a) the suspension or cancellation applies only to 50% of the applicable rate of the benefit before any abatement on account of income; and
(b) the person's spouse or partner is entitled to receive 50% of that rate of the benefit, and the appropriate Income Test applies to that rate, but at half the abatement rate in that Income Test.

Clearly there was little, if any, substantive simplification achieved by the change. Furthermore, a comparison of the complete texts of each version of the subsection reveals that the 'simplified' version introduced by the 2007 Act is slightly (three words) longer than its predecessor.

In 2012, the National Party Government embarked on a comprehensive programme of welfare reform. The Minister for Social Development, Paula Bennett, announced that the reforms to 'fundamentally change the welfare system' would be 'complex and substantial, so legislation will be introduced in two stages'.[69] The first stage would involve a Bill covering young people and lone parents and was intended, inter alia, to impose stricter controls on payments to the former (such as direct payments of rent and utility costs)[70] and increased work expectations on the latter.[71] The Bill, the Social Security (Youth Support and Work Focus) Amendment Bill (now Act 2012), was

---

[68] This work test sanction is imposed under s 117 of the Social Security Act 1964.

[69] See the New Zealand Government website: www.beehive.govt.nz/release/welfare-reform-legislation-be-introduced (posted 27 February 2012).

[70] Young people will be assigned to one of 43 'youth service providers' selected by the Ministry of Social Development. A Youth Service was established in August 2012 to help young people 'find the best option for education, training or work-based learning that will help [them] build [their] skills and find a job': see the Youth Service website, www.youthservice.govt.nz/.

[71] The principal benefit, 'Domestic Purposes Benefit – Sole Parent', was reformed from 15 October 2012 so that, for example, a lone parent with a child aged 5–13 would be expected to take a part-time job if offered, and if the child was aged 14 or over, a full-time job.

introduced in March 2012. The second stage of reform will involve a Bill to overhaul benefit categories and reduce fraud. The latter legislation, published in Bill form in September 2012 – the Social Security (Benefit Categories and Work Focus) Amendment Bill – is concerned with simplification of the structure and the closer alignment of rules, although another aim behind the measures is to tighten up further on work conditionality.[72] An underlying principle of reform is:

Rules should be simple for beneficiaries and the public to understand.

- Consistency and alignment in rules promotes greater clarity and understanding of what is expected of people in return for receiving benefits.
- This also promotes administrative efficiencies, which can free case managers up to work with beneficiaries.[73]

Under the reform, three new benefit categories would replace the seven existing categories. The new categories are 'Jobseeker Support' for people 'actively seeking and available for work', 'Sole Parent Support' for lone parents with a child under age 14 and 'Supported Living Payment' for people who are significantly restricted by illness, disability or injury. Those entitled to sickness benefit would not be in the last category but would be placed in the Jobseeker Support group, although the precise expectations on them in terms of working would depend upon the extent of their work capability.[74]

The reforms, which are due to come into effect in July 2013, are comparable with aspects of the universal credit reforms in the United Kingdom, which are due to be fully implemented by 2017. The New Zealand reforms are also expected to simplify particular parts of the legal framework, such as the rules governing the commencement and ending of entitlement.[75] The much amended and complex Social Security Act 1964[76] will remain the principal statute; the legislation effecting the above reforms will amend but not replace it.

[72] For example, work-related requirements for jobseekers would include passing drug tests where they were required by employers in relation to certain employments: see Office of the Minister of Social Development, *Welfare Reform Paper D: Pre-Employment Drug Testing Requirements* (27 July 2012), www.msd.govt.nz/documents/about-msd-and-our-work/newsroom/media-releases/2012/welfare-reform-paper-d-pre-employment-drug-testing-requirements.pdf.

[73] Office of the Minister for Welfare Reform, *Welfare Reform Paper B: Design of the New Benefit Categories* (27 July 2012), www.msd.govt.nz/documents/about-msd-and-our-work/newsroom/media-releases/2013/wr-cab-paper-b-design.pdf, para 18 (original emphasis). See also Office of the Minister for Welfare Reform, *Welfare Reform Paper A: Overview* (27 July 2012), www.msd.govt.nz/documents/about-msd-and-our-work/newsroom/media-releases/2013/wr-cab-paper-a-overview.pdf, para 44.

[74] Minister of Social Development, 'Second Stage of Welfare Reforms Introduced', press release (17 September 2012), beehive.govt.nz/release/second-stage-welfare-reforms-introduced. In addition to sickness benefit, Jobseeker Support will also replace unemployment benefit, domestic purposes benefit (DPB) for lone parents looking after under-14s and DPB for 'women alone' and widow's benefit for women with children aged 14-plus or those without dependent children.

[75] New Zealand Government, *Social Security (Benefit Categories and Work Focus) Amendment Bill Explanatory Note* (2012), 6.

[76] Various sets of regulations have also been amended by this amendment legislation.

IV. Germany: The *Sozialgesetzbuch*

Social security in Germany is based around a social insurance model supplemented by means-tested social assistance (*Sozialhilfe*). As in the United Kingdom (at least until the introduction of universal credit), assistance with rented housing costs has been a discrete form of support.[77] Redress in respect of social security decisions is based around initial review by the administrative authority and then appeal to a social court (*Socialgerichte*)[78] or sometimes by application to an administrative court.[79] Germany is said to have 'one of the most developed social security systems in the world',[80] and not surprisingly therefore, the system rests on a complicated legislative framework.[81] A codification reform of Germany's social security legislation aimed at making the legislation more coherent, clear and comprehensible[82] long predated the comparable efforts made in Australia.[83]

This reform, commencing in 1975–76, comprised the introduction of the *Sozialgesetzbuch* (SBG) (Social Code).[84] The Code covers all areas of social security, although constitutional law in the form of the German Basic Law, which has an important bearing on the responsibilities and functions of the state, is also important in shaping the state–citizen relationship, including the state's duty to provide social protection.[85] The 12 books of the SBG (SGB

---

[77] For further background on Germany and for UK–Germany comparisons, see J Clasen, *Paying the Jobless: A Comparison of Unemployment Benefit Policies in Great Britain and Germany* (Aldershot, Avebury, 1994); and F McGinnity, *Welfare for the Unemployed in Britain and Germany: Who Benefits?* (Cheltenham, Edward Elgar, 2004) ch 3.

[78] There may be an appeal from the local social courts to a regional social court (*Landessocialgerichte*) and then, on a point of law and with leave to appeal, to a federal court (*Bundessocialgerichte*).

[79] B Schulte, 'The Institutional Framework, Legal Instrument and Legal Techniques Relating to the Promotion of Access to Social Security to Non-Citizens: A German Perspective' in U Becker and MP Oliver (eds), *Access to Social Security for Non-citizens and Informal Sector Workers: An International, South African and German Perspective* (Stellenbosch, African Sun MeDia, 2008) 121–23.

[80] LG Mpedi, 'Promoting Access to Social Security to Informal Sector Workers' in Becker and Oliver (eds) (ibid) 234.

[81] CJ Jewell, 'Assessing Need in the United States, Germany, and Sweden: The Organization of Welfare Casework and the Potential for Responsiveness in the "Three Worlds"' (2007) 29(3) *Law & Policy* 380, 384 and 392.

[82] See B Maydell, 'The Codification of Social Law in Germany' in KD Kremalis (ed), *Simplification and Systemisation of Social Protection Rules* (Athens, Ant N Sakkoulas, 1996) 125.

[83] See above s II.

[84] Available at www.sozialgesetzbuch.de/.

[85] See U Becker and S von Hardenberg, 'Country Report on Germany' in U Becker et al (eds), *Security: A General Principal of Social Security Law in Europe* (Groningen, Europa Law, 2010) 100–4.

I–XII), which have been introduced over three decades, contain common principles and rules relating to specific parts of the system, such as social insurance (SGB IV) and administration (SGB X), while many books have specific focuses, such as support and facilities for children and youth (SGB VIII) and rehabilitation of disabled persons, including provision of benefits (SGB IX).[86] General provision made by SGB I includes principles applicable across the various benefits. According to Bernd Schulte, 'These principles take into account the difficulties people experience in understanding their rights in a very complicated social security system.'[87] Thus, for example, SGB I also contains an obligation on the authorities to make the public aware of their rights and obligations under the Code.[88] In response to the legal duty to inform the public about their rights, the social security authorities have been publishing information leaflets, which, reassuringly, are 'better to understand than the law itself'.[89] One of the main aims of the SGB is to ensure transparency and accessibility of social law in Germany, yet the parts of the Code are complex in themselves.[90]

There is also complexity arising from a general provision stating that the rules within the individual parts of the Code, governing specific schemes, are to take precedence over common rules.[91] Thus, for example, while the SGB IX aims at a co-ordinated approach towards rehabilitation and support for disabled people by establishing a basis for cooperation, coordination and convergence, benefits for disabled people are governed in various ways by seven of the individual books.[92] A further cause of complexity is the interface (*Schnittstellen*) between the different parts of the SGB.

The prevalent view in Germany appears to be that its social security law is very complex, but that in the post-SGB era, there is little government interest in wholesale simplification or rationalisation.[93] Specific reforms to parts of the system have nevertheless been taking place, such as changes to provision for the unemployed, designed to extend activation and reorganise assistance among this category (see SGB II).[94]

---

[86] See F Welti, 'Systematische Stellung des SGB IX im Sozialgesetzbuch – Zusammenarbeit der Leistungsträger und Koordinierung der Leistungen' ('The Systematic Role of the SGB IX in the Social Security Code: Cooperation of Social Security Service Providers and Coordination of Services') (2008) *Die Sozialgerichtsbarkeit* 321.

[87] Schulte, 'The Institutional Framework, Legal Instrument and Legal Techniques' (above n 79) 117.

[88] SGB I §13.

[89] Schulte, 'The Institutional Framework, Legal Instrument and Legal Techniques' (above n 79) 117.

[90] See, for examples, Becker and von Hardenberg (above n 85) 97–146.

[91] SGB I, para 37.

[92] See Welti (above n 86).

[93] The author is especially indebted to Professor Felix Welti of the University of Kassel and Professor Eberhard Eichenhofer of the University of Jena for discussion of social security in Germany.

[94] See E Eichenhofer, 'Hartz Reforms: Hard Reconstructions?' in Stendahl, Erhag and Devetzi (eds) (above n 1) 133–43.

V. Sweden: Codifying Social Insurance Law and Reforming Sickness Benefits

Sweden's social security system, despite its increasing attempts to emphasise personal responsibility through strict activation measures affecting those in receipt of unemployment benefits,[95] continues to epitomise the institutional model of welfare 'characterised by far-reaching public or state responsibilities for the social security of its citizens'.[96] It still conforms to Gøsta Esping-Andersen's classification (noted in chapter one) of a social democratic welfare state, despite the increasing retrenchment of state welfare there, as in other Scandinavian states. Insurance benefits such as unemployment insurance, old-age pension and sickness insurance remain central to the Swedish welfare system. But citizens also have access to locally administered social assistance providing a nationally set amount covering daily living costs apart from expenses such as housing and utility costs, which are instead eligible for coverage through local discretion on the basis of what is considered reasonable. Other national benefits include disability allowance and attendance allowance for people with needs arising out of disability. For challenges to decisions on insurance benefit, there is an internal review stage. Appeal in these and in social assistance cases lies to the administrative court and from there to the administrative court of appeal, provided the latter court grants leave to appeal. The final tier of appeal is the Supreme Administrative Court, also accessed only with leave.

Two aspects of social security law in Sweden are of particular relevance so far as the issue of complexity is concerned. The first concerns the reformulation of general social insurance legislation, while the second is concerned specifically with changes relating to provision for those with work incapacity.

As noted above in chapter one, Sweden is one of the states to have considered a wholesale reform of welfare (more particularly of social insurance), but as in the case of Germany, it is the legal structure of benefits that has been the focus of wide-ranging reform rather than the system itself. In January 2011, a new Code of Social Insurance was introduced, bringing together a wide range of separate legislative measures. The aim of establishing this comprehensive Code was reflected in the Inquiry on the Coordination of Social Insurance Legislation (SamSol) which preceded it, although a change of government following the Inquiry report's publication in 2005 contributed to a delay in the process of reform.

---

[95] See Van Aerschot (above n 1) ch 3.
[96] T Erhag, 'Country Report on Sweden' in Becker et al (eds) (above n 85) 483.

The Inquiry had been established to undertake a technical review of Sweden's social insurance statutes and to devise proposals for new legislation 'to give improved clarity and better assurance against lack of consistency as regards rules and concepts common to social insurance' and which would be 'easier to take in and apply' than the existing provisions.[97] The Inquiry acknowledged the influence on its thinking of the codified social security leg-islation of France and Germany, among others. The Inquiry's overall recom-mendation was for the incorporation of the legislation into a single Code, divided into eight separate parts.[98] It would include most of the social insur-ance legislation (but not unemployment insurance – see below), comprised in approximately 30 separate Acts. Such a Code was seen as conducive to improved understanding of social security among citizens. It was also seen as likely to facilitate better administration of benefits, and the report argued that the Code's structure and the 'more accessible' language of the individual provisions would aid decision-making by officials,[99] leading to 'a more legally secure and consistent application of social insurance'.[100] The usability and coherence of the Code would be enhanced due to the possibility of cross-referencing, enabling 'the connections between and consequences of various regulations and measures' to be more easily identified.[101] The use of common provisions where possible, a key feature of the German Social Code noted above, was also proposed. A further advantage of codification would relate to the updating of the legislation; it was considered that altering the Code would be easier than having to amend numerous separate statutes simultaneously.

Although the Inquiry Report considered that it would be feasible for the new Code to be in force by January 2008, the fall of the Government in 2006 contributed to delay in its implementation. Nevertheless, in late 2007 the draft Social Insurance Code was handed over to the Council on Legislation (*Lagrådet*), a constitutional body consisting of judges from the Swedish Supreme Court and the Supreme Administrative Court. By this stage, the proposed implementation date of the Code was set at January 2009. The role of the Council on Legislation is to scrutinise bills prior to their submission to Parliament for consideration. The Council is charged with identifying any of a Bill's provisions that may be regarded as being in contravention of the fun-damental laws of the Constitution. The Council's written opinion on the draft Code[102] was prepared by June 2008, thus representing reasonably swift

---

[97] Statens Offentliga Utredningar, *Socialförsäkingsbalk Del 1* (Stockholm, Statens Offentliga Utredningar, 2005) 35.

[98] The eight parts, or 'Titles', comprise: A. general provisions; B. family benefits; C. benefits in the event of sickness or work injury; D. special benefits in the event of disability; E. benefits in old age; F. benefits to surviving dependants; G. housing allowances; H. certain common provisions.

[99] See Statens Offentliga Utredningar (above 97) 38.

[100] Ibid.

[101] Ibid, 36.

[102] Lagrådet, *Utdrag ur protokoll vid sammanträde 2008-06-17* (2008), www.lagradet.se/yttrand en/Socialforsakringsbalk.pdf.

progress given that, according to the Council's then Chairman, Judge Rune Lavin, it was set to be the largest single legislative measure in Swedish history, comprising around 1,900 articles.[103]

In its report, the Council acknowledged the need for the previous law, which evolved over several decades and had been amended and supplemented on numerous occasions, to be 'systematically reviewed, coordinated and modernised'.[104] The Council noted that in order to make the law more 'precise, transparent and easy to apply', the draft gave attention to its structure and verbal expression, including the employment of indexes and the use of shorter paragraphs and more everyday terminology.[105] In the Council's assessment, 'mixed results' were achieved, since while there had been undoubted improvements in important provisions previously governed by rules that were 'characterised by being very long and complicated', it had seemingly been impossible to simplify the language without altering the substance of the rules themselves. Moreover, the Council made reference to the need for cross-referencing on a wide scale: 'numerous provisions include references to yet other provisions in other chapters in the Social Insurance Code'.[106] The Council saw this as particularly problematic for ordinary citizens. They would often 'have to rely on several different provisions thereof, and will consequently also need to be able understand its various components. This may be perceived as difficult, especially for a non-legally trained audience.'[107]

One significant omission from the Code was unemployment benefits. According to the Council's report on the draft, this was because the Code's primary purpose was to govern all benefits administered by the Swedish Social Insurance Agency (*Försäkringskassan*) and reflected the Agency's Implementation Guidelines on the law. As the Agency is not responsible for unemployment benefits, these benefits were excluded from the Code. The Council regarded this as unfortunate, since the benefit was considered to be a component of social insurance.[108] Even without these provisions, however, the Code was a very large and wide-ranging instrument, and this drew the criticism from the Council that the attempt to consolidate numerous and distinct legal frameworks into a single measure had given rise to 'serious deficiencies' by making it over-complicated and unwieldy. To help to avoid this, stated the Council, the rules on administration and procedure could

---

[103] Email to the author (29 April 2012). I am very grateful to Judge Lavin for explaining the role of the Council and forwarding a copy of its report on the social insurance fund, of which an English translation was commissioned with the aid of the author's Leverhulme Research Fellowship grant.

[104] Lagrådet (above n 102) General Observations (English translation).

[105] Ibid.

[106] Ibid.

[107] Ibid.

[108] Ibid, part 1 'A Social Insurance Code or other legal solutions'.

have been placed in a separate instrument, and in order to ensure clarity and accessibility, partitioning of the Code was necessary.[109]

Another aspect of the Code on which the Council concentrated was the language used. It was noted that there had been a real effort to make the rules as simple as possible to read and, as mentioned above, to use everyday language. There had in that regard been an attempt to meet the political commitment to place the focus on the perspective of individual citizens. However, since the Code was still a legal instrument, it was necessary for it to meet the test of consistency and certainty. The Council found many examples of expressions that, across at the Code as a whole, had diverse meanings. The Code also contained some drafting errors, although that is not perhaps surprising given its overall length and complexity. In its overall assessment of the draft Social Insurance Code, the Council on Legislation pulled no punches. The Code was 'riddled with serious inadequacies on various levels in terms of accuracy, language use, disposition, delimitation and technical analysis'.[110] The Council nevertheless concluded that the problems could be rectified, and so it decided not to reject the proposed reform. However, it did not consider that the Code could be made ready for implementation before January 2010, particularly in view of the adjustments needed to the Swedish Social Insurance Agency's Implementation Guidelines and the modifications needed to the Agency's information technology systems.

Minor corrections and various other structural and clucidatory adjustments were made to the draft Swedish Social Insurance Code in the light of these comments, and in its final form, the Code was published in 2010. As noted above, the Code came into operation in January 2011. The drafting of such a large and wide-ranging instrument of some technicality was clearly problematic, and the experience demonstrates how simplification of the law can be a complex task. As to whether the Code has improved the accessibility and intelligibility of Swedish social insurance law, the Council on Legislation regarded its achievement in that regard as limited, as noted above. Anecdotal evidence gathered recently from judges and academics in Sweden[111] indicates that the Code is considered to have aided professionals who deal with this area of the law since it has combined previously fragmented laws and provided clearer definitions of various key concepts. It has enhanced their understanding of the law, including among decision-makers. A particular benefit is the Code's computer-accessibility. The creation of the Code is also considered to have emphasised the public importance of social insurance itself. However, the failure to include legal areas outside the Social Insurance

---

[109] Ibid.

[110] Ibid, 'Overall assessment by the Council . . .'

[111] The author acknowledges with thanks the assistance of Thomas Erhag of the University of Göteborg for reporting on informal discussions on this subject with judges at a recent conference in Sweden. The author is also grateful for the views expressed to him by two retired judges of the administrative court in Sweden.

Agency's remit is considered a weakness. Furthermore, the Code is still considered to be very complex and not readily intelligible to the general public, who must continue to rely on guidance from the relevant agencies.

So far as individual benefits are concerned, one highly significant reform in Sweden aimed to rationalise and give a more rehabilitative focus to sickness insurance benefits (also incorporated into the Code). As in other states, including the United Kingdom, there was concern at governmental level at the numbers of people dependent, on a long-term basis, on sickness benefits. Reforms in 1992 that gave employers a degree of responsibility for the rehabilitation to work of their sickness benefit recipient employees marked 'the beginning of a policy aiming to reactivate the long-term ill that was to become very important in the following decades'.[112] Further reform in 1997, for example, sought to tighten access to sickness benefits by, in particular, making the key entry condition that of 'incapacity' rather than sickness per se – a reform which mirrors the incapacity benefit reforms in the United Kingdom in 1994–95.[113] This did not, however, halt the increase in numbers receiving these benefits in Sweden. Consequently, political interest in this area of social security grew.[114] The Reinfeldt Government, which came to power in 2006, sought to tackle what was perceived as a problem through a reform of sickness insurance. The reform, introduced in July 2008, comprised the establishment of a 'rehabilitation chain' linking different stages in possible entitlement over time, as occurs under the equivalent system in the United Kingdom. Thus a claimant's incapacity was assessed with reference to his or her usual occupation and then, after 180 days, with reference to his or her capacity for any kind of work on the regular labour market. Moreover, a maximum duration of entitlement to sickness insurance protection was prescribed at 364 days, though with a possible continuation in some cases by a further 550 days. Entitlement to a separate 'temporary disability benefit' was also abolished.[115]

The 2008 reforms resulted in a simpler framework of protection. According to Sara Stendahl, viewed with a 'lawyer's eye, the reform . . . could be interpreted as being embedded in an optimistic notion of the possibility of introducing clarifications to a muddled and complex system'.[116] The criteria for entitlement were intended to be clearer; and along with the set time limits, the overall goal was one of increased predictability.[117] 'Law . . . was the main instrument through which simplification was to be achieved.'[118] The more

---

[112] S Stendahl, 'The Complicated Made Simple? The Reinfeldt Government's 2006–10 Reforms of Swedish Social Security Protection for Those with Reduced Capacity for Work' in Devetzi and Stendahl (eds) (above n 4) 100.

[113] Under the Incapacity for Work Act 1994. See, eg, N Wikeley, 'Social Security and Disability' in N Harris et al, *Social Security Law in Context* (Oxford, Oxford University Press, 2000) ch 12.

[114] Stendahl (above n 112) 101 and 103.

[115] Ibid, 103–4.

[116] Ibid, 104.

[117] Ibid.

[118] Ibid.

sharply defined and restrictive basis for entitlement nevertheless gave rise to political difficulties due to the numbers of claimants who soon fell out of protection, with media reports of 'individuals who were sick with cancer or other indisputably difficult illness and who, because of the Reinfeldt reform, were claimed to be forced to register at the unemployment office'.[119] As a result, amendments were introduced to soften some of the restrictions, for example by making it possible for claims to continue beyond the maximum of 914 days or 2.5 years.

So far as simplification and related clarity are concerned, there are doubts whether the Reinfeldt reforms as a whole have had such net effect. Stendahl has highlighted the following as being inconsistent with any claim of simplification: the criterion of 'serious illness' as a basis for continued entitlement to benefit beyond 364 days; that of receiving 'extensive treatment in hospital or elsewhere' as the ground for staying on benefit beyond the 550-day extended period; and the introduction of the concept of 'gainful employment on the regular labour market' to which work capacity is now linked.[120] She has concluded, 'If the aim of the reform was to reduce complexity and increase predictability, these changes do very little to support such a development.'[121]

Further reforms were made to sickness insurance in 2012, including increased opportunities for extension of the duration of entitlement, on the basis of individual assessment. The Swedish government has also announced an intention to 'simplify the regulations' governing sickness insurance.[122]

VI. Simplification Tendencies Elsewhere

Aside from the broadly based reforms to the legal frameworks or benefit structures illustrated above, there have been efforts in some states to simplify specific parts of their benefit systems where the problems due to complexity are considered most acute or at least where simplification is most practicable. Simplification tendencies have emerged across a range of states in relation to the shape and administration of their welfare systems.

Since pensions comprise one of the most complex areas of welfare, it is perhaps unsurprising that they have been the subject of simplification reforms in several states. Reforms to pensions have, for example, included new pensions

---

[119] Ibid.
[120] Ibid, 117.
[121] Ibid.
[122] See the government website at www.government.se/sb/d/15472/a/184141.

legislation in the Netherlands. In particular, the Pensions Act (*Pensioenwet*),[123] introduced in 2007, had the aim of making the system 'easier to understand, by creating a clearer legal framework'.[124] Pensions in the Netherlands comprise a 'three-pillared' system of an insurance-based (ie, contributory) state retirement pension with a second-tier pension (such as an occupational pension or company based pension) and, thirdly, any private pension arrangements.[125] The new Act replaced the Pension and Savings Fund Act 1952, which had been amended on numerous occasions, and it extended accrual of pension rights to younger workers.[126] It aimed not only to provide better safeguards for employees and retirees regarding the future or current payment of pensions but also to provide them with a statutory right to receive clear information about their entitlements.

Other reform trends include rationalisation of benefit schemes or streams within them, such as the merger of separate schemes of housing supplement and home-keeping supplement in Iceland, or administrative arrangements, as in Denmark's new centralised benefit payment and administration body (*Udbetaling Danmark*) in place of commune administrations (a reform that is expected to save approximately DKK300 million per annum)[127] and the *Arbeids-og velferdsetaten* (Labour and Welfare Service) (NAV) in Norway. The NAV was established in 2006 to combine the functions of the Employment Service and the National Insurance Administration, which it replaced. The aim was not only to emphasise further the notion of progression to work as a social norm for those out of employment but also to provide a 'stronger user-orientation' to services.[128] NAV manages Norway's National Insurance scheme, which provides a wide range of benefits, including unemployment benefit, parental benefit, child benefit, sickness benefit, disability pension and war pension.

Italy is another state to have shown simplification tendencies in relation to parts of its social security system. According to one study, 'a certain degree of complexity is encountered in all the Italian social security schemes'.[129] Social security law in Italy is in itself complex due to its level of detail.[130] One

---

[123] Act of 7 December 2006 containing rules concerning Pensions (Pensions Act).

[124] See the newsletter published by the International Social Security Association (ISSA), entitled *Trends in Social Security* (2006) No 4, www.issa.int/layout/set/print/content/download/53040/973895/file/06-4-E.pdf, 30–31.

[125] L van der Meij, 'Pensions Crisis in the Netherlands' (2011) 16 *Pensions* 13.

[126] Employees aged 21 or over could not be excluded from pension arrangements.

[127] International Social Security Association, 'Denmark: Centralizing the Management and Payment of Benefit' (20 October 2012), www.issa.int/Observatory/Country-Profiles/Regions/Europe/Denmark/Reforms/Centralizing-the-management-and-payment-of-benefits.

[128] H Johansson and B Hvinden, 'Extending the Gap between Legal Regulation and Local Practice? Legal and Institutional Reforms in the Field of Activation in the Nordic Countries' (2007) 14 *Journal of Social Security Law* 131, 146.

[129] E Bakirtzi, *Case Study in Merging the Administrations of Social Security Contribution and Taxation* (Washington, DC, IBM Centre for the Business of Government, 2011) para 3.3.1.

[130] S Vernile, 'Complexity, Simplification and Social Security', paper presented at the conference *Complexity, Simplification and Social Security*, Università Commerciale Luigi Bocconi (23 November 2012).

specific area of complexity is that of transitional arrangements, particularly in relation to changes to the law governing pensions, a dominant field of legislative reform in the area of social security over the past few decades.[131] The 'continuous changes in the field of pensions schemes have significantly increased the level of complexity and inconsistency' in the legislation.[132] Piecemeal reforms to insurance benefits and social assistance in Italy have also occurred, 'making the system even more complicated'.[133] An example of a small-scale simplification is Article 24 of Statute Law 214 of 2011, involving a merger of the three different pension agencies. But in general, reforms to pensions have comprised relatively immediate responses to economic trends and their consequences, whereas comprehensive simplification requires more time and planning.

Another development in Italy, this time in the field of unemployment benefits, has been Statute Law 92 of 2012, which introduces, on a phased basis, a new unemployment benefit, *assicurazione sociale per l'impiego* (ASPI). This new benefit replaces a large number of existing benefits and aims to provide a floor of protection for all those who lose their employment, subject to conditions attached via activation measures. This reform has been described as a 'first step towards simplification' in this area.[134] In general terms, however, much of the recent legislation in Italy 'seems to be connected . . . to the financial troubles of the national budget, more than being the result of a well thought out social security policy'.[135]

In Ireland, where the law on social security is also complex,[136] the Social Welfare (Consolidation) Act 2005 incorporated statutory amendments included in some 26 Acts, 18 of which were social welfare Acts, made since the law was previously consolidated in 1993. The 2005 Act comprises 364 sections and seven schedules and represents a kind of Code, although supplemented by regulations. While the introduction of the Act did not constitute an attempt at simplification per se, the Department of Social and Family Affairs published a lengthy (128-page) official guide, intended to present the key provisions of the Act 'in a readily understood form'.[137] Yet the guide's structure follows that of the Act itself, and while it uses straightforward language, it cannot avoid all the technicality of some the Act's provisions. A typical example is its explanation of how unemployment benefit is linked to a

[131] M Borzaga, 'Country Report on Italy' in Becker et al (eds) (above n 85) 313–14.

[132] M Borzaga, 'The Complexity of the Italian Social Security System: Features, Reasons, Trends', paper presented at the conference *Complexity, Simplification and Social Security*, Università Commerciale Luigi Bocconi (23 November 2012).

[133] Ibid.

[134] Ibid.

[135] Borzaga, 'Country Report on Italy' (above n 131) 299.

[136] For the legal framework, see M Cousins, *Social Security Law in Ireland*, 2nd edn (Alphen aan den Rijn, Wolters Klewer, 2012).

[137] Department of Social and Family Affairs, *Social Welfare Consolidation Act 2005 Explanatory Guide* (November 2005), www.welfare.ie/en/downloads/swcact_exp_05.pdf, 'Foreword from the Minister'.

period of interruption of employment (as has also been the case under UK social security law):

> Unemployment Benefit is payable for any day of unemployment which forms part of a period of interruption of employment. A day of interruption of employment means any day, other than a Sunday, on which a person is unemployed or is unable to work due to illness. Any 3 days of interruption of employment within a period of 6 consecutive days are treated as a period of interruption of employment and any two such periods not separated by more than 26 weeks are treated as one period of interruption of employment.[138]

The guide does manage to express complex legislative provisions in a less technical way, but in view of its format, structure and language, it is likely to have far greater utility to advisers than to the general public. Moreover, some of the terminology is not explained. For example, the condition of being 'habitually resident in the State' is attached to a whole list of benefits by the Act. In the guidelines, the term is referred to as 'habitually *living* in the State' (emphasis added), presumably in order to make it slightly clearer, and is referred to as such in each of the relevant parts of the guidelines. But there is no reference to the meaning of the term, whose complexities are covered in detailed 'Operational Guidelines' intended for decision-makers.[139] According to Mel Cousins, the definition adopted by the Irish authorities is that found in the EC law test for habitual residence, but he has argued that 'the legal position on habitual residence is somewhat unclear and . . . we are likely to see a considerable number of appeals and possibly court cases in the coming years'.[140]

VII. Conclusion

The response to the complexity of social security law and systems has varied across states. In the case of Australia, Germany and Sweden, simplification and greater clarity have been sought through the codification of the law, a difficult process in view of the volume and complexity of the rules which a code needs to incorporate. The evidence from Germany and especially Australia shows that codification is unlikely to simplify the law as a whole to

---

[138] Ibid, 25.
[139] See the Department of Social Protection website, www.welfare.ie/en/Pages/Habitual-Residence-Condition_holder.aspx.
[140] M Cousins, 'The Habitual Residence Condition in Irish Social Welfare Law' (2006) 13 *Irish Journal of European Law* 187, 206.

any significant degree, although it certainly has the advantage of enhancing coherence by locating all or most of the relevant rules in one place, even if the need for cross-referencing (as in both the German and Swedish Codes) can undermine the benefits of such consolidation. Furthermore, the experience in Sweden shows that attempts to rewrite the law in everyday, simpler language may not necessarily reduce its complexity because it may introduce greater ambiguity or uncertainty. The recasting of parts of social security law in New Zealand has offered further evidence that simplification through redrafting cannot always be guaranteed to succeed.

There has also been selective simplification of the benefits structures, whether fairly broadly based, as in the case of New Zealand's Social Security (Benefit Categories and Work Focus) Amendment Bill, or narrower in scope, as in the pension reforms in the Netherlands and Italy. Mergers of administrative frameworks, as witnessed in both Denmark and Norway, have also aimed to make things simpler from the claimant's perspective while achieving managerial efficiencies. This particular trend is reflected in the UK universal credit reforms, whose reduction in benefit schemes is also mirrored in the current reforms in New Zealand and in some of the proposals emanating from the Henry Review in Australia. Whether, in view of the experience of and results achieved by codification of social security law in other states, such a reform would be beneficial in the United Kingdom is certainly open to question. Meanwhile, the evidence from a range of states with welfare systems that have similar features to those in the United Kingdom has not provided any peerless examples of significant or holistic simplification of social security and its legal framework. Rather, it has revealed limited progress, although account must be taken of the only partial commitment to simplification that has been in evidence in most cases.

8

Conclusion: The Complex State of Welfare

Managing the complexity of the welfare system has become a key task for government in the United Kingdom. The current Government's redesign of large parts of the system reflects an acknowledgement that significant reform offers perhaps the only means of effecting meaningful simplification. However, in a field governed by extensive, complicated and often highly technical rules, the arrangements for the transition to a new structure are in themselves liable to be complex and to involve expansive new legislation, as has undoubtedly proved to be the case with the Coalition's reforms. Moreover, as we have seen, while some of the rules on the new universal credit are rationalised versions of those which have governed the separate schemes, the fundamental character of social security law has not changed. Government has proclaimed the introduction of universal credit as 'sweeping away the complexities of the current benefit system',[1] but such a claim does not stand up to scrutiny now that the legislative framework is coming into place.

Since the law and structure of modern welfare must continue to reflect the system's role in identifying and responding to diverse social circumstances and individual needs, while also furthering various social and economic policy agendas, the complexities can surely only be reduced, not eliminated. Despite the simplification achieved by combining different elements of support and administrative structures, and redrafting some of the rules, the law of universal credit necessarily has a very broad span and contains a level of technicality that is customary in this field. As the Social Security Advisory Committee stated after the new draft regulations were referred to it:

---

[1] Department for Work and Pensions (DWP), 'Iain Duncan Smith: Early Roll-Out of Universal Credit to Go Live in Manchester and Cheshire', press release (24 May 2012), www.dwp.gov.uk/newsroom/press-releases/2012/may-2012/dwp057-12.shtml.

Social security legislation can often be complicated. Even to those familiar with regulations, the volume of complex and inter-related detail involved in benefit law can be challenging. This was particularly true of the Universal Credit (and related) draft regulations which the Committee was invited to scrutinise . . .[2]

There are also complexities in other welfare reforms. For example, as noted in chapter two, there are new local schemes for council tax support[3] and for discretionary support in place of part of the social fund; replacing two national benefit frameworks are fragmented systems based on numerous separate schemes. Complexity is also increasing as a result of the shift to online claiming and the taxation charge attached to child benefit in families with at least one high earner. Furthermore, other changes being made – to disability benefits and pensions, even if partly aimed at simplification – will place the whole system in a state of transition over many years to come. The universal credit system itself is liable to further change over time, given the propensity for policy shifts and new initiatives in this sphere.

I. Defending Complexity

Complexity, then, is inevitable, but to what extent is it defensible? The case for complexity in the law and structure of welfare must rest on the desirability of ensuring that entitlement is moulded as closely as possible to the diverse requirements of each individual or family unit that the system aims to support. In that way, complexity serves one of the traditional ends of the welfare state. In directing what the state deems an appropriate level of support to its intended targets, the system operates on the basis of detailed, mostly bright-line rules rather than through the exercise of (structured) discretion. Bright-line rules need not be complex – indeed, some rules are based around simple distinctions such as may be found in straightforward time limits – but in the field of social security very many of them are. This is not merely because of the diverse individual circumstances to which welfare schemes need to be responsive but also because of the underlying policy aims to which they are directed, such as to encourage various forms of behaviour, most notably work-seeking, and to target support in various ways. As discussed in section II of chapter three, the use of these bright-line rules also aims to ensure that

---

[2] Social Advisory Committee, 'Universal Credit Report Published' (10 December 2012), ssac. independent.gov.uk/news/universal-credit/.

[3] As noted above ch 2, s III, this has been specifically singled out as a cause of complexity by the Institute for Fiscal Studies.

first-tier decision-making is directed and controlled.[4] It is a means of managing some of the risks – such as inconsistency, bias and arbitrariness – associated with a process in which public resources, on a very considerable scale, are distributed by frontline administrators.

At the same time, however, complexity in itself tends to generate risks. As was shown in chapter three, it can be difficult for complex rules always to be applied correctly, while the complex ways in which different parts of the system interrelate may result in an increased risk of error in decision-making. As Jeremy Lonsdale has commented, 'Complex benefits are difficult to administer tautly.'[5] By hindering the effective administration of a system of support that is of critical importance to most of the individuals who claim entitlement, complexity can undermine welfare's central goal of meeting social needs. The application of complex rules can, however, be facilitated to some extent by the use of information technology (IT), as discussed in chapter two. Using IT in this way may be conducive to the formalistic approach upon which the application of rules in a modern bureaucratic process is predicated, although the effectiveness of such an approach in this context is limited not only by an IT system's own technical limitations but also by the way that, no matter how carefully they are drafted, the rules 'can never completely specify all the possible variations' in circumstances to which the system ought to be responsive.[6] Moreover, within social security law, many difficult issues of interpretation and judgment arise to which IT programs are unsuited: decision-making can be a highly complex task, particularly in cases concerning issues of work capacity or disability. In such cases, even though the legal framework is based on bright-line rules, a wide range of facts have to be determined and considered, and the law is difficult to apply to them with certainty and precision. Moreover, as discussed in previous chapters, such factors contribute to the increased costs involved in administering benefits.

Equally, the way in which rules at the simpler end of the scale provide a broader, less sophisticated basis on which to allocate or deny state support is also problematic. Rules that apply relatively simple criteria to determine entitlement may ease the administration of a benefit, but they offer a somewhat crude basis of response to social need. As Martin Partington has argued,

> [A] social security system that attempts to offer a highly individualized range of social security benefits, directed at satisfying a high variety of clearly defined individual needs (which might be thought to be an appropriate, even laudable, objective for a social security system) is likely to be extremely complex; by contrast a system

---

[4] See also C Harlow and R Rawlings, *Law and Administration*, 3rd edn (Cambridge, Cambridge University Press, 2009) 197.

[5] J Lonsdale, 'Dealing with the Complexity of Benefit Regulations' (2004) 40 *Benefits* 135, 135.

[6] J Seldon and B O'Donovan, 'The Achilles' Heel of Scale Service Design in Social Security Administration: The Case of the United Kingdom's Universal Credit' (2013) 66(1) *International Social Security Review* 1, 10.

which offers 'rough justice' may be simpler, because less individual cases need to be satisfied and thus be the subject of specific rules.[7]

Age thresholds in the rules determining levels of entitlement to mainstream benefits such as jobseeker's allowance or housing benefit, for example, have been much criticised for being predicated on broad and simplistic assumptions about how people do or should live their lives – for example, that young people below a particular age could live in their parents' homes and thus retain a degree of dependence on their families.[8] Unfairness may result from such rules, even if the policy and resource factors underlying them, including efficiency considerations, may nevertheless enable them to satisfy the test of justifiability and proportionality applicable to Article 14 of the European Convention on Human Rights (ECHR) so that their discriminatory effect would not constitute a violation of Convention rights (in particular, the rights in Article 1 of the First Protocol).[9]

In *Humphreys*,[10] for example, the rule in question provided that child tax credit was payable to only one person in respect of any particular child. The parents had two children but were not living as a couple; the care of the children was shared between them. The father looked after the children for at least three days per week under the terms of the court order governing residence. The mother received child tax credit in respect of the children, as Her Majesty's Revenue and Customs had decided that she had the main responsibility for their care and thus should receive it.[11] The father complained that the rule was discriminatory, contrary to Article 14 of the ECHR read with Article 1 of the First Protocol.[12] The rule was clearly simpler to administer than one that would have required apportionment of the credit between the parents, particularly in cases where the care-sharing arrangements were less well defined. This was acknowledged by Lady Hale in the UK Supreme

---

[7] M Partington, 'The Juridification of Social Welfare in Britain' in G Teubner (ed), *Juridification of Social Spheres* (Berlin, Walter de Gruyter, 1987) 429.

[8] See, eg, N Harris, 'Social Security and the Transition to Adulthood' (1988) 17 *Journal of Social Policy* 501.

[9] See P Sales and B Hooper, 'Proportionality and the Form of Law' (2003) 119 *Law Quarterly Review* 426; M Cousins, 'The European Convention on Human Rights, Non-discrimination and Social Security: Great Scope, Little Depth? (2009) 16(3) *Journal of Social Security Law* 120; and, eg, *R (Reynolds) v Secretary of State for Work and Pensions; R (Carson) v Secretary of State for Work and Pensions* [2005] UKHL 37 (see ch 4 s I). See also *Stec v United Kingdom* (Application Nos 65731/01 and 65900/01), where the Grand Chamber stated: 'Because of their direct knowledge of their society and its needs, the national authorities are in principle better placed than the international judge to appreciate what is in the public interest on social or economic grounds, and the Court will generally respect the legislature's policy choice unless it is "manifestly without reasonable foundation"' ([52]). See also *R(RJM) v Secretary of State for Work and Pensions* [2008] UKHL 63, discussed above ch 3, n 25.

[10] *Humphreys v The Commissioners for Her Majesty's Revenue and Customs* [2012] UKSC 18; [2012] 1 WLR 1545.

[11] Per reg 3(1), Child Tax Credit Regulations 2002 (SI 2002/2007), as amended. Child benefit is also covered by a no-splitting rule: see the Social Security Contributions and Benefits Act 1992, ss 143 and 144 and Sched 10.

[12] See above ch 1, n 50.

Court, giving the only substantive judgment, concluding that the discrimination was justified for the purposes of Article 14. She said:

> The state is, in my view, entitled to conclude that it will deliver support for children in the most effective manner, that is, to the one household where the child principally lives. This will mean that that household is better equipped to meet the child's needs. It also happens to be a great deal simpler and less expensive to administer, thus maximising the amount available for distribution to families in this way.[13]

In this case, therefore, the policy aim behind the benefit of supporting children in poorer households was better served by a simple no-splitting rule than a more complex rule seeking to tie entitlement to precise caring arrangements, which could vary enormously across different sets of parents.

II. Trade-Offs

The unfairness to which a simple rule can give rise, compared with the use of more complex criteria to determine the entitlement of claimants in particular circumstances, was an issue covered in recent research commissioned by the Department for Work and Pensions (DWP), which examined the public's views on pension reform.[14] As discussed in chapters one and two, a single-tier universal pension was proposed by the Government and is currently set for introduction in 2016. The flat-rate weekly sum will be set at a higher level than the basic pension credit, and this will obviate the need (and right) for many to receive this means-tested top-up. However, as a result of the abolition of some of the additional pension elements for which some people have been able to qualify under the current state pension system, some will lose out. The research found that some people were concerned about the trade-off between fairness and simplicity in pension reform. Nonetheless, 'simplicity was generally seen to be more important than fairness as a means of ensuring that pensioners receive the money to which they are entitled'.[15] Thus the benefit of having a simple pensions framework that can more easily be grasped outweighed the fairness of a more complex system that relates entitlement more closely to people's actual contributions but is more diffi-

---

[13] *Humphreys* (above n 10) [29].
[14] A Thomas, J Hunt and A Coulter, *A Simpler State Pension: A Qualitative Study to Explore One Option for State Pension Reform*, Department for Work and Pensions, Research Report No 787 (2012).
[15] Ibid, 42.

cult for people to understand. The opposite view has been observed in people's attitudes to taxation systems: 'there is clear evidence that taxpayers can have a very strong preference for a fair tax rather than a simple one.'[16]

There are other potentially difficult trade-offs in any simplification of the benefit system. For example, fraud can sometimes be more easily masked in a complex system, as noted in chapters one and two. But introducing a simpler less intrusive application process may in fact undermine the goal of reducing fraud, since there may be less chance of detecting a false claim. Similarly, as noted in chapter two, there is a trade-off between tightly targeted benefits, which are associated with complexity, and the potential impact of simpler schemes in terms of raised take-up levels, reduced administrative costs and increased incentives to work.[17] Yet the cost argument at least, which is based on the potential for increased simplicity to ease the administration of a benefit, is also more balanced than one might expect. Take the 'living together as husband and wife' (LTAHAW) rule (also known as the 'cohabitation rule') and its equivalent rule for people living as though civil partners.[18] The rule, which was discussed in chapter three, determines whether for the purposes of income related benefits, two people in a relationship should be assessed on the basis that their level of basic need is the same as if they were married or civil-partnered to each other. The effect of the rule is that a couple's level of entitlement corresponds with a rate of benefit which is less than double that to which each would be entitled independently if not in a couple. As was noted, the LTAHAW rule is a complex one to administer because of the wide range of factors that must be considered in classifying the relationship. As was also noted, the matters to be examined are in effect derived from case law, which in turn draws on and to some extent endorses departmental guidance issued in the 1970s. A calculation by the DWP that was published in 2005 indicated that if the LTAHAW rule were abolished and all couples were simply paid double the single person's rate regardless of whether they were in fact living together or separately, it would cost £2.2 billion per annum in additional benefit payments whilst saving just £190 million in administrative costs.[19]

---

[16] S James and A Edwards, 'Developing Tax Policy in a Complex and Changing World' (2008) 38(1) *Economic Analysis and Policy* 35, 45.

[17] National Audit Office (NAO), *Means Testing: Report by the Comptroller and Auditor General* (2010–12, HC 1464) 24, para 3.3.

[18] See Social Security Contributions and Benefits Act 1992, s 137(1), as amended.

[19] NAO, *Department for Work and Pensions: Dealing with the Complexity of the Benefits System*, HC 592 (London, Stationery Office, 2015), 54.

III. Basic Income?

There would also be trade-offs involved in adopting a scheme of a universal 'basic income' or 'citizen's income' as an alternative to the present framework of largely targeted benefits, with its attendant complexity. Basic income involves the payment of a set sum by way of income to every citizen. The income would essentially be unconditional and paid to people 'no matter what their circumstances'.[20] Such a system would operate in place of the current basic welfare benefits. Thus, as Paul Spicker has stated, 'There would be no cohabitation rule, no separate means test and no conditions about work.'[21] The system would, in contrast to the benefits system, be 'simple, easy to administer and should achieve complete coverage and take-up'.[22] Ease of administration, as well as lower administrative costs,[23] would result in part from the scheme's universality and partly from the absence of a need for 'checking on people'.[24] However, gains relating to increased take-up and 'target efficiency' may have been overstated in view of the need to maintain efficient lists or registers of payees and for a 'robust oversight mechanism' to ensure that 'those fail to receive their basic income are identified, the error is swiftly rectified, and a feedback mechanism prevents the same error from occurring again'.[25]

There are also some fundamental problems with basic income. First, the overall cost would be high, and although there would be significant offsetting by not having to pay welfare benefits and credits, it would require large tax revenues from those in employment to cover the basic needs of the population. This could, secondly, diminish the incentive to work among many of those in employment. Moreover, although part of the case for basic income is that it increases the incentive to work, since earnings do not offset any of it, there is also an argument that those receiving basic income would be discouraged from seeking work by virtue of having their needs met.[26]

---

[20] K Rowlingson, '"From Cradle to Grave": Social Security and the Lifecourse' in J Millar (ed), *Understanding Social Security: Issues for Policy and Practice* (Bristol, Policy Press, 2009) 145.

[21] P Spicker, *How Social Security Works: An Introduction to Benefits in Britain* (Bristol, Policy Press, 2011) 121.

[22] Ibid.

[23] Although not as low as proponents suggest: see J De Wispeleare and L Stirton, 'The Public Administration Case against Participation Income' (2007) 81(3) *Social Service Review* 523; and J De Wispeleare and L Stirton, 'The Administrative Efficiency of Basic Income' (2010) 39(1) *Policy and Politics* 115.

[24] Rowlingson (above n 20).

[25] J De Wispeleare and L Stirton 'A Disarmingly Simple Idea? Practical Bottlenecks in the Implementation of a Universal Basic Income' (2012) 65(2) *International Social Security Review* 103, 105 and 115.

[26] Rowlingson (above n 20).

Although the election of a Labour Government committed to welfare reform in 1997 generated a belief that there were enhanced prospects for the introduction of some form of basic income,[27] and such schemes still have their proponents,[28] governments have not warmed to or taken up the idea. The cost and uncertainty as regards the effects of such schemes are likely to be the major reasons. But another must be their inability to fulfil the wide role that social security now plays. As Spicker has pointed out, 'simplified schemes' of this kind 'tend to assume that social security is about redistribution and the relief of poverty', but '[s]ocial security is not just about giving money to poor people; it does lots of other things, including for example compensation for disability, encouraging or discouraging different patterns of behaviour, or helping to maintain the economy'.[29]

IV. The Claimant

Analysing the so-called 'customer journey' was identified in earlier chapters as the most fruitful means of assessing and understanding the impact of complexity on claimants and their rights to welfare. Chapters four to six identified various ways in which complexity presents difficulties during each stage of a potential journey, affecting matters such as a claimant's knowledge and understanding of his or her rights in making a claim, the capacity to bring an effective challenge to an unfavourable decision, and the degree of awareness both of the obligations attached to continuing entitlement and the potential consequences of failure to meet them. Complexity throughout these stages also has a tendency to generate dissatisfaction and a feeling among clients of the welfare system that they are being treated unfairly. In any event, insufficient understanding of their potential entitlement or how to claim it, the basis on which benefit has been denied or the effect that a change in circumstances may have one's eligibility for various kinds or levels of support, would probably fuel among claimants a similar preference for simplicity to that expressed by respondents in the research on attitudes towards the single-tier pension, noted above.

---

[27] See, eg, B Jordan et al, *Stumbling Towards Basic Income* (London, Citizen's Income Study Centre, 2000). One form of basic income scheme involves 'participation' income, which takes account of various social contributions such as caring for children or taking active steps to secure work: Rowlingson (above n 20) 145.

[28] See, eg, G Monbiot, 'Communism, Welfare State: What's the Next Big Idea?' *The Guardian* (2 April 2013) 25.

[29] Spicker (above n 21) 123.

A good illustration of why claimants have cause to dislike the welfare system's complexity is their experience of funeral expenses payments, discussed in chapter three. As we saw, the rules governing this benefit are particularly complicated, and the struggle faced by recently bereaved claimants to understand the benefit's complexities can impact on their grief. More generally, it has also been noted at various points how the complicated claims forms for certain benefits are considered burdensome by claimants. The claimant experience also offers a useful benchmark against which to gauge the impact of any simplification strategies. Since complexity in the welfare system is difficult to measure in any scientific sense,[30] it might nevertheless be possible to judge how much simplification has been achieved with reference to the degree of improvement in the customer journey. Government attention around the issue of reform to the welfare system is now focused on this journey, although it is still fixed most closely around the route from welfare to work. One of the chief aims of universal credit, as we have seen, is to ease that transition by enabling state support to continue at an adjusted level when a claimant takes up employment, thereby obviating the need which existed under the previous arrangements to start claiming tax credits in place of social security benefits.

It may be concluded that, overall, the detrimental impact of complexity on the customer journey justifies attempts to reduce it, as do the difficulties it generates for the accurate and efficient administration of claims. Yet the system has evolved, following a period of 'dramatic growth in benefits' which began in the 1970s,[31] into one in which there is a range of sophisticated programmes designed to cope with people's diverse, wide-ranging and complicated financial and personal circumstances. Its schemes of support must be responsive to the transitions in people's lives which affect their capacity for self-reliance. Citizens can be assumed to want the welfare system to help to insulate individuals from the financial effects of, for example, living with disability, bringing up children in a workless household, or reaching the end of working life due to old age or infirmity. At the same time, they would expect benefits to be targeted only on those considered to have real needs and they would want treatment to be consistent. They would also want decisions to be accurate, with an effective process for correcting errors. A system designed to meet all these objectives is not going to be simple, particularly if, as in the United Kingdom, there are traditional divisions in the main basis of entitlement between insurance-based and non-contributory benefits (notwithstanding the decline in the former, although the principle of contributory welfare has growing political support) and between means-tested and non-means-tested benefits. It is also a system that is subject to continual adjustment in the face of social and economic trends, policy shifts and the impact of judicial decisions.

[30] See above ch 3.
[31] P Alcock, *Poverty and State Support* (Harlow, Longman, 1987) 99. See also N Harris et al, *Social Security Law in Context* (Oxford, Oxford University Press, 2000) chs 4–6.

So, a degree of complexity may be not only inevitable but in some respects also desirable. Nevertheless, simplification is a worthy goal, particularly if it helps to ensure that individuals will have access to their proper entitlement and above all if it supports the accepted values of the benefit system and its rules. These values, some of which were alluded to above, may be considered to include: operating fairly and on a basis of equality; targeting relevant needs effectively; ameliorating rather than reinforcing incapacity and dependency; and enabling erroneous decisions to be corrected. They should also include accessibility for citizens and a system with 'low compliance costs for claimants'[32] and that provides effective assistance to those who need help to navigate it.[33]

V. The Law and Its Role

The law is perhaps the greatest source of complexity in the welfare system. At the same time, it offers tools of simplification. Not only could social security legislation be reformulated to improve its coherence, for example, through the swift republication of complete versions of amended primary legislation, but more importantly, it could be redrafted in simpler and clearer language to make it more intelligible to ordinary citizens.

The law may have played a major part in the benefits 'maze', but it may also have a potential role in demystifying it. Anette O'Neill, evaluating the degree of clarity and accessibility achieved by the codification of social security law in Australia,[34] has argued, for example, that the 'use of plain English in legislation reduces the need for interpretation, reduces the cost of administration and enables those subject to the law to be aware of their obligations and rights'.[35] Similarly, the UK Office of the Parliamentary Counsel has called for a focus on the language and style of legislation as part of its 'good law' initiative and, referring to legislation in general, has indicated that while simplification may not be achievable, improving how legislation is presented, made

---

[32] J Millar, 'Simplification, Modernisation and Social Security' (2005) 13(1) *Benefits* 10, 14.

[33] B Schulte, 'Defending and Enforcing Rights to Social Protection', International Social Security Association (ISSA) Initiative Findings & Opinion No 16 (2004), www.issa.int/pdf/initiative/2find-op16.pdf.

[34] Discussed above ch 7.

[35] A O'Neill, 'Plain English and the 1991 Social Security Act' in J Disney (ed), *Current Issues in Social Security Law* (Canberra, Centre for International and Public Law at Australian National University, 1994) 153.

available and explained can at least reduce public perception of complexity and thereby facilitate access and understanding.[36]

The case for adopting such an approach is strong, given the fundamental importance of welfare provision for so much of the population and the ways that the underlying legal complexity hinders ordinary citizens' utilisation of and participation in the relevant processes surrounding entitlement.[37] Lord Renton's view, cited in chapter one, that if statutes are unintelligible, it represents a 'disservice to our democracy'[38] is equally relevant to secondary legislation; so much of social security law is in this form, contained in statutory instruments, which, by their nature, tend to be more arcane, technical and frequently amended. As it stands, the law in this field contributes to and underlines the system's overall complexity, which, as we have seen, is considered – even by government – to be disempowering of citizens. It hinders choice and limits people's ability to take proper control of and order their own lives.

Whether consolidation, or codification, of the law, which Lord Neuberger (in common with many others) has advocated as likely to benefit statute law in general,[39] would make a useful contribution in this field is open to question. The experience in Australia, Germany and Sweden, discussed in chapter seven, raises doubts about the effectiveness of such reform as a simplification mechanism. The codification reforms in these states have brought about increased legal coherence and – through the updating of online versions of the codes as changes have been introduced – some improvement to the accessibility of the legislation. But they have failed to address to any meaningful degree the difficulties caused to citizens by the complex legal forms in which rules of entitlement are set out. The problem, however, is that in rewriting rules that, by virtue of their purpose, need a level of detail and precision, it can be very difficult to find appropriate simpler language that does not alter their meaning or potential effect. Nevertheless, while the Tax Law Rewrite project in the United Kingdom may not have been an unequivocal success, it has illustrated the feasibility of devising a more comprehensible whilst accurate manifestation of legislative intent.[40] Indeed, 'the revised format and use of plain English had made the [tax] legislation more logical and readable, at

---

[36] Office of the Parliamentary Counsel, *When Laws Become Too Complex: A Review into the Causes of Complex Legislation* (London, Cabinet Office, 2013) 18 and 29; Office of the Parliamentary Counsel, *Good law*, www.gov.uk/good-law?utm_source=Sign-Up.to&utm_medium=email&utm_campaign=1317-221121-Judicial+Intranet+update+19+April+2013.

[37] See above ch 1.

[38] D Renton, 'Failure to Implement the Renton Report', speech at the Statute Law Society (6 April 1978), www.francisbennion.com/pdfs/fb/1979/1979-004-002-renton-part1.pdf, 8.

[39] Lord Neuberger of Abbotsbury, 'General, Equal and Certain: Law Reform Today and Tomorrow', Annual Lord Renton Lecture at the Statute Law Society (28 November 2011), www.judiciary.gov.uk/Resources/JCO/Documents/Speeches/mr-speech-lord-renton-lecture-28112011.pdf.

[40] See above ch 1.

least for those new to tax'.[41] While the length of the legislation itself may increase, 'longer legislation can be clearer and easier to use'.[42] Reducing the length of laws can merely increase their denseness,[43] which, as previously noted, is associated with complexity.

Complex and obscure legal rules could be regarded as part of a broader disconnect between law and the social realm, one which autopoietic theory has conceptualised in terms of law being a separate sphere – in Niklas Luhmann's terms a 'normatively closed system' operating to its own principles and logic.[44] The rules governing social security are part of the '"juridification" of welfare'[45] in terms of the changes in both the quantity and quality of the legislation in the field. Gunther Teubner has emphasised that juridification is not merely a facet of the extension and intensification of law but relates also, and in particular, to the qualitative aspects – the nature of the changes in the content of the law.[46] A combination of these elements could be evidenced in the subjection of citizens to an increasing number of tightly drafted rules affording rights to welfare that are highly conditional, whilst also constituting those to whom the rules apply as objects of a decision-making process.[47] The law has thus been seen as playing a key part in the 'continual reshaping of social security claimants as "others" who are further marginalized'.[48] Although the contractual character of welfare-to-work arrangements and the idea of a 'claimant commitment' (discussed in chapter six) imply that individuals have personal capacity as determining, independent actors, the reality is that there is little choice for claimants, particularly given the punitive consequences under complex sets of rules[49] of a failure to adhere to the obligations to which they effectively sign up.[50]

The instrumentality of law in the area of welfare policy can support a somewhat sinister viewpoint regarding complexity. Cornelius Kerwin has said that some people see the rules governing eligibility for health care benefits under the federal Medicaid programme in the United States as being 'so

[41] C Turnbull-Hall and R Thomas, *Length of Tax Legislation as a Measure of Complexity* (London, Office of Tax Simplification, 2012), www.hm-treasury.gov.uk/d/ots_length_legislation_paper.pdf, 2.

[42] Ibid.

[43] Ibid.

[44] N Luhmann, *A Sociological Theory of Law* (London, Routledge, 1985).

[45] H Dean, *Welfare Rights and Social Policy* (Harlow, Prentice Hall, 2002), 157. See also J Habermas, *Legitimation Crisis* (Boston, Beacon Press, 1975).

[46] G Teubner, 'Juridification: Concepts, Aspects, Limits, Solutions' in Teubner (ed) (above n 7) 6–7.

[47] Dean (above n 45) 158–59.

[48] G McKeever, 'Social Citizenship and Social Security Fraud in the UK and Australia' (2012) 46(4) *Social Policy and Administration* 465, 480. See also the discussion of citizenship above ch 1, ss III and IV.

[49] See above ch 6, s III.

[50] See, eg, K Veitch, 'Law, Social Policy, and the Constitution of Markets and Profit Making' (2013) 40(1) *Journal of Law and Society* 137, 149–52.

complex and laden with qualifications that their effect, if not their intent, has been to make it easier for the government to find some basis on which to deny benefits'.[51] According to him, some people consider that 'complexity may be a tactic used by those with ulterior motives'.[52] This is a somewhat cynical perspective, but in reality, complex rules do broadly serve a purpose of enabling government to direct support towards its intended targets, thereby providing a rational legal justification, if not necessarily a moral one, for denying entitlement. Of course, simple rules – or rather rules that target entitlement on a simple basis, especially those governing categorical or universal benefits such as winter fuel payments[53] – can also serve this purpose and, as previously noted, are relatively easy to administer. They have the obvious advantage of enabling the legal basis for a decision refusing entitlement to be more easily explained and understood than it would be where located in more complex provisions. Yet within an apparently simple rule there may, by virtue of the rule's inherent flexibility, lie much hidden complexity providing scope for the kind of oppressive denial of support that Kerwin has discussed. Indeed, there is an argument that flexible rules used to implement complex policy goals may have less democratic legitimacy than firm rules with this purpose, as the public may lack confidence in laws that appear to give too much scope to officials.[54] Furthermore, if one accepts the view that juridification at least partly involves an intensification of legal rules, such as occurs when detailed rules progressively replace discretion,[55] one can on that basis derive support for Partington's view that it may in fact be a positive force by protecting social welfare rights.[56] He notes that juridification has negative connotations: 'it implies a value judgment – that there is too much law, that the "life world" of the individual is being "colonized"', and it is manifest in legislation which is 'unnecessarily complex'.[57] Yet he concludes that in helping to ensure protection against the 'unbearably harsh realities of social life, . . . juridification of the welfare state . . . on balance represents a social achievement of profound importance in a civilized world'.[58]

---

[51] CM Kerwin, *Rulemaking: How Government Agencies Write Law and Make Policy* (Washington, DC, CQ Press, 2003) 97.

[52] Ibid.

[53] However, there is growing political pressure for these payments, for which (in essence) all pensioner households are eligible (see above ch 2 s II and ch 3 n 7), to be scrapped or perhaps means-tested, on the grounds that as wealthy as well as poor pensioners are eligible to them they represent an inappropriate allocation of public funds. In 2011–12 and 2012–13, an estimated 500,000 pensioners liable to higher rate (40%) income tax, were in receipt of them. See HL Deb 23 January 2013, vol 742, col WA237 (per Lord Freud).

[54] See Sales and Hooper (above n 9) 447.

[55] See H Zacker, 'Juridification in the Field of Social Law' in Teubner (ed) (above n 7) 404.

[56] Partington (above n 7) 436. Note also Teubner's own view that we should not be blind to the 'freedom guaranteeing function of juridification processes in the intervention state . . . [J]uridification in welfare states should be accepted as such.' Teubner (above n 46) 13.

[57] Partington (above n 7) 421 and 436.

[58] Ibid, 436.

VI. Danger Ahead?

As we have seen, one of the key objectives behind the introduction of universal credit in the United Kingdom is to simplify the social security system by
combining a range of different benefits and credits, concentrating their
administration in one agency, and aligning and consolidating the rules governing entitlement and claims. The Government's impact assessment for universal credit includes an estimated saving in administrative costs of more
than £200 million per annum as a result of 'reduced complexity'.[59] The
reduced level of fraud and error which is expected to result from the simpler
framework is also predicted to generate savings.[60] In terms of the impact on
appellants, the Government has admitted that universal credit will benefit
some but not others: 'the move to a simpler system will mean that some
households will be entitled to more than under the current system, while
some will be entitled to less.'[61] Transitional protection will, however, prevent
existing claimants from reductions in support in the short term. Indeed, there
is a government commitment that they will be no worse off, provided their
circumstances do not change,[62] although over time the value of their underlying benefit entitlement will be eroded.[63]

As we have seen, part of the case for universal credit has also been to make
the system easier for claimants to understand so that, for example, they are
less likely to be deterred from moving into work due to ignorance of how
benefit entitlement will be affected. While it remains to be seen how far this
advantage materialises in practice, on the face of it, a simpler system that is
easier and less expensive to administer, generates less error and risk of fraud,
and reduces barriers to the take-up of employment, would seem to be incon-
trovertibly beneficial.[64] Yet as the discussion at various points throughout this

---

[59] Department for Work and Pensions (DWP), *Universal Credit: Impact Assessment* (December 2012) 5.

[60] Ibid, 9, para 18.

[61] Ibid, 18, para 55.

[62] Ibid, para 56. See also Department for Work and Pensions (DWP), *Transitional Protection: Universal Credit Policy Briefing Note* (10 December 2012).

[63] DWP, *Transitional Protection* (ibid) 2: 'For example, if a claimant qualifies for £20 cash protection and subsequently sees a rise in their underlying Universal Credit award, perhaps through a small fall in income or through uprating of the Universal Credit award, the total award will not increase until the £20 cash protection is used up. This approach ensures that peo-ple move eventually to their new rate but without seeing any cash reductions in the amount.'

[64] But see a recent analysis by the Child Poverty Action Group, which has warned that univer-sal credit 'is likely to prove anything but simple', and 'many complexities will remain': L Judge, *Will Universal Credit Work?*, Economic Report Series (London, Trades Union Congress, 2013), www.tuc.org.uk/tucfiles/586.pdf, 9 and 14.

book has indicated, there are new complexities as a result of the reforms as a whole, especially when one takes account of the localised council tax support and social fund arrangements. Furthermore, the legal framework remains, despite some areas of rationalisation and rewriting, one of the most complex across the whole field of public law, in part reflecting the complexity of the underlying policy, as has similarly been noted in the context of tax law reform.[65]

The quest for a simpler welfare system has long been pursued by government, but with varying degrees of commitment. The current policy preoccupation with it echoes that occurring in the period of welfare reform in the 1980s. At that time, Partington commented: 'In the current political and economic climate in Britain it must be stressed that the overt quest for simplicity . . . masks a more or less covert search for ways to cut (or at least prevent rises in) levels of social security expenditure.'[66] Due to the scale of the current universal credit reforms, which will have an enormous impact on the welfare system and affect vast numbers of citizens, and have required extensive new legislation to bring them into effect, there has necessarily been wide-ranging consultation and fairly close scrutiny of the changes. As a result, even though some elements of the universal credit reforms, including some of the extensions to conditionality (estimated to have the effect of subjecting a further one million claimants to work-search conditions[67]), have not received a great deal of public attention thus far, simplification cannot be considered to have masked cutbacks in entitlement. Other important changes to the welfare system such as the reduced number of rates of benefit under the new personal independence payment, the curbs on housing support, and the proposed single-tier state pension, have not exactly avoided public attention.

Despite the similarity of the current political and economic environment surrounding welfare reform with that of the 1980s, one thing that is different is the increased capacity of government to play openly to the economic case for rationalisation of the welfare system and to use it to trump with relative political ease many of the social concerns about the impact of reform. Even if the financial imperative to rein in expenditure diminishes in the years ahead, if and when significant economic recovery occurs, it is unlikely to reduce political interest in reducing further the role of the welfare system and simplifying it as a means of achieving further savings.

In recent years there has been recognition that the functionality of the welfare system has been reduced by the level of complexity affecting it. The adverse impact of complexity on the administration of benefits and credits and on the 'claimant journey' is widely acknowledged as unacceptable both within and outside government and Parliament. As we have seen, there is

---

[65] James and Edwards (above n 16) 44.
[66] Partington (above n 7) 429.
[67] DWP, *Universal Credit: Impact Assessment* (above n 59) para 102.

often a trade-off between fairness and simplicity. Now that comprehensive overt reforms to the welfare system are occurring, the danger to be guarded against in the years ahead, as government perhaps seeks further reductions in complexity by establishing sharper whilst simpler boundaries to entitlement, of the kind that age limits and other broad classifications can provide, is that some of the benefits of complexity in terms of the responsiveness of the system to particular levels of need will be lost.

Index